International Environmental Law and Economics

P. K. Rao

BLACKWELL
Publishers

The right of Krishna Rao Pinninti to be identified as the author of this work has been asserted in accordance with the Copyright, Designs and Patents Act 1988.

First published 2002

2 4 6 8 10 9 7 5 3 1

Blackwell Publishers Inc.
350 Main Street
Malden, Massachusetts 02148
USA

Blackwell Publishers Ltd
108 Cowley Road
Oxford OX4 1JF
UK

1002466151 /

Library of Congress Cataloging-in-Publication Data
Rao, P. K.
    International environmental law and economics / P. K. Rao.
      p. cm.
    Includes bibliographical references and index.
    ISBN 0-631-21892-0 (alk. paper) – ISBN 0-631-21893-9 (pb.)
    1. Environmental law, International. 2. Sustainable development –
Law and legislation. 3. International economic relations. I. Title.
    K3585 .R36 2002
    341.7′62—dc21

                             2001018132

British Library Cataloguing in Publication Data
A CIP catalogue record for this book is available from the British Library.

This book provides the economics of international environmental law but does not purport to provide legal advice, an area of licensed lawyers.

Typeset in 10/12pt Meridien
by Graphicraft Limited, Hong Kong
Printed in Great Britain by TJ International Ltd, Padstow, Cornwall

This book is printed on acid-free paper.

Contents

Boxes

Preface and Acknowledgments

This book is motivated by the need for a work that synthesizes the rapid advances in the literature on the economics of the global environment (and of "law and economics") on the one hand, and of international environmental law on the other. Undoubtedly, a series of three or more volumes would be an ideal way of presenting such a synthesis. However, this book encompasses a vast amount of information for its size. As the first textbook on the subject, it is an essential supplement to the literature that is currently available.

The book offers a judicious balance between insights from the economics of international environmental law and those from the law and economics of the global environment. The salient features of major international environmental laws are explained and the important contributions of economic analysis at different levels of law development are presented throughout. Although it would have been possible to explore some of the analytical models of economics in greater detail, this would have necessitated omitting other material at the expense of a fuller understanding of the issues.

One of the guiding principles for the selection of material for the book has been to provide analyses that lead to operationally meaningful and potentially pragmatic environmental policies and international laws governing the global environment. Fancy complex models tend to offer little guidance if they are based on least robust assumptions and/or lead to hypersensitive prescriptions that have no practical relevance on this planet. The book endeavors to incorporate some of the significant theoretical economic insights, although it does so largely at a nontechnical level. While some analytical models are more useful than others, the book generally takes the view that the new area of international environmental law and economics can be enriched with a meaningful integration of the relevant legal framework with a mix of economic analyses that lead to pragmatic and practicable environmental policies and laws governing the environment. Several case laws and practical applications have been incorporated in some of the box items, in addition to their presentation in the text. These illustrate the operational features of the law and economics of the global environment. This book will be of interest to a wide readership: professionals in environmental law, environmental economics, international relations, and students of law, economics, and the environment. A previous course or exposure to economics and/or international law would be useful, but not essential, for the study of this book.

I wish to thank the following institutions for permission to quote material: the European Court of Justice, the International Court of Justice, the UN Framework Convention for Climate Change, the UN Division for Sustainable Development, and the UN Publications Board. I gratefully acknowledge the active support of Blackwell Publishers, especially that of the executive editor, Al Bruckner, and editor, Colleen Capodilupo. I also benefited from a set of reviewers; their views provided useful inputs for my revisions. Brigitte Lee provided helpful editorial review of the text. My family support has been unlimited (whether or not this obeys norms of bounded rationality) in my publication activities.

Pinninti Krishna Rao
pkrao@att.net

Overview of the Book

Is this book about the economics of international environmental law, or the law and economics of the international (i.e., global) environment? In fact it is about both, although the focus is greater on the first. This sounds an ambitious agenda because it is one. The onus of presenting a nonpartisan analysis is such that it should remain open to all reasonable methods of enquiry and presentation. However, bounded resource constraints tend to restrict the treatment to a practicable extent and level only. A series of books could possibly address all the relevant aspects. This being the first textbook on the subject, perhaps this could constitute a modest beginning for more expanded products in the future.

Conventional environmental economics tends to be of limited use in a global environmental policy context, mainly for the reason that several institutional complexities have also to be considered in the economic analysis and design of relevant policies. As a result, an appropriate mix of welfare economics, environmental economics, institutional economics, and the theory of international relations is required for arriving at meaningful economic policy analyses. An important aspect of economic enquiry common to both the economics of the international environmental law (IEL) and the law and economics of the global environment is that of the role of transaction costs, broadly included in the field of new institutional economics. Properly interpreted, the contributions of law and economics do not always lead to the prescription of market-based solutions to all economic problems. Rather, they do not rule out such possibilities, should they be in the societal interest. In the milieu, several techniques of analysis such as game theory, optimization, and decision-making under uncertainty assume significant roles. These approaches, features, and ingredients form part of the foundations of this text. Does this imply that the reader is expected to be familiar with these inputs, before a study of this book? No, to a large extent; some familiarity is, of course, useful. The role of neoclassical economics in the economic approaches is complemented by the insights of new institutional economics, in order to appreciate the role of economics in the field of international environmental law. If we start directly with the benchmarks of law and economics tradition (which itself is not of high vintage), it may involve losing sight of a few other economic insights. The expanded horizons of modern economics remain relevant for the study of international environmental law and the global environment.

These features have outlined the economics and/or law and economics aspects so far. The presentation and analyses of international environmental law are themselves subject to inputs from several sources. Among these are: international public laws, international economic laws, and international environmental laws *per se*. The first component of these comprises several sources of law, including customary international law (CIL), international treaties, and related agreements. The second component includes aspects of international finance and trade, among other issues – all with direct and indirect implications on the legal interpretations of environmental policies at national and international levels. The third component relates to international environmental agreements between countries, and other agreements/conventions/conferences among different combinations of countries at regional/multilateral/bilateral levels. Some of these are explicit in their mandatory requirements of environmental and related compliance; others tend to form ingredients of "soft law," which sometimes graduates to form binding/hard law on states. The indirect role of agreements and other international consensual resolutions regarding environmental governance in all cases is that of behavioral regularity conditioning, or formation of expectations of state parties' environmental conduct and international cooperation.

Unlike domestic laws of most countries, there are no law-making bodies nor lawmakers for international environmental law. In addition to the lack of a single (and perhaps comprehensive) set of legal statutes, the absence of an apex court and law-enforcement machinery or institutional framework for the governance of international environmental law suggests the role of pragmatic and strategic approaches to the design and implementation of the relevant legal norms. Even these relative shortcomings do not necessarily lead to a legal void. On the contrary, the provisions of international environmental law run into several thousands of pages. The legal aspects of state responsibility and governance of greenhouse gases alone form substantial segments of books. Environmental phenomenon-specific and geographic or other group-specific international environmental laws have proliferated over the years since about the 1970s. Are these simply on the law books, or did a mechanism of enforcement emerge? Is there a concern for compliance and noncompliance at the state and international levels? How effective are the relevant laws? Is there a strategic approach or catalytic role for international organizations to effect the desired environmental compliance? Based on the study of legal provisions, institutions, and economic criteria, what improvements are desirable and feasible in global environmental governance? These are some of the key issues to be addressed in the course of this book. This evolving area will continue to be enriched with greater insights and approaches over the years, and this book could form one of the contributions for such progress.

Turning to significant developments in the area of global environmental governance, the past decades have witnessed substantial understanding of complex environmental phenomena. During the 1990s rapid economic globalization and the design of measures for international environmental cooperation have been substantially founded. Perhaps the globalization of the environment and internationalization of the economy would have been more appropriate than globalization of the economy and internationalization of the environment. This would be useful both in popular parlance and in policy coordination among states.

The focus of environmental economics during the 1970s to 1990s shifted substantially from domestic environmental economics to global environmental economics. This can be seen also from the large segment of research publications in these areas throughout this period. These trends continue into the twenty-first century. One of the critical issues at this juncture is to sensitize policies affecting international economic interdependencies with those of global environmental interdependencies. Current international laws and other policy settings may not be readily conducive to such computabilities, but the task has still to be addressed in the developments of economics and law.

The role of international environmental law is important for the achievement of various environmental as well as economic goals. Unlike the domestic laws of many countries, international public law tends to be relatively incomplete (though not less perfect). The specific field of international environmental law is more complex than its counterparts in most other areas. This is because of inadequate understanding of some environmental phenomena, relatively fewer trained judiciary in the environmental arena, and a lower quality of information for decision-making.

A few salient features of the book's contents are summarized below.

Part I deals with the important aspects of global environmental economics, including sustainable development, the economics of international cooperation, and principles of environmental governance. After providing a brief background of international public law (developed further in chapter 4), chapter 1 explains the fundamentals of ecological and environmental economics and the concept of sustainable development, along with the economics of environmental sustainability. The significance of environmental protection is explained, both in concept and in relation to intergenerational welfare issues, including some of the international environmental laws. In a primarily intragenerational context (with potential intergenerational spillovers), the role of the environment in protecting public health is examined. The historical evolution of some of the important environmental principles is also outlined in this chapter. Broadly, the contributions of the Brundtland Commission Report of 1987 (which led to the advocacy of the concept of sustainable development) and the Rio Declaration of 1992 (which led to a fairly comprehensive set of principles constituting environmental soft law) are seen as the milestones for further developments.

Management of the global environment in general, and that of the global commons in particular, requires international cooperation. The economics of property rights and liability rules, as well as the role of transaction cost economics, provide significant contributions to an understanding of the relative efficacy of global environmental policies and international environmental laws. These issues, in addition to the economics of contracts and the theory of international environmental agreements, constitute important aspects of the contents of chapter 2. These analyses are useful in the design and implementation of international treaties and environmental laws.

Chapter 3 of Part I sets out a few basic concepts of decision-making under risk and uncertainty. The evolution of the precautionary principle (PP), an important standard of international environmental law, is discussed in detail, including the analytical basis of the principle. Later, the methodology of cost–benefit analysis (CBA) is discussed as a tool in decision-making, subject to clarifications on its limitations. The critical roles of time preferences and changing time discounting of future values are also discussed in this chapter.

Part II of the book deals firstly (chapter 4) with the main elements of international public law on which much of the legal basis for international environmental law can be founded. The roles of state sovereignty and international relations theories in the formation of international environmental law are also discussed in chapter 4. This chapter also deals with treaty reservations and other provisions in the design and implementation of international environmental agreements. Chapter 5 focuses on biological resources and related international environmental law. The main elements here include the important features of the Convention on International Trade in Endangered Species (CITES), the Convention on Biological Diversity (CBD), the UN Conference on the Law of the Sea (UNCLOS), and a few other agreements/conventions. Chapter 6 deals with those aspects of international environmental law that are focused around recognized environmental phenomena: global warming and the control of greenhouse gas emissions, ozone depletion and the regulation of substances that affect it, desertification, regulation of hazardous materials, international water resource management, and related issues. The discussion is supported by a number of case studies and applied analyses.

Lastly, Part III provides an integration of economic and environmental laws, and of the economics of international environmental law. Chapter 7 discusses the complementary provisions of international laws for maximizing global welfare. The role of international economic organizations in global environmental management and the scope for improvements are briefly explored. Chapter 8 deals with the interface of international trade and environmental laws. The role of economic factors in the complementarity of environmental and trade policies is explained. Applications of the polluter pays principle (PPP) and the precautionary principle are also examined. The final chapter addresses issues of environmental compliance, dispute resolution, and the effectiveness of international environmental law. The roles of incentives and disincentives in these features, and of nongovernmental organizations (NGOs), are also examined. Scope for further improvements in international environmental law is suggested in chapters 7 through 9.

Abbreviations

AIJ	activities implemented jointly
CBA	cost–benefit analysis
CBD	Convention on Biological Diversity
CC	carrying capacity
CDM	clean development mechanism
CFCs	chlorofluorocarbons
CIL	customary international law
CITES	Convention on International Trade in Endangered Species
COP	Conference of Parties
CTE	Committee on Trade and Environment of the WTO
CV	contingent valuation
DPG	domestically prohibited good
DSB	Dispute Settlement Body of the WTO
DSU	Dispute Settlement Understanding of the WTO
ECE	European Commission for Europe
ECJ	European Court of Justice
EEZ	exclusive economic zone
EIR	endogenous institutional response
EKC	environmental Kuznets curve
EMIT	environmental measures and international trade
EPA	Environmental Protection Agency
ER	environmental resilience
ESA	Endangered Species Act
EU	European Union
FAO	Food and Agriculture Organization
FDI	foreign direct investment
GAE	generalized allocative efficiency
GATS	General Agreement on Trade in Services
GATT	General Agreement on Tariffs and Trade

GE	greenhouse effect
GEF	Global Environmental Facility
GET	Global Environmental Trust
GHG	greenhouse gas
GPE	generalized productive efficiency
GWP	global warming potential
HCFC	hydrochlorofluorocarbons
IBRD	International Bank for Reconstruction and Development
ICJ	International Court of Justice
ICSU	International Council of Scientific Unions
IDA	International Development Association
IEA	international environmental agreement
IFC	International Finance Corporation
IFF	Intergovernmental Forum on Forests
ILC	International Law Commission
ILO	International Labor Office
IMF	International Monetary Fund
IMO	International Maritime Organization
IOC	International Oceanographic Commission
IPCC	Intergovernmental Panel on Climate Change
IPD	iterated prisoner's dilemma
IPR	intellectual property right
IR	international relations
ITLOS	International Tribunal for the Law of the Sea
IUCN	World Conservation Union
JI	joint implementation
LDC	less developed country
LR	liability rule(s)
MCPF	marginal cost of public funds
MDB	multilateral development bank
MEA	multilateral environmental agreement
MED	marginal environmental damage
MFN	most favored nation
MMPA	Marine Mammal Protection Act
MTN	multilateral trade negotiations
NAFTA	North American Free Trade Agreement
NGO	nongovernmental organization
NNP	net national product
NPV	net present value
NTB	nontariff trade barrier
ODA	official development assistance
OECD	Organization for Economic Cooperation and Development

OLG	overlapping generations
PD	prisoner's dilemma
PEM	positive environmental measures
PFC	perfluorocarbons
PIC	prior informed consent
POP	persistent organic pollutants
PP	precautionary principle
PPM	process and production method
PPP	polluter pays principle
PR	property right(s)
QELRO	quantified emissions limitation and reduction objective
RRA	relative risk aversion
SCBA	social cost–benefit analysis
SD	sustainable development
SPS	Sanitary and Phytosanitary
SRTP	social rate of time preference
TBT	Technical Barriers to Trade
TCE	transaction cost economics
TC	transaction cost(s)
TEP	tradable emission permit
TPR	total productivity rule
TREM	trade-related environmental measure
TRIM	trade-related investment measure
TRIPS	trade-related aspects of intellectual property rights
UN	United Nations
UNCED	UN Conference on Environment and Development
UNCLOS	UN Conference on the Law of the Sea
UNCOD	UN Convention on Desertification
UNCTAD	UN Conference on Trade and Development
UNDP	UN Development Program
UNEP	UN Environment Program
UNFCCC	UN Framework Convention on Climate Change
USEPA	US Environmental Protection Agency
VOC	volatile organic compounds
WCED	World Commission on Environment and Development
WHO	World Health Organization
WMO	World Metereological Organization
WTO	World Trade Organization

part I

Global Environmental Economics

International environmental law, a relatively new aspect of international public law, is largely founded on global environmental phenomena and international collective measures to address adverse environmental changes. The latter are significantly affected by various economic and other anthropogenic influences. The role of economic factors is such that they contribute to environmental changes and also possess the potential to mitigate the consequences. An appreciation of global economic factors, along with their underlying microeconomic factors, enables a meaningful formulation of globally relevant international policies, including laws and their implementation. Environmental upkeep is relevant not necessarily for its own sake. Rather, it is important because neglecting the role of the environment as the major contributing factor to economic and biological sustainability could prove prohibitively expensive for society. Thus environmental sustainability is a prerequisite for most economic activities. Environmental sustainability does not imply sustainable development; the latter involves an active concern for economic development relevant for intergenerational economic welfare. International cooperation in the protection of the global environment can take several forms. International and regional agreements/treaties to regulate environmental changes and their consequences, formulation of legal institutions and instruments, and exchange of information, technology, and other resources are some of the significant ingredients of this cooperation. Economic analysis has an important role in most of the above aspects of global environmental governance. Relevant economic principles and methods are explained throughout this book, in context-specific analyses. Part I provides the major segment of economic concepts and fundamentals involving global environmental economics and its microfoundations.

The next three chapters address issues relating to the complementarity of the economy and the environment, the critical role of environmental features in sustainable development, the salient features of global common resources, broad features that affect global governance, and analytical methods for risk management and environmental decision-making.

Various major developments in the evolution of international environmental policy during the past few decades, along with concerns for intergenerational welfare and justice, are summarized in chapter 1. The important foundations of ecological and environmental economics, leading to the concept and interpretation of sustainable development, the role of environmental stability in the quality of public health and human welfare, and principles of environmental rights are also discussed. The main features of the global commons, the roles of international treaties and other agreements in their governance, the economics of transaction costs and the economics of cooperation as well as strategic behavior are among the major issues discussed in chapter 2.

The prevalence of scientific and economic uncertainty as well as incomplete information are special elements of decision-making relating to varying attributes of risk-aversion, the role of the precautionary principle, and pragmatic approaches to the assessment of costs and benefits of alternative policies. These issues are the focus of chapter 3. Economic and environmental decision-making is better facilitated with the use of modern analytical tools. Pragmatism in international policy-making requires a judicious assessment of institutional and technical factors. International environmental law and economics fits into such a framework.

The debate on environmental resource management at the global level was formally founded with the 1972 Stockholm Declaration of various countries, and strengthened later with the 1992 Rio Declaration involving more countries. Several regional and international activities geared toward the phenomenon of sustainable development have engaged attention ever since. Free-market systems were not seen as self-correcting institutions for the purpose of environmental management, in the absence of regulations or other catalytic interventions. The second half of the twentieth century witnessed considerable intervention mechanisms from governments as well as from civic action groups, at national and international levels. Environmental law became another method of controlling unregulated and uncompensated harm-inducing activities (also described as external-ities) in the industrial countries. After a fair recognition of the interdependencies of environmental features cutting across national boundaries, several important international agreements were for-mulated which laid the foundations for some of the global environ-mental policies and development of the law. The feature-specific and problem-specific international environmental agreements at the international level are discussed in Part II (chapters 5 and 6).

The conceptual and analytical foundations of economics provided by the first three chapters are useful for an understanding of global environmental problems and international environmental law, espe-cially in relation to various issues discussed in subsequent chapters.

chapter one

Sustainability and Sustainable Development

▮ 1.1 INTRODUCTION

The earth's capacity to supply various resources to support life in all forms tends to be fixed in physical terms in any given period of time. This feature is more obvious in the case of exhaustible resources, and perhaps less obvious in the case of renewal capacities or assimilative (sink) capacities dealing with several pollutants. The planet's sinks, which provide the function of assimilation of wastes and the renewal of environmental assets for uninterrupted supply of nature's services, are constrained by unsustainable patterns of anthropogenic inter-ferences, while the availability of resources is constrained by the en-hanced costs of resource appropriation (for example, deep-sea fishing) and excessive consumption (for example, of ozone-depleting substances such as chlorofluorocarbons). The potential diminution below critical threshold limits in the effective supply of biogeochemical resources for supporting life on the planet poses a threat. This threat applies to both sustenance of life and prosperity. Such processes lead to the accumulation of environmental bads, in lieu of environmental goods, and also result in major adverse biogeophysical feedback effects with potentially irreversible consequences (see Rao, 2000).

This chapter provides the basic ingredients of ecological and envir-onmental economics, leading to the broad concepts and approaches for sustainable development. Among the important ecological con-cepts are resilience, carrying capacity, and ecosystem services. In terms of economic approaches, a few broad directions toward environmental management are briefly presented. It may be seen that economic growth and environmental sustainability are integrally interlinked, and that sustainable development is the product of these and other institutional provisions. Relevant concepts and definitions are included later in this chapter. The role of international public law in governing global environmental policies is explained in the general context so as to provide necessary background for more specific applications in later chapters.

Some of the historical highlights in the formation of international public law in general, and environmental law in particular, are provided in some of the sections in this chapter. The regional evolution of multilateral environmental policies in the European Community (EC) and the recognition of environmental rights in some of the national constitutions of several countries are also noted. The main issues of interest in this chapter include the role of intragenerational and intergenerational concerns for environmental sustainability and economic development.

■ 1.2 INTERNATIONAL PUBLIC LAW, ENVIRONMENT, AND ECONOMICS

There were a few bilateral and regional agreements between select groups of countries before the World War II era (1939–45). However, much of the progress in international law formation took shape after the war. The institutional formation of the United Nations Charter facilitated some of these developments. Nonetheless, the environment was not necessarily a priority issue at the beginning of this institutional governance of global issues. The original Charter of the UN does not mention the word "environment." The stated purposes of the 1946 UN Charter include, *inter alia*, the following:

> To achieve international co-operation in solving international problems of an economic, social, cultural, or humanitarian character, and in promoting and encouraging respect for human rights and for fundamental freedoms for all without distinction as to race, sex, language, or religion. (Article 3)

However, during the subsequent years, a number of UN Resolutions and UN-coordinated international agreements, among other institutional developments (including judicial verdicts), led to the formation of international environmental laws and policies (see the appendix to this chapter for a summary of the chronology of international environmental agreements). Environmental and ecological interdependence is such that policies and practices within national boundaries or other political entities are not sufficient to ensure optimal quality of the global environment. Also, it is much harder to control and regulate the consequences of changes in the global environment. Over the years, treaties and international agreements (such as the 1946 Whaling Commission and the 1972 World Heritage Convention) have been explicitly and implicitly seeking to recognize the need for global co-operation and to incorporate the interests of future generations, and increasingly providing for more specific obligations on the part of the nation-states.

It was not until 1972 that the important role of environmental factors was accorded formal international recognition. At the global level, the Swedish initiative supported by the US led to the first global environmental conference, the United Nations Conference on the Human Environment at Stockholm in 1972. The launching of the United Nations Environment Program (UNEP) followed as a byproduct. The conference led to the Stockholm Declaration, with 29 Principles, and provided a permanent basis for international environmental coordination and diplomacy. The Declaration paved the way for the formation of guidelines and nonbinding (soft law) commitments to environmental policy in a transboundary context among states. Principle 1 of the Declaration sought a "solemn responsibility to protect and improve the environment for present and future generations."

It is useful to note that the Stockholm Conference did not emphasize what was to become, within the next two decades, the dominant social paradigm: addressing global warming and related greenhouse gas (GHG) issues. This is indicative of the ever-changing dynamics of environmental problems (including scientific understanding of complex environmental interdependencies) and the need for a flexible policy framework that included a dynamic legal institutional infrastructure.

The UN Charter in its 1975 Resolution formally endorsed its mandate on the environmental responsibilities of states. The 1975 UN Charter of Economic Rights and Duties of States, specifying "Common Responsibilities towards the international community," provides in its Article 30 (UNGA Res. 3281, UN Doc. A/9631, 1975; reprinted in 14 ILM 251, 1975):

> The protection, preservation and enhancement of the environment for the present and future generations is the responsibility of all States. All States shall endeavor to establish their own environmental and developmental policies in conformity with such responsibility. The environmental policies of all States shall enhance and not adversely

affect the present and future development potential of developing countries. All States have the responsibility to ensure that activities within their jurisdiction or control do not cause damage to the environment of other States or of areas beyond the limits of national jurisdiction. All States should cooperate in evolving international norms and regulations in the field of the environment.

In international law, the 1982 World Charter for Nature (UN General Assembly Resolution on a World Charter for Nature, GA Res. 37/7, UN GAOR, UN Doc. A/RES/37/7; 1983) dealt with some clear ingredients of international soft law and ecocentrism. Its preamble referred to humankind as "part of nature," and encouraged a respect for nature "regardless of its worth to man." It is highly unlikely that most societies can afford to ignore the costs of nature's preservation in all its original form. However, a more pragmatic anthropocentric specification emerged a decade later at the Earth Summit. Principle 1 of Agenda 21 declared that: "Human beings are at the center of concerns for sustainable development. They are entitled to a healthy and productive life in harmony with nature." This assertion seeks to maintain a reasonable balance between the interests of human prosperity in the short and medium time horizons, and the long-term interests of nature and hence humankind itself.

These landmark developments in the arena of public international law have been further strengthened over the years. Principle 21 of the 1972 Stockholm Declaration, which preceded the above assertion, and later Principle 2 of the 1992 Rio Declaration (see below) maintained a similar stand on the issue of transboundary damages to the quality of the environment:

> States have, in accordance with the Charter of the United Nations and the principles of international law, the sovereign right to exploit their own resources pursuant to their own environmental and developmental policies, and the responsibility to ensure that activities within their jurisdiction or control do not damage the environment of other States or of areas beyond the limits of national jurisdiction.

The 1992 World Conference on Environment and Development held at Rio de Janeiro was very well represented by the heads of state of most countries. This conference led to the Rio Declaration, which contained Agenda 21 for its implementation by member states. This formed another major segment of soft law, which is in the process of transforming into hard law, as later chapters will show. (For a detailed account of the history and evolution of laws and environmental values and perspectives, see, for example, Wells, 1996.)

A number of broad policy measures were sought to be prescribed under the Rio Declaration of the Earth Summit, 1992. These included eight "Economic Principles," including the following three important ones:

1 The right to development must be fulfilled so as to equitably meet developmental and environmental needs of present and future generations. (Principle 3)
2 All States and all people shall cooperate in the essential task of eradicating poverty as an indispensable requirement for sustainable development, in order to decrease the disparities in standards of living and better meet the needs of the majority of the people of the world. (Principle 5)
3 To achieve sustainable development and a higher quality of life for all people, States should reduce and eliminate unsustainable patterns of production and consumption and promote appropriate demographic policies. (Principle 8)

All these principles emphasize economic development in addition to sustainability. The concept of sustainability admits varying notions and definitions (see later in this chapter). Development is fundamentally a broad-based specification of economic progress. The resulting concept of "sustainable development" is thus fraught with a multitude of potentially conflicting requirements. The concept of "sustainability" in one of its definitions could lead simply to some kind of "safe minimum standards" in resource use (including preservation of environmental quality and its assets). Other variations allow for varying types and degrees of substitution of natural resources in favor of economic development.

Some of the countries, developing as well as developed, enshrined the significance of the environment and its contribution to current and future generations in their national constitutions. Such provisions in the form of environmental rights (including environmental public health rights) or human rights enable judicial institutions to play a role whenever basic violations occur in this regard. The new Constitution of South Africa (adopted in May 1996), for example, states in Article 24 of Chapter 2:

> Every person has the right
> a) to an environment that is not harmful to their health or well-being; and
> b) to have the environment protected, for the benefit of present and future generations, through a reasonable legislative and other measures that

i) prevent pollution and ecological degradation;
ii) promote conservation; and
iii) secure ecologically sustainable development and use of natural resources while promoting justifiable economic and social development.
(Cited in Storm, 1997)

The Philippines Constitution, Section 16 of Article II of 1987, provides
that "[t]he State shall protect and advance the right of the people to a
balanced ecology in accord with the rhythm and harmony of nature"
(cited in Stone, 1996).

In a landmark case in the Philippines, minors as plaintiffs sued on
their own behalf and on behalf of unborn generations to nullify timber-
harvesting licenses so as to "prevent the misappropriation or impair-
ment" of Philippine rainforests. The Supreme Court upheld the
complaint in July 1993 (*Oposa v. Secretary of the Department of Environment and Natural Resources of the Philippines*, July 30, 1993; reprinted in
33 ILM 173, 1994), with due recognition of the "environmental rights"
of future generations (see also Stone, 1996).

The process of evolution of environmental concerns and environmental rights (as may be protected by appropriate national laws in
terms of property rights and liability aspects covering environmental
harm) has been gradual in most countries and regions. This applies to
the European Union (EU) as well. Box 1.1 summarizes the evolution
of environmental policies and their complementarity with economic
development policies in the EU. In this context, it is also useful to
note that 35 countries of the European region including the EC adopted
the 1998 Aarhus Convention on Access to Information, Public Participation in Decision-making, and Access to Justice in Environmental
Matters. In its preamble, the Convention states, *inter alia*, that
"adequate protection of the environment is essential to human well-
being and the enjoyment of basic human rights, including the right to
life itself."

The role of economic analysis

The identified role of economic analysis in the study of international public law, and in particular international environmental
law, is of relatively recent origin. International law and economic
scholarship was portrayed as "the new kid on the block" (Cass, 1997).
It was also noted that one of the 1990s *Bibliography of Law and Economics*

BOX 1.1

Evolution of environmental policies: The European Union

When the Treaty of Rome was written in 1956–7, there was no perceived need to provide for a common policy on the environment. In October 1972, a conference of heads of state or government proposed a common environmental policy. About 200 items of Union legislation on the environment have been enacted since 1972. Environment policy was built into the Treaty by the Single European Act of 1987 and its scope was extended by the Treaty on European Union of 1992. This permitted the use of majority voting on environmental legislation and introduced as a principle of Treaty law the concept of sustainable growth which respects the environment. While providing for national action and allowing member states to take even tougher protection measures than those agreed at Union level, the Treaty stated that the Union policy should contribute to the pursuit of:

- preserving, protecting, and improving the quality of the environment;
- protecting human health;
- ensuring a prudent and rational utilization of natural resources;
- promoting measures at the international level to deal with regional or worldwide environmental problems.

The Treaty requires Union policy to aim "at a high level of protection," at rectifying environmental damage at source, and to be based on taking preventive action and making the polluter pay. The Declaration of the heads of state and government, meeting in Council on June 26, 1990, calls for a further action program for sustainable development, meaning a policy and strategy for continued economic and social development without detriment to the environment and the natural resources essential for human activity. The fifth program of action in relation to the environment for 1998–2000 in the EU stated that the program sets out a new approach to Community environmental policy based, *inter alia*, on the following principles:

- the adoption of a global, proactive approach aimed at the different actors and activities which affect natural resources or pollute the environment;

- determination to change current trends and practices which harm the environment for current and future generations;
- establishing the concept of shared responsibility;
- using new environmental instruments.

In regard to international cooperation, Article 130r (1) of the Treaty on European Union includes the promotion of measures at international level to deal with regional or worldwide environmental problems, including global climate change, ozone depletion, biodiversity loss, and deforestation. The cooperation can be either multilateral, in the framework of different international institutions, or bilateral, in the framework of aid to developing countries and combating transboundary pollution, or both.

Source: www.eu.int/ (March 1, 2000)

deals with this theme in fewer than two pages out of listings of 550 pages of bibliography on law and economics by subject areas. A survey paper, "Economic Analysis of Law" by Kaplow and Shavell (2000), admittedly did not include international law, much less any mention of international environmental law. The general trend remains that there is considerable scope to enrich the field and contribute to legal scholarship and policy-making in the relevant areas of the international environment and its integral relationship with modern economics.

The integration of modern economic analyses and international environmental law is meaningful when there are well-defined laws for operation at the global level and when there is fairly robust economic analysis (including the analytical methods that provide the underpinning). The use of traditional economics is subdued since the complexity of the environmental–ecological–institutional interactions involved call for a judicious mix of neoclassical economics (especially welfare economics), institutional economics, and behavioral economics.

The role of institutions and ethics cannot be isolated in the process of applying economic principles. As Baxter (1974, p. 4) argued, every human being's welfare must be regarded "as an end rather than as a means to be used for the betterment of another." This assertion brings to the surface some of the assumptions of neoclassical economics and questions the ethical foundations of these assumptions. The free-market institutions themselves may not be sufficient to ensure the attainment of a socially optimal tradeoff between anthropocentric benefits and ecological costs (where there do not exist relevant markets for some of the natural resources such as the biogeochemical renewal capacity of the planet or the global commons). Also, as Coase (1960, p. 43) rightly pointed out, "problems of welfare economics must ultimately dissolve into a study of aesthetics and morals."

Two of the basic norms of economic foundations are relevant here: economic efficiency and economic equity or fairness. Normally, efficiency refers to resource allocative efficiency: maximizing output for a given set of inputs, or minimizing inputs for a given level of output. The Pareto-optimality criterion is also of interest. This requires that the welfare of different sections of society improves (under specified settings), without allowing any section to be worse off. This is considered by some as a "soft criterion," since a marginal or negligible cost to some could well be worth a substantial benefit to many others (as long as the second-round effects of any such moves do not contribute adversely to any section of society), but this would disqualify under the Pareto-optimality criterion (see chapter 3 for more details of this criterion).

Two new concepts are relevant in any consideration of efficiency aspects. The conventional concepts are:

- **Productive efficiency**: This refers to the efficacy of input–output relationships among resources and their corresponding primary outputs. Output is sought to be maximized with a given set of resources, or, in some contexts, input cost is sought to be minimized for a given level of output.
- **Allocative efficiency**: This refers to the value-maximizing allocation of resources among competing alternative resource uses. Economic value maximization is itself subject to a few alternative methods, such as the Hicks–Kaldor criterion or the Pareto criterion (see below and also chapter 3 for an explanation and applications of these concepts).

In general, efficiency is a relatively inefficient concept in the arena of international environmental law (IEL), although it has a good deal of relevance in the application of economic analyses in the domestic law context. This is because of the limitations in the concept's applicability when substantially heterogeneous countries are involved, and because of the impossibility of monetized evaluation of several environmental resources (especially those related to the sink and assimilative capacities of the planet). An extended set of related economic concepts could possibly be useful in their applications for IEL. These are normative economic criteria, to be used as possible norms for the first-best approaches, without any consideration of factors such as the political economy and institutional constraints. Realistic adjustments relative to the "ideal" potential (according to these efficiency norms) will still be useful, at least for understanding the extent of deviations from the first-best and for evaluating alternatives in arriving at closest approximations to policies leading toward the fulfillment of these norms. These new concepts are defined below.

- **Generalized productive efficiency (GPE)**: This refers to the relationship between resource inputs (market-related and non-market goods/services together) and output in production processes, usually in a market-related output system.
- **Generalized allocative efficiency (GAE)**: This refers to the relative usage of resources (both market-based and nonmarketed goods/services) to achieve desired objectives such as profit or income maximization.

Both GPE and GAE are expanded versions of the conventional economic definitions where, typically, only marketed goods/services are considered for inputs and outputs. In the traditional versions, it is thus presumed that most ecological and environmental goods and services have neither market value nor scarcity. The point of departure for the purpose of environmental economic analyses starts here when we seek to deploy the generalized criteria to include all resources, whether they follow a market price evolution path or not. Just because these do not often show up in the marketplace does not mean that they are worth nothing, neither does it imply that a major shortfall in any of the implicitly freely assumed goods and services will not surface in the regular market features for traditional goods and services.

GAE admits two additional categories of evaluation. The first is the Pareto-improvement criterion under which any change in the GAE should allow improvement in the welfare of society subject to the requirement that no member is made worse off as a result of such changes. The second is called the Hicks–Kaldor criterion. Under this category, any improvement in the welfare of some sections of society is admissible if such gains (to whomever these accrue) can *potentially* offset any losses to some others. This criterion itself does not warrant the occurrence of any actual compensation, as long as such a potential exists. This criterion remains the fundamental basis for traditional cost–benefit analysis of projects (see chapter 3). In other variations on the theme of economic justice, Ogus (1995) provided an illustrative review of attempts to apply conventional efficiency criteria in the British legal system, including the roles of "distributive justice," "corrective justice," and "procedural justice."

The above discussion on efficiency also brings to light the role of institutions in governing efficiency. Transaction costs (see chapter 2) continue to play a significant role in achieving alternate levels of efficiency (Rao, 2001). Transaction cost economics (TCE; see chapter 2) suggests that "efficiency will guide the development of international institutions" (Aceves, 1996). The new institutional economics, built on neoclassical economics and incorporating TCE and game theory, promises to be the right direction for further application in the integration of international law and economics. An appropriate expansion of analytical methods, integrating relevant directions in both economic inquiry and law and economics, will enrich international legal scholarship. For a brief survey of some of the issues, see also Dunoff and Trachtman (1999).

Equity or fairness remains a highly contentious issue. This could mean different things. The most important lacuna of much economic analysis lies not in the absence of a reasonably precise criterion of optimal equity, but rather in simply ignoring the equity considerations altogether. Undoubtedly, a meaningful selection of fairness or equity criteria depends on the adoption of a social-value framework, the articulation of comprehensive multifaceted considerations, and the development of relevant legal regimes for implementation. The latter becomes unfeasible if the bases for such developments are themselves weak or nonexistent. In many analytical settings, the role of philosophical principles and sociopolitical considerations (including contemporary social paradigms) remain the guiding posts for economic criteria reflecting the type and degree of desirability (if any) of equity, whichever way it is defined. Broadly, equity considerations could center around the following segments for comparison and comparative/relative fairness: intergenerational, intragenerational, interregional, and intersectoral.

In related analytical economics, there has until recently been very minimal recognition of the role of formal game theory in the arena of legal analysis. One of the significant applications to legal studies is by Baird et al. (1994). The foundations of game theory date back to the 1940s and have been actively expanded over the years to examine strategic decision-making and analysis of decisions to maximize strategic economic or other objectives. International cooperation and related issues have been examined in this light by a number of authors. The role of game theory in international economics has been principally focused on strategic trade policies (see chapter 8). Some of the fundamentals of game theory and applications to international environmental issues and international cooperation aspects are discussed in chapter 2. In addition to the choice of appropriate methods of economic analysis, an important prerequisite for laying relevant foundations is an effective integration of principles of the environment/ecology with those of modern economics. Economic analysis tends to attain greater specificity and focus in the context of law and economics when the fundamentals are applied to ecological and environmental systems. These are explained in the following section.

■ 1.3 ELEMENTS OF ECOLOGICAL AND ENVIRONMENTAL ECONOMICS

A few preliminaries in the foundations of alternate approaches may be clarified here. These are important for an understanding of some of the complex interrelationships among environmental and ecological resources, with a clear implication that policies and laws devised to protect a specific element of the environment need to recognize interactions among other related environmental factors. This is to be called simply an ecosystem approach.

Environmental governance principles, approaches, and objectives originate either explicitly or implicitly in the fundamental approaches of ecocentrism and anthropocentrism. Ecocentrism is an environmental philosophy which views human activities in terms of their implications for the ecological ingredients, their relative effects, and ecological balances. Ecosystem approaches are more readily endorsed under this philosophy. Anthropocentrism, on the other hand, is based on the view that any and all human activities must be in the primary interests of humans for achieving society's desired objectives and goals, regardless of whether some features of the environment and ecology are kept intact or disturbed. In this approach, the preservation of wildlife, for example, is relevant if and only if wildlife resources contribute to wealth or other benefits to humans. Despite this polarization, every analysis (whether scientific or otherwise) need not be viewed in terms of the dichotomy of these two approaches. This is because a blatantly anthropocentric approach could eventually reach a critical stage, when ecological and biogeophysical limitations in the systems' functioning would act as impediments to the continuity of human prosperity, stability, and survival. Perhaps there is sufficient room on the planet to accommodate a reasonable balance between both anthropocentric and ecocentric approaches. The real issue is to find the right balance and the means to achieve and maintain it forever – on a sustainable basis.

There have been varied philosophical and ethical proponents of interspecies equity and biotic rights. These constitute an application of the ecocentric approach. For example, Nash (1993, p. 238) argued that "the underlying concern of biotic rights is human responsibility to the rest of nature," and that the emphasis on "rights provides an objective moral basis for this responsibility." The closest approximation for the provision of appropriate protection would be to devise a code of global and national animal rights laws, which has yet to be done on a comprehensive basis. On the other hand, most of the provisions of international law are still centered around anthropocentric foundations of law and nature. The primary justification for this is human self-interest, and such conditions are necessarily conducive to environmental protection (Gillespie, 1997). To quote Harremoes (1996, p. 391), "it is in the anthropocentric interest of man to incorporate ecocentric aspects in religion and philosophy . . . Ecocentric approaches have to be argued within the context of anthropocentric interests, in order to have impact."

It has been argued that the acclaimed philosopher and mathematician René Descartes (1596–1650) was perhaps not holistic in his axiomatic prescription, "Cogito, ergo sum" (quoted in Harremoes, 1996, p. 390), which means that everything starts with humanity and humanity's visualization of values and concepts for its utility. Even when such a position is taken, it is often founded on the fallacy that such disintegration from the natural laws of life on the planet could work against the ultimate human self-interest paradigm. The prerequisites for survival – such as ecological resilience, limits on the planet's carrying capacity or sink capacity (which determines the pollution renewal capacity, which in turn directly affects the phenomenon of accumulation of pollutants, causing severe damage to ecological functions and impeding ecosystem services), and the stability and integrity of the ecosystem which affects these features of the socioeconomic system (for a summary of ecological interdependencies and the limitations in terms of the identifiability of cause-and-effect relationships in this context, see Gregory, 1999) – manifest themselves in catastrophic phenomena (including global warming and depletion of the ozone layer). (See box 1.2 for some definitions of concepts.)

BOX 1.2

Ecology and environment: Concepts and definitions

Biophilia: Genetically based inherent human need to affiliate deeply and closely with the natural environment, especially its living organisms; seen as part of the mental and emotional apparatus of humans (see Wilson, 1992, for many interesting details).

Biosphere: The segments of the earth and its surrounding atmosphere that can, in principle, support life: the region on land, in the oceans, and in the atmosphere inhabited by living organisms.

Biota: The collection of all living things, including plants and animals.

Carrying capacity (CC): The maximum size of a specific population of species that a given habitat can support for a specified period of time, without disrupting the equilibrium in the long run. A dynamic concept, the CC is expressible in terms of relevant parameters (see pp. 20–2).

Ecosystem: The set of all life forms and their physical environment, including the entire set of entities interacting between them. Ecosystems are products of the interactions of all living and nonliving factors of the environment and the biosphere. The functioning of an ecosystem results in several interactions, which lead to what is known as the "balance of nature" at any given time.

Ecosystem services: These include: (1) maintaining biodiversity and production of ecosystem goods, such as food, fiber, biomass fuels, pharmaceuticals, industrial products, and their precursors; (2) life-support functions such as environmental cleansing, recycling, and renewal; and (3) providing intangible aesthetic and cultural benefits (for a detailed description of the ecosystem, its functions, services, and potential approaches to their evaluation, see Daily, 1997).

Resilience: The ability of the ecosystem to absorb perturbations (of different scales and in different time periods) without changing its structural features (see pp. 19–20).

Stress: The result of an environmental change that reduces the survival fitness of an organism. This is usually governed by a nonlinear relationship between the influence and fitness.

> **Threshold limits**: The limits of factors beyond which growth and equilibrium/stability of populations, or other survival features of life forms and organisms, are likely to be adversely affected. These limits constitute critical levels for survival.

Sustainability

Sustainability refers to the phenomenon of being able to maintain resources or assets forever. Environmental sustainability refers to the preservation of all aspects of the environment, qualitatively and quantitatively, for infinite time horizons. Two distinctions in this concept are relevant, however. These are:

- **Weak sustainability**: Patterns of sustainability that allow for substitutions (of varying types and degrees, with little consensus on the details) among environmental resources.
- **Strong sustainability**: Patterns of sustainability that sustain every asset undiminished in quality and quantity forever.

The strong version is usually advocated by vigorous environmentalism, and the weak form is suggested by some industrial enterprises and other free-market advocates. Substitution among sources and sinks and stock and flow aspects need to be understood in the context of the role of technical progress and human capital in order to arrive at a pragmatic framework for sustainability (for broad surveys, see Pezzey, 1992; Rao, 2000). The concept of irreversibility remains an area of critical importance in all forms of sustainability. Support for the merits of weak sustainability or any form of pragmatic sustainability should not ignore this feature.

Two of the most important concepts of ecological sciences relevant for the study of environmental sustainability are resilience and carrying capacity (CC). These are explained below.

Resilience

An important concept that describes environmental or ecological sustainability is founded on the role of perturbations on environmental systems or ecosystems, expressed in terms of the resilience of relevant systems. Ecosystem resilience or environmental resilience (ER) refers to the ability of a system to absorb disturbances and the magnitude of disturbance that can be absorbed before a system changes its structure

– its influences and processes that control behavior (see also Holling, 1995). In a simpler conventional framework, this may be interpreted as the ability of systems or species and organisms to respond to various disturbances (internal and/or external influences) to their environment, and to restore *status quo ante* features. Usually, resilience is not retained when the ranges of tolerance for variations in environmental factors are crossed by the disturbances or external influences. It is relevant to note that the ranges of tolerance differ significantly across different species and organisms, and a common factor may not be applied to the entire biota. The tolerance level of a system for any environmental or ecological stress tends to be reduced when other stresses exist, including those that are relatively remotely related. This exacerbates the vulnerability of the system to multiple or cumulative disturbances, and the linkages obey nonlinear relationships (for details, see Myers, 1993). Loss of resilience tends to shift a system toward its thresholds, and eventually leads to its flip from one equilibrium state to another.

Biogeophysical systems possess different levels of adaptability to changes, as do some other subsystems of ecological systems. These are likely to suffer irreversible consequences when their resilience features are lost. This has been seen, for example, in almost all groundwater systems when water withdrawal has exceeded critical limits without appropriate attention being given to replenishing the water table.

ER is a useful indicator of environmental sustainability. The characteristics of resilience include some components of adaptivity of the system. In order for humanity to be sustainable ecological systems must remain resilient, and any significant loss of ecosystem resilience (as, for example, in cases of desertification) could imply an irreversible change in the set of available options for the continued enjoyment of life in both present and future generations. Such phenomena exacerbate the adverse environmental consequences of economic activities as well.

Among the ecological problems that challenge the ability to achieve sustainable development are: (1) pollution problems cumulatively formed by human influences on air, land, and oceans that trigger sudden changes affecting the vitality of societies; (2) the ecological components of these features that possess features of irreversibility. These issues warrant greater attention in any approach to sustainability.

Carrying capacity (CC)

The complexity of source and sink problems as impediments to ecological sustainability can be better appreciated if we recognize that these

impose limitations of the planet's CC. This CC is defined as the maximum potential to support life forever on the planet without jeopard-
izing any major features. The CC is a dynamic function of various
resources, transformation methods, and outputs. Factors that contribute
to the changing levels of the CC include human and other disturbances, adaptation and evolutionary mechanisms, and technical innovations. The quality of nature and its assets affect its ability to provide
life-supporting services, including the supply of environmental
resources, as well as assimilation of wastes and pollution (environmental "bads"). Most of the definitions of the CC have been advanced
by ecologists and do not explicitly refer to a specific time horizon.
Such concepts are less useful for any design of long-term policy.

The CC tends to be adversely affected by the impact of cumulative
environmental effects (see also Rees, 1995): the additions of cumulative environmental effects of a persistent causal agent over time, or by
several similar agents or activities at a given time juncture. Here the
additivity does not imply the absence of nonlinear interactive effects
that accentuate the adverse environmental effects.

Some of these adverse effects such as the greenhouse effect are
illustrated below. The capacity of global sinks to assimilate environmental bads is also a form of natural capital which should be protected,
and "development that would add to the aggregate pollution load
imposed on the ecologically critical sinks may well be uneconomic in
a total social cost framework" (Rees, 1995). Thus, in essence, CC is
integrally linked to some of the features of sustainable development
(SD, discussed later in this chapter) and is a dynamic concept – as is
the "flux of nature" (the static version of which is the conventional
"balance of nature"). The dynamics of anthropogenic influences (including endogenous preference changes) play a major role in affecting
the CC. A formal analytical definition of the CC would seek (Rao,
2000) to explicitly recognize the objective function (maximal sustainable size of population) subject to the dynamics of economy–ecology
and specify the time horizon (whether infinity, i.e., forever, or a
foreseeable time period, such as a thousand years), as well as specify
meaningful constraints or stipulations (such as perceived levels of the
planet's sink capacities for greenhouse gases) that are sought to be
maintained. The sensitivity of the CC with respect to each of these is
very significant.

The role of sources and sinks is perhaps the single most important
fundamental characteristic underlying the dynamics of nature, its
resilience, and the carrying capacity of the planet. Let us recall that
ecosystem resilience may be broadly expressed in terms of its ability

to return to a normal equilibrium configuration after any small disturbance. When this does not happen, i.e., when its self-renewing and absorptive capacities are severely constrained, the loss of resilience could pose serious problems, including discontinuities with catastrophic consequences. This is the context in which the source and sink features interface directly with potential problems arising from loss of system resilience and hence of SD. Any discontinuous change in ecosystem functions leads the system to flip from one equilibrium to another, with the possible sudden loss of biological productivity. This diminishes the potential CC and may also result in an irreversible change in the set of options open to both present and future generations (examples include loss of the groundwater table, desertification, and loss of biodiversity).

The scarcity values of the environment and resources are better appreciated in terms of the apparent finiteness and increasing scarcity of many individual components of the systems. It is also important to realize that many of the current problems affecting the environment and development are critically linked to the self-renewing or regenerative and absorptive capacities of the biosphere, geosphere, and ecological system. Thus, the problems of atmospheric and biogeophysical regenerativeness are adversely affected by the recyclability of various ingredients of environmental "bads" such as atmospheric pollution, greenhouse gases, water pollution, and solid wastes.

Ecosystem discontinuities and the irreversible nature of changes adversely and significantly affect the source and sink problems of the planet. The resulting costs cannot be easily estimated. The focus on constraints affecting sustainable development has shifted from "source" limits to "sink" limits since the 1970s. Some limits are more amenable to substitution and more localized than others, as in the case of alternate sources of energy in some regions. Some features are tractable and are being tackled, such as the phasing out of chlorofluorocarbons (CFCs) under the Montreal Protocol. Sink capacity utilization features have a lot to do with the free-rider nature of open access to the common pool.

Trends in resource availability and the planet's sink capacity (the most significant environmental facet) both suggest a significant decline, while greenhouse gas emissions are increasing in most countries, mainly as a result of various applications of fossil fuel and biomass energy use. Economic growth and these emissions are highly correlated in these countries. Energy conservation and greater technological innovations are required to mitigate the effects. Important possibilities in this direction include a drastic reduction in deforestation and steps to produce effective carbon sequestration through significant afforestation operations.

The various impediments to sustainability (in biogeophysical and ecological terms) and SD are centered around global environmental factors. The ramifications cut across national boundaries. Global environmental problems undoubtedly have their roots at local, regional, and subregional levels, and at the levels of individual consumers and producers. However, such problems warrant collective coordinated actions whereby different societies, countries, and individual entities contribute to alleviate the common current and potential future problems. Any such coordinated or cooperative effort requires the participation of all potential contributors to the problems, and presumes that there are common perceptions and objectives, with participants having comparable means for achieving these objectives. These conditions are usually not met in most scenarios. Yet, to the extent that commonalities could be derived, the approach merits being adopted in terms of devising policies, programs, and actions for implementation. The analytics of strategic cooperative behavior draw upon game-theoretic formulations (see chapter 2), and some of these analyses suggest that in repeat transaction settings with interface between countries (possibly coordinated under agreements like the Montreal Protocol), there is much greater scope for cooperative behavior. It has also been established that this institutional arrangement is particularly relevant when the valuation of the future is not heavily discounted (see chapter 3 for discounting future values and time preferences).

Economic growth

Economic growth is conventionally measured in terms of increases in income. We are interested in the dynamics of sustainable economic growth with the requirement that desirable environmental features (specified type and degree) are sustainable. This formulation incorporates the inevitable link between the economy and the environment. The inverted U-relationship (often called the environmental Kuznets curve, EKC) that has been posited by some authors to link rises in economic growth (or growth of average per capita income) and declines in per capita emissions of pollutants is still somewhat hypothetical. This premise ignores, among other things, that income inequality creates a gap between a country's ability to pay for environmental protection and its willingness to pay for it (Magnani, 2000). Besides, not all pollutant emissions tend to behave in the same way in all countries or in response to rises in income in each year. Carbon dioxide, industrial water pollution, and municipal waste are some of the pollutants whose trend hardly obeys a relative decline per unit income growth. Furthermore, any presumption of the reversibility (using recycling or other measures) of pollution damage is unlikely to be meaningful (on the empirical findings on the EKC, see the survey by Jayadevappa and Chhatre, 2000). Some observations made by Rao (2000) are relevant here: (1) various methods used in the estimation of the interrelationship between economic growth and environmental quality are still largely too weak in their information base and analysis to be able to offer any significant policy guidance; (2) to the extent that the results can be viewed as robust, the analysis so far suggests that the possibility of economic growth itself taking care of environmental sustainability is very remote; (3) this does not imply that economic growth is not a necessary prerequisite for improved quality of life, especially in less developed regions; and (4) a realistic intervention policy in terms of incentives and disincentives for sustainable development can make an important contribution toward achieving desired goals, at global, national, and local levels.

Regarding a qualitative relationship between economic growth and environmental concerns, Vellinga (1999) derived the following conclusions, using an analytical optimizing model wherein the utility objective admits the role of environmental factors (that is, the broad utility function of society is not independent of the quality of the environment):

> The conditions under which environmental preservation has an influence on the long-term economic growth rate include the requirement that the quality of the environment/nature should influence the marginal utility of consumption.

The interrelationship of economic growth and environmental quality is largely the concern of the current generation of the population, with implications for future generations. In addition, there are several issues of resource use and resource access equity across generations. These are addressed in the next section.

■ 1.4 INTERGENERATIONAL AND INTRAGENERATIONAL WELFARE

It is not entirely meaningful to dichotomize the debate between intergenerational and intragenerational issues. This is because, at any given time point, there are overlapping generations, and the problems thereby concern a set of about at least four generations almost simultaneously. The classification, then, could mean unborn future generations and the current four generations. Approximated on a timescale, this would imply concerns spanning the next century for the population currently on the planet (although there would be few persons whose lifespan exceeded a century), and beyond a century for future populations.

Let us begin with an assessment traced back to Aristotle: human well-being is realized only partly by satisfying whatever people's preferences happen to be at a particular time; it is also necessary that successive generations leave behind sufficient resources to ensure that future generations are not constrained in their preferences. Thus, the set of meaningful choices in the future (not necessarily "for the future" as assessed at the current time) should be at least as good as the set available to the current generation. Since the choices include those of economic and noneconomic factors, possibly with limited interdependencies between them, this scenario is not amenable entirely to economic interpretations alone.

The Rawlsian theory of "justice as fairness" (Rawls, 1972) seriously considers issues of intergenerational justice. This theory was considered "contractarian" in the sense that it is posited on a requirement of ethical tradition where the relevant moral behavior is agreed upon by members of the society as a social contract. The three main ingredients listed for recognition under intergenerational transfer of rights are: the right to an appropriate return on savings, to the conservation of natural resources and the environment, and a sensible genetic preservation. These are all clearly interdependent, in an ecological sense. Sustainability of the resource base is a necessary prerequisite for achieving a productive output from savings, and biodiversity preservation is the key to healthy genetic potential over the generations. Consistent with the preservation of intergenerational equity, Rawlsian justice seeks to bring in distributional fairness with clear preference for policies which attend to improvement of the least well-off sections. This is also referred to as the Rawlsian maximin criterion, seeking maximization of the welfare of the least well-off sections or generations of society.

The concern for future generations is vividly expressed in several international environmental agreements. Box 1.3 provides an illustrative list of extracts from these agreements and declarations of principles. Having examined some of the major issues of intergenerational and intragenerational importance in the economic and environmental aspects of life on the planet, we need to address the concept and application of sustainable development.

BOX 1.3

Future generations and multilateral agreements

The following is an illustrative though not necessarily exhaustive list, with relevant summary extracts, of the explicitly stated provisions in various multilateral agreements between states.

1   International Convention for the Regulation of Whaling, 1946.

> Recognizing the interest of the nations of the world in safeguarding for future generations the great natural resources represented by the whale stocks. (p. 74)

2   UN Charter of Economic Rights and Duties of States, adopted by the UN General Assembly Resolution 3281, 1974.

> The protection, preservation and enhancement of the environment for the present and future generations is the responsibility of all States. All States shall endeavour to establish their own environmental and developmental policies in conformity with such responsibility. (Article 30)

3   Convention on the Conservation of Migratory Species of Wild Animals, 1980.

> Aware that each generation of man holds the resources of the earth for future generations and has an obligation to ensure that this legacy is conserved and, where utilized, is used wisely. (p. 1)

4   UN Convention on Biological Diversity, 1992.

> Sustainable use means the use of components of biological diversity in a way and at a rate that does not lead to the long-term decline of biological diversity, thereby maintaining its potential to meet the needs and aspirations of present and future generations.

5   Statement of Principles for a Global Consensus on the Management, Conservation, and Sustainable Development of all Types of Forests, UN Conference of 1992.

Forest resources and forest lands should be sustainably managed to meet the social, economic, ecological, cultural and
spiritual human needs of present and future generations.

6   The Rio Declaration on Environment and Development,
1992.

The right to development must be fulfilled so as to equitably
meet developmental and environmental needs of present and
future generations. (Principle 3 of the Declaration)

7   The United Nations Framework Convention on Climate
Change, 1992. Article 3 (1) Principles state the following:

In their actions to achieve the objective of the Convention
and to implement its provisions, the Parties shall be guided,
inter alia, by the following:

The Parties should protect the climate system for the benefit
of present and future generations of humankind, on the basis
of equity and in accordance with their common but differentiated responsibilities and respective capabilities. Accordingly,
the developed country Parties should take the lead in combating climate change and the adverse effects thereof.

8   North American Agreement on Environmental Cooperation,
1993.

The objectives of this Agreement are to . . . foster the protection
and improvement of the environment in the territories of the
Parties for the well-being of present and future generations.

9   Aarhus Convention on Access to Information, Public Participation in Decision-making, and Access to Justice in Environmental Matters, 1998 (in the region of the United Nations
Economic Commission for Europe (ECE)). It was signed by
35 states and the EC. The preamble states, *inter alia*, that:

every person has the right to live in an environment adequate to his or her health and well-being, and the duty, both
individually and in association with others, to protect and
improve the environment for the benefit of present and
future generations . . .

> Article 1 (Objective) declares:
>
> In order to contribute to the protection of the right of
> every person of present and future generations to live in an
> environment adequate to his or her health and well-being,
> each Party shall guarantee the rights of access to information,
> public participation in decision-making, and access to justice
> in environmental matters in accordance with the provisions
> of this Convention.

A broad definition of sustainable development

One of the general requirements of SD seeks to improve the quality
of human life while living within the carrying capacity of supporting
ecosystems (World Conservation Union, UNEP, and Worldwide Fund
for Nature, 1991). The broad definition, widely accepted since its
enunciation in 1987, is given in the Report of the World Commission
on Environment and Development (Brundtland Commission of 1987).
This Report contributed to much of the ongoing concern for sustainable development. It stated:

> Sustainable development is development that meets the needs of the
> present without compromising the ability of future generations to meet
> their own needs. It contains within it two key concepts: the concept of
> "needs," in particular the essential needs of the world's poor, to which
> overriding priority should be given; and the idea of limitations imposed
> by the state of technology and social organization on the environment's
> ability to meet present and future needs. (p. 43)

It must be recognized that this definition explicitly acknowledges the
roles of intergenerational as well as intragenerational welfare while
securing a sustainable quality of life forever. However, most of the
literature on SD and its applications quotes only the first sentence of
the above definition, thus constituting a gross distortion of the integrity of the concept. As Solow (1996) suggested, the concept of SD
should be relevant not because of its vagueness, but in spite of it.

A closer approximation to a workable definition or approach can be
attempted in several directions. According to Vellinga et al. (1995),

> The concept of sustainable development can be defined as maintenance
> and sustainable utilization of the functions (goods and services) pro-
> vided by natural ecosystems and biospheric processes. Conversely, in

BOX 1.4

Broad approaches to sustainable development

1   **Neoclassical economics**: Nondeclining human welfare or quality of human life; sustainable growth based on technical progress and substitution possibilities; optimizing environmental externalities; maintaining aggregate or subgroup-specific stocks of natural and economic capital with substantial reliance on market factors (possibly with specifications of legal and other institutional regulations); predominant role of individual enterprises and individuals in decisions affecting income generation, consumption, and environmental implications.

2   **Evolutionary ecology**: Maintaining resilience of natural systems; allowing for variations and biological cycles; learning from uncertainty in natural processes; humans forming only a component of the list of biological species, with no presumed dominant role; fostering genetic/biotic/ecosystem diversity.

3   **Human ecology**: Remaining within the carrying capacity, with limitations on scales of material throughput for economic activities, including human consumption; considering multiple effects of human actions over regional and temporal dimensions and in relation to ecological features.

4   **New institutional economics**: Recognizing the roles of institutions and transaction costs (including adaptation and transformation costs), information-processing, and rational decision-making constraints; devising incentives as well as disincentives to regulate anthropogenic influences of all decision-making entities in order to ensure sustainable development.

a situation of unsustainability, where the limits of the biosphere's carrying capacity are exceeded, not all of the environmental functions can be fully fulfilled anymore.

Several broad perspectives have emerged over the years to describe environmental problems and to prescribe solutions. Box 1.4 summarizes some of the important approaches in this regard; note that this does not constitute an exhaustive list. This book relies heavily on perspectives 1 (neoclassical economics) and 4 (new institutional economics), as outlined in the box, and attempts to complement rather than polarize the two perspectives. The role of ecological perspectives remains an underlying structural concern in the context of the application of one or more of these economic approaches.

Economic definition of sustainable development

A formal definition may be stated (see also Rao, 2000):

Sustainable development (SD) is the process of socioeconomic development which is built on the environmental sustainability approach (defined above), with an additional requirement that the worth of the capital stocks vector (valued at appropriate shadow prices) is maintained constant or undiminished at each time interval forever.

This definition seeks an evaluation of resources at their "true worth" or shadow prices. This is usually conditioned upon the specification of at least two major criteria: the metric on which these monetized and nonmonetized values have to be measured, and the degree of unsustainability or sustainability under which the above valuations occur. These empirical exercises are not necessarily easy to implement, but an application of the concept even at the qualitative level can provide insights and policy guidelines. The role of ecological interdependencies, for example, comes to the surface in the process of any application of the definition. It may also be clarified that any static assessment of the "shadow prices" of resources could be on their valuation under unsustainable conditions; the prescription then becomes less relevant. In other words, these evaluations need to be carried out with reference to exogenously determined sustainable conditions.

The important distinction between sustainability and sustainable development allows one to examine more real-life solutions to identified and potential problems that affect the welfare of human society. Some advocate assigning equal importance to all species on the planet. It is suggested here that we accept the premise that humans remain the dominant species, but we will need greater realization and action to ensure that other constituents of ecosystems are preserved if their life-supporting nature is not to be disturbed to the detriment of the human population. Thus, sustainable development continues to play a dominant role over sustainability, and the latter is deemed as a binding constraint on the socioeconomic development processes. Even after accepting such a premise, a number of factors, such as the valuation of the future and of resources, perceptions, and the role of uncertainty, contribute to alternative interpretations and policy guidelines.

Within the above framework the concept of sustainability, impro-vised with additional considerations of unique and irreplaceable as-sets (biological or other), can offer guidance to policies for pragmatic sustainable development. This approach, strengthened by the use of comprehensive methods of optimal development, promises appropri-ate directions for economic inquiry that are applicable in a wide vari-ety of socioeconomic systems. This is attainable with the application of select approaches for sustainable development.

Environmental irreversibilities, cumulative effects, and nonlinearities in environmental responses to resource use pose major potential prob-lems that require extensive application of the precautionary principle (see chapter 3) and related decision-making mechanisms for environ-mental governance. All these salient features of life on earth should form the ingredients of comprehensive approaches to sustainable de-velopment.

Economic growth remains a necessary requirement for the above development, but it is not sufficient on its own (Rao, 2000). A non-interventionist free-market approach to these processes is unlikely to mitigate the problems of environmental degradation. Environmental improvement does not automatically follow economic growth, despite some arguments in the environmental economics literature that sug-gest the possible existence of inflection points which, once reached, show declines in environmental pollutants per unit economic growth thereafter (for a brief survey and discussion of these studies, see Rao, 2000). It remains imperative that active policies and implementation mechanisms are needed for achieving desirable environmental quality and sustainable standards of living.

The issues of sustainability and sustainable development are based on concerns about all of the following global environmental problems: the rise of global mean temperatures, deforestation, ozone deple-tion, emissions of greenhouse gases, the expanded scale of operations influenced by the growing population and consumption, and general environmental pollution. The combined interdependent effects of these phenomena are simultaneously at work, to an extent never before experienced on the planet. The problem is one of loss of ecosystem resilience. The synergism here is of an interwoven nonlinear relation-ship, the potential outcome of which could be unprecedented cata-strophic problems that engulf every aspect of life (as we know it) and its sustainability. Humanity may not be fully prepared to face such large-scale adverse phenomena, and there is the problem of "the fear of the unknown." One of most important areas of concern relates to the role of environmental changes in affecting human health. Some of the important elements of these interdependencies are discussed in the next section, although it should be stated that there are still several major unknowns in our emerging understanding of these complex interrelationships.

■ 1.5 ENVIRONMENT AND PUBLIC HEALTH

Aristotle argued for a right to health: "if we believe men have any personal rights at all as human beings, they have an absolute right to such a measure of good health as society, and society alone, is able to give them" (quoted in Willis, 1996, p. 197). Thus, human health may be seen as a natural right, at both the individual and community level.

The Constitution of the World Health Organization defines health as "a state of complete physical, mental and social well-being, and not merely the absence of disease or infirmity." The UN Charter recognizes the right to health in its human rights documents. The Universal Declaration of Human Rights states (UN Charter Ch. 9, Art. 25, December 10, 1948, GA Res. 217, UN GAOR, 3rd Session, 1948): "Everyone has the right to a standard of living adequate for the health and well-being of himself and his family." The second component of the international bill of human rights is the International Covenant on Economic, Social, and Cultural Rights. Its Article 12 declares: "State parties to the present Covenant recognize the right of everyone to the enjoyment of the highest attainable standard of physical and mental health." The UN Commission on Human Rights in its 1994 Report, *Human Rights and the Environment*, advocated the "human right to a healthy environment" (46th Session, UN Doc. E/CN.4/Sub.2/1994/9).

Among the international environmental agreements that make explicit mention of the role of environmental protection and human well-being is the 1998 Aarhus Convention on Access to Information, Public Participation in Decision-making, and Access to Justice in Environmental Matters. In its preamble, the Convention states, *inter alia*, that "adequate protection of the environment is essential to human well-being and the enjoyment of basic human rights, including the right to life itself."

Biogeophysical and public health economics

The role of the environment in affecting health status is fairly well documented when the factors are determined in terms of local biophysical environment. The evolution of global environmental features, their changes over time, and their potentially iniquitous incidence (in terms of the possible lack of a direct relationship between contributors to the changes and victims of such changes) need considerably greater attention. Transboundary transmissions of environmental problems, causing externalities of production and consumption systems of different sectors and countries, tend to accentuate the following global environmental phenomena: the accumulation of GHGs, ozone depletion, and the loss of biodiversity. Each of these phenomena plays a serious role, independently and jointly. The environment and public health are more closely dependent in the current era than ever before. This is because of the elevated levels of environmental quality and its sensitivity to enhanced economic activities as well as to other anthropogenic influences. Among the adverse contributors to environmental health problems are some toxic pesticides, hazardous wastes and their deposits, the continued use of ozone-depleting substances, transboundary river pollution, the release of persistent and volatile organic pollutants, and emissions of GHGs leading to an enhanced greenhouse effect (GE). Box 1.5, based on US Environmental Protection Agency (USEPA) information, summarizes some environment-related health problems in terms of their direct effects; other major indirect effects include those attributable to global warming and other large-scale phenomena.

One of the direct effects of the GE is the warming of surface temperatures and the consequent severity of heatwaves in most regions of the world. Heat stress lowers productivity and raises morbidity of populations. The richer countries could possibly partly safeguard themselves against this effect by using energy-intensive technologies, but this only provides another multiplier effect or enhanced GE. To that extent protection against climate change can contribute to enhanced economic as well as environmental externalities. Poorer regions of the world can ill afford any worsening of their climate since their adaptation costs are unaffordably high, and these regions generally lose out for lack of any meaningful protection against the severity of the climate and its health effects. These effects may be either direct or indirect, operating via disease burden or other indirect consequences such as the depleted quantity and quality of water resources and access to gainful employment.

Whenever an aggregate estimate of temperature rise due to global warming is estimated, the magnitudes involved, such as a third of a centigrade per decade, convey only part of the emerging scenario. Such magnitudes have serious implications in terms of a significant increase in the number of days with higher night-time temperatures,

BOX 1.5

Environment and health

The effects of some environmental features on human health are summarized below.

1 **Ozone (O₃)**
   Source: chemical reaction of pollutants, volatile organic compounds (VOCs), and nitrogen oxide (NO$_x$).
   Health effects: breathing problems, reduced lung function, asthma, reduced resistance to infections, stress on lung tissues.
2 **Volatile organic compounds (VOCs)**
   Source: releases from burning fuel, solvents, paints, glues, and other products.
   Health effects: in addition to ozone effects, many VOCs can cause serious health problems such as cancer.
3 **Nitrogen oxide (NO$_x$)**
   Source: burning of gasoline, natural gas, coal, oil, etc.
   Health effects: lung damage, illnesses affecting breathing passages and lungs.
4 **Carbon monoxide (CO)**
   Source: burning of gasoline, natural gas, coal, oil.
   Health effects: reduces ability of blood to bring oxygen to body cells and tissues (cells and tissues need oxygen to work); hazardous to people with heart or circulatory problems.
5 **Sulfur dioxide (SO₂)**
   Source: burning of coal and oil, especially high-sulfur coal from the eastern United States; industrial processes (paper, metals, and others).
   Health effects: breathing problems, damage to lungs.

Sources: USEPA and other sources

with a consequently drastic increase in the disease vectors that transmit infectious diseases. Mosquitoes, flies, rodents, and other insects flourish in the increased warming of the regions. Loevinsohn (1994) observed the marked increase in the incidence of malaria in Rwanda during the 1980s in close relation to observed increases in the temperatures of the region. The mechanisms of enhanced transmission of malarial diseases due to climate change were also documented by Lindsay and Birley (1996). A rapid increase in the incidence of serious illness due to dengue fever epidemics is predicted from many of the global models (see Patz et al., 1998). Among the major diseases that are expected to expand their incidence are malaria, dengue fever, schistosomiasis, and onchocerciasis. Global climate models suggest that, with regard to malaria alone, a 3°C increase in global mean temperature by 2100 could lead to substantial widening of the malarial zones and an addition of 50 to 80 million cases per annum globally (Stone, 1995).

The emergence of new diseases is tied to the changes in the climate that affect the survival of parasites and alter the ratios of prey–predator combinations (see Epstein, 1995). The emergence of a greater variety and incidence of diseases due to global warming is indicated by Bradley (1997). This constitutes an ever-increasing problem when the ongoing phenomenon of biodiversity loss reduces the potential for obtaining medical solutions to emerging health problems. The health impact of climate change depends on various interactive phenomena: multiple and continued disturbances to the ecosystem leading to public health effects, variations in the adaptation (autonomous or planned intervention-based) of different societies to health issues, and global climatic changes with differential impacts on local areas and systems, and other feedback effects of continued changes. McMichael and Martens (1995) listed the main types of potential health impact of global climatic change as follows:

- **Direct impacts**: Morbidity and mortality due to increased and severe heatwaves; respiratory illnesses as a result of increased air pollution and pollen content of the air; skin and eye problems as a result of increased ultraviolet radiation from stratospheric ozone depletion; aggravated weather extremities leading to destruction of life and property.
- **Indirect impacts**: Altered range and diffusion of vector-borne infectious diseases such as malaria, and contagious diseases such as cholera; adverse effects on food-production systems leading to malnutrition and loss of health, demographic disruption, and a compromised quality of life in most regions.

An integrated approach to any assessment of health impacts of climatic change involves appreciation of the effects of climate change directly, and its effects via environmental change. Interactive feedback mechanisms of climate change and environmental change must be recognized in this context. Direct climatic influences include disturbances to ecological systems, habitat loss for humans and other biota, agronomic effects on food production and human survival, and heat stress and consequent morbidity and mortality. The effects of climatic change that operate via consequential environmental change include changes in air pollution chemistry leading to severity of known and unknown diseases, aggravated effects of ozone depletion, the increased deployment of pesticides of all varieties which, in turn, tend to contribute to further health problems, and the loss of biodiversity and its effects on potential health remedies. In addition, the interaction of climate change and environmental change aggravates multiply the above effects in unknown proportions. Some of the relevant integrated analytical models in this context are summarized by McMichael (1997). The state of this knowledge requires continued and greater attention from institutions such as the World Health Organization (WHO).

The problem of the extended and accelerated spread of many diseases is the expected economic burden in both developed and developing regions of the world. The magnitude of illness, its effects on productivity, costs of prevention and of treating the affected populations, those of morbidity and mortality, and adverse implications on sustainable development are only a partial list of considerations. Some estimates of monetary costs are proposed in a few studies (some are cited in the special focus of *World Resources 1998–99*), but none is comprehensive. At this stage, even a qualitative understanding of the likely effects provides greater insight into the economic and human costs of climate change.

■ 1.6 SUMMARY

International environmental laws should recognize fully the role of ecological principles, ecology–economy relationships, and the application of alternative economic approaches and critical concepts in the formulation and effectiveness of various provisions and their operational interpretation. This chapter lays the groundwork for some of the historical and evolutionary aspects of international environmental and economic policies, especially the role of sustainability and sustainable development. The imperatives of ecological principles are also to be recognized since natural laws form the scientific bases for economic formulations, with the latter guiding some of the ingredients of international environmental law.

Environmental change tends to impose known and unknown costs on most sections of contemporary and future societies, unless proper attention is paid toward prevention, adoption, and mitigation. This is particularly significant when the rapid pace of climate change or changes in environmental phenomena allows scarcely sufficient time and resources for adaptation, adoption, and mitigation. As Wood (1996) argues, "accelerated climate change threatens to overwhelm the capacity of natural systems to adapt."

Global economic welfare and enhancement and their sustainability require environmental security and stability. Small perturbations which might be economically justified as "efficient" necessitate the existence of resilient environmental phenomena. In the absence of the requisite resilience, what was conceived as a small disturbance could imply major environmental losses, and hence economic losses as well. Continued use of resources on a sustainable basis and the application of the principles of generalized productive efficiency and generalized allocative efficiency are the imperatives for global welfare enhancement when several global environmental goods and services are nonmarketized. The role of scientific and informational uncertainties warrants greater concern for the precautionary principle (see chapter 3), which would seek to "err on the safe side" in such situations. In the absence of any single global entity to ensure the observance of environmental sustainability, a series of internationally coordinated measures is required to achieve the desirable global objective. These areas are discussed in the remaining chapters of the book.

The global environment is the resultant of anthropogenic influences, which are not necessarily confined to individual national boundaries. Global interdependencies are influenced by the economic and environmental policies of nations and collective international arrangements, in addition to market forces. The need for and feasibility of global cooperation to protect the environment is already widely established. The role of international institutions, in general, and legal institutions, in particular, remains to be explored further, however. The distinctions between environmental sustainability and sustainable development enable the assessment of the relative roles of institutions and policy instruments in the modulation of the global environment. Similarly, the concerns of current and future generations also require careful attention, as they cannot be expected to be attended to by market institutions alone. International diplomacy and law remain focal points of action for the future and depend heavily on the articulation of issues in the management of global environmental resources, with interdisciplinary perspectives and economic assessments.

Appendix: International Environmental Agreements

Dates represent date of adoption.

Global climate change

- Kyoto Protocol on Climate Change, November 1997
- United Nations Framework Convention on Climate Change (UNFCCC), May 9, 1992
- UN Conference on Environment and Development
  - Agenda 21, June 3–14, 1992
  - Rio Declaration, June 3–14, 1992

Stratospheric ozone depletion

- Adjustments and Amendment to the Montreal Protocol on Substances that Deplete the Ozone Layer, November 23–5, 1992
- Adjustments and Amendment to the Montreal Protocol on Substances that Deplete the Ozone Layer, June 29, 1990
- Montreal Protocol on Substances that Deplete the Ozone Layer, September 16, 1987
- Vienna Convention for the Protection of the Ozone Layer, March 22, 1985

Desertification and land cover change

- United Nations Convention to Combat Desertification in those Countries Experiencing Serious Drought and/or Desertification, Particularly in Africa, September 12, 1994
- United Nations Conference on Desertification (UNCOD) Plan of Action to Combat Desertification and General Assembly Resolutions, August 29, 1977

Conservation of biological diversity

- Agreement Establishing the Inter-American Institute for Global Change Research, May 13, 1992
- Convention on Biological Diversity, June 5, 1992
- Protocol on Environmental Protection to the Antarctic Treaty, October 4, 1991
- European Convention for the Protection of Pet Animals, November 13, 1987
- ASEAN Agreement on the Conservation of Nature and Natural Resources, July 9, 1985

- International Tropical Timber Agreement, November 18, 1983
- Protocol to Amend the Convention on Wetlands of International Importance Especially as Waterfowl Habitat, December 3, 1982
- Benelux Convention on Nature Conservation and Landscape Protection, June 8, 1982
- World Charter for Nature, 1982
- Convention on the Conservation of Antarctic Marine Living Resources, May 20, 1980
- Convention on the Conservation of European Wildlife and Natural Habitats, September 19, 1979
- Convention on the Conservation of Migratory Species of Wild Animals, June 23, 1979
- Agreement on Conservation of Polar Bears, November 15, 1973
- Convention on International Trade in Endangered Species of Wild Fauna and Flora, March 3, 1973
- Convention for the Protection of the World Cultural and Natural Heritage, November 23, 1972
- Convention for the Conservation of Antarctic Seals, June 1, 1972
- Convention on Wetlands of International Importance Especially as Waterfowl Habitat, February 2, 1971
- Benelux Convention on the Hunting and Protection of Birds (as amended), June 10, 1970
- International Convention for the Protection of Birds, October 18, 1950

Transboundary air pollution

- Convention on the Transboundary Effects of Industrial Accidents, March 17, 1992
- Convention on Environmental Impact Assessment in a Transboundary Context, February 25, 1991
- Basel Convention on the Control of Transboundary Movements of Hazardous Wastes and their Disposal, March 22, 1989
- Protocol to the 1979 Convention on Long-range Transboundary Air Pollution on Long-term Financing of Cooperative Program for Monitoring and Evaluation of the Long-range Transmissions of Air Pollutants in Europe (EMEP), September 28, 1984
- Protocol Concerning Cooperation in Combating Pollution in Cases of Emergency, March 21, 1981
- Convention on Long-range Transboundary Air Pollution, November 13, 1979

Hazardous waste management

- Bamako Convention on the Ban of the Import into Africa and the Control of Transboundary Movements and Management of Hazardous Wastes Within Africa, January 30, 1991
- Basel Convention on the Control of Transboundary Movements of Hazardous Wastes and their Disposal, March 22, 1989

Ocean resources

- Agreement for the Implementation of the Provisions of the United Nations Convention on the Law of the Sea of December 10, 1982 Relating to the Conservation and Management of Straddling Fish Stocks and Highly Migratory Fish Stocks, August 4, 1995
- Agreement Relating to the Implementation of Part XI of the 1982 United Nations Convention on the Law of the Sea, July 28, 1994
- Agreement to Promote Compliance with International Conservation and Management Measures by Fishing Vessels on the High Seas, November 29, 1993
- Agreement Establishing the South Pacific Regional Environment Program (SPREP), June 16, 1993
- Convention for the Conservation of Southern Bluefin Tuna, May 10, 1993
- Annex III to the Protocol of February 17, 1978 Relating to the International Convention for the Prevention of Pollution from Ships of November 2, 1973 (MARPOL 73/78), as amended on October 30, 1992
- Protocol on Protection of the Black Sea Marine Environment Against Pollution from Land-based Sources, April 21, 1992
- Convention for a North Pacific Marine Science Organization (PICES), December 12, 1990
- International Convention on Oil Pollution Preparedness, Response, and Cooperation, November 29, 1990
- Amendment to the Annex to the Convention for the Prevention of Marine Pollution by Dumping of Wastes and Other Matter, November 3, 1989
- Protocol Concerning Marine Pollution Resulting from Exploration and Exploitation of the Continental Shelf, March 29, 1989
- Protocol for the Prevention of Pollution of the South Pacific Region by Dumping, November 25, 1986

- Protocol Concerning Cooperation in Combating Pollution Emergencies in the South Pacific Region, November 25, 1986
- Convention for the Protection of the Natural Resources and Environment of the South Pacific Region, November 24, 1986
- Protocol to Amend the International Convention on Civil Liability for Oil Pollution Damage, May 25, 1984
- Protocol to Amend the International Convention on the Establishment of an International Fund for Compensation for Oil Pollution Damage, May 25, 1984
- Agreement for Cooperation in Dealing with Pollution of the North Sea by Oil and Other Harmful Substances, September 13, 1983
- United Nations Convention on the Law of the Sea, December 10, 1982
- Convention for the Conservation of Salmon in the North Atlantic Ocean, March 2, 1982
- Amendments to the Convention on the Prevention of Marine Pollution by Dumping of Wastes and Other Matter Concerning Settlement of Disputes, October 12, 1978
- Protocol of 1978 Relating to the International Convention for the Prevention of Pollution from Ships, February 17, 1978
- Protocol to the International Convention on Civil Liability for Oil Pollution Damage, November 19, 1976
- Protocol to the International Convention on the Establishment of an International Fund for Compensation for Oil Pollution Damage, November 19, 1976
- Interim Convention on Conservation of North Pacific Fur Seals, February 9, 1957 (as amended on May 7, 1976)
- Protocol for the Prevention of Pollution of the Mediterranean Sea by Dumping from Ships and Aircraft, February 16, 1976
- Convention on the Prevention of Marine Pollution from Land-based Sources, June 4, 1974
- Nordic Environmental Protection Convention, February 19, 1974
- Protocol Relating to Intervention on the High Seas in Cases of Pollution by Substances Other than Oil, November 2, 1973
- International Convention for the Prevention of Pollution from Ships, November 2, 1973
- Convention on Fishing and Conservation of the Living Resources in the Baltic Sea and Belts, September 13, 1973
- Convention on the Prevention of Marine Pollution by Dumping of Wastes and Other Matter, December 29, 1972

- Convention for the Prevention of Marine Pollution by Dumping from Ships and Aircraft (as amended), 15 February 1972
- International Convention on the Establishment of an International Fund for Compensation for Oil Pollution Damage, December 18, 1971
- Agreement Concerning Cooperation in Taking Measures Against Pollution of the Sea by Oil, September 16, 1971
- International Convention on Civil Liability for Oil Pollution Damage, November 29, 1969
- International Convention for the Conservation of Atlantic Tunas, May 14, 1966
- Convention for the International Council for the Exploration of the Sea (as amended), September 12, 1964
- Agreed Measures for the Conservation of Antarctic Fauna and Flora, June 2, 1964
- Fisheries Convention, March 9, 1964
- Treaty Banning Nuclear Weapon Tests in the Atmosphere, in Outer Space, and Under Water, October 10, 1963
- Convention on Fishing and Conservation of the Living Resources of the High Seas, April 29, 1958
- Convention on the Continental Shelf, April 29, 1958
- Interim Convention on Conservation of North Pacific Fur Seals, February 9, 1957
- International Convention for the Prevention of Pollution of the Sea by Oil (as amended on April 11, 1962 and October 21, 1969), May 12, 1954
- International Convention for the Regulation of Whaling, December 2, 1946
- MARPOL Optional Annex Annex IV: Regulations for the Prevention of Pollution by Sewage from Ships

International trade and the environment

- Rio Declaration and Agenda 21, June 3–14, 1992
- Bamako Convention on the Ban of the Import into Africa and the Control of Transboundary Movements and Management of Hazardous Wastes Within Africa, January 30, 1991
- Basel Convention on the Control of Transboundary Movements of Hazardous Wastes and their Disposal, March 22, 1989
- Convention on the Regulation of Antarctic Mineral Resource Activities, June 2, 1988
- International Tropical Timber Agreement, November 18, 1983

- European Convention for the Protection of Animals Kept for Farming Purposes, March 10, 1976
- Convention on International Trade in Endangered Species of Wild Fauna and Flora, March 3, 1973
- Convention for the Protection of the World Cultural and Natural Heritage, November 23, 1972

Sources: Fridtjof Nansen Institute (1996); UN (1997); http://sedac.ciesin.org/pidb/texts-subject.html (April 20, 2000)

Review Exercises

1 Explain the role of intragenerational equity in the contexts of (a) environmental sustainability; (b) economic sustainability; and (c) sustainable development.

2 If ecological resilience is unaltered, is sustainable development assured? If not, what are the additional requirements for this purpose?

3 If the original UN Charter did not explicitly include its role in the environmental arena, what legitimizes or governs the UN's role in international environmental law?

4 How are international public laws and international private laws interrelated in the context of global environmental governance?

5 If adverse environmental public health is attributed to the role of pollution emissions, discuss the role of different economic criteria relevant in (a) internalizing environmental costs of consumption and production; and (b) maximizing the value of economic output.

6 Explain the concepts of generalized productive efficiency and generalized allocative efficiency with applications in environmental resource management.

7 What are the information requirements for an operational interpretation of the economic definition of sustainable development?

8 Elucidate the Rawlsian concept of social justice and compare it with the underlying principles of justice in the Brundtland Report's definition of sustainable development.

REFERENCES

Aceves, W. J., 1996, An economic analysis of international law: Transaction cost economics and the concept of state practice, *University of Pennsylvania Journal of International Economic Law*, 17, 995–1068.

Baird, D. G., Gertner, R. H., and Picker, R. C., 1994, *Game Theory and the Law*, Cambridge, MA: Harvard University Press.

Baxter, W. F., 1974, *People or Penguins: The Case for Optimal Pollution*, New York: Columbia University Press.

Bradley, D. J., 1997, From chilly summer afternoon to global warming: Climate as a determinant of human disease (editorial), *Tropical Medicine and International Health*, 9, 823–4.

Cass, R. A., 1997, Economics and international law, *New York University Journal of International Law and Politics*, 29, 473–522.

Coase, R. H., 1960, The problem of social cost, *Journal of Law and Economics*, 3, 1–44.

Daily, G. (ed.), 1997, *Nature's Services: Societal Dependence on Natural Ecosystems*, Washington, DC: Island Press.

Dunoff, J. L. and Trachtman, J. P., 1999, Economic analysis of international law, *Yale Journal of International Law*, 24, 1–59.

Epstein, P. R., 1995, Emerging diseases and ecosystem instability: New threats to public health, *American Journal of Public Health*, 85 (2), 168–72.

Gillespie, A., 1997, *International Environmental Law, Policy and Ethics*, Oxford: Clarendon Press.

Gregory, R., 1999, Identifying environmental values, in V. H. Dale and M. R. English (eds.), *Tools to Aid Environmental Decision-making*, New York: Springer-Verlag, pp. 32–58.

Harremoes, P., 1996, Dilemmas in ethics: Towards a sustainable society, *Ambio*, 25, 390–2.

Holling, C. S., 1995, Sustainability: The cross-scale dimension, in M. Munasinghe and W. Shearer (eds.), *Defining and Measuring Sustainability: The Biogeophysical Foundations*, Washington, DC: The World Bank/UN University, pp. 65–76.

Jayadevappa, R. and Chhatre, S., 2000, International trade and environmental quality: A survey, *Ecological Economics*, 32, 175–94.

Kaplow, L. and Shavell, S., 2000, Economic analysis of law, in A. J. Auerbach and M. Feldstein (eds.), *Handbook of Public Economics*, New York: Elsevier Science.

Lindsay, S. and Birley, M., 1996, Climate change and malaria transmission, *Annals of Tropical Medicine and Parasitology*, 90, 580–8.

Loevinsohn, M. E., 1994, Climatic warming and increased malaria incidence in Rwanda, *Lancet*, 343, 714–17.

McMichael, A. J., 1997, Integrated assessment of potential health impact of global environmental change: Prospects and limitations, *Environmental Modeling and Assessment*, 2, 129–37.

McMichael, A. J., Haines, A., Slooff, R., and Kovats, S., 1996, *Climate Change and Human Health*, Geneva: World Health Organization.

McMichael, A. J. and Martens, W. J. M., 1995. The health impacts of global climate change: Grappling with scenarios, predictive models, and multiple uncertainties, *Ecosystem Health*, 1, 23–33.

Magnani, E., 2000, The environmental Kuznets curve, environmental protection policy and income distribution, *Ecological Economics*, 32, 431–43.

Myers, N., 1993, *Ultimate Security: The Environmental Basis of Political Stability*, New York: W. W. Norton.

Myers, N., 1995, Environmental unknowns, *Science*, 269, 358–60.

Nanda, V. P. and Ris, Jr., W. K., 1976, The public trust doctrine: A viable approach to international environmental protection, *Ecological Law Quarterly*, 5, 296–410.

Nash, J. A., 1993, The case for biotic rights, *Yale Journal of International Law*, 18.

Ogus, A., 1995, Economics and law reform: Thirty years of Law Commission endeavor, *Law Quarterly Review*, 111, 407–20.

Patz, J. A., Epstein, P. R., Burke, T. A., and Balbers, J. M., 1996, Global climatic change and emerging infectious diseases, *Journal of the American Medical Association*, 275, 217–23.

Patz, J. A., Martens, W. J. M., Focks, D. A., and Jetten, T. H., 1998, Dengue fever epidemic potential as projected by general circulation models of global climate change, *Environmental Health Perspectives*, 106 (3), 147–53.

Pezzey, J., 1992, Sustainability: An interdisciplinary guide, *Environmental Values*, 1, 321–62.

Rao, P. K., 2000, *Sustainable Development: Economics and Policy*, Oxford: Blackwell.

Rao, P. K., 2001, *The Economics of Transaction Costs*, London: Palgrave.

Rawls, J., 1972, *A Theory of Justice*, Cambridge, MA: Harvard University Press.

Rees, W. E., 1995, Cumulative environmental assessment and global change, *Environmental Impact Assessment Review*, 15, 295–310.

Solow, R. M., 1996, Intergenerational equity, yes – but what about inequity today?, in *Human Development Report 1996*, UNDP Publication, New York: Oxford University Press, p. 16.

Stone, C. D., 1996, Locale and legitimacy in international environmental law, *Stanford Law Review*, 48, 1279–91.

Stone, R., 1995, If mercury soars, so may health hazards, *Science*, 267, 957–8.

Storm, J. A., 1997, South Africa's new environmental policies: Making green the new dominant color, *Georgetown International Environmental Law Review*, 9, 641–62.

Taylor, P. E., 1998, From environmental to ecological human rights: A new dynamic in international law?, *Georgetown International Environmental Law Review*, 10, 309–97.

Vellinga, N., 1999, Multiplicative utility and the influence of environmental care on the short-term economic growth rate, *Economic Modeling*, 16, 307–30.

Vellinga, P. et al., 1995, An ecologically sustainable biosphere, in *The Environment: Towards a Sustainable Future*, Boston: Kluwer Academic Publishers, pp. 317–46.

Wells, Jr., R. N., 1996, *Law, Values, and the Environment*, Lanham, MD: Scarecrow Press.

Willis, F. M., 1996, Economic development, environmental protection, and the right to health, *Georgetown International Economic Law Review*, 9, 195–220.

Wilson, E. O., 1992, *The Diversity of Life*, Cambridge, MA: Belknap/Harvard University Press.

Wood, J. C., 1996, Intergenerational equity and climate change, *Georgetown International Environmental Law Review*, 8, 293–332.

World Commission on Environment and Development (Brundtland Report), 1987, *Our Common Future*, Oxford: Oxford University Press.

World Conservation Union, UNEP, and Worldwide Fund for Nature, 1991, *Caring for the Earth: A Strategy for Sustainable Living*, Gland, Switzerland: IUCN.

World Resources Institute, 1998, *World Resources 1998–99*, New York: Oxford University Press.

chapter two

The Global Environment and International Cooperation

▌ 2.1 INTRODUCTION

Environmental interdependencies require cooperative and coordinated solutions among nations. This does imply some degree of influence of international policies on domestic policies, and vice versa. Much of the concern in the global environmental arena relates to the governance of global commons, in addition to transboundary environmental problems that affect states directly in terms of environmental impacts. As discussed in chapter 1, the governance of global commons resources, constituted by the sources and sinks of the planet's biogeochemical and other resources, remains a critical issue of international significance. For the purposes of further analyses, it is useful to categorize global commons resources into two broad types: common property resources (*res communis*) and open-access resources (*res nullius*). The former denotes the existence of collective as well as individual rights and duties (even if these are not very well defined), and the latter refers to resources not owned or regulated by any entity.

In this chapter, the phenomenon of the "tragedy of the commons" is explained and its limited role examined. Several concepts related to externalities are briefly introduced for their further use in this and later chapters. Similarly, a few basic concepts of strategic behavior among states and the application of game-theoretic and other analytical approaches (and their limitations) are outlined. Common to almost all the international laws in their formulation and implementation are a few ingredients of state cooperation. These structural elements are explored, especially with the use of analytical methods of economics.

The role of property rights and liability regimes is important in the governance of environmental resources, especially in the containment of environmental externalities. Global environmental externalities are a byproduct of the limited effectiveness (or nonexistence, in some cases) of these rights and duties. This chapter addresses issues of transboundary environmental effects leading to environmental externalities, economic institutions and instruments for the governance of global environmental resources and their problems, and the economics of cooperation and coordination. The roles of strategic behavior affecting varying types of cooperation among nations, and of transaction costs (often not considered in the economics literature on conventional cost–benefit calculus) influencing the decisions of nations in international environmental policy, are among the key components of these issues. In addition, some of the limitations of the commonly proposed "Coasean-bargaining" for global environmental negotiations are also important. By addressing these aspects, this chapter provides a framework for the discussion in later chapters of the more detailed arrangements of international cooperation in specific areas.

■ 2.2 ENVIRONMENTAL EXTERNALITIES

The existence of uncompensated and unsustainable environmental externalities is often the single most important reason for policy intervention, whether at global or state level, and whether the interventions are sought through market mechanisms, through regulatory mechanisms, or through a combination of both. A variety of externalities can be distinguished; these are summarized in box 2.1. These classifications are useful in applied environmental problems and their policy analyses.

In the environment arena, transboundary environmental externalities with a geographic proximity feature (among neighboring regions and countries) include acid rain deposits, deterioration in riverwater quality, and the movement of hazardous wastes, to cite a few. However, a broader category of problems is that of continued aggravation of the global environment by individual nations (which may or may not imply geographically determined externalities in terms of proximity to the sources of pollution) affecting the global commons, as explained below.

BOX 2.1

Concepts in public economics

Externality: The phenomenon of generating products/outputs that are not intended in an interrelationship among specified entities; for example, ozone depletion as a result of use of chlorofluorocarbons (CFCs).

- *Economic externality*: Characterizes the economic aspects of an externality.
- *Environmental externality*: Refers to environmental features of an externality.
- *Positive externality*: Refers to the positive contribution of an externality in relation to a specific context or objective; for example, the regional (but not necessarily global) cooling effects of the production of aerosols.
- *Negative externality*: Converse of the above; for example, the greenhouse effect of continued emissions of carbon dioxide.
- *Stock externality*: Externality that arises from changes or accumulations of the inventory or stock of a specific commodity or other physical entity; a similar concept holds for a "flow" externality. The atmospheric concentration of greenhouse gases is a stock pollutant with negative externalities. Urban smog is a stock externality as well as a flow externality.
- *Strategic externality*: The impact of strategic behavior on other components of a system in relation to specific activities undertaken by direct participants; occurs especially in the recourse to resource consumption with limited liability or cost-sharing.
- *Static externality*: Refers to an externality arising out of a single instance or single period process; for example, the role of local high temperatures in dry forest fires.
- *Dynamic externality*: Refers to an externality that is carried over time, as in the process of deforestation and its externality on the biodiversity of species.

Free-ride: The possibility of using goods/services without having to pay for their use.

Incentive-compatible: The responsiveness of an entity to the provision of incentives, usually with reference to one or more stated objectives of the system or its functions.

> **Market failure**: The inability of market institutions to attain socially/economically desirable efficiency objectives, such as social welfare maximization.
> **Market inefficiency**: The suboptimal role of market institutions in the realization of social efficiency or other aggregate objectives.
> **Public goods**: Those goods which are not necessarily provided by the market in response to demand and supply factors and which possess the properties of nonexcludability (the goods provided are accessible to all potential users) and nonrival usage (their consumption does not always reduce availability to other potential consumers).
> **Club goods**: Goods that possess partially rival benefits which can be excluded at a small cost to enable usage to be monitored.

The global commons

The global commons are defined (Rao, 2000a) as the global environmental resources that cut across national boundaries which are affected across all regions by direct and indirect interventions in any one or more regions. The global commons possess varying features over time due to the changing interface between humans and the environment. The main problems of concern in the global commons are atmospheric gases that accumulate and cause the greenhouse effect, leading to climate warming; the thinning of the ozone layer, leading to increased ultraviolet-B (UV-B) radiation; transboundary pollution in the air and water; and loss of biodiversity.

The roots of anthropogenic contributions in the global commons are largely founded in the open-access and free-rider problems of public goods. Thus, the concern about the emerging problems in the global commons generally focuses on the legitimacy of appropriations of sink capacities without any obligations being imposed on the part of the users/polluters. This leads to the issue of legitimacy of any exercise of property rights. Property configurations can be broadly classified in terms of private property, state property, common property, and open access. Various resources such as fresh water and the biological pool constitute examples of common property, whereas atmospheric concentrations of greenhouse gases and the ozone layer are examples of global commons with open access. We refer to these commons simply as global commons. They possess open-access characteristics.

Even those who believe in the universal role of free markets for resource allocation and efficiency (of one type or another) are brought up short by the issue of creating a fair global market for a relatively scarce resource. Emissions trading in greenhouse gas regimes is a mechanism that is strongly advocated, but the creation of benchmarks for the initial market conditions and the role of the state in regulating the market are far from being resolved. It is not presumed here that markets are the only suitable forms of global governance for the sustainable management of the global commons. A mix of institutional and market factors is required for this purpose. There are hardly any features of property in the open-access case, unless some restraints such as emissions trading and quotas are imposed institutionally.

The "tragedy of the commons"

The phenomenon of the "tragedy of the commons" (Hardin, 1968) is applicable here since the planet's sink capacity is tampered with by human contributors who do not have to pay for its destruction. In their open-access use of common resources, people could usher in their collective doom, according to the "tragedy of the commons" hypothesis. This is similar to the "free-rider" problem analyzed by economists in the economics of public goods, but in that case the public goods are paid for by various institutions; in the case of the global environment, nature provides the goods and responds somewhat belatedly with potentially irreversible adverse consequences.

The problem of the tragedy of the commons arises in the context not of common property but of no clearly defined property rights and the lack of repeat interactions among participants that establish an interlinking appreciation of dependencies or reciprocity. The proper terminology for a potential application of the phenomenon is free-access resources, or *res nullius*, rather than common property resources. These features are conventionally applied to the problem of governance of commodities or resources arising from one or more common pools of sources, with no cost to the users. Hardin sought to explain the processes of extinction of some of the fish stocks in terms of the "philosophy of the commons." However, the reasoning extends to the problems of the governance of sinks, which is the main concern here. In all such cases, the processes underlying the free-rider and open-access phenomena need to be addressed. Alternatively, from an equivalent economic-pricing perspective, the costs of externalities should be internalized. Users or beneficiaries should be made to pay some kind of "tax," based on their value-added "output," for the loss of sink capacity and for any losses and damage to ecosystems or reduction in ecosystem services.

It is useful to note that any dichotomous treatment of property simply in terms of common (nonprivate) property and private (exclusive) property is a simplification of the issues involved. Another categorization, "anticommons," was suggested by Heller (1998) as an added alternative. Anticommons is a property regime in which multiple owners hold effective rights of exclusion to a scarce resource, and the ownership of anticommons property includes the ability by each owner to prevent other owners from obtaining a core bundle of rights in an entity. In this direction of inquiry, nonprivate property may be analyzed as follows: (1) anticommons property if the predominant feature is one of rights of exclusion in the use of resources, and (2) common property if the exercise of privileges of inclusion remains the dominant feature. Can a tragedy of anticommons occur? Heller suggested that this is possible when too many entities have rights of exclusion in a relatively scarce resource. However, it is the club structure and its features of collusive behavior (or cartelization) that possesses the potential for a kind of tragedy: suboptimal resource use in a global welfare-maximizing sense. Is the real alternative to potential problems in the global commons to be seen in terms of globally representative institutions such as those under the UN Framework Convention on Climate Change (UNFCCC) (see chapter 6)? The answer is obviously in favor of strengthening such a forum for effective global environmental management. Some of these issues will be discussed in later chapters (especially chapters 4 and 9).

International public goods include, as an important category, environmental public goods. This, by implication, allows the existence of "free-riders." By the nature and characteristics of public goods, the users are usually nonexcludable (whether or not they "pay" or participate in a "responsible" manner) and are nonrival or indivisible: the usage of one party does not always reduce the usage for another. However, there are costs of provision for these environmental public goods, and the classical public goods analogy soon loses its relevance when we recognize the following interlocking phenomenon at the international level: some of the costs of provision of the environmental public goods under the broad group of global commons (such as the ozone layer) are transformed for the free-riders into those of other resource costs (such as trade restrictions under another environmental or economic regime for the free-riders or nonparticipating parties to a specific public good). Additional operative details of such provisions are outlined in chapters 6 through 8. Thus, it is important to design new policy instruments as well as new institutional arrangements for effective global environmental governance. Let us recognize that both stock externality and strategic externality are relevant in the design of international agreements for the governance of both *res communis* and *res nullius*.

The complementary aspects of property rights and liability rules in the governance of the global commons are explained in the next section. These concepts are particularly useful in the choice of policy instruments for international cooperation and the development of environmental law.

■ 2.3 PROPERTY RIGHTS AND LIABILITY REGIMES

Fundamental to economic and environmental implications of global activities are the institutions of property rights and liability laws. The role of property rights (PR) is fairly common when regulating economic resources, especially when they are perceived as relatively scarce (hence the use of the term "economic"). Most environmental resources are perceived to be relatively abundant in supply, and thus do not seem to attract allocation of property rights in general. In the extreme form of allocation of PR, it could lead to some form of privatization or state control that may not be conducive to resource allocative efficiency or equity. The role of specifying PR is not to render exclusive control or ownership, but rather to identify the stakeholders and their rights and duties in the sustainable use of specific resources. The stakeholders could be various categories of entities: individual, group, state-regulated, or other.

Global commons broadly fit into two groups of environmental resources: *res communis* and *res nullius*. PR as well as liability rules (LR) apply to the resources in the *res communis* category. However, by definition, PR do not apply to the resources in the *res nullius* category. LR can still be made relevant by a global provision under an appropriate legal framework for these resources; this can be accomplished by making it inapplicable to invoke *non liquet*, and providing for a standby clause of accountability and stakeholder responsibility. Source and sink aspects of PR and LR are also important distinguishing characteristics under each of the main components of the global commons. These additional distinctions tend to be useful in the formulation of appropriate PR and LR.

Global environmental resources, under both *res nullius* and *res communis* categorizations, are, in effect, not governed if there are no well-defined and enforceable rights and duties on the resource-exploiter nations (or other entities). In the absence of any legally valid methods of global environmental accounting and sharing of responsibilities, even the features of *res communis* degenerate into those of *res nullius*. In such a system, global environmental externalities remain the norm rather than the exception, thus leading to uncompensated infliction of environmental and consequential damage on known or unknown victims. Thus, the role of well-defined PR complemented by an enforceable liability regime is often a prerequisite for a meaningful design of sharing responsibilities in the governance of the global environment. The economics of PR and LR are of interest in issues of management of the global commons and in international cooperation.

One of the definitions of PR is an "exclusive right to the use, control, and enjoyment of a resource" (Landes and Posner, 1987, p. 29), and this does not entail any further calculation of potential benefits of transfer of PR to others. In contrast, the liability rule allows a claim for damages caused to the resource.

A primary function of PR is that of "guiding incentives to achieve a greater internalization of externalities" (Demsetz, 1967), where internalization refers to a process (usually a change in the specifications of property rights). It was also noted that the costs of internalizing externalities is smaller with a small set of decision entities. By implication, it may be argued that the process may be severely constrained when it comes to solving global environmental pollution and related problems of the global commons where several state parties have roles to play.

PR refer to the "sanctioned behavioral relations among men that arise from the existence of things and pertain to their use . . . defining the position of each individual with respect to the utilization of scarce resources" (Furubotn and Pejovich, 1972, p. 1139). PR are inextricable from technology resources (Stubblebine, 1975) and tend to provide an expanding set of choices of instruments, with technological or development progress. It is useful to include administrative and regulatory inputs as well as other institutional inputs in the characterization and specifications of technology to admit its relevant generalization. It is thus important to recognize the role of institutional governance, especially that of the state, in any analysis of PR regimes. Absent the role of the state, a PR regime might be devoid of any meaning. Let us recall that a regime, in general, consists of "norms, rules and procedures agreed in order to regulate an issue area" (Haas, 1980, p. 357). Thus, a PR regime presumes the existence of an appropriate regulatory/enforcement mechanism.

In an early study, Demsetz (1966) identified three implications (similar to those of the Coase theorem, see below) of a PR regime when the costs of exchanging and enforcement are zero (which is unlikely in any realistic setting): (1) the value of all "harmful and beneficial effects" of alternative specifications of PR will be brought to bear on the asset-holders; (2) PR will be efficiently used if the asset-holding decision-makers are rational utility maximizers; and (3) the mix of output that is produced will be independent of the distribution of PR among asset-holders but for the effects of changes in wealth holdings of these on relevant demand schedules. Some of these idealized insights are useful as a starting point to examine the role and implications of PR. In a real-world setting, the complexity of issues warrants a greater comprehension of the role of transaction costs and behavioral characteristics of the economic decision-making entities.

The main characteristics of PR are: exclusivity, transferability, divisibility, duration and well-defined boundaries of rights, and enforceability. For the role of PR in the context of private markets (global, local, or regional) and environmental marketization for resource management, see Devlin and Grafton (1998). Property rights in the context of global environmental resources are rights exercisable by globally agreed participating entities at the national and international levels with delineated rights and duties to the consumptive use and replenishment of environmental resources, both in the areas of sources and sinks of environmental goods as well as their externalities.

The above interpretation brings to the forefront the limitations of Principle 21 of the Rio Declaration, which provides "the sovereign right to exploit their own resources pursuant to their own environmental policies." The role of externalities or depletive consumption of the sink features of the planet remain problematic areas, if these are not fully integrated with the Principles. Clearly, Principle 21 must be interpreted in conjunction with the precautionary principle set out under Principle 15 of the Rio Declaration, and the right to exploit resources is to be balanced against sovereignty rights. It is reasonable to infer that environmental property rights of the global commons tend to be residual rights in the sense that these are applicable only after national laws regarding private property rights and their protection are fully exhausted. Also, as Taylor (1998, p. 121) argued, "as regards environmental harm isolated to a state's own environment, no competing property rights are involved and therefore there is no legal solution – the environment receives no protection." As a result, it was suggested that the law of state responsibility for environmental protection may not be strong enough beyond providing "indirect protection" of the environment, balancing it against the priority needs of protection of the exercise of other (and usually well-defined, relative to those concerning the environment) property rights.

A theory of PR is usually incomplete without an accompanying theory of the state and the role of LR. Liability rules seek to offer protection to an interest (if it is well defined), and do not directly support protection of exercise of rights or duties in any PR regime. In its operative form, a liability rule that specifies a penalty clause in an agreement or other legal stipulation is an *ex ante* formulation that signals the costs of violating a legal imperative, and thus tends to contribute to self-enforcement of the required obligations, provided the penalty clause remains enforceable (at reasonably low transaction costs; see section 2.5). A theory of property rights that gives the proper role to liability rules is a crucial requirement to enable efficient functioning of entities or activities under any meaningful decentralization of resource management (see also Mattei, 1997).

The existence of well-defined, transparent, and enforceable liability regimes generally send the right signals to decision-making entities. Often, some of the important elements of such factors are either missing in practice, or the corresponding transaction costs are very high. The result is the achievement of limited efficiency in regulating externalities or undesirable environmental consequences. In addition, liability regimes may not suffice to preserve global environmental features. Such provisions, if credibly enforceable, are likely to supplement the role of various rules/standards or other preventive measures developed under international law. Liability regimes are unlikely to restore *status quo ante*, however, as in the case of problems involving loss of biodiversity or genetic resources. Thus, in environmental resources that are potentially irreversible in their quality/existence, the impact of liability rules remains rather insignificant. Besides, the existence of significant magnitudes of transaction costs implies that liability regimes will play a somewhat limited role; the practicality of rules of liability should act as a guiding principle for substitution rules in relation to negotiated solutions (Demsetz, 1972).

An integrated view of property rights and liability rules suggests the use of the concept of "entitlements" (Calabresi and Melamed, 1972). While this integration serves the purpose of examining the distributive aspects of resources, the operational aspect involving the costs of devising relevant regimes, institutions, and organization – including the role of different elements of transaction costs – is still a major factor in selecting one component over the other in PR versus liability approaches. These aspects can be better examined in relation to specific contexts and issues, in addition to the objectives of these regimes. The reasons for greater use of the PR approach in international legal systems include (Dunoff and Trachtman, 1999): (1) the costs of creating PR versus dispute resolution systems; (2) the costs of determining and levying damages from offenders; (3) operative features of "excessive costs," and net benefits of liability regimes; and (4) the collective public goods nature of the provision of liability systems, with potential free-riding behavior by some countries.

Property rights are usually oblivious of the role of these rights in constructive or destructive aspects of the environment or the economy. The potential environmental hazards of some bioproducts or genetic manipulations provide examples of the lack of a mechanism or the application of precautionary principles in these patenting and licensing regimes. In the same context, as Gollin (1991) suggested, it is feasible to use intellectual property rights to enhance environmental protection. The roles of some features of various national-level laws under the Patent Acts, Public Information Acts, and Licensing Acts need to be evaluated and reformed for this purpose.

Liability for injurious consequences should be examined in both a bilateral and a multilateral context. The latter becomes relevant when negative externalities exist which affect other states beyond recognized injured states, and/or affect the global commons.

The US Restatement (Third) of Foreign Relations Law (Section 601) (1987) noted that "a state is obligated to take all necessary precautionary measures where an activity is contemplated that poses a substantial risk of a significant transfrontier injury." The 1991 ILC Draft Articles (International Law Commission, 1991) provide a set of guidelines for the imposition of liability for various injurious transboundary consequences, including environmental damage, caused by a state party. These seek to deploy the role of the offending state to negotiate (Article 21) with the "affected State or States to determine the legal consequences of the harm, bearing in mind that the harm must, in principle, be fully compensated." The ILC Draft Article 24 on harm to the environment and resulting harm to persons or property states that "[i]f the transboundary harm proves detrimental to the environment of the affected State: a) The State of origin shall bear the costs of any reasonable operation to restore, as far as possible, the conditions that existed prior to the occurrence of the harm. If it is impossible to restore these conditions in full, agreement may be reached on compensation, monetary or otherwise, by the State of origin for the deterioration suffered."

Lack of identifiability and accountability in international environmental damage remains one of the serious obstacles in the governance of the global commons. The implementation of liability laws and the assessment of damage costs may not be feasible when affected states and their environments are interconnected in a fuzzy and uncertain manner. Usually, global environmental phenomena tend to pose problems of distant (if not remote), diffuse, or indeterminate linkages (Handl, 1990; Rao, 2000b).

Principle 22 of the Stockholm Declaration asserts that states "cooperate to develop further the international law regarding liability and compensation" for the victims of transboundary pollution. This was followed by a consistent pattern of resolutions asserting the need for such provisions (specific environmental agreements provide a few provisions; see chapter 9). However, this remains the area of greatest vacuum, even in the twenty-first century. Some of the most recent reports of the International Law Commission indicate the prevalence of continued disagreements among many of the UN member states regarding the specification of measures governing state liability in transnational environmental damage. The design and implementation of LR critically depends upon the role of transaction costs in effecting this. This is particularly relevant in the international public law arena. Accordingly, the next section provides a description of the ingredients and implications of varying transaction costs on policy design and institutional arrangements.

■ 2.4 Economic Instruments and Institutions

The roles of economic institutions (including PR and LR, discussed earlier) and of economic instruments (market-based, regulatory, or both) need to be viewed in terms of their consistency: a policy instrument cannot be dissociated from an institutional configuration that aligns with it. In other words, it is a package deal of choice of instruments and institutional arrangements (if not institutions) that is to be explored in a cost-effective sense. Costs include direct and indirect costs, especially transaction costs over the relevant time horizon.

Relative effectiveness of different policy instruments can possibly be examined in terms of the following (see Mabey et al., 1997): efficiency, stability, and potential for realistic achievement. The roles of behavioral factors, transaction costs, and institutions remain a parallel stream of elements of concern in each of the above.

Market failure and institutional or nonmarket failure are only convenient dichotomies of analysis for some economists. The role of specific agency maximands, rather than socioeconomic objectives, generally acts as the guiding factor for the conduct of activities in the latter group (Wolf, 1988).

Regulation in one form or another continues to be relevant even under free-market systems; it is only a matter of degree rather than of category. Global environmental regulation must be conceived differently from national environmental regulation. As Wiener (1999, p. 681) argued, (1) "legal institutions matter in the choice among regulatory instruments"; and (2) "the economics of instrument choice are embedded in and contingent on the underlying legal system."

One of the most common economic instruments for containing environmental harm and for internalizing environmental externalities is taxes, whether they are incremental or marginal. When instituted in relation to the objective of protecting the environment, they are often called green taxes. These have been deployed in one form or another with varying success in some European countries. An examination of the economics of green taxes is useful, not necessarily to seek their scope for the international arena, but to explore the harmonization of any such tax proposals in a collective action in each of the participating countries.

The economics of green taxes

The terms green taxes, environmental taxes, and pollution taxes are used interchangeably for the present, although they do not mean precisely the same thing. Although the above categories include carbon taxes, the converse does not hold. Historically, Pigou (1932) was among those economists who advocated pollution taxes. A Pigouvian tax is tax levied on each unit of pollution output and the tax amount equals the marginal damage the pollution causes to the economic system, at an efficient level of production system or output level. This tax tradition may have some feasibility if the source of pollution and its relative contribution and damage are known. Baumol and Oates (1988) classified two alternative bases within the above tradition of taxes: (1) the assessment of tax on the basis of optimal production (implying an "optimal tax rate"), which may not provide an incentive to the polluting firm to alter the emission pattern of pollution; and (2) levy of the tax rate iteratively adjusted to relate it to the current magnitudes of marginal damage, which may provide incentives to the polluter to alter the magnitudes of pollutant emissions. Both these approaches to taxation pose limitations arising out of availability of relevant information and practical implementation problems or enforcement.

Much of the literature on Pigouvian taxes did not address the issue of revenue mobilization or the consequent decisions of levying pollution taxes. Similarly, the role of these taxes in improving distributive justice or Pareto-optimal resource allocation methods is often ignored. Pollution taxes possess the potential to offer an environmentally sensitive tax structure for an economy, if the tax instruments are properly formulated and implemented. This is, in principle, a case of double dividend. It is also useful to note a Pigouvian subsidy also can, in principle, be devised to provide an incentive for reduction in pollution emissions or enhancement of environmental quality. In general, it is relevant to note that whereas the subsidy tends to be financed out of a preexisting distortionary tax structure and possibly enhance distortionary taxes, the converse could be achieved when proper Pigouvian taxes are imposed, effecting a reduction in the distortions of the preexisting tax system (Ballard and Medema, 1993).

Most of the economic models and policies for addressing environmental concerns ignored the interactions of new taxes with the existing tax system. This simplistic approach, including the classic Pigouvian tax method, tends to overestimate the requisite tax for achieving desired ecological goals. The overall effect of the tax consists of (1) the Pigouvian or the partial equilibrium effect; (2) the tax interaction effect; and (3) the revenue-recycling, or more generally, the fiscal effect. The basic partial equilibrium analysis of optimal environmental tax invokes the Pigouvian method, where the optimal tax rate equals the marginal external costs or marginal environmental damage (MED); this implies the gross marginal cost or marginal abatement cost associated with an environmental tax equals the tax rate. However, in a general equilibrium setting, the presence of prior taxes imposes higher gross costs from the environmental tax, even when revenues are recycled through cuts in the distortionary tax. Parry's (1995, 1997) results support these conclusions since the tax interaction effect is of greater magnitude than the revenue-recycling effect under plausible values of parameters. The optimal environmental tax worked out to be about 70 percent of the Pigouvian tax, or of the MED.

In addition, the results of Bovenberg and Goulder (1996) suggest that optimal carbon taxes decline with the level of preexisting taxes. The general equilibrium model results of Bovenberg and Goulder (1996) suggest that the tax equals the ratio between MED from the use of this good and the marginal cost of public funds (MCPF). It is useful to note that MCPF depends on the configuration of the entire tax kit containing all taxes.

The above indicates the role of preexisting taxes whenever ecotaxes or green taxes are considered for their imposition. In general, an optimal green tax induces the level of emissions at which marginal welfare benefits from reducing emissions equals the marginal welfare cost of achieving such reductions. In the absence of preexisting distortionary taxes, the rule simplifies to that involved in Pigouvian taxes: optimality requires that the green tax be set equal to the marginal benefit from reducing environmental damage. It is seen from the above that the Pigouvian tax rate is optimal if and only if the MCPF equals unity. Usually, the MCPF exceeds unity, and this warrants the optimal green tax being less than its Pigouvian counterpart.

Again, it is important to note that the role of transaction costs (see section 2.5 for details, including Coasean analyses) remains significant in all taxation efforts; there are countries where the costs of tax collection exceed the official collection of tax revenues, and in many scenarios these provide yet another source of private provision of fiscal resources where the bureaucracy tends to misappropriate the tax revenues. However, to the extent that mechanisms of cost-effective green tax harmonization (for example on internationally traded goods) exist, the role of these taxes and the optimal levels of such taxes may be appreciated. In terms of national policies, interactions between economic externalities and environmental policies can be viewed as a byproduct of political self-interest; internalization of economic externalities occurs as a result of interest group lobby activities and exercise of political power for self-sustenance of the incumbent regime. Aidt (1998) argued that a "self-interest policy-maker" with regulatory power tends to trade off the general interest of society with the interests of lobby groups. In this sense "the public-choice axiom of political self-interest bridges the Coasean and Pigouvian approach to environmental policy" (Aidt, 1998, p. 2). While such a bridge might exist, this proposition exposes the fact that the result of political compromises might be such that it does not lead to a Pareto-improvement of social welfare.

The origins, concepts, role, and limitations of transaction cost economics are explained in the next section. It is relevant to note that the field of "law and economics" has deep roots in transaction cost economics. Accordingly, it is important that the relevant concepts and results of analysis are carefully interpreted for possible use in its applications to the area of international environmental law.

■ 2.5 TRANSACTION COST ECONOMICS (TCE)

Transaction costs (TC) raise the issue of economic (and political) organization as a problem of formal and informal (or explicit and implicit) contracting. Transaction costs include (but are not limited to) the following: *ex ante* costs of negotiating and forming a contract or agreement; *ex post* costs of monitoring and enforcing a contract or agreement, and search and information costs. It is important to recognize that the two sets of cost elements are usually interdependent, and hence an attempt to minimize one set of transaction costs should also consider the corresponding implications for the entire vector of cost elements. It is not uncommon that lopsided approaches to these cost-reducing problems result in net additions to costs, direct and indirect. For example, in order to reduce the costs of violations by individuals or other entities one might conceive of greater "powers" for the law-enforcement machinery, but this could imply greater liability costs (at the administrative unit level) or victimization costs (at the society level, based on social costs) later when the enlarged scope for exercise of power is accidentally or intentionally misused.

The transaction costs paradigm offers a general framework for examining the choice of policy instruments and/or regimes for the management of resources/entities of relevance among contracting and other parties. In the international relations context, transaction costs include both contracting and information costs, in addition to monitoring or related costs of enforcement, even in the absence of a single entity for enforcement purposes. An illustrative case study of bilateral contracting over transboundary natural resource issues involving South Africa and Lesotho may be found in Boadu (1998).

The underlying principle of TC is the principle of bounded rationality:

> The capacity of the human mind for formulating and solving complex problems is very small compared with the size of the problems whose solution is required for objectively rational behavior in the real world – or even for a reasonable approximation to such objective rationality. (Simon, 1957, p. 198)

According to Williamson (1985, p. 30), "transaction cost economics assumes that human agents are subject to bounded rationality, whence behavior is 'intendedly rational, but only limitedly so.'" Williamson also suggested (p. 45) that bounded rationality is "the cognitive assumption on which transaction cost economics relies."

Although Ronald Coase is best known for recognizing the role of property rights and bargaining without governmental intervention (for which he received a Nobel Prize), it should also be well known that these prescriptions emerged based on the conscious assumption of zero transaction costs and admittedly in an ideal world. Coase's contribution (mainly Coase, 1960) was to recognize the role of transaction costs, without which the predictions of the economic working of institutions/property rights could hold true.

The Coase theorem generally states that if there are no transaction costs, the most efficient solution is to clearly define the property rights. Thus, property rights and markets offer solutions to problems of externalities (or social costs that are different than private costs). Although Coase did not call this assertion a theorem, many others did. In one of its variations, the theorem was stated by Posner (1993, p. 195) as follows: "If transaction costs are zero, the initial assignment of a property right – for example, whether to the polluter or to the victim of pollution – will not affect the efficiency with which resources are allocated."

This assertion is supposed to be an answer to the externality problem, and supposedly an alternative to the initial allocation of property rights, subject to a set of explicit and implicit assumptions about the system. A well-functioning legal system and a "level playing field" for the bargaining parties are among the implicit prerequisites, lest the "mighty" bargaining party (polluter or victim) extract a socially suboptimal price for the offense committed. An application of loss-aversion criteria suggests that the Coase theorem could not hold when allocation of the legal entitlements influences the outcome, as those individuals who are "initially allocated an entitlement are likely to value it more than those without the legal entitlement" (Sunstein, 1997, p. 132).

Coase (1988) also noted that there are a number of limitations on the applicability of the original Coase theorem, especially the original suggestion that economic efficiency holds under varied legal rules as long as bargaining is undertaken between contending parties; the emphasis is still that bargaining exists between contending parties. But the latter suggestion is founded on the assumption that there is no other externality in the form of strategic behavior. However, when multiple and often unidentified parties are involved in causing environmental problems or related externalities, there is little possibility of bargain in any form. There is no single coordinating entity that could meaningfully (including seeking the attainment of global welfare maximization) assign property rights regarding various environmental assets and their stocks and flows. In general, bargaining scenarios may not induce contending parties to declare their preferences and ranking of alternatives, and this implies bargains may not be optimal (Farber, 1997). By now it should be clear that the Coase theorem has extremely limited applicability in the context of problems arising from global environmental externalities. Inada and Kuga (1973) disproved the original claim that the introduction of "markets" for externalities can lead to Pareto-optimal resource allocation. In case there is still doubt regarding the possibility of application, let us recall Coase's own observation and note its limitations for nonmarketized environmental resources. Coase (1960, p. 15) stated that the "economic problem in all cases of harmful effects is how to maximize the value of production." Clearly, this does not correspond to an ecologically or environmentally meaningful system (described in terms of sustainability and sustainable development in chapter 1).

Coase's efficiency concept seeks to maximize the total wealth or "total product rule" (TPR) (White, 1987), where the total is not necessarily that of the society but is that of the contesting parties. In the Coasean tradition, parties tend to enhance economic efficiency in the Pareto-welfare-improving sense, based on "efficient bargaining." Coasean propositions are oblivious to the real-world features of differential transaction costs or asymmetric transaction costs, which invariably induce suboptimalities even in the Paretian sense. Besides, the contesting parties may jointly contribute toward externalities, extended to another set of parties (who may or may not be identifiable). In its best scenarios of applicability, the Coase "theorem" ignored the general or economy-wide effects of "efficient" solutions to bargaining problems arising out of economic damage and property rights (or their absence). Thus, the Coasean approach remains largely unsuitable for applications in the global environmental arena. It may also be observed that TPR tends to favor the economically advantaged (see White, 1987). However, to prevent possible misinterpretation of some of these concerns, it is relevant to quote Coase (1960, p. 43): "it is . . . desirable that the choice between different social arrangements for the solution of economic problems should be carried out in broader terms than this and the total effect of these arrangements in all spheres of life should be taken into account."

There are also additional clarifications to the validity or otherwise of the Coasean proposition. If utility maximization or social welfare maximization rather than wealth maximization is being sought in a negotiating situation, the Coase theorem is of little help (even when it holds good). Thus, even in the ideal case of zero transaction costs, the magnitude of social utility is still influenced by the initial assignment of rights and entitlements, as argued by Hovenkamp (1990). Let us also recognize that the Coasean motive of joint wealth maximization or maximization of TPR can at best be reflective of short-term market terms, prices, and incomes. This cannot in any way lead toward a path of sustainable development when these factors are obtained from unsustainable production and consumption settings and imperfect markets.

Dixit and Olson (2000) undertook a detailed analytical investigation of these issues, using their formulation of the Coase theorem (p. 310): "If transaction costs are zero, rational parties will necessarily achieve a Pareto-efficient allocation through voluntary transactions or bargaining." They found that the relevance of the Coase theorem is very limited as it might not lead to efficiency in the context of voluntary cooperative arrangements in the provision of public goods (including global environmental goods), when one interpretative version of the theorem asserts that only transaction costs can prevent voluntary negotiations from attaining Pareto-efficient outcomes. On the other hand, as argued by Cooter (1989), the Coase theorem assumes the validity of optimism that there exists cooperative behavior between contending parties, when the transaction costs of bargaining are nil; this ignores, among other things, the commonly observed role of strategic behavior. The fact that bargaining itself is a transaction cost (Usher, 1998) suggests there are inherent fundamental flaws in the assertions with Coasean proposals. Some of the strongest logical objections to the validity of the Coase theorem have been enunciated by Usher (1998). Olson (1996) argued that Coasean-style bargaining is inconsistent with rational individual behavior. An interesting perspective on the role of rationality arises from Simon (2000), who suggested the search for broader invariant laws of economic or other behavior may be better handled by paying attention to "historical conditions and localized patterns of interaction." This assertion is particularly relevant in the context of international environmental agreements.

Much of the literature on law and economics so far remains focused on the applicability of the Coase theorem. Similarly, considerable literature in the area of environmental economics has sought to suggest a significant role for the Coase theorem in resolving environmental management problems using the property rights approach, including market-based instruments such as emissions trading. There are two major limitations on most of these approaches: (1) the role of significant transaction costs, which invalidate the theorem's applicability;

and (2) the lack of a distinction between local environmental externalities (where presumably there is a small number of identifiable contributors to pollution and its victims) and global environmental externalities (where the contributors to environmental problems are atomistic and where actual and potential victims, numbering millions, are scattered and diffused). In an analytical investigation, DeSerpa (1994) asserted that the Coase theorem may be valid, if at all, only in some situations governing local environmental externalities. It was also suggested that a global environmental externality differs from a local one in that individual victims are adversely affected not by individual culprits' activity, but by the "collective action of a large number of culprits." See Rao (2001) for a detailed analytical and applied treatment of TC.

When it is costly to transact, the role of institutions surfaces very prominently. Institutional features, especially property rights, affect the efficiency of markets and overall economic performance. Institutions are composed of legal regimes, rules and standards, conventions and informal traditions, and enforcement features (North, 1992). This generalized view of enforcement allows a combination of legal and informal enforcement mechanisms to establish and sustain different sets of property rights. The role of law and the need for an "efficient" legal system as a prerequisite for minimization of transaction costs in modern societies deserve particular emphasis, however. TC based on LR govern the distribution of the burdens of negotiation; these costs are typically asymmetric between contesting parties. The principle that TC are a function of LR is very important (Samuels, 1992). The TC approach tends to bridge the gaps in the dichotomous approaches of economic efficiency assessments of market and regulatory functions or the failures of these institutions. Since policies are generally viewed as institutional arrangements, TC analysis plays a role in each case.

Nalebuff (1997) established the following relevant findings:

1 The existence of transaction costs means that a market-based property rights approach is not a universal solution for environmental problems.
2 At efficient levels of pollution, both Pigouvian taxes and Coasean property rights tend to coincide: the marginal damage equals the Pigouvian tax and this equals the market price for pollution rights (see also section 2.4 above).

TC thus play an important role in affecting economic behavior and influence the specifications of different economic instruments to govern environmental resources. The role of TC in the design of "efficient" contracts and environmental agreements remains profound. Section 2.7 below clarifies the joint roles of TC and "incomplete contracts" in their operational impacts affecting international environmental governance. Absent TC, any number of ideal solutions exist, but the existence of TC constrains the choices for solving real-world problems. However, due recognition of the role of TC enables the design and implementation of "efficient" systems. Coase's contributions remain significant in directing attention to the evaluation of pragmatic alternatives, even though some of the pointed results (such as the so-called Coase theorem) fail to meet several requirements toward realistic applications. Also, it should be stressed that it is unfair to Coase to denote the Coasean world as one of zero transaction costs (as several writers seem to do), since Coase's greatest contribution was to clarify the role of transaction costs. Some of these features will be reflected in the following sections.

Economics of standards and norms

Established or well-defined standards (whether established under a legal regime or by commonly accepted norms of conduct) that are shared by different economic entities and states tend to reduce transaction costs and uncertainties of transactions by expectations formation and greater predictability of outcomes; these tend to enhance efficiency in the production of goods and services (for a variety of microeconomic institutions, see also Platteau, 1994). The role of trust and tested/repeat cooperation also remains similar. Buchanan (1987) suggested that economic efficiency must be judged by evaluating the processes through which transactions are carried out, and thus required greater focus on the issue of standardization and institutional development. For a formal definition, let us state that standardization refers to a well-defined characterization or specification of features verifiable with reference to an entity – physical, economic, environmental, institutional, organizational, or other. One of the key ingredients of standardization is transparency, which reduces informational asymmetry between participant decision-makers and facilitates minimization of transaction costs involved in the conduct of interactive activities, direct or indirect, planned or unplanned. Such a background facilitates behavioral prescriptions and compliance and enforcement.

Interaction, if not entirely strategic interaction, among decision-making entities is facilitated when it is standardized. The broadly defined utility of increasing marginal standardization yields decreasing marginal utilities, with the implication that there is an optimal degree of standardization in any given institutional and physical configuration. The role of the state is to exploit the economies of standardization, with a dynamic framework, both in internal and external activities (see also Blankart and Knieps, 1993). The latter include international environmental and economic cooperation and harmonization of standards. Again, it should be clear that harmonization does not imply identical standards as these may not fit all societies or activities equally. There is an optimal degree of harmonization of standards, economic or environmental or other. The critical determinant of these standards should include the need to optimize resources with few externalities.

The relative importance of rules versus standards depends to some extent on the role of legal mechanisms and whether the law is given content *ex ante* or *ex post*. Standards are usually given a well-defined content when they are applied to a specific conduct or activity. It may be argued that the only distinction between rules and standards is "the extent to which efforts to give content to the law are undertaken before or after individuals act" (Kaplow, 1992, p. 560). Kaplow also suggested (p. 588) that "[w]hether a complex standard is preferable to a simple rule depends on the combined effects of complexity and promulgation of the law as a rule versus as a standard (*ex ante* versus *ex post* creation)." The example of environmental management of hazardous substances was given to suggest that management might be better facilitated as a complex standard than as a set of simple rules. A simple rule, often based on the presumption of the "one size fits all" norm, could overdeter whereas a simple standard may be underinclusive relative to the features to be managed or regulated. The role of these alternatives and a combination of both in affecting incentives/disincentives motivating behavior should be the guiding factor for placing relative emphasis on rules versus standards. In addition, the latter can be made more dynamic with changes in technology, preferences, or other meaningful factors. As pointed out by Kaplow (1992), the main factor determining the relative desirability of rules versus standards is the frequency with which a given law is expected to govern the conduct of the actors or participants. The economies of rule-making and of the specification of standards are also influenced by the transaction costs involved in either specification, as well as the available information base. Static versus dynamic aspects of these features are also important in the ever-changing technological and environmental setting of the world. In general, the specification of rules affords economy in processing information but could compromise the efficiency-enhancing role of providing incentives for eligible participants for innovation or cost-effective compliance. Standards also tend to be transformed into rules in the legal system whenever it relies on precedents of legal decisions.

While statements of relevant principles, general procedures, and standards are important, a note of caution is relevant (HLRA, 1991): international environmental law could be rendered ineffective if state adherence to rules and procedures bears little relation to actual reduction in the levels of transboundary pollution; this could imply emphasis on form over substance and could thus constitute a futile exercise. The optimal design of rules and standards should largely devise methods of implementation that minimize TC and explore the scope of such specifications in any exercise of global harmonization of environmental standards.

2.6 THE ECONOMICS OF CONTRACTS

Cooperative and coordinative management of global environmental problems, especially those of the global commons, is usually carried out through a series of environmental and economic agreements. These are called treaties, protocols, agreements, or contracts. In all cases they possess the characteristics of a contract between parties and seek to obligate the parties to fulfill their provisions. A British court in the nineteenth century opined that international treaties are simply one form of contract and should be interpreted as such for operational purposes. The main differences between domestic commercial contracts and international treaties lie in the role of the sovereignty factor and in the enforceability (including access to verifiable information) of the agreements between parties. Since international environmental agreements form a group of special contracts, it is useful to study the common features of contracts in general, and later examine the specific features of various agreements. For a detailed comparison of similarities and dissimilarities between standard (domestic law-based) contracts and international treaties, see Dunoff and Trachtman (1999).

One motivation for studying the economics of contracts is to achieve better insights into the potential behavioral and welfare implications of alternate arrangements of future commitments (and their potential deviations), and to assess the role of incentives and disincentives for compliance with contractual specifications. Parties can collectively benefit from provisions of pragmatic rules by which interrelationships among participants are governed.

Legal contract theory vs. economic contract theory

Legal contract theory details "authoritative decision-makers how to regulate contracting behavior" procedurally and substantively (Schwartz, 1992, p. 76), whereas economic contract theory focuses on the design of optimal contracts, leaving the details of such contracts for their existence and working (usually based on normative considerations, assuming "rational parties" as the contracting parties) to be devised by various institutions. Despite their widespread usage, contracts literature in the legal and economic arenas remains incomplete, which explains the substantial utilization of judicial institutions. A wide variety of categorizations of contracts is relevant for gaining greater insights. These are summarized below.

Complete vs. incomplete: A contract is incomplete if (1) there are contractual gaps, *ab initio*, or in its interpretation *ex post*, and/or (2) it does not exhaust the contracting possibilities that could be ideally envisioned in the complete contracting case. A key aspect for the formation of "complete contracts" is the feature relating to "perfectly contingent contracting." This feature is itself conditioned by (Tirole, 1999): (1) adverse selection, when some of the decision-makers possess (at the initial stage of contract formation) private information not shared in the contract setting; (2) informational asymmetry, when some parties accumulate additional information (after contract formation) contributing to informational asymmetry among contracting parties; and (3) moral hazard, when contracting parties take actions which are inconsistent with the contract's objectives but which may not be verifiable. The existence of transaction costs affect, in addition to incomplete information, the possibility of forming "complete" contracts. These factors contributing to (relative or absolute) incompleteness of contracts include: unforeseen contingencies; undescribable states of events and other stochastic developments surrounding the system affecting or affected by the contract specifications (Anderlini and Felli, 1994); increasingly high costs of enumerating what are considered *ex ante* as rather remote or "less important"; potential or *ex post* costs of contract enforcement.

Inevitably incomplete contracts and legally incomplete contracts: A contract is "inevitably incomplete" (Schwartz, 1992, p. 79) if "the optimal solution to a contracting problem would require the parties to condition on information that is unobservable to one or both of them *ex post* or that decision maker could not verify"; a contract is legally incomplete to the extent that "its terms require the parties to condition on unverifiable information" (ibid., p. 81). In general, courts (or other third-party institutions) are required to fill in the contractual gaps, both *de jure* and *de facto*, to bring some operational meaning to the incomplete contracts. These interpretative gap-filling methods elude any sense of uniformity across locations, sectors, and time. This is because of the substantial vacuousness of criteria to adopt in such situations.

It is useful to note that in the complete contracts framework, optimal contracts can be specified contingent on all observable information, even after the original starting time period of the contract. Conversely, incomplete contracts are largely founded on the existence of unobservable and/or asymmetric information among contracting parties on the one hand, and third parties (for the purpose of verifiability or coordination) on the other. As pointed out by Saussier (2000), the nonverifiability feature remains an important provider of incompleteness in contracts. Strategic uncertainty remains a significant contributor to the phenomenon of incomplete contracts. This feature is largely unexplored in the literature on the theory of incomplete contracts and also in the role of TC. TC play a role in mitigating the effects of incomplete information by suggesting relevant guidelines for the design of "optimally incomplete contracts." This is largely due to explicit recognition of the role of bounded rationality in decision-making and its existence in complex scenarios. The role of contract renegotiation and the attendant costs, in addition to the costs of contract design and enforcement, are pertinent issues in the application of TC analysis. Contract adaptation and *ex post* flexibility issues are also required for consideration in the TC approach. Thus, the complementary application of contract theories and TC approaches are essential for the design of optimal contracts.

Other categories of contracts

Explicit and implicit contracts: These are distinguished by the features of the stated explicit contract, and by the underlying (usually unwritten) linkages with other activities (outside the contractual provisions) of the contracting parties that affect one or more of the parties. It may be noted here that there is a distinction between implicit contracts and implied contracts. The latter are often interpreted in courts and other institutions in relation to the objectives of the contract or other relevant provisions (even if the interpretation may not admit its unique or only one particularity), but implicit contracts are usually non-verifiable or enforceable by third parties. The interaction between implicit and explicit contracts is an area of considerable further study relevant in international relations. An apparent suboptimal choice is consciously made by some parties since it becomes optimal when viewed in the broader context that includes other interrelationships between parties. This is not necessarily a "give-and-take" summing situation, but could be a systematic submission of some parties to the implicit coercive measures of more dominant parties in the contract scenario (assuming such a contract was deemed necessary by the relatively weaker parties in the first place).

Short-term vs. long-term contracts: These relate to the nature of specifications of the time horizon over which the contract is sought to be implemented, including any clarification of terminal-period specifications such as targets fulfillment.

Static vs. dynamic contracts: These differ in the nature of specifications of contractual duties/rights that are functions of time, changing over time in accordance with a specified schedule (usually time-based, but it could also be in relation to the magnitudes of various parameters involved in any given time interval).

Renegotiable vs. negotiation-proof contracts: These characterize any contract provisions allowing renegotiation in relation to various contingencies and/or specified time periods, in contrast to fixed nonrenegotiable (closed) contracts. Contract modifications based on renegotiations apply differently to the major categories (Schwartz, 1992): (1) renegotiation of complete contracts; (2) modification of "completable" contracts (based on *ex post* states of the situation); and (3) modification of inevitably incomplete contracts using renegotiations.

Optimal contracts: These are defined in terms of normative features which enable the maximization of stated objectives to be attained subject to relevant constraints, and which provide enforceable specifications of actions for implementation by parties to the contracts, clarified in terms of time horizons, verifiable information features, contingencies for alternative scenarios, and the provision of nonfulfillment of clauses. Obviously, these are transaction-specific, although methodologically common formulations can be advanced.

Contracts involving third-party externalities (efficiency properties for contracting parties with or without externalities) are yet another group of complex agreements. As long as these externalities are positive externalities, benefits are provided to nonparties when costs are not incurred; but when they are negative externalities, the problem requires further attention to compensate the affected parties. In the global sense, these contracts require formulations that seek to maximize global welfare and need to be developed on an explicit ethical basis and on principles of justice when the activities of the contracting parties generate spillover externalities to nonparties.

Dynamic contract theories (see, for example, Crawford, 1985), implicit and explicit contract theories, and strategic cooperative behavior (sometimes described in terms of cooperative game theory; see the next section) play a prominent role in most studies of short-term and long-term cooperation among state parties in international environmental regimes.

2.7 THE ECONOMICS OF COOPERATION AND COORDINATION

Cooperative behavioral features (due to reciprocity and issue linkage, or other factors) among states, even when operating at less than perfect (or optimal) levels, tend to reject Hardin's (1968) "tragedy of the commons" hypothesis. This is partly attributable to global interdependencies recognized by states. As suggested by Barrett (1997), the active and dynamic (rather than isolationist) structure of interactions facilitates a narrowing of the gap between cooperative and noncooperative outcomes. It is this interactive structure that should facilitate the design of "optimal contracts" and agreements to the advantage of all states (and avoid the unjustified components of free-rider phenomena). Several analytical models, especially with the use of game-theoretic formulations, have been advanced over recent years (see, for example, Barrett, 1997) for the study of international cooperation in relation to economic and environmental issues. However, the current state of knowledge falls short in offering relatively robust prescriptions for direct application in the legal implementation of international agreements. The so-called "self-enforcing" models often assume full compliance with a contract or with the provisions of a treaty. However, in reality this is a somewhat rare occurrence. What can be proposed, instead, as a desirable feature relevant for most countries and most environmental problems is to seek the direction of compliance rather than full compliance.

It is logical to visualize potential compliance aspects at the stage of designing agreements. Most models use the dichotomous descriptions "compliance" and "noncompliance" as two binary states of state actions.

The realist description warrants the compliance measure to be described as a function of several relevant parameters (usually dynamic), including incentives at international and state levels for compliance, the costs of compliance, and the limitations of the available institutional and other infrastructure. The combined effect of structural and strategic features contribute to varying degrees of compliance and enforcement of international agreements in states. It is not accurate to depict every element of noncompliance as a willful strategic decision by respective states (unless such a position is explicitly stated). The degree of compliance, even with best intentions, is conditioned by preexisting conditions (socioeconomic and legal, among others). Modeling behavior in game forms is usually founded on assumptions of "level playing fields" and equality of competence among parties to formulate relevant strategies. These features are hard to obtain, given the substantial diversity among states. Thus, we still await further development of formal meaningful models for suggesting more realistic prescriptions of policy. Typically these tend to form a new class of complex "differential games," based on "fuzzy information" and asymmetric decision-making capabilities.

The design content of an international environmental agreement (IEA) is a critical determinant of the size and composition of signatories and ratifiers. The design also influences the potential "entering of reservations" by these parties as well as the degree of commitment in the implementation of the agreed provisions of the IEAs. International agreements or problem-specific Conventions seek to address global issues. Even if they do not accomplish their stated goals in the immediate horizon, they tend to promote cooperative behavior. One of the underlying behavioral factors for such an impact is due to the influence of these Conventions or agreements on the behavioral expectations of both participating or signatory states as well as eligible new parties. The role of economics in the design of international environmental policies and of international environmental agreements is significant. The behavior of participating and nonparticipating states is substantially governed by economic factors and corresponding strategies amenable for economic interpretations. Hence the need for an in-depth analysis of the relevant issues.

Cooperative agreements vs. self-enforcing agreements

The general potential for free-riding phenomena (and other features of conventional public goods) affecting international environmental resources tends to be controlled or minimized when we assess the problem in an integrated framework, where states are viewed and influenced via several interlinking factors such as financial incentives for controlling environmental externalities and provision of concessional international loans in developing countries for related or unrelated development projects. Contrary to the predictions of some of the (static) game-theoretic formulations of the "tragedy of the commons" (see, for example, Hardin and Baden, 1977), several IEAs have been designed and ratified during the 1990s. It is also noted that most of these do not necessarily entail any incentives such as direct resource transfers to some or any of the participating states. This real-world evidence points to the limitations (fortunately) of the free-riding phenomena. Increased environmental awareness and voluntary cooperation among states remain relevant factors in the explanation of conditional/partial cooperative behavior. When a state decides to participate in an agreement it does not necessarily undertake a calculation of the benefits and losses of participation or nonparticipation in relation to the provisions of the specific agreement *per se*. Rather, it makes an assessment of the comprehensive implications of forward and backward linkages to the political, economic, and environmental arena. The international standing of a state constitutes an element of infrastructure leading to potential transaction cost minimization in respect of various areas of international cooperation (for example, easier access to international credit and humanitarian relief). Perceptions by individual states in this approach facilitate their cooperation and motivation for joining a specific IEA or coalition in related areas among states. Carraro and Siniscalco (1998) outlined an analytical formulation of coalition formation in IEAs in the international political economy context. Their approach suggests that states' interactions are not necessarily described by the prisoner's dilemma models of game theory. Issue linkage and resource transfers are among the key elements of inducing cooperation among states in a dynamic setting. However, one of the main limitations of Carraro and Siniscalco's (1998) approach needs comment here. This limitation arises from their adoption of the definition of coalition stability from oligopolistic markets literature regarding cartel formation where one of the usual assumptions states that there is no incentive to broaden the coalition. In the arena of IEAs the problem of a relatively fixed market and the focus on market shares for profit maximization is not posed, as in the case of cartels and their members' motivations for collusive coalitions. Rather, the expanding size of an environmental coalition is likely to enhance the size of the total benefits available to participating as well as other states, and thus is a desirable feature of the agreement's stability. In fact, the larger the size of the coalition, the more unlikely it is that a state will defect from the agreement (or from its obligations) and thus face relatively conspicuous isolationism and its consequences.

The distinction between "consummate cooperation" and "perfunctory cooperation" becomes relevant in the design of international agreements. The former refers to the phenomenon where initiatives are taken by the participating states and decision-makers to fill in any gaps in the contractual arrangements and actions are initiated in order to fulfill the objectives of specific agreements, not merely seeking a sense of compliance with the agreed norms of conduct. Fehr and Gachter (1998) used these concepts largely in the context of employee job performance and inducing workers' voluntary cooperation. The role of reciprocity as norm is also found relevant in many contexts, provided a critical minimum number of decision entities accept such norms for the conduct of activities. This leads to the proposition that "positive reciprocity implies a conditionally cooperative behavior" (Fehr and Gachter, 1998). Fehr et al. (1997) suggested substantial potential for reciprocity norms in contract enforcement mechanisms, where contracts tend to be completed with both implicit and explicit specifications. This is an area of economic behavior that requires further attention applied to sovereign agreements among states.

The prevalence of the phenomena of conditional cooperation and partial cooperation acts as a significant barrier to a potential "tragedy of the commons" by invoking an element of voluntary cooperation and another of positive reciprocity. Gains from partial cooperation can enable expansion of coalitions of state parties in some of the environmental agreements with the use of self-financed resource transfers acting as incentives for compliance with desired environmental actions as well as ensuring some degree of stability of these group coalitions (see Carraro and Siniscalco, 1993).

States are deemed to be coordinating their policies if each chooses its national policies to maximize the global welfare function. This is equivalent to seeking that each state takes into account the features obtaining in every other state and chooses its own policies (domestic and international). A substantial degree of information-sharing among states is presumed here. In uncoordinated scenarios, environmental public goods are likely to be undersupplied and the optimal environmental quality may not be achieved. In such scenarios, each state tends to ignore its own contribution to negative externalities affecting the environment but suffers the consequences of such actions by itself and by others.

There are two types of inefficiencies in uncoordinated policy regimes, in addition to costs of externalities: biases of incomplete information and uncertainty. Let us distinguish the main types of uncertainty (see, for example, Ghosh and Masson, 1994):

- **Additive uncertainty**: Random changes which affect the target variables directly while leaving policy multipliers unchanged; this may not lead to benefits of coordination.
- **Multiplicative uncertainty**: Uncertainty about the effects of policy instruments on target variables, possibly reflecting structural changes; coordination gives rise to welfare improvement. This phenomenon should act as an incentive to coordinate macroeconomic policies (Ghosh and Masson, 1994).

It is important to distinguish two types of incentives: myopic incentives and strategic incentives. International institutions involved in the area of global environmental policies and agreements need to draw upon the roles of incentives so as to enable the "framing of a strategic situation in the most advantageous way to foster international cooperation" (Ecchia and Mariotti, 1998, p. 578). Since the participant states' payoffs are not merely based on economic considerations, it is useful to include strategies that are effective in an "issue-linking" approach. An example of this approach includes provision of financial or technological resources for appropriate state parties to implement desirable environmental policies. The structure of negotiations toward an agreement could include direct and indirect integration of environmental, economic, and other issues in a coherent global welfare-maximizing manner. This might sound like a tall order for the coordinating institutions, especially since these are themselves products of some of the participating states. Experiences in the global environmental policy formation and negotiation processes suggest that additional preparatory steps along these lines are usually cost-effective in the short run and in the long run. The theory of the design of treaties or IEAs should help provide a framework on which treaty negotiation strategies can be developed (Barrett, 1998). However, negotiation strategies constitute only one aspect of the design of efficient and effective treaties. The approach of game theory tends to be of some use, but several additional elements of analysis are essential even to meaningfully apply game theory.

The main elements of treaty design for IEAs are:

- pre-agreement analyses and eliciting cooperation among various (preferably all) states;
- contract/treaty design and *ab initio* assent of parties; ratification of the agreement by these parties;
- provision of incentives for expanded membership of parties;
- provision of incentives for compliance and effective implementation by members (which include features relevant for sustaining membership);
- provision of disincentives for nonmembers so as to ensure that free-rider phenomena are controlled and nonmembers find it more in their own self-interest to join the coalition under the treaty;
- provision of disincentives for noncompliance among members;
- optimal provision of "reservations" clauses so as to avoid the "least common denominator problem" and enhance the levels of environmental protection at the aggregate level; meaningful provision of renegotiation clauses based on future information and experiences among members;
- minimization of transaction costs of treaty formation and implementation, including time-lags in treaty design, ratification, and entry into force;
- effective mechanisms of information exchange, monitoring, and evaluation;
- provision of mechanisms to resolve disputes arising out of implementation of the treaty or of conflicts with other treaties.

These are some of the normative considerations of the economics of coordination. In addition, a broad group of international cooperation and coordination strategies is founded on strategic considerations. These aspects and their foundations are described next.

Game theory and iterated transactions

Game theory, a product of the World War II era, formalizes the strategic conceptualization and analytics of decision-making in competitive or other situations involving one or more decision-makers. Although such formalized analysis by itself may not solve legal or economic decisions, it provides a logical basis for understanding some of the issues. Interactive choices that affect decision-makers' payoffs (not necessarily purely financial or economic) to be interdependent are termed strategic; strategic behavior usually incorporates the role of such interdependencies. In the simplest case, a unitary decision-maker views the states of the world as if they were being played by "nature" or an unknown entity, using a range of options. The key elements in the game analysis are: players, payoffs, and strategies. Games are categorized broadly, in terms of cooperative or noncooperative features, complete or incomplete possession of information, one-time or repeat iterations, played under deterministic or uncertain conditions, and a few other classifications. Games of incomplete information and games of imperfect information differ. The former deal with situations where players are not fully informed about rules or payoffs or other related information, whereas in the latter the players may be imperfectly informed about the history of strategies or other background. As Baird et al. (1994) observed, an understanding of the implications of differential informational possessions of parties is an essential element in any legal or coordination problem when parties tend to act strategically.

The two key principles of game theory are those of "strict dominance" and the "Nash equilibrium" (see box 2.2). The existence of multiple Nash equilibria in many complex real-world configurations is an important feature and usually warrants invoking additional criteria for the selection of "solution" concepts (see also Salant and Sims, 1996). An important element of strategy articulation for states is the existence of strategic uncertainty: parties may not be able to specify or even foresee strategy alternatives at different time instants into the future (especially in a long time-horizon scenario, as in the case of most environmental negotiations or agreements); this is complicated by the varying implicit time horizons of states and their representative regimes whose time horizon of concern is partly influenced by their perceptions of impending change in political institutions and regimes holding the relevant positions of power or representation.

There is a vast literature in game theory and its applications to various fields; see, for example, Rasmusen (1989) for a general approach; Baird et al. (1994) for applications in various areas of law; and Hanley and Folmer (1998) for an edited collection of papers examining applications in the environmental field. A few illustrative analyses may be stated here. Compte and Jehiel (1997) and Myerson (1997) offer a few elementary game-theoretic models for international negotiations affecting the global commons. Carraro and Siniscalco (1998) examine the role of game models for analyzing the evolution of IEAs. In addition, Missfeldt (1999) provides a survey of game-theoretic modeling efforts for analyzing transboundary pollution.

BOX 2.2

Game theory: Concepts and definitions

Best response: A strategy that gives the highest payoff to the player, in response to the strategies chosen by the other players; rational players are assumed to adopt such strategies.

Payoff: The utility a player derives from any specific strategy or combination of strategies.

Extensive form game: Description of a game in terms of its structure, comprising: (1) the players in the game; (2) rules regarding when each player can take decisions and what constitute choices in the set of available options; (3) information about each player's actions; and (4) the payoffs to each player resulting from any specific combination of strategies.

Normal form game: Game description specifying three elements: (1) the players in the game; (2) the strategies at each player's disposal; and (3) the payoffs corresponding to each potential combination of strategy choices among players.

Subgame: Comprises a part of the game with these elements: starts at one or more decision nodes; includes all the decision nodes and terminal nodes that follow a given decision node contained in the subgame; does not include nodes outside these links.

Cooperative game: Game in which players can make binding nonspiteful moves, in contrast with a noncooperative game, where they cannot.

Dominant strategy: A player's best response to any strategies that other players choose; in this case his or her payoff is highest relative to all other strategies in combination with all the alternatives of the other players. A player chooses a strictly dominant strategy and will avoid any strategy that is strictly dominated by another (nontrivial) set of strategies; for clarity, it may be added here that when a specific strategy is always worse than some other strategy, then it is strictly dominated.

Dominant strategy equilibrium: An array of the dominant strategies of each player.

Nash equilibrium: A strategy combination where no player has an incentive to deviate from his or her strategy given that the others do not deviate from such a combination; this comprises a combination of strategies that players choose such that no player could obtain a greater payoff by choosing a different strategy, given the set of strategies others choose. This concept was introduced by John Nash (1950) and led to the award of the Nobel Prize in Economics in 1994. The way to approach the Nash equilibrium is to propose a strategy combination and to examine "if each player's strategy is a best response to the other's strategies" (Rasmusen, 1989, p. 33). Nash-equilibrium strategies are further developed and classified into open-loop strategies (where each player precommits to an entire path of strategies at the beginning of the game), and feedback strategies (where strategies vary as functions of time lapse, state of new information, and decisions of the previous period).

Subgame perfect Nash equilibrium: A Nash equilibrium constituted by the selection of strategies in a subgame.

Bayesian Nash equilibrium: A combination of strategies such that for each player, the strategies are best responses to the probability distributions of other players' strategies, preceding moves, and private information of each player.

Zero-sum game: Game in which the sum of the payoffs of all the players is zero in any combination of strategies they choose.

Management of the global commons can be viewed as a multistage game, with strategic interactions from various countries in their differential access to the commons and their differential contribution to the externalities problems or free-rider phenomena. Some of the problems of management of the commons at regional and local levels can also be examined in such a framework. International environmental agreements are seen as games (Barrett, 1992; Carraro and Siniscalco, 1998), and European problems of acid rain are seen in a similar setting as well (Maler, 1989). Some of the qualitative results of the common property regime for the management of a large natural aquifer were derived by Negri (1989). It was concluded that, in the absence of a coordination mechanism, feedback equilibria led to a more rapid aggregate extraction of resources relative to the conventional open-loop solution of the dynamic game. Let us recall that open-loop equilibria correspond to the assumption that players commit themselves during the initial period of the game to a specific strategy (considered the optimal strategy for the entire duration); feedback equilibria vary the optimal strategies in response to the observed state of information at each time instant or for each successive move.

The role of game theory in customary international law (CIL) can also be examined. One of the theories of CIL (see chapter 4) assumes that "states act rationally and strategically in pursuit of their perceived self-interest" (Goldsmith and Posner, 1998, p. 53). This assumption regarding state rationality is somewhat dubious in its standing, especially when we recognize that the state is not always to be viewed as a unitary player, and that the representative mechanisms for the state's interests are pluralistic in their pursuit of individual as well as state interests. In other words, the motivational and behavioral factors of the representative agents of the state are the key to the characterization of so-called state rationality. In general, however, the roles of mutual cooperation and strategic interaction among state representatives tend to be better understood using appropriate game-theoretic formulations. Lewis (1969) asserted that in a cooperative game where the participants' behavior allows a reasonable predictability and hence coordination, preferences then become rather a secondary requirement: once a process gets launched, a metastable self-sustaining system of preferences, expectations, and actions is generated, which remains capable of being sustained indefinitely, and this phenomenon is defined as a convention. In an operational sense, it may be observed that even if some international treaties or Conventions do not accomplish their goals in the short run, they tend to promote cooperative behavior through their influence on behavioral expectations.

A few analytical aspects based on simple game-theory methods may be stated. The following propositions from Axelrod (1984) are useful:

1   If the discount factor is sufficiently high, there is no best strategy independent of the strategy of the other player/participant. (p. 15)
2   Any strategy which may be the first to cooperate can be collectively stable only when the discount factor is sufficiently large. (p. 61)

Also, in the "iterated or repeat prisoner's dilemma," the potential for cooperation is enhanced when there is high probability of future interaction between parties (Mesterton-Gibbons, 1992). The prisoner's dilemma (PD) is explained in box 2.3.

The above insights suggest that when countries and institutions perceive their continued interaction and potential gain by acting credibly, genuine cooperation is more likely. In addition, if the effects, especially the benefits, of cooperation are likely to occur, cooperation is more likely.

The traditional contributions (see, for example, Ostrom, 1990) of the global commons describe countries' environmental interaction as

BOX 2.3
Prisoner's dilemma (PD) and iterated PD (IPD)

A simple static (one-period) description of a noncooperative two-player game with two alternatives at each player's command is described in terms of a prisoner's dilemma (PD), illustrated here. PD is a game in which the two players believe they have incentives to defect, no matter what the other player does in terms of cooperation or defection. There are two choices for each player: cooperate or defect. Let us use the notation DC to represent the payoff to the first player when that player defects and the other player cooperates; similar explanations hold for the notations CC, CD, and DD. In this game, if the first player cooperates, the other player prefers to defect: CD > CC. If, however, the first player prefers to defect, the other player still prefers to defect: DD > CD. The dilemma is that, if both defect, they both do worse than in the cooperative case: CC > DD. Thus the PD possesses a ranking of the combination of strategies DC > CC > DD > CD. An additional restriction (see Axelrod and Keohane, 1986) is also usually to be ensured for the existence of the "dilemma': CC > (DC + CD)/2. This condition provides that it is better to mutually cooperate than to allow an even chance of being fooled or fooling the other. A prisoner's dilemma with no additional features of communication, cooperation, and commitment constitutes an illustration of a noncooperative game. A cooperative game is a game in which the players can make binding commitments, but this does not happen in a noncooperative game.

In a multiperiod or repeat game, the role of time discounting enters the calculus of each player's valuation of the outcomes at different stages and future time instants. In such a game, the discount rate and discount factor (see chapter 3) play a critical role; some of these implications are seen in Axelrod's propositions stated above.

a nonrepetitive PD where the free-riding nature of resource exploitation leads to the "tragedy of the commons." Sandler (1997) summarized a variety of applications of PD in environmental and other aspects of international cooperation. The set of possible equilibrium outcomes is much larger and the possible set of cooperative outcomes relevant for international environmental agreement or consensus is greater in a repeat or iterated prisoner's dilemma (IPD) situation. Such a description of global scenarios is included in a few works (see, for example, Barrett, 1992; Sandler, 1997; Carraro and Siniscalco, 1998).

The so-called folk theorem (see, for example, Friedman, 1986) states, in one of the versions, that the players can achieve their utilities in the Nash-equilibrium sense if the game is iterated with an infinite time horizon and players do not significantly discount future values. Five conditions have been identified for overcoming PD (Goldsmith and Posner, 1998): low discount on time or future iterations or both, indefinite or infinite continuity of the game, very limited payoffs for noncooperative defections, substantial knowledge of each other's payoffs and strategies, and absence of spiteful behavior and inclusion of strategic, potentially cooperative behavior. The role of continued interaction or repeat transactions was also seen as a prerequisite for relative stability of cooperation in an IPD scenario (Mesterton-Gibbons, 1992).

Constrained rationality and incomplete information tend to severely limit the practical application of most models of game theory. Much of the assumed normative behavior in these models is also somewhat unrealistic. The assumption of knowledge of reasonable, meaningful, and comprehensive sets of strategy choices as well as of their corresponding payoffs over time is usually very restrictive and at times "self-validating" (Stein, 1999). For a review of the role and limitations of game theory in legal interpretations and law development, see Salant and Sims (1996), and in international relations see Stein (1999).

■ 2.8 SUMMARY

The issue of environmental externalities is the single most important factor behind the imperatives of international environmental law. The phenomenon of global environmental interdependence requires global cooperation and coordination of environmental and economic policies. Free-riders generally inflict additional costs on others. If there are no meaningful and effective international mechanisms for the governance of the global commons, in the long-run, free-riders as well as others would suffer the effects of the lack of optimal provision of environmental goods and services. While admitting the importance of strategic behavior among parties, mechanisms for the design and implementation of relevant policies with cooperative arrangements are significant in the management of global environmental resources. Repeat transactions and the relatively low discounting of valuations of future benefits are among the motivating factors for improved cooperation between state parties. International environmental agreements should employ these characteristics in the provision of appropriate incentives for treaty participation and compliance.

The "tradition" of "law and economics" relies heavily on Coasean propositions. It is rather ironic that these propositions have been found to be of least relevance in the field of international environmental management, yet we continue with the "law and economics" direction. This book proceeds with another set of variants of "law and economics" which are relevant for the problems of concern rather than proposing misapplications of traditional principles.

A judicious combination of the specifications of property rights and liability rules is an important aspect of the design of international environmental agreements. Transaction costs play a critical role in the development of such provisions and in their enforcement. Diplomatic, economic, and legal institutions need to take these features into account for policy formulation and implementation purposes.

"Properly designed contracts" are important to eliminate the several imperfections and features of incompleteness that remain the reality of a treaty or agreement if requisite attention is not paid to assessing the implications of these aspects.

Review Exercises

1   (a) Explain the role of the "tragedy of the commons" theme in a repeat transaction setting with (i) a fixed time horizon and fixed participating parties; (ii) a fixed time horizon and random participating parties; and (iii) an infinitely long time horizon and fixed participating parties.
    (b) Can environmental "free-riders" also be victims of environmental externalities?

2   Explain the contributions of Pigou and Coase to the problem of managing environmental externalities using economic criteria, using an example of interstate riverwater pollution.

3   Identify reasons why the Coase theorem is irrelevant for international environmental assets management.

4   Discuss the role of rules versus standards in the management of chemical pollution, at transboundary or regional levels.

5 Discuss the relative merits (or lack thereof) in utilizing property rights regimes and liability regimes in the management of global greenhouse gas emissions. Examine these aspects first in a static, then in a dynamic multiperiod framework.

6 What are the cooperation-enhancing factors in an IPD scenario? Examine the potential interdependence of some of the identified factors among themselves.

7 Yarbrough and Yarbrough (1994, p. 260) proposed the following extended Coase theorem in the context of global resource management. Discuss its role, limitations, and validity, if any.

"With zero transaction costs resources would flow to their highest valued user and control over resources would be independent of both the initial allocation of property rights *and control over territory.*"

REFERENCES

Aceves, W. J., 1996, An economic analysis of international law: Transaction cost economics and the concept of state practice, *University of Pennsylvania Journal of International Economic Law*, 17, 995–1068.

Aidt, T., 1998, Political internalization of economic externalities and environmental policy, *Journal of Public Economics*, 69, 1–16.

Anderlini, L. and Felli, L., 1994, Incomplete written contracts: Undescribable states of nature, *Quarterly Journal of Economics*, 109, 1085–1124.

Axelrod, R., 1984, *The Evolution of Cooperation*, New York: Basic Books.

Axelrod, R. and Keohane, R. O., 1986, Achieving cooperation under anarchy: Strategies and institutions, in K. A. Oye (ed.), *Cooperation under Anarchy*, Princeton: Princeton University Press, pp. 226–54.

Baird, D. G., Gertner, R. H., and Picker, R. C., 1994, *Game Theory and the Law*, Cambridge, MA: Harvard University Press.

Ballard, C. L. and Medema, S. G., 1993, The marginal efficiency effects of taxes and subsidies in the presence of externalities: A computable general equilibrium approach, *Journal of Public Economics*, 52, 199–216.

Barrett, S., 1992, International environmental agreements as games, in R. Pethig (ed.), *Conflicts and Cooperation in Managing Environmental Resources*, Berlin: Springer-Verlag, pp. 18–33.

Barrett, S., 1997, Towards a theory of international environmental cooperation, in C. Carraro and D. Siniscalco (eds.), *New Directions in the Economic Theory of the Environment*, Cambridge: Cambridge University Press, pp. 239–80.

Barrett, S., 1998, On the theory and diplomacy of environmental treaty-making, *Environmental and Resource Economics*, 11, 317–33.

Baumol, W. J. and Oates, W. E., 1988, *The Theory of Environmental Policy*, Englewood Cliffs, NJ: Prentice-Hall.

Blankart, C. B. and Knieps, G., 1993, State and standards, *Public Choice*, 77, 39–52.

Boadu, F. O., 1998, Relational characteristics of transboundary water treaties: Lesotho's water transfer treaty with the Republic of South Africa, *Natural Resources Journal*, 38, 381–409.

Bovenberg, A. L. and Goulder, L. H., 1996, Optimal environmental taxation in the presence of other taxes: General equilibrium analyses, *American Economic Review*, 86, 985–1000.

Buchanan, J. M., 1987, *Economics: Between Predictive Science and Moral Philosophy*, College Station, TX: Texas A&M University Press.

Bugge, H. C., 1996, The principles of "polluter-pays" in economics and law, in E. Eide and R. van den Bergh (eds.), *Law and Economics of the Environment*, Deidrecht: Kluwer, pp. 53–74.

Calabresi, G. and Melamed, A. D., 1972, Property rules, liability rules, and inalienability: One view of the Cathedral, *Harvard Law Review*, 85, 1089.

Carraro, C. and Siniscalco, D., 1993, Strategies for international protection of the environment, *Journal of Public Economics*, 52, 309–28.

Carraro, C. and Siniscalco, D., 1998, International environmental agreements: Incentives and political economy, *European Economic Review*, 42, 561–72.

Coase, R. H., 1960, The problem of social cost, *Journal of Law and Economics*, 6, 1–44.

Coase, R. H., 1988, *The Firm, the Market and the Law*, Chicago: University of Chicago Press.

Compte, O. and Jehiel, P., 1997, International negotiations and dispute resolution mechanisms: The case of environmental negotiations, in C. Carraro (ed.), *International Environmental Agreements: Strategic Policy Issues*, Cheltenham: Elgar.

Cooter, R. D., 1989, The Coase theorem, in J. Eatwell, M. Milgate, and P. Newman (eds.), *Allocation, Information, and Markets*, London: Macmillan, pp. 64–70.

Crawford, V. P., 1985, Dynamic games and dynamic contract theory, *Journal of Conflict Resolution*, 29, 195–234.

Demsetz, H., 1966, Some aspects of property rights, *Journal of Law and Economics*, 9, 61–71; reprinted 1975 in H. G. Manne (ed.), *The Economics of Legal Relationships: Readings in the Theory of Property Rights*, New York: West Publishing, pp. 184–93.

Demsetz, H., 1967, Towards a theory of property rights, *American Economic Review*, 57, 347–60; reprinted 1975 in H. G. Manne (ed.), *The Economics of Legal Relationships: Readings in the Theory of Property Rights*, New York: West Publishing, pp. 23–36.

Demsetz, H., 1972, When does the rule of liability matter?, *Journal of Legal Studies*, 1, 13–28; reprinted 1975 in H. G. Manne (ed.), *The Economics of Legal Relationships: Readings in the Theory of Property Rights*, New York: West Publishing, pp. 168–83.

DeSerpa, A. C., 1994, Pigou and Coase: A mathematical reconciliation, *Journal of Public Economics*, 54, 267–86.

Devlin, R. A. and Grafton, R. Q., 1998, *Economic Rights and Environmental Wrongs: Property Rights for the Common Good*, Cheltenham: Edward Elgar.

Dixit, A. and Olson, M., 2000, Does voluntary participation undermine the Coase theorem?, *Journal of Public Economics*, 76, 309–35.

Dunoff, J. L. and Trachtman, J. P., 1999, Economic analysis of international law, *Yale Journal of International Law*, 24, 1–59.

Ecchia, G. and Mariotti, M., 1998, Coalition formation in international environmental agreements and the role of institutions, *European Economic Review*, 42, 573–82.

Farber, D. A., 1997, Parody lost/pragmatism regained: The ironic history of the Coase theorem, *Virginia Law Review*, 83, 397–428.

Fehr, E. and Gachter, S., 1998, Reciprocity and economics: The economic implications of *Homo Reciprocans*, *European Economic Review*, 42, 845–59.

Fehr, E., Gachter, S., and Kirschsteiger, 1997, Reciprocity as a contract enforcement device, *Econometrica*, 65, 833–60.

Friedman, J. W., 1986, *Game Theory with Applications to Economics*, Oxford: Oxford University Press.

Furubotn, E. G. and Pejovich, S., 1972, Property rights and economic theory: A survey of recent literature, *Journal of Economic Literature*, 10, 1138.

Ghosh, A. R. and Masson, P. R., 1994, *Economic Cooperation in an Uncertain World*, Oxford: Blackwell.

Goldsmith, J. L. and Posner, E. A., 1998, Notes toward a theory of customary international law, *American Society of International Law Proceedings of the 92nd Annual Meeting*, 53–7.

Gollin, M. A., 1991, Using intellectual property to improve environmental protection, *Harvard Journal of Law & Technology*, 4, 193–235.

Goulder, L. H., 1995, Environmental taxation and the double dividend: A reader's guide, *International Tax and Public Finance*, 2, 157–83.

Haas, P., 1980, Why collaborate? Issue linkage and international regimes, *World Politics*, 32, 355–67.

Handl, G., 1990, Environmental security and global change: The challenge to international law, *1990 Yearbook of International Environmental Law*, 2–23.

Hanley, N. and Folmer, H. (eds.), 1998, *Game Theory and the Environment*, Cheltenham: Edward Elgar.

Hardin, G. H., 1968, The tragedy of the commons, *Science*, 162, 1243–8.

Hardin, G. and Baden, J., 1977, *Managing the Commons*, New York: Freeman.

Harvard Law Review Association (HLRA), 1991, Developments in the law: International environmental law, *Harvard Law Review*, 104, 1484–1639.

Heller, M. A., 1998, The tragedy of anticommons, *Harvard Law Review*, 111, 621–88.

Hovenkamp, H., 1990, Marginal utility and the Coase theorem, *Cornell Law Review*, 75, 783–810.

Hurwicz, L., 1972, On informationally decentralized systems, in C. McGuire and R. Radner (eds.), *Decision and Organization*, Amsterdam: North-Holland, pp. 297–336.

Inada, K.-I. and Kuga, K., 1973, Limitations of the "Coase theorem" on liability rules, *Journal of Economic Theory*, 6, 606–13.

International Law Commission (ILC), 1991, *Draft Articles on Liability for Injurious Consequences of Acts Not Prohibited by International Law*, UN Doc. A/CN.4/428.

Kaplow, L., 1992, Rules versus standards: An economic analysis, *Duke Law Journal*, 42, 557–629.

Landes, W. M. and Posner, R. A., 1987, *The Economic Structure of Tort Law*, Cambridge, MA: Harvard University Press.

Lewis, D., 1969, *Convention: A Philosophical Study*, Cambridge, MA: Harvard University Press.

Mabey, N., Hall, S., Smith, C., and Gupta, S., 1997, *Argument in the Greenhouse*, London: Routledge.

Maler, K. G., 1989, The acid rain game, in H. Folmer and E. Ireland (eds.), *Valuation Methods and Policy Making in Environmental Economics*, New York: Elsevier, pp. 188–205.

Manne, H. G. (ed.), 1975, *The Economics of Legal Relationships: Readings in the Theory of Property Rights*, New York: West Publishing.

Mattei, U., 1997, *Comparative Law and Economics*, Ann Arbor: University of Michigan Press.

Mesterton-Gibbons, M., 1992, On the iterated prisoner's dilemma in a finite population, *Bulletin of Mathematical Biology*, 54, 423–43.

Missfeldt, F., 1999, Game-theoretic modeling of transboundary pollution, *Journal of Economic Surveys*, 13, 236–87.

Myerson, R. B., 1997, Game-theoretic models of bargaining: An introduction for economists studying the transnational commons, in P. Dasgupta, K. G. Maler, and A. Vercelli (eds.), *The Economics of Transnational Commons*, Oxford: Clarendon Press, pp. 17–34.

Nalebuff, B., 1997, On a clear day, you can see the Coase theorem, in P. Dasgupta and K. G. Maler (eds.), *The Environment and Emerging Development Issues*, Oxford: Clarendon Press, pp. 35–47.

Nash, J., 1950, The bargaining problem, *Econometrica*, 18, 155–62.

Negri, D. H., 1989, The common property aquifer as a differential game, *Water Resources Research*, 25, 9–15.

North, D., 1992, Institutions and economic theory, *American Economist*, 36, 3–6.

Oates, W. E., 1995, Green taxes, the environment, and the tax system, *Southern Economic Journal*, 61 (4), 915–22.

Organization for Economic Cooperation and Development (OECD), 1995, *Environmental Principles and Concepts*, OECD Document OECD/GD(95)124, Paris: OECD Secretariat.

Olson, Jr., M., 1996, Big bills left on the sidewalk: Why some nations are rich, and others poor, *Journal of Economic Perspectives*, 10, 3–24.

Ostrom, E., 1990, *Governing the Commons*, Cambridge: Cambridge University Press.

Parry, I., 1995, Pollution taxes and revenue recycling, *Journal of Environmental Economics and Management*, 29 (3), 564–77.

Parry, I., 1997, Environmental taxes and quotas in the presence of distortionary factor markets, *Resource and Energy Economics*, 19, 203–20.

Pigou, A. C., 1932, *The Economics of Welfare*, London: Macmillan.

Platteau, J.-P., 1994, Behind the market stage where real societies exist, I and II, *Journal of Development Studies*, 30, 533–77 and 753–817.

Posner, R., 1993, Nobel laureate: Ronald Coase and methodology, *Journal of Economic Perspectives*.

Rao, P. K., 2000a, *Sustainable Development: Economics and Policy*, Oxford: Blackwell.

Rao, P. K., 2000b, *The Economics of Global Climatic Change*, Armonk, NY: M. E. Sharpe.

Rao, P. K., 2001, *The Economics of Transaction Costs*, New York: Palgrave.

Rasmusen, E., 1989, *Games and Information*, Oxford: Blackwell.

Salant, S. W. and Sims, T. S., 1996, Game theory and the law: Ready for the prime time?, *Michigan Law Review*, 94, 1839–82.

Samuels, W. J., 1992, *Essays on the Role of Government*, Vol. 2, New York: New York University Press.

Sandler, T., 1997, *Global Challenges*, Cambridge: Cambridge University Press.

Saussier, S., 2000, When incomplete contract theory meets transaction cost economics: A test, in C. Menard (ed.), *Institutions, Contracts and Organizations*, Cheltenham: Edward Elgar, pp. 376–98.

Schwartz, A., 1992, Legal contract theories and incomplete contracts, in L. Werin and H. Wijkander (eds.), *Contract Economics*, Oxford: Blackwell, pp. 76–108.

Simon, H. A., 1957, *Models of Man*, New York: John Wiley.

Simon, H. A., 2000, Barriers and bounds to rationality, *Structural Change and Economic Dynamics*, 11, 243–53.

Stein, A. A., 1999, The limits of strategic choice: Constrained rationality and incomplete explanation, in D. A. Lake and R. Powell (eds.), *Strategic Choice and International Relations*, Princeton: Princeton University Press, pp. 197–228.

Stubblebine, W. C., 1975, On property rights and institutions, in H. G. Manne (ed.), *The Economics of Legal Relationships: Readings in the Theory of Property Rights*, New York: West Publishing, pp. 11–22.

Sunstein, C., 1997, *Free Markets and Social Justice*, New York: Oxford University Press.

Taylor, P., 1998, *An Ecological Approach to International Law*, London: Routledge.

Tirole, J., 1999, Incomplete contracts: Where do we stand?, *Econometrica*, 67, 741–81.

Usher, D., 1998, The Coase theorem is tautological, incoherent or wrong, *Economics Letters*, 61, 3–11.

von Neumann, J. and Morgenstern, O., 1944, *Theory of Games and Economic Behavior*, Princeton: Princeton University Press.

White, B., 1987, Coase and courts: Economics of the common man, *Iowa Law Review*, 72, 577–636.

Wiener, J. B., 1999, Global environmental regulation: Instrument choice in legal context, *Yale Law Journal*, 108, 677–800.

Williamson, O. E., 1985, *The Economic Institutions of Capitalism*, New York: Free Press.

Wolf, Jr., C., 1988, *Markets or Governments: Choosing Between Imperfect Alternatives*, Cambridge, MA: MIT Press.

Yarbrough, B. V. and Yarbrough, R. M., 1994, International contracting and territorial control: The boundary question, *Journal of Institutional and Theoretical Economics*, 150, 239–64.

chapter three

Economic and Environmental Decision-making

■ 3.1 INTRODUCTION

A number of key factors, principles, and methods need to be incorporated in the processes of environmental management. International environmental law is generally strengthened by analytical methods. The selection of "optimal risk acceptance" under relatively limited information, the evaluation of alternatives (with the use of cost–benefit or other methods of assessment), and a recognition of the explicit and implicit roles of time preferences (or discounting future costs and benefits, not necessarily in monetary terms only) are among the key ingredients of economic and environmental decision-making. These are relevant at the state as well as international levels for policy and law development, and also in devising operational guidelines for implementation. These issues form the main concern of this chapter.

The development of relevant laws and their adoption in practice are both subject to frequent problems of incomplete information and systemic uncertainties. These features require greater awareness of alternative approaches to decision-making under uncertainty. The economics of risk-taking behavior has implications for the environmental consequences of economic policies. Similarly, risk-averse behavior in environmental management has implications for economic performance. Besides, specific risk-acceptance levels (in relation to any resource use or conservation, for example) in either fields should be sensitive to the changes in other risks since the latter interact with the former. This chapter presents various concepts and definitions relevant in this context. Their prudent application in specific environmental management areas remains a task for the future, as is that of more detailed methodological analyses than those presented here.

The most common features of economic and environmental decision-making, especially those involving longer time horizons, relate to a wide variety of uncertainties and incompleteness of information. The complex interrelationships among system components tend to evolve over time, with the influences of exogenous and endogenous factors. It is useful to examine some of the important analytical methods and concepts to gain additional qualitative insights into decision-making approaches relevant to global environmental systems. A few approximations of analytical methods of decision-making under uncertainty have filtered through for practical application, such as the precautionary principle. Some of these emanated from intuitive logical reasons to safeguard against unknowns and uncertainties. This chapter provides both a historical perspective on the evolution of this principle and several related formal analytical methods/concepts for formulating international environmental policies.

Another major aspect of economic analysis included in this chapter is that of economic evaluation. An important economic ingredient relevant for the pragmatic ranking of alternatives among policy choices is cost–benefit analysis and the economic evaluation of alternate proposals. To the extent that monetization or other valuation methods permit comparability of different alternatives, the use of such assessments enables selection of cost-effective elements. Critical in the time-discounted valuation of future costs and future benefits of any proposed policy or regulation is the selection of the discount rate applicable over the relevant time horizon. Several analytical investigations are summarized for understanding this issue. A few applied cases and examples illuminate the analytics of decision-making.

3.2 UNCERTAINTY AND INCOMPLETE INFORMATION

Economic and environmental decision-making requires proper recognition of various quantifiable and unquantifiable uncertainties. Incomplete availability (even after excluding strategic incompleteness) of information remains a common feature as well. Even with the best intentions, policy formulations and their implementation measures can be constrained by these complexities. The relevance of some of the fundamentals of decision-making under uncertainty and incomplete information is thus apparent. Box 3.1 outlines economic concepts that are pertinent in this context.

BOX 3.1

Economic concepts for decision-making under uncertainty

Certainty equivalent: The comparison of an uncertain quantity X in relation to the probability of its attainment of different values and then comparing the resultant with its certainty c, i.e., if the expected value $E(X) = c$ then X is considered the certainty equivalent of c. In the discrete version case the expected value is given by the sum $p_1 x_1 + p_2 x_2 + \ldots + p_n x_n$, where $p_j s$ are the probabilities of realization of values x_j in all the n states which cover the possible alternatives.

The concepts of concavity, convexity, and linearity of a function are defined by comparing the function value associated with a linear combination of values of its argument with the linear combination of the corresponding function values. For a linear combination formed by the expected value operator E relative to a given probability distribution, and utility function U, the following relation holds:

$E[U(V)] < U[E(V)]$, under concavity;
the reverse inequality holds under convexity; and
equality holds for linearity.

Thus a rational decision-maker with a concave utility function would be inclined to exchange a random asset for a nonrandom level of asset which equals the expected value of the exchanged asset.

The certainty equivalent $C(V)$ is defined by:

$$U[C(V)] = E[U(V)]$$

The difference between the expected value and the certainty equivalent is called the (subjective) price of risk r, representing the "risk premium" a decision-maker is willing to offer in order to eliminate the risk (also see, for example, Sinn, 1989):

$$r(V) = E(V) - C(V)$$

Consumer surplus: The additional utility that might be available to a consumer as a result of a change in price or non-price intervention relative to the scenario without such a change.

Exogenous: Any variable or influence which is prescribed without any direct influence of the system under its influence.

Expected value: The added sum of the products of quantities with their corresponding probabilities of occurrence or realization.

Endogenous: The dependent entity which responds to an evolving or changing feature or structural relation in the system affected by the factor or the entity under consideration.

Nonadditive utility: The utility levels which do not simply add from one period to another without their interperiod dependency.

Recursive utility: The emergence of successive periods of utility in terms of the preceding ones.

Risk-averse behavior: The decision-making approach where the certainty equivalence is not enough to offset the involved uncertainties, and the decision situation warrants greater risk premium g to compensate for the uncertainties, i.e.,

$$E(X) + g = c$$

Risk-taking behavior is the converse of the above. Here $E(X) - g = c$. These definitions are based on the approach of "expected values" for decision-making, sometimes called first-order risk-aversion criteria. There are other alternative criteria for decision-making, which lead to a different set of estimates for the risk premia.

Risk-neutral behavior: The acceptance of certainty equivalence as a relevant decision criterion, i.e., being indifferent between the certainty-equivalent quantity and the corresponding level of quantity with certainty.

Time consistency: In a multiperiod decision-making process, sticking to the multiperiod decision at the end of each successive period as if the original decision still holds for the remaining periods, even with new information or other changes. Consistency of preferences over time was also defined by Becker (1998) as being when the choices an individual would like to make in the future, if he or she knew at the current time what would happen in the interim, are exactly the same as the choices he or she will actually make then.

Three main types of decision-making attitudes or behavioral characteristics influenced by risk/uncertainty deserve to be summarized. These are risk neutrality, risk aversion, and risk-taking. It is feasible to argue that the dual of risk aversion could be visualized as risk-taking, and hence its subclassification requires attention. Most of the analytical literature focuses on the former, with any inferences regarding the latter remaining residual. Thus, it largely suffices to understand one of the two systems in their subclassifications, outlined in box 3.2. In terms of the relevance of specifications of the utility functions for

BOX 3.2

Concepts in risks and decision-making behavior

Uncertainty: A situation typically characterized by pure uncertainty with little sense of degree of uncertainty, its frequency, and evolution over time. In other words, a probabilistic assessment of the event or its consequences is usually not feasible using available information, but it is known that the system is not to be described in terms of certainty of events and/or responses. It is also useful to categorize uncertainty in terms of its sources and functional aspects: cumulative uncertainty, uncertainty over time, spatial uncertainty, damage uncertainty, and a few others (see, for example, Watzold, 2000, for a taxonomy of environmental uncertainties).

Risk: An uncertain situation that plausibly admits its characterization in terms of different probability estimates (whether subjective or objective), leading to various measures of risk corresponding to varying levels of their probability of materialization; "the combined effect of the probability of occurrence of an undesirable event and its magnitude."

Risk premium (r): $r = a - b$, the difference between the expected value of the payoff (a) and its certainty equivalent (b).

Risk-seeking or risk-favoring: Decision-making where a negative risk premium is assigned for selection among alternatives.

Risk-neutral: This position corresponds to zero risk premium, or the recognition of certainty equivalence with the expected value of payoff; the decision-maker would be indifferent between allowing a risk x^- and obtaining the nonrandom amount of payoff equal to $E(x^-) - r$, where E denotes the expected value (for a given probability distribution).

Risk aversion: This broad feature corresponds to a positive risk value, whether constant or exhibiting dynamic properties.

- *Constant risk aversion*: Decision scenario where the risk premium is a positive constant.

- *Absolute risk aversion*: $R_{1x} = -U^{II}(x)/U^{I}(x)$.
- *Relative risk aversion (RRA)*: $R_{2x} = -x\,U^{II}(x)/U^{I}(x)$.
  RRA can be seen as an elasticity of risk-aversion measure. In an application of this concept, Gollier et al. (2000) proved that the precautionary principle (see section 3.3) becomes relevant in the prevention of future risks when RRA remains constant at a level less than 1.
- *Increasing relative risk aversion*: The relative risk aversion is an increasing function of x.
- *Decreasing risk aversion*: The risk premium shows a declining trend with increasing values of x.
- *Decreasing absolute risk aversion (DARA)*: Absolute risk aversion is a decreasing function of x; as an illustrative application of this concept (see Pratt, 1964), let us note that under DARA, exogenous contributions to the general risk situation in a decision-making environment (or added riskiness scenarios in general) lead a rational decision-maker to take more care (or remain more risk-averse) elsewhere in areas where such decisions could make a difference.
- *Standard risk aversion*: This is a combination of decreasing absolute risk aversion and decreasing absolute prudence; the latter given by the requirement that the ratio $-U^{III}(x)/U^{II}(x)$ decreases with increases in x; this feature recognizes that the economic phenomenon of the "precautionary savings" motive decreases in intensity with wealth or resource accumulation (Kimball, 1990, 1993).

Loss aversion: This concept originates in behavioral sciences, using "prospect theory" (Kahneman and Tversky, 1979); it is based on the assumption that individuals are averse to losses and react differently to a decrease in gains as opposed to an increase in losses – even if the magnitudes of the quantities involved in either case are the same. The role of loss aversion and prospect theory tends to be greatly amplified in the law and economics of "trusts." Various court rulings on the standards of prudence in investment decisions of trusts in the US under the US trust laws (see Scott, 1999) suggest that trustees should not view gains and losses in a symmetric fashion and that risks should be minimized (less than what standard portfolio theories of traditional economics allowing tradeoff between mean and variance of returns to investments would indicate).

> An application of loss-aversion criteria suggests that the Coase theorem (see chapter 2) could not hold when the allocation of legal entitlements influences the outcome, since those individuals who are "initially allocated an entitlement are likely to value it more than those without the legal entitlement" (Sunstein, 1997, p. 132). This raises the issue of effective design (including appropriate institutional arrangements for governance) of property rights regimes and liability rules, with less reliance on "bargaining" solutions in such situations.

decision-making, it is useful to note that a risk-neutral decision-maker will have a linear utility function, a risk averter a concave utility function, and a risk-seeking decision-maker a convex utility function.

Multivariate risks

Multivariate risk decisions arise due either to multiple decision-makers or to multiple entities of concern (each obeying a different path of risky evolution), or to a combination of both. It is no easy task to rank alternative scenarios, in the absence of a uniform and consistent agreement among participant decision-makers regarding the criteria for ranking them, which also implies the need for an agreement on the nature of tradeoffs among potentially conflicting risks and their implications on the multiple payoff functions. Kihlstrom and Mirman (1974) established that a prerequisite for the comparison of attitudes toward risk and risk aversion is that the utility functions being compared represent the same set of preferences (or preference ordering) among alternatives.

Background risks or those risks exogenous to the system and not within the control of decision-makers are to be recognized as real-world phenomena whenever risks of environmental or related problems are analyzed for mitigating or prevention. Decreasing absolute risk aversion suggests the need to take more care wherever such care makes a positive difference in risk minimization (see Pratt, 1964).

The reasoning that bearing one risk should tend to lead to greater risk aversion in respect of other independent risks led Kimball (1993) to suggest the criterion of "standard risk aversion." "Standard risk aversion is when, in the case of statistical independence, *every loss-aggravating risk aggravates every undesirable risk.*" In cases with decreasing absolute risk aversion, all undesirable risks are loss-aggravating. Considerations of standard risk aversion enable decision-makers to recognize the sensitivities of undesirable independent risks to primary risk characteristics of phenomena or events. The application of some of these concepts and approaches of multivariate and multiperiod risks in the global environmental field suggests that whenever we discover a greater risk (such as the larger extent of ozone depletion or accumulation of greenhouse gases, or greater links between global warming and deforestation), we need to take steps consistent with enhanced relative risk-aversion criteria. Given environmental inter-dependencies, more precautions must be taken in such scenarios. The sensitivity of economic and environmental policies and laws should be such as to recognize the role of changing perceptions of risks and their implications for prudent behavior at the state and international levels. Some of the concepts of risk and decision-making under uncertainty need to be applied in future developments of IEL; they are presented here and will be applied in later chapters, although a few illustrations are offered toward such applications.

Admittedly, despite substantial advances in the theory and methods of stochastic decision-making, some tend to form parts of analytical tools for decision-making rather than providing comprehensive solutions to general problems (for a partial review, see Buschena and Zilberman, 1994). In other words, in addition to the application of some of these concepts and methods, sound judgment remains an imperative for decision-making under uncertainty.

One of the important applications of decision-making under uncertainty is in the area of precautionary decisions or the role of prudence. These aspects are discussed in the next section, with a historical and applied policy perspective.

▋ 3.3 THE PRECAUTIONARY PRINCIPLE (PP)

Environmental unknowns and surprises constitute part "ignorance" and part "ignore-ance" (Myers, 1995). Let us recall that at the time of the first major international conference on the environment in Stockholm in 1972, there was little mention of the currently recognized problem of global warming, although global warming was recognized as early as 1896 by the Swedish scientist Svante Arhenius. System uncertainties or stochastic features of biogeophysical (and economic) systems, combined with potentially irreversible phenomena, do call for a very cautious approach, largely expressed in terms of the

BOX 3.3

Analytical aspects of the precautionary principle

The expected utility theorem states that it is possible to rank alternative utility functions defined on the space of random outcomes,
using real-number valuations, in such a way that the expected
value utility does capture the preferences (relevant for the decision-
making entity) among alternatives.

In the social utility function context, Harsanyi (1955) established
that if every individual preference as well as social preferences
conform to expected utility theory, the sum of utility functions
representing the preferences of individuals constitutes the social
utility function, provided social preferences satisfy the Pareto criterion. More rigorous refinements of these results were established
by Broome (1990), leading to the conclusion that unless all economic decision-makers agree about the estimates of probability of
occurrence of various events, a social expected utility function may
not be meaningfully constructed. Analogous results have also been
established in comparing multiple risks. Kihlstrom and Mirman
(1974) showed that a prerequisite for the ranking of outcomes
based on multivariate risks is that decision-makers possess the same
ordinal preferences over the outcome vectors for each of the ingredients of the commodity space (see also Levy and Levy, 1984).

Risk aversion becomes an important feature in decision-making
when a large number and/or magnitudes of risks are involved. Can
gambling be consistent with risk aversion? It is possible, if merely
subjective rather than objective probabilities of occurrence of
favorable events are included. Let us note that the gambler is one
who believes and acts on the belief that the odds are more favorable
to him or her than they really are, as stated by Arrow (1974). If
individual rationality is to be interpreted, an additional risk factor
projected as likely to occur in the future is usually responded to
with an increase in capacity building (including savings or other
related measures to address future needs), indicating prudence is
warranted in all such cases of increase in uncertainty. An analogy
holds at the aggregate level in environmental protection as well.

Gollier et al. (2000) argued, on the basis of a number of analytical investigations, that the effect of increased uncertainty on current actions entails a "precautionary effect" even when there is no
significant problem of environmental irreversibility. They provided

an interpretation of the PP in the standard Bayesian framework for the revision of decisions based on new information. They suggested on the basis of these formulations that significant scientific uncertainty about future environmental risks should warrant greater use of the PP at this juncture if: RRA $< c < 1$, where c is a constant.

precautionary principle (PP). The PP is based on the idea that any uncertainty should be interpreted toward a measure of safeguard. In a sense, it is equivalent to the "better safe than sorry" principle, or a "no regrets" policy. When formally adopted into the relevant legal provisions, the PP shifts the burden of proof to the accused party. The polluter, potential polluter, or resource user bears the onus of proving that the contested activity is not harmful to the environment before any precipitative actions are initiated by the party. The PP favors erring on the side of risk aversion (OECD, 1995).

Some of the analytical foundations of the PP are provided in box 3.3. The PP is equivalent to "risk-averse" behavior in cases that involve irreversibility or extremely high costs in socioeconomic or biogeophysical or other terms. The principle could lead to a caution that may be attained at the expense of substantial potential gains. It would be similar, for instance, to imposing a ban on driving an automobile because the activity of driving involves a positive probability of accident. However, the risk-averse nature of the PP is extremely relevant where scientific knowledge is too limited to quantify uncertainty and thus cannot establish probability distributions of potential outcomes (see also Bodansky, 1991).

The historical origins of the PP in the international context are summarized below (for more details, see Cameron et al., 1998; Weintraub, 1992).

The evolution of precautionary measures

The first international formulation of the precautionary principle was in the statements of the First International Conference on the Protection of the North Sea in 1984, when the focus was on emissions into the marine environment. The PP has played an increasingly significant role since its endorsement by the Second International Conference of the North Sea in 1987. The final report of the ministers to the 1987 London Conference declared: "accepting that in order to protect the North Sea from possibly damaging effects of the most dangerous substances, a precautionary approach is necessary which may require action to control inputs of such substances even before a causal link has been established by absolutely clear scientific evidence" (Second International Conference on the Protection of the North Sea (London Declaration), London, 1987; 27 ILM 835).

In May 1990, 34 states in the Economic Conference for Europe (ECE) adopted at Bergen, Norway, a Ministerial Declaration on Sustainable Development in the ECE region. The Bergen Declaration proclaimed: "In order to achieve sustainable development, policies must be based on the precautionary principle. Environmental measures must anticipate, prevent and attack the causes of environmental degradation. Where there are threats of serious or irreversible damage, lack of full scientific certainty should not be used as a reason for postponing measures to prevent environmental degradation" (UN Doc. A/Conf.151/PC/10). Later in the same year, the Second World Climate Conference (with the participation of 137 states) held in Geneva adopted a Ministerial Declaration similar to the Bergen Declaration:

> In order to achieve sustainable development, policies must be based on the precautionary principle . . . Where there are threats of serious or irreversible damage, lack of full scientific certainty should not be used as a reason for postponing cost-effective measures to prevent such environmental degradation. The measures adopted should take into account different socioeconomic contexts.

The preamble to the Montreal Protocol of 1987 stated that "the parties are determined to protect the ozone layer by taking precautionary measures to control equitably total global emissions of substances that deplete it." Furthermore, it declared that it is relevant to utilize the "precautionary measures . . . that have already been taken at the national and regional levels."

The Maastricht Treaty of the European Union included the PP as a legal obligation for environmental policy, asserting that Community policy (Article 130r) "shall be based on the precautionary principle and on the principles that preventive action should be taken, that environmental damage should, as a priority, be rectified at source and that the polluter should pay."

The 1990 UN Environment Program's Governing Council recommended member countries to adopt "alternative clean production methods including raw material selection, product substitution, and clean production technologies and processes as a means of implementing a precautionary principle in order to promote production systems which minimize or eliminate the generation of hazardous wastes."

The 1991 Bamako Convention on the Ban of Import into Africa and the Control of Transboundary Movement of Hazardous Wastes Within Africa declared: "Each Party shall strive to adopt and implement the preventive, precautionary approach to pollution problems which entails, *inter alia*, preventing the release into the environment of substances which may cause harm to humans or the environment without waiting for scientific proof regarding such harm."

Article 3 (3) of the 1992 UN Framework Convention on Climate Change (UNFCCC) states:

> The Parties should take precautionary measures to anticipate, prevent or minimize the causes of climate change and mitigate its adverse effects. Where there are threats of serious or irreversible damage, lack of full scientific certainty should not be used as a reason for postponing such measures, taking into account that policies and measures to deal with climate change should be cost effective as to ensure global benefits at the lowest possible cost.

Principle 15 of the Rio Declaration of the Earth Summit, 1992 maintained that: "In order to protect the environment, the precautionary approach shall be widely applied by States according to their capabilities. Where there are threats of serious or irreversible damage, lack of full scientific certainty shall not be used as a reason for postponing cost-effective measures to prevent environmental degradation." The PP was also proposed for hazardous waste management in the 1992 Rio Declaration (Agenda 21, Chapter 22.5).

The 1973 CITES Convention does not directly refer to the PP, but in the 1994 Fort Lauderdale Resolution that arose from the meeting of the state parties it was agreed to adopt the PP when any review of the lists of endangered species is considered.

The 1994 WTO Agreements on Technical Barriers to Trade (TBT Agreement) and the Application of Sanitary and Phytosanitary Measures (SPS Agreement) also recognize the role of the PP. As an illustration of the PP in the governance of food safety issues within the framework of multilateral trade under the WTO, the provisions under the SPS Agreement are largely contained in its Article 5 (Assessment of Risk and Determination of the Appropriate Level of Sanitary or Phytosanitary Protection), which states, *inter alia*, the following:

- Section 6: "when establishing or maintaining sanitary or phyto-sanitary measures to achieve the appropriate level of sanitary or phytosanitary protection, Members shall ensure that such measures are not more trade-restrictive than required to achieve their appropriate level of sanitary or phytosanitary protection, taking into account technical and economic feasibility."

- Section 7: "In cases where relevant scientific evidence is insufficient, a Member may provisionally adopt sanitary or phytosanitary measures on the basis of available pertinent information, including that from the relevant international organizations as well as from sanitary or phytosanitary measures applied by other Members. In such circumstances, Members shall seek to obtain the additional information necessary for a more objective assessment of risk and review the sanitary or phytosanitary measures accordingly within a reasonable period of time."

The 1995 UN Agreement for the Implementation of the Provisions of the UN Convention on the Law of the Sea 1982 Relating to the Conservation and Management of Straddling Fish Stocks and Highly Migratory Fish Stocks (called simply the Fish Stocks Agreement) states in its preamble that parties are "conscious of the need to avoid adverse impacts on the marine environment, preserve biodiversity, maintain the integrity of marine ecosystems and minimize the risk of long-term or irreversible effects of fishing operations." The 1995 Fish Stocks Agreement in its Article 5 (c) provides for the application of the PP, and its Article 6 and Annex 2 state the details of operational aspects of the PP (see also Hewison, 1996). The agreement requires its parties to be "more cautious when information is uncertain, unreliable or inadequate. The absence of adequate scientific information shall not be used as a reason for postponing or failing to take conservation and management measures" (Article 6 (2)).

The provisions in several other international agreements also include somewhat similar concerns for precautionary measures to safeguard environmental features.

The PP in policy formulations

The broad evolution of the PP over the years indicates that the PP has been most frequently advocated in governing marine resources and pollution. It is also relevant to note that most international environmental laws were founded in the high seas, in the sense that they pertain to the management of oceans and marine life. Since many environmental problems are fraught with system uncertainties and incomplete information about system characteristics, the PP tends to be equally applicable. The increasing role of PP suggests that it is ripening into a norm of international law, especially into customary international law. Some of the key elements of a legal definition rely upon: (1) a threshold of perceived threat against which advance action would be deemed justifiable; and (2) the burden of proof on the activity contributor or entrepreneur to show that a proposed action will not cause actual harm (see also Barton, 1998; Cameron and Abouchar, 1991). The PP implies the current commitment (with certainty) of resources in order to safeguard against the likelihood of future occurrence (with varying degrees of potential uncertainty) of adverse outcomes of activities. This approach implicitly seeks tradeoffs in the interests of the present with those of the future, and thus depends on implicitly assumed time discounting and future resource valuation. Current practices in the application of the PP do not seem to examine these factors explicitly. This is because the role of the PP remains confined so far to providing guidance on policy judgment and providing benefit of the doubt in favor of environmental resources. For a wide variety of endorsements of the PP among international organizations and their interpretations, see Cameron et al. (1998) and Hohmann (1994).

Any formulation of the PP is considered a "tool for decision-making in a situation of scientific uncertainty" (Freestone, 1994). As Hey (1992) stated: "the concept requires that policy makers adopt an approach which ensures that errors are made on the side of excessive environmental protection." The Rio Declaration seeking the PP as a guiding principle promises to lead to its adoption as an ingredient of general customary international law. Cameron et al. (1998) suggested the role of two types of precautionary measures in law and policy: (1) those seeking *de facto* precaution and (2) those stipulating *de jure* precautionary standards. In reality, however, a combination of both types of actions are relevant, depending on the nature of the problem and the pragmatic considerations surrounding the implementation of solutions. An important operational aspect of the implications of adopting the PP is the process of "shifting the burden of proof": an alteration of environmental assets by a defendant requires the defendant to prove the absence of adverse environmental impact rather than the entity pointing to such a problem; the presumption of innocence until proven otherwise (as in common law) does not hold.

The European Union (EU) paper on the PP (Document EU/G/SPS/GEN/168; 2000) maintained the broad-based acceptance and application of the PP within the EU and also in its interactions with international activities, trade or other. For policy purposes it was clarified that the degree of emphasis on the PP remains a result of "political" decision, a function of risk level that is "acceptable" to the society on which the risk is imposed. The European Council Meetings of December 2000 held at Nice adopted a Council Resolution on the PP and made further clarifications to the European Treaty provision regarding the PP for environmental policy formulation under its Article 174 (2). It also noted that the PP is gradually asserting itself as a principle of international environmental law, and sought its greater use in the governance of the global environment.

Having advocated in some detail the role and relevance of the PP, its potential limitations may be provided. Although qualitatively a very useful approach, the PP cannot offer specific directions of policy since its role is primarily to set the direction of activities rather than the corresponding magnitudes. It is also important to ensure that the application of the PP involves both sides of the equation. For example, some pesticides can be avoided if organic substitutes or other less harmful alternatives exist. However, a total ban on the former may not do much good if it leads to significant crop losses and food shortages. In seeking to apply the PP to protect people and the environment against the adverse effects of using such chemicals, one may be ignoring the relevance of applying the same principle to save lives through the provision of increased food supplies or basic hygiene. Regulations adopting the PP must accord due recognition of (1) the meaningful availability of alternatives or substitutes and (2) ensuring that a parallel illegal market does not arise as a byproduct of the regulation. A judicious balance is necessary in applying the PP and assessing the consequences both with and without its application. Misapplication of the principle can lead to peril, and the remedy may not always be a superior solution (Cross, 1996).

Use of the PP for sustainable development requires areas of applicability to be appropriately identified, such as in the cases of the atmospheric concentration of greenhouse gases, loss of biodiversity, and soil degradation and desertification. This is not to suggest that the principle is any less relevant in apparently "nonenvironmental" sectors. In all such cases, "help cannot wait" and adequate safeguards are essential. The role of the PP in all such situations is to enable advance preventive measures, possibly with improved resource distribution mechanisms. An illustration of one application of the PP in the domestic environmental law of Australia is given in box 3.4.

BOX 3.4

The precautionary principle in Australian law

The use of the PP in environmental protection in Australia illustrates the influence of international environmental law on domestic national and local laws as well as the interface of environmental laws with economic laws. The PP is incorporated into several federal policies of the Australian government and is also emerging as a common law doctrine (Barton, 1998).

The 1992 Intergovernmental Agreement on the Environment (IGAE) established the broad framework for environmental policies in Australia, including guidelines for the federal, state, and territory governments. The IGAE stated (Chapter 3.5): "Where there are threats of serious or irreversible environmental damage, lack of full scientific certainty should not be used as a reason for postponing measures to prevent environmental degradation." The additional guidelines include: "(i) careful evaluation to avoid, wherever practicable, serious or irreversible damage to the environment; and (ii) an assessment of the risk-weighted consequences of various options."

A few significant developments were initiated in 1992 and later. The National Strategy for Ecologically Sustainable Development deployed the PP as a guiding principle. The Forest and Timber Inquiry Report also proposed "adopting a precautionary approach to potentially irreversible consequences of particular uses." The National Forest Policy Statement, evolved in 1992 (and endorsed by all states except Tasmania), declared that in "keeping with the 'precautionary principle,' the State Governments will undertake continuing research and long-term monitoring so that adverse impacts that may arise can be detected and redressed."

The PP is not, however, too extensive in federal environmental laws. Barton (1998) identified three main reasons for this: (1) the PP tends to directly conflict with "the traditional conceptions of property that categorize the environment as a resource to be exploited rather than an asset to be conserved"; (2) the PP is not seen in terms of standards for adoption; and (3) there is limited appreciation of regulatory measures or the need for cleaner technologies.

Sources: Barton (1998); www.erin.gov.au/portfolios/esd/igae.html; www.erin.gov.au/portfolio/esd/nsesd.html; www.rfa.gov.au/nfps/contents.html

The PP case law

The PP seeks to "shift the burden of proof" to the party that seeks to undertake potentially harmful activities. In a sense this principle could minimize transaction costs in establishing the case against a potential wrongdoer (in the traditional sense). "The value shift which the precautionary principle reflects might herald the willingness of states to sacrifice some autonomy for the sake of environmental protection. . . . To the extent that the . . . principle reflects a revaluation of state sovereignty, it may become 'customary international law'" (Weintraub, 1992). Proof of *opinio juris*, which is the expressed intention of a state to abide by a custom as law, is relevant to establish the premise of practice of international customary law. Custom usually implies a sustained time-honored practice. However, in the *North Sea Continental Shelf* cases (*FRG v. Den.; FRG v. Neth.*, 1969 ICJ 3, February 20), the International Court of Justice (ICJ) observed (Id. at 4): "Even without the passage of any considerable period of time, a very widespread and representative participation in the convention might suffice as proof of (*opinio juris*), provided it included that of the States whose interests were specially affected."

In Hungary's application to the ICJ in the Danube dams case (Gabcikovo-Nagymaros project), the PP was invoked in paragraph 31, which stated:

> States shall take precautionary measures to anticipate, prevent or minimize damage to their transboundary resources and mitigate adverse effects. Where there are threats of serious or irreversible damage, lack of full scientific certainty shall not be used as a reason for postponing such measures. Art. 2, paragraph 5(a) of the Convention on the Protection and Use of Transboundary Watercourses and International Lakes, signed in Helsinki on 17 March 1992, as well as the IUCN Draft Art. 6 and Brundtland Report, Art. 10, provide support for the obligation in general international law to apply the precautionary principle to protect a transboundary resource. (Quoted in McIntyre and Mosedale, 1997, pp. 231–2)

This assertion constitutes an important milestone in the application of the PP. McIntyre and Mosedale (1997) suggest that the principle has already evolved as a norm of international law. They also contend that some of the important prerequisites for the effective implementation of the principle are precautionary assessment, setting of precautionary standards, and fulfillment of information requirements both in collating data and conducting relevant research activities. Uncertainty arising from ignorance, inadequate data, or indeterminacy should also be considered in the interpretation of the expression "scientific uncertainty"; thus it is prudent to generalize this to include statistical uncertainty as well. It is not unusual that scientific uncertainties tend to require long time spans (decades in some cases) to resolve.

The role of the PP extends to several areas of environmental decision-making. A new standard of proof – that of "reasonable ecological or medical concern" – was adopted in a number of cases in the US judicial system. One of the earliest was in *Reserve Mining Co. v. EPA* (514 F.2d 492, 520, 8th Circuit, 1975). Defendants, under this standard, are required to prove in the negative any valid reasonable ecological or medical concern in order to be allowed to implement an activity that interferes with *status quo ante*. Some US cases that refer to a precautionary approach include: *TVA v. Hill* (437 US 153, 1978); *Lead Indus. Ass'n v. EPA* (449 US 1042, 1980); and *Beanal v. Freeport-McMoran Inc.* (969 F. Supp. 362, E. D. La., 1997).

Structural or technical aspects are largely covered in the treatment of uncertainty and potential applications of the PP to facilitate pragmatic environmental decision-making. The important issue of economic evaluation of policies (including regulations and alternative proposals for environmental management) is examined in the remainder of this chapter.

3.4 RECONCILING ECONOMIC AND ENVIRONMENTAL CRITERIA

An overview of anthropocentrism and the role of economics needs to be provided before seeking methods of economic analysis relevant for optimal decision-making. In utilitarianism, things have value to the extent that they confer satisfaction to humans, but this does not necessarily imply abuse of the planet's resources or a lack of interest in, say, the rights of animals or concern for various segments of nature. It asserts that we can assign value only in so far as we as humans take satisfaction from doing so. But this line of valuation can only go this far. It may not be consistent with the biogeophysical or ecological approach required for sustainable development, hence the need for normative scientific considerations, which ensure resilience of the planet's ecosystems. In other words, any features of a potential loss of resilience are unlikely to be reflected in market signals such as scarcity prices until it is too late to rectify the problems. It may be concluded that utilitarianism has its place if this premise can be broadened to include concerns for system-wide implications of alternative choices and anthropogenic influences on resilience features. In some specific cases involving irreversibility, as in the potential loss of biospecies, alternative criteria for decision-making include the specification of "safe minimum standards" (SMS), a critical threshold below which no amount of economic reasoning could possibly allow standards to fall. However, a good deal of economic analysis, in addition to ecological concepts, is useful in establishing such standards. For a review of the role of SMS (including their relationship with game-theoretic strategies), see Palmini (1999).

The valuation of natural resources

We need to clarify the distinctions between the main categories of natural resources: renewable, nonrenewable, and exhaustible. A renewable resource such as water or marine fish has its thresholds. When these thresholds are crossed, the renewal characteristics of the resource are physically diminished (with excessive mining of groundwater or overfishing), as argued in Rao (2000a). The consequences of such reductions tend to be generally reflected in their market prices, wherever markets exist for the resources. A nonrenewable resource differs from an exhaustible resource in so far as the former asserts only its depletive feature without reference to the possible exhaustiveness itself. An exhaustible resource is a nonrenewable resource, but the converse need not hold true; this is because of potential technical and economic barriers in exhausting the resource (Rao, 2000a). Valuations are usually linked to some market mechanisms. Markets constitute part of the mechanisms affecting resource prices, and it is only rarely that prices approximate to the "real value" of any resource. This is because the interlinking of market and nonmarket institutions and their operating efficiencies affect any observed market prices.

The utilitarianism approach allows valuation of resources when it utilizes both direct use values and indirect use values. It also includes nonuse values (values that do not involve any actual direct or indirect physical involvement with the natural thing in question), which could be the greatest of all values. It is this sink or source which generates relevant flows of ecosystem services that support the functioning of economic systems. It is thus a misnomer to classify much of the worth of the ecosystem as a "nonuse value," as is done in some studies.

The array of services provided by ecosystems spans all of these category values. The pest-control and flood-control services they offer have direct use value to nearby agricultural producers. Their provision of habitats for migratory birds implies an indirect use value to people who enjoy bird-watching or birdsong, and, depending on whether the birds are being observed or hunted, the indirect value to the consumer may be consumptive or nonconsumptive. There are two forms of utilitarianism (see, for example, Goulder and Kennedy, 1997). The first, called a weak form, asserts that the value of a given species or form of nature to an individual is entirely based on its ability to yield satisfaction (directly or indirectly) to the person. The second is a strong form of utilitarianism, which assigns values to natural entities based on their benefit to society; this is usually carried out by cost–benefit analysis methods.

Traditionally, total economic value (TEV) has been a useful concept. TEV is defined as the sum of use value UV (direct plus indirect), option value OV, existence value EV, and other nonuse value $ONUV$ (Rao, 2000a):

$$TEV = UV + OV + EV + ONUV$$

The existence value differs from preservation value. The latter corresponds to the continued existence of an entity for reasons other than any expected benefit for the people valuing it. It is meaningful to expect the preservation value to be reflected in the $ONUV$. Nonuse values comprise two components, existence value and option value. The existence value is the value that derives from the sheer contemplation of the existence – apart from any direct or indirect uses of goods and services; survey approaches such as contingent valuation assessments are considered relevant. The option value can be interpreted in two ways. In the first this refers to a premium that people are willing to pay to preserve an environmental amenity, over and above the mean value (or expected value) of the use values anticipated from the amenity. This premium reflects individual risk aversion. In the absence of the latter, people's willingness to pay would equal the mean use value, and option value equals zero. In the second approach, the future value is not necessarily assessed by individual members of the society but the system realizes the benefits. This would be the case, for example, when the commercialized medicinal value of a plant variety is exploited at some time point.

One important clarification that is relevant for much of traditional economic valuation methods is that they presume relative fixed and closed ecosystems and environmental influences so that they enable insensitivity of products and services (and hence their valuations) to the latter factors. "Openness" or exposure to the rest of the global interactions (not necessarily via market factors) makes most economic valuations questionable (Hodgson, 1997).

The main element of economic evaluation methodology is cost–benefit appraisal. This needs to be carried out even when some of the variables and factors are not monetized or governed by market factors. Some of these aspects are the focus of the next section.

■ 3.5 COST–BENEFIT ANALYSIS AND INCOMMENSURABILITY

The foundations of the methods of cost–benefit analysis (CBA) arose from the Hicks–Kaldor criterion of efficiency maximization (Hicks, 1939; Kaldor, 1939). This criterion requires that a project or activity merits consideration or remains desirable when the total benefits exceed total costs. This criterion merely requires that those who gain from an activity be able to compensate losers and still remain better off; it does not, however, ensure in any manner that losers are in fact compensated. It is also important to note a fundamental economic assumption of this process: the marginal utility of income is constant and remains the same among all people (including gainers and losers in any activity). Several foundations and applications remain somewhat shaky, but a few rudiments and qualified applications of CBA are useful when they can throw light on the relative economic merits of alternatives. Blackorby and Donaldson (1990) argued in an analytical framework that some of the assumptions need to be modified to accommodate concerns of economic equity and income distributional aspects, in addition to conventional "economic efficiency" aspects (where a "dollar is a dollar" irrespective of the utility value to different sections of the society). Environmentalists generally criticize most applications of CBA as they attempt to monetize all resources and discount their future valuation, thus leaving little value for the long-term future.

The standard financial methods of cost–benefit calculations draw upon the calculation of the discounted stream of cash flows, both the sequences of costs C_t and of benefits B_t, for the period of concern T for a project or component of economic activity. The discounted lumped sum is called the net present value (NPV) and depends on the choice of the discount rate r. This is given by the expression:

$$\text{NPV} = \sum_{t=1}^{T} (1 + r)^{-t} [B_t - C_t]$$

If the inflation needs to be taken into account, r is replaced by $r - i$, where i is the rate of annual inflation. The new measure $r - i$ corresponds to the real rate of interest wherever the formulation is carried out only in financial terms.

This description is relevant when monetary values are used for the CBA. In general, true worth of resources is hardly reflected in the above estimates of benefits and costs. At the minimum, one needs to assess the shadow prices for each of the inputs and outputs involved in the flows of benefits and costs. A standard form of social cost–benefit analysis (SCBA) starts with the formulation of the main objective or frame of reference for the analysis: that of maximizing social welfare or an equivalent social objective. It is not always possible to construct and solve complex optimizing models to generate these shadow prices. Instead, approximations are often made to assess these "true values" of resources with an intuitive approach. This requires an assessment of opportunity costs (benefits), albeit in a partial equilibrium sense, of each of the inputs involved in the SCBA. If, for example, groundwater is supplied at a government-fixed price P, this is transformed into $G(P)$ where G reflects the costs of providing a unit supply of the resource, and $G(P)$ may be more or less than P depending on (1) the existence of a subsidy or other distortion to the real costs of provision of the resource; and (2) the set of direct and indirect costs and their apportionment methods, constituting the cost function. Similarly, the benefit of this input is its total social contribution in the consumption and/or production function, including the linkages of this input to the rest of the relevant system. Since many inputs/resources in the context of the environment are not in the market or even directly connected to the market characteristics, a series of nonmarket valuations such as the TEV approach or others discussed above become relevant. The formula for computing the benefits net of costs with "appropriate" discounting (see the next section) over time remains very much similar to the cash-flow-based formula given above.

CBA methodology (in various forms) has been playing an important role in various aspects of public and private decision-making. In the context of global environmental issues, especially in the management of the global commons, the methods require considerable further strengthening because of the following factors: (1) the time horizons involved are usually a hundred years or longer; (2) there is no unitary decision-making mechanism; (3) most factors to be considered are largely outside market parameters, as they are not necessarily affecting market signals at the present instant in time; (4) there are significant unknowns and uncertainties in the cost and benefit configurations;

and (5) assigning numerical values to bring the multiple factors to a common numéraire and scale is extremely complex and possibly founded on many potentially arbitrary assumptions. The ranking of alternative projects based on a common scale of measurement or numéraire presumes the existence of a "complete ordering" of alternatives for the purpose of this ranking. However, such an ordering may not exist in the presence of uncertainties and unforeseen contingencies. This situation enables the use of "partial orderings" only (i.e., all the alternatives cannot be completely ranked, there remain indeterminate cases) and is akin to the problem of bounded rationality (see chapter 2). Besides, there are serious problems in using a "consumer surplus" argument-based CBA for dealing with uncertain economy–environment interactions when the implications of alternative activities or policies differ in their relative risk attributes. Based on a rigorous analysis, Stennek (1999) established that the use of expected consumer-surplus methods does not approximate to welfare of consumers (or other groups of society) in the presence of risk-averse behavior by such societies. In one of the necessary conditions, the relative risk-aversion coefficient must be zero in order that such measures approximate welfare.

It must be noted that cost-effectiveness analysis is likely to be more useful than most valuation methods and CBA, since it can enable a combination of prescriptions of ecological principles with those of economics, warrants less information in many cases, and can evaluate cost-minimizing alternatives. As Spash (1997) noted, environmental management is largely an exercise in cost-effective control of the source and sink functions of planetary resources; the latter do not usually admit application of CBA methods.

Much of the economics literature suggests that society can generally be risk-neutral relative to individuals when considering future costs and benefits of project investments and various policies and programs. This was suggested because in society, a large number of people tend to share the burden of costs and provide some kind of risk-pooling; some activities can be very productive while others effect drag on the system. However, these arguments are unhelpful when it comes to analyzing some of the problems of the global commons where collective doom is a real possibility following from inaction or wrong actions.

Incommensurability

The plurality of values and concerns for noneconomic objectives suggests the potential limitations of using a common numéraire and converting all environmental and economic goods and services into these common unitary-scale units. Some of the dangers of forcing such a unitary-scale approach are noted mainly by philosophers and others seeking to expand the scope of economic analyses. O'Neill (1996, p. 101) argued that "attempts to force a measuring rod of any kind onto rational deliberations lead to arbitrariness, contrivance and obstruction of the process of reasoned debate." It must, however, be considered an imperative for ranking major projects involving large resource outlays that a scalar or vector metric for measurement of the "value" be used as a comparative yardstick facilitating rational decision-making. A broader approach than that commonly practiced in conventional cost–benefit analysis would incorporate indicators covering impacts on nonmonetized aspects of the physical, social, cultural, and human environment in the configurations of interest.

Much of the application of CBA presumes some type of "commensurability." This tends to make sense in a pure corporate private sector context with profit maximization as the underlying objective and driving force, but not in general. Strong commensurability assumes the existence of a common numéraire which enables assigning numerical values to each factor and function involved in the decision-making context, models, and policies. The preferences are usually based on the magnitudes of the numerical values assessed. The numbers also assist in arriving at tradeoffs, wherever necessary, in compromising otherwise conflicting objectives. This approach could directly contrast some of the requirements of sustainable development, unless this is used only in relatively well-defined monetized sections of the system, with the sustainability criteria serving as the binding constraints.

A "weak commensurability" approach relies only on the ordinal ranking of preferences amongst alternatives and does not require assigning numerical values to all the parameters involved, but it may not be enough to suggest relevant policies and the scale of operations or interventions in environmental governance. None of the approaches can make sense devoid of the institutional implications, constraints, and effectiveness. The constellations of market and state institutions provide the relevant background, but their relative effectiveness makes a difference as to how far they can operate in an ecologically rational manner.

CBA must take into account sustainability requirements at different stages of valuation, and one of the key elements in this process is to choose an appropriate discount function. This critical issue is developed in subsequent sections of this chapter. It is also important that the valuation of environmental and other resources must first be done within a framework of sustainability and then converted into appropriate equivalents using a common numéraire like consumption. This broader approach is usually ignored when tried by some of the conventional but controversial methods such as contingent valuation (CV) and surveys of willingness to pay (WTP). Some of the valuations for various resources which have generated numerical values and which can be seen in part of the literature claiming to deal with sustainability issues are usually carried out in a very narrow context. They ignore the hypersensitivity of estimates with respect to small changes in market and nonmarket institutional settings, and thus are unreliable. Often valuations are generated based on existing unsustainable conditions and then attempts are made to apply them for the purpose of obtaining some kind of sustainability. These methods tend to be ones where precision up to the tenth or higher decimal is possible, but where the basic premise is wrong. In other words, it is a configuration where one could be precisely right, if only one were right at all! It serves no useful purpose to generate such numbers and use them for project valuation and CBA. The critical ingredients that need to be clarified are those that relate to the analytical or logical decision model or structure (with or without the deployment of mathematical methods) and clarify the objectives, constraints, factors, and institutions, in addition to the choice of an appropriate discount rate. Both efficiency and equity issues must be taken into account together (see also Page, 1997).

Intergenerational efficiency and SCBA

Can we rely on markets and related institutions to lead to intergenerational efficiency? The most significant bottleneck in this regard is the absence of informational and institutional settings, especially missing markets. Markets are missing in the sense that there is no interaction and exchange for mutual gain taking place between present and future generations. Missing markets, like other missing institutions, make it hard to realize intergenerational efficiency. The well-known problem of "market failures" in terms of their inability to correct for "externalities" such as pollution in industrial processes is an additional issue to be taken into account. Problems of excessive environmental misuse can also be viewed in terms of the failure of intergenerational product and environmental markets (Rao, 2000a).

Formulations involving "overlapping generations" (OLG) models where the interests of different generations are simultaneously considered with forward and backward linkages relative to the dominant generation are, in principle, capable of examining the potential implications of the existence of relevant markets. One of the major impediments to some formal models is how to ensure what is known as "time consistency." In an intergenerational setting, this means the problem of how to make sure that future decision-making systems will, in fact, respect continuity and ensure furtherance of future interests at every point in time or point of departure of new decision horizons. This issue is better resolved by noting that in the OLG approach, each set of age-cohort people are themselves "multiple selves" over time: the role of each generation changes over time and thus it does not carry an unintersecting line of interest relative to other generations.

▊ 3.6 APPRAISAL AND EVALUATION METHODS

An appraisal of a project or proposal that involves economic and environmental factors is feasible in the absence of significant uncertainties. In addition to reconciling economic and environmental parameters onto a common scale, the issue of intergenerational aggregation based on time discounting is of importance here.

Some economists argue against any type of future discounting, but then go on to imply that the discount rate should be zero. This is an illogical position, because zero then becomes the chosen rate of discounting future values and is required to remain a constant forever, irrespective of any changes in the tastes or well-being of future generations. Goodin (1982) suggested that discounting methods are possibly devoid of sound logic. Contrary to Goodin's notion that discounting amounts to ignoring future generations, the productive utilization of resources at current and foreseeable future periods gives scope for accommodating the interests of the present and future if resources are properly utilized and due attention is paid to future generations (Rao, 2000a). An enlightened and/or egalitarian society can do better than others. A society which does not discount the future at all but is capable of efficiently utilizing its resources is unlikely to protect the interests of the current as well as future generations. Goodin stated that "a constant discount rate across all periods and all goods . . . seems without psychological warrant, just as psychological discounting is itself without moral warrant" (1982, p. 56). There should be little disagreement that the discount rate should be the same in each future period. Goodin further declared that "outcomes that are equidistant in time would have to be discounted equally" (ibid., p. 57). There is neither an observed behavioral justification for such behavior nor an economic rationale for maintaining such a position. This issue is better resolved below in the discussion on "hyperbolic discounting" (see Rao, 2000a). However, Goodin could be correct in suggesting that "in a declining economy, the logic of diminishing marginal utility leads to weighting future payoffs more heavily than present ones." According to Goodin, discounting may be applied only to "interest-bearing" resources. This position presumes that the resources are readily monetized in the valuation process. It was also suggested that the rate and structure of discounting applied to nontradable goods should match the corresponding features of investments in those goods.

It is doubtful whether Frank Ramsey (1928) – an important contributor to the development of modern neoclassical growth theory – remains correct in asserting that pure time preference is a "practice which is ethically indefensible and arises merely from the weakness of the imagination." Efforts are needed to deal with the distant future, even with several unknowns and uncertainties, and to grapple with a limited information base so that the direction of progress may be at least approximately right; the alternative would possibly be to neglect due recognition of the future in the presumption that the complexities involved were too great to handle.

Changing preferences and discounting

In classical economics, Fisher (1930) argued that the pure rate of time preference should not be independent of the size and shape of the consumption profile. However, in the conventional intertemporal utility maximization approach, independence arises from the strong separability property of utility: marginal rates of substitution for consumption at any two time instants are independent of the rest of the consumption profile. Constant time discounting does imply that the discount factor at any instant is independent of the underlying consumption path. This may not be a realistic description of real-life features.

Another related viewpoint on recognizing changes in consumption and tastes suggests that it is the satisfaction of wants as they arise that matters: tomorrow's satisfaction matters, not simply today's assessment of tomorrow's satisfaction (see also Goodin, 1986).

A relevant ingredient in the definition of sustainability relates to a possible change in preferences of future generations relative to the present mix of generations regarding consumption and preservation of environmental assets. This suggests the need for specifying discount factors, endogenized with respect to consumption and resource stock levels at different future time instants. This is easier to state than to implement in any analysis, however. The information requirements of such approaches are complex, perhaps to the point of merely shifting the original formulation of the problem into unknown territory. The discount rate must reflect the rate of return on alternative sustainable uses, and not any uses, of capital if we are to have a policy consistent with sustainable development. Application of an unsustainable discount rate, i.e., a discount rate based on an alternate use of capital that is unsustainable (Daly, 1991, p. 255), can hardly be a useful start for exercises in global environmental management that involve long time horizons. The relevance, scope, and technical aspects of nonconstant discounting of future values have been analytically examined by Harvey (1994, 1995), Laibson (1997), and Rao (2000b).

Intergenerational discounting issues are not necessarily separable from intragenerational issues, mainly because different generations (four or more) overlap at any given time when society as a whole is considered. As a result of this overlap, it is sometimes suggested that optimal provisions for the welfare of all those currently living tend to give some weight for the future.

In respect of cases of "latent harm" to human public health caused by problems of environmental quality, Revesz (1999, p. 1016) suggested that "discounting raises no significant ethical objections that are independent of those that could be raised against cost benefit analysis in general and the valuation of human lives in particular." In respect of future generations, "discounting gives rise to daunting ethical issues." In October 1985, a subcommittee of the US House of Representatives on Oversight and Investigations noted, while seeking to reduce the discount rate, that discounting at the then prescribed Office of Management and Budget (OMB) rate of 10 percent per annum over a 40-year period would reduce the $1 million value per life saved to just over $22,000, and this figure changes to $208,000 when the rate drops to 4 percent per annum. Various ramifications of discount rates in US environmental law are briefly discussed in box 3.5.

In the US courts, many judicial decisions gave public entities flexibility in choosing a discount rate for their valuation of monetary-equivalent resources and project appraisal. Morrison (1998) offers a

BOX 3.5

Discounting and environmental law: The USA

The issue of appropriate discounting concerns all institutions and sectors, both legally and indirectly. In respect of a partial ban on asbestos, the USEPA was challenged regarding its use of discount rate. Under the 1984 Reagan administration Executive Order No. 12,291, mandated cost–benefit studies of all major regulations in the US are coordinated by the US Office of Management and Budget (OMB). In the *Corrosion Proof Fittings v. EPA* case (947 F.2d 1201, 1218–19, US Fifth Circuit, 1991), the matter was reviewed in detail (for an analysis of the case, see Wecker, 1994; Revesz, 1999). In October 1991 the US Fifth Circuit Court vacated the EPA regulation, with the following statement: "Because the EPA must discount costs to perform its evaluations properly, the EPA also should discount benefits to preserve an apples-to-apples comparison, even if this entails discounting benefits of a non-monetary nature." The court upheld the EPA discount rate of 3 percent per annum. It implicitly assumed the relevant rate was the real rate of interest (the nominal long-term rate of interest minus the average rate of inflation).

Until 1992, the OMB deployed a discount rate of 10 percent. Discounting $1 million damage occurring at 100 years from now at this rate gives its current worth at $72, and this amount changes to $52,033 when the rate is reduced to 3 percent (this rate was used and recommended in a few studies; see Page, 1997). The discount rate was later reduced to 7 percent, with a stated justification that this rate represents "the marginal pretax rate of return on an average investment in the private sector in recent years" (OMB Circular No. A-94, 57 Federal Register, at 53, 522–523, 1992). However, the OMB uses a different rate for carrying out cost-effectiveness analysis, in the range 3 to 4 percent per annum. This is based on the real return on long-term government bonds (the corresponding interest rate adjusted for the rate of inflation). The discrepancy in discount rates can alter the ranking of projects and is unwarranted. Let us also note that, as Heinzerling (1999) observed, even at the OMB's prescribed 7 percent discount rate, a regulation will count every ten-unit gain or any benefit accruing after 35 years as a single unit's worth today.

Table 3.1 Choice of discount rates by US federal agencies

Agency	Regulation	Discount rate	Time horizon (yrs)
EPA	Emissions Standards for Locomotives and Locomotive Engines 62 Fed. Reg. 6366, 6401–02 (1997)	7	41
EPA	Protection of Stratospheric Ozone 61 Fed. Reg. 45778, 45808 (1996)	3	50
Fish and Wildlife Service	Endangered and Threatened Wildlife and Plants 60 Fed. Reg. 17296, 17301–303 (1995)	3	45
Bureau of Reclamation	Change in Discount Rate for Water Resources Planning 62 Fed. Reg. 60267, 60269 (1997)	7.125	–
FDA	Food Labeling Regulations 58 Fed. Reg. 2927, 2929 (1993)	5	20

Source: Summarized from Morrison (1998)

detailed account of the different discount rates chosen by various US federal government entities; see table 3.1 for a summary. It was also observed that the practice of the US Environmental Protection Agency (USEPA) "appears arbitrary because it often chooses relatively high discount rates (between 7 and 10 percent) for regulations imposing future costs and low rates (around 3 percent) for regulations creating future benefits."

Before concluding this section, it is important to note the analytical basis for the choice of lower rather than higher discount rates when stochastic features are involved; see Rao (2000b) for detailed mathematical derivations on this issue. Also, it is desirable to deploy hyperbolic discount factors which allow declining discount rates over time so that longer-term inputs and outputs also are accounted rather than reduced to zero levels under the "tyranny" of discounting!

 ## 3.7 SUMMARY

Risk perceptions and risk-bearing attitudes are among the primary influences of decisions under uncertainty. Most long-term decisions in the management of the global environment are structurally built on system uncertainties. In addition, there are several unknowns in the complex interrelationships among various components of the global environment and ecology. These features make it imperative to adopt appropriate precautionary measures, and the optimal degree of such precautions can be based on a pragmatic assessment of the risks of inaction and the costs of alternative feasible actions.

Despite serious shortcomings in the application of cost–benefit analysis and in the choice of proper discount rates in the valuation of future costs and benefits, some robust exercises in this regard can be useful guides for choosing alternate policies and actions. It is by no means an easy task to extend the exercise to a global scale where considerable differences exist in valuations, including the magnitudes of the marginal utility of various resources. The choice of discount rates indicates wide variations in the valuation of future resources. However, a firm prescription here is the choice of relatively low discount rates and/or declining discount rates (over future time horizons) in order to ensure the long-term optimality of environmental resource-management regimes.

Review Exercises

1   Discuss the role and limitations of the precautionary principle with special reference to select fish species that are location-specific. Examine the potential roles of adjacent coastal states and the rest of the world in managing such resources, in the absence of a clearly delineated international law.

2   Discuss the role and limitations of cost–benefit analysis for project decisions involving preservation (*in situ* and *ex situ*) of biological species with no known direct beneficial effects to humans.

3   When are environmental and economic criteria likely to be (a) congruent, and (b) conflicting? Examine this issue in spatial, temporal, and other classifications of socioeconomic systems and provide illustrative examples. What factors tend to reconcile conflicting or potentially conflicting scenarios? Is there a role for national governments and global institutional arrangements in effecting a greater complementarity of the objectives of economic and environmental management?

4 Discuss the relevance of alternate measures of risk aversion in relation to each of these major environmental phenomena: ozone depletion in relation to the use of CFCs; global warming in relation to emissions of GHGs; loss of biodiversity in relation to land-use changes; and transboundary water pollution in relation to the application of agrochemicals. In each case, suggest potential pragmatic and cost-effective alternatives, including incremental changes, to address the identified problem. Explain the role of different measures of risk aversion in each context.

5 Discuss the merits of lower discount rates in environmental decision-making.

REFERENCES

Arrow, K. J., 1974, *Essays in the Theory of Risk Bearing*, New York: North-Holland.

Barton, C., 1998, The status of the precautionary principle in Australia, *Harvard Environmental Law Review*, 22, 509–58.

Blackorby, C. and Donaldson, D., 1990, A review article: The case against the use of the sum of compensating variations in cost–benefit analysis, *Canadian Journal of Economics*, 23, 471–94.

Blackwell, D., 1951, Comparison of experiments, in J. Neyman (ed.), *Proceedings of the 2nd Berkeley Symposium on Mathematical Statistics and Probability*, Berkeley: University of California Press.

Becker, G., 1998, *Accounting for Tastes*, Cambridge, MA: Harvard University Press.

Bodansky, E., 1991, Scientific uncertainty and the precautionary principle, *Environment*, 33 (7), 4–7.

Broome, J., 1990, Bolker–Jeffrey expected utility theory and axiomatic utilitarianism, *Review of Economic Studies*, 57, 477–502.

Buschena, D. E. and Zilberman, D., 1994, What do we know about decision-making under risk and where do we go from here?, *Journal of Agricultural and Resource Economics*, 19, 425–45.

Cameron, J. and Abouchar, J., 1991, The precautionary principle: A fundamental principle of law and policy for the protection of the global environment, *Boston College International and Comparative Law Review*, 14, 1–27.

Cameron, J., Wade-Gery, W., and Abouchar, J., 1998, Precautionary principle and future generations, in E. Agius and S. Busuttil (eds.), *Future Generations and International Law*, London: Earthscan Publications, pp. 93–113.

Cross, F., 1996, The perils of the precautionary principle, *Washington & Lee Law Review*, 53, 851–83.

Daly, H. E., 1991, *Steady-State Economics*, Washington, DC: Island Press.

Fisher, I., 1930, *The Theory of Interest*, New York: Macmillan.

Foster, J. (ed.), 1997, *Valuing Nature?*, London: Routledge.

Freestone, D., 1994, The road to Rio: International environmental law after the Earth Summit, *Journal of Environmental Law*, 6, 193–223.

Gollier, C., Jullien, B., and Treich, N., 2000, Scientific progress and irreversibility: An economic interpretation of the precautionary principle, *Journal of Public Economics*, 75, 229–53.

Goodin, R., 1982, Discounting discounting, *Journal of Public Policy*, 2 (1), 53–72.

Goodin, R., 1986, *Protecting the Vulnerable*, Chicago: University of Chicago Press.

Goulder, L. H. and Kennedy, D., 1997, Valuing ecosystem services: Philosophical bases and empirical methods, in G. Daily (ed.), *Nature's Services*, Washington, DC: Island Press, pp. 23–47.

Harsanyi, J., 1955, Cardinal welfare, individualistic ethics, and interpersonal comparisons of utility, *Journal of Political Economy*, 63, 309–21.

Harvey, C., 1994, The reasonableness of nonconstant discounting, *Journal of Public Economics*, 53, 31–51.

Harvey, C., 1995, Proportional discounting of future costs and benefits, *Mathematics of Operations Research*, 20 (2), 381–99.

Heinzerling, L., 1999, Environmental law and the present future, *Georgetown Law Journal*, 87, 2025–78.

Hewison, G. J., 1996, The precautionary approach to fisheries management: An environmental perspective, *International Journal of Marine and Coastal Law*, 11, 301–32.

Hey, E., 1992, The precautionary concept in environmental policy and law: Institutionalizing caution, *Georgetown International Environmental Law Review*, 4, 303–18.

Hicks, J. R., 1939, The foundations of welfare economics, *Economic Journal*, 49, 696.

Hodgson, G., 1997, Economics, environmental policy and the transcendence of utilitarianism, in J. Foster (ed.), *Valuing Nature?*, London: Routledge, pp. 48–63.

Hohmann, H., 1994, *Precautionary Legal Duties and Principles of Modern International Environmental Law*, London: Graham and Trotman.

Kahneman, D. and Tversky, A., 1979, Prospect theory: An analysis of decision under risk, *Econometrica*, 47, 263–92.

Kaldor, R. N., 1939, Welfare propositions of economics and intertemporal comparisons of utility, *Economic Journal*, 49, 549.

Kihlstrom, R. E. and Mirman, L. J., 1974, Risk aversion with many commodities, *Journal of Economic Theory*, 8, 361–388.

Kimball, M. S., 1990, Precautionary savings in the small and in the large, *Econometrica*, 58, 53–73.

Kimball, M. S., 1993, Standard risk aversion, *Econometrica*, 61, 589–611.

Laibson, D., 1997, Golden eggs and hyperbolic discounting, *Quarterly Journal of Economics*, 62 (2), 443–77.

Levy, H. and Levy, A., 1984, Multivariate decision-making, *Journal of Economic Theory*, 32, 36–51.

McIntyre, O. and Mosedale, T., 1997, The precautionary principle as a norm of customary international law, *Journal of Environmental Law*, 9, 221–41.

Morrison, E. R., 1998, Judicial review of discount rates used in regulatory cost–benefit analysis, *University of Chicago Law Review*, 65, 1333–69.

Myers, N., 1995, Environmental unknowns, *Science*, 269, 358–60.

Organization for Economic Cooperation and Development (OECD), 1995, *Environmental Principles and Concepts*, OECD Document OECD/GD(95)124, Paris: OECD Secretariat.

O'Neill, J., 1996, Cost–benefit analysis, rationality and the plurality of values, *Ecologist*, 26, 98–103.

O'Riordan, T. and Cameron, J. (eds.), 1995, *Interpreting the Precautionary Principle*, London: Earthscan Publications.

Page, T., 1997, On the problem of achieving efficiency and equity, intergenerationally, *Land Economics*, 73, 580–96.

Palmini, D., 1999, Uncertainty, risk aversion, and the game theoretic foundations of the safe minimum standard: A reassessment, *Ecological Economics*, 29, 463–72.

Pratt, J. W., 1964, Risk aversion in the small and in the large, *Econometrica*, 32, 122–36.

Ramsey, F., 1928, The mathematical theory of savings, *Economic Journal*, 38, 543–59.

Rao, P. K., 2000a, *Sustainable Development: Economics and Policy*, Oxford: Blackwell.

Rao, P. K., 2000b, *The Economics of Global Climatic Change*, Armonk, NY: M. E. Sharpe.

Rawls, J., 1972, *A Theory of Justice*, Oxford: Clarendon Press.

Revesz, R. L., 1999, Environmental regulation, cost–benefit analysis, and the discounting of human lives, *Columbia Law Review*, 99, 941–1017.

Scott, A., 1999, Trust law, sustainability, and responsible action, *Ecological Economics*, 31, 139–54.

Sinn, H.-W., 1989, *Economic Decisions under Uncertainty*, Heidelberg: Physica-Verlag.

Spash, C., 1997, Environmental management without environmental valuation?, in J. Foster (ed.), *Valuing Nature?*, London: Routledge, pp. 170–85.

Stennek, J., 1999, The expected consumer's surplus as a welfare measure, *Journal of Public Economics*, 73, 265–88.

Sunstein, C., 1997, *Free Markets and Social Justice*, New York: Oxford University Press.

Sunstein, C. R., 1999, Behavioral law and economics: A progress report, *American Law and Economics Review*, 1, 115–57.

Watzold, F., 2000, Efficiency and applicability of economic concepts dealing with environmental risk and ignorance, *Ecological Economics*, 33, 299–311.

Wecker, R. L., 1994, Case comment. A "hard look" at a soft analysis: Corrosion Proof Fittings v. Environmental Protection Agency, *Boston University Public International Law Journal*, 4, 145–60.

Weintraub, B. A., 1992, Science, international environmental regulation, and the precautionary principle: Setting standards and defining terms, *New York University Environmental Law Journal*, 1, 173–223.

part II

International
Environmental Laws

This part describes the foundations of international public law in general, and of international environmental law (IEL) in particular. After an explanation of the sources of international law, several important concepts and definitions in this context are provided. The evolution of customary international law and the interactions of environmental values, human rights, and the provisions of international law are some of the broad issues discussed in chapter 4. The salient features of treaties and the laws governing treaties, including the implications of special features such as "reservations" in various treaties, are examined. The principles of soft law and hard law and their development into modern IEL are also discussed in chapter 4. The roles of transaction cost economics and international relations theory (including strategic behavioral factors) in explaining the formation and implementation of international environmental agreements are also explored.

The issue of state sovereignty and the lack of an apex law-making/ enforcement apparatus at the international level indicate the need for a greater recognition of the roles of multivariate relationships among states at any given point of time and of repeat interactions among states over time. This suggests the significance of reciprocity and issue linkages, both in explicit treaty provisions and in implicit contracts. A desirable element of such features is the incentive mechanism for greater cooperation among states, whether or not this is explicitly warranted by the legal provisions. The role of appropriate law development in this context is, therefore, one of recognizing behavioral interdependencies at the international level, while seeking to apply principles of ecology and economics for the design and implementation of elective international environmental laws. The issues of state participation in treaties and treaty breaches are also to be viewed in terms of the above features, whereby a breach is not usually involved in the calculus of costs and benefits of compliance with a treaty versus a breach of the treaty provisions. Rather, the behavioral attitudes of state parties include a number of interrelated considerations, partly deliberated in modern theories of international relations and strategic decision-making. These topics are examined in various sections of chapter 4.

After laying these foundations, the discussion focuses on important specific features of laws affecting different aspects of the environment and ecology. Some stipulate binding obligations (such as the Montreal Protocol to the Vienna Convention for the Protection of the Ozone Layer), while others are still components of soft law (such as the Forest Principles). For convenience of presentation, laws are categorized into those that attempt to seek international actions in a rather preemptive or precautionary approach (chapter 5), and those that address identified global environmental problems to arrest deterioration and also take further precautionary measures (chapter 6). Clearly, the set of parties in each treaty or other agreement comprises different states in different agreements (even after excluding regional agreements and confining the category to "global" agreements). It is thus simplistic to assume the global significance of each of these laws when a significant number of states are nonparties to several of the agreements. This raises a variety of economic and institutional factors. The roles of economic incentives (as in the case of the Montreal Protocol applied to developing countries) and disincentives (as in the case of trade with nonparties in the case of CITES) for participation are important.

After a review of the salient legal features, suggestions are made as to the role of economic analysis. The gaps identified in this direction warrant considerable additional research and global coordination.

chapter four

Soft Laws, Treaty Provisions, and the Law

■ 4.1 Introduction

International public law has several special features relative to the typical domestic laws of most countries. Enforcement of the law is not expected to follow from a judicial ruling; the apex global judicial institutions have their own statute limitations. Verifiable and credible information on any issue is subject to the cooperation and compliance of sovereign states. Besides, there are gaps in the specifications of rights and obligations of states in relation to specific issues and in areas where there are no existing laws (*non liquet*). The provision and enforcement of penalties for violations, assuming these can be determined or traced to the source(s) with foolproof evidence, remain major impediments to the effectiveness of international laws. This is even more pertinent in the environmental sector, since the basis of information for liability regimes is usually weak and the role of property rights regimes is also feeble as these rights may not even exist in several environmental resources in the global commons. In general, the operation of the rule of law in the international arena is dissimilar to that of the domestic laws of states. An appreciation of the various important features of international law lays a foundation for understanding the framework governing the formation and practice of international environmental law (IEL).

In this chapter we examine the following important aspects: the sources of the relevant law; interactions between environmental values and IEL; the evolution of modern IEL, with a review of the relevant historical foundations, concepts, and principles; an assessment of the role of transaction costs analysis and game-theoretic strategic analysis for international treaty design and implementation; the role of state sovereignty and state practice; and the interaction between domestic and international public laws. Other issues included here are the use of reservations in treaties, the limitations of "efficient breach theory" in treaties, the juxtaposition of domestic and international environmental laws, and the role of multiple repeat interactions among states in facilitating cooperation. International public law is governed by a set of international norms and institutions such as the International Court of Justice (ICJ) and the WTO's Appellate Body. These features are summarized in the next few paragraphs. After setting out the legal background, the chapter subsequently explores the behavioral aspects of states and the roles of soft law and binding laws in the structure of IEL.

■ 4.2 SOURCES OF INTERNATIONAL PUBLIC LAW

There are several sources of international public law. The principal sources include "law-making" treaties and other material sources, the statute of the ICJ, international customary practices, general principles of law, judicial decisions, and scholarly writings (sometimes termed the writings of "publicists").

Among treaty sources, all treaties do not possess the same legal standing. Those treaties that provide binding provisions on a few states only are called "particular international law." In contrast, "general international law" comprises multilateral law-making treaties to which a majority of states are parties (Brownlie, 1990). Treaties constitute sources of obligation (beyond voluntary acceptance of moral obligation *opinio juris*) and not general rules of application. Law-making treaties create "general norms for the future conduct of the parties in terms of legal propositions, and the obligations are basically the same for all parties" (Brownlie, 1990, p. 12). Bilateral treaties may also be treated alike, especially if they provide an element of customary practice. Resolutions of the UN General Assembly are not necessarily laws in themselves, but they constitute evidence of the opinions of governments. Important law-making resolutions include, for example, the 1962 Declaration on Permanent Sovereignty over Natural Resources (see section 4.5). The "Final Act" or the Conclusions of international state-represented conferences also provide sources of law, sometimes even before these products are ratified by states because of the indicated intentions of wide-ranging parties. Drafts adopted by the International Law Commission also are treated as sources of law. For some periods of time, a multilateral treaty waiting for ratification by its parties may also be construed as evidence of generally accepted rules.

The elements constituting customary practice include (Brownlie, 1990): (1) duration of practice (usually one of the sufficiency conditions but not always one of the necessary conditions to qualify); (2) substantial (if not complete) uniformity and consistency of practice; (3) generality (not necessarily universality, general acceptance, and/or lack of previous objections) of the practice; and (4) *opinio juris et necessitatis* (the role of obligatory practice, "a general practice accepted as law").

The Statute of the ICJ was annexed to the Charter of the UN, signed at San Francisco, June 26, 1945. The ICJ was constituted under Article 92 of the UN Charter. Of particular significance is ICJ Article 38:

> 1. The Court, whose function is to decide in accordance with international law such disputes as are submitted to it, shall apply:
> a. international conventions, whether general or particular, establishing rules expressly recognized by the contesting states;
> b. international custom, as evidence of a general practice accepted as law;
> c. the general principles of law recognized by civilized nations;
> d. subject to the provisions of Article 59, judicial decisions and the teachings of the most highly qualified publicists of the various nations, as subsidiary means for the determination of rules of law.
> 2. This provision shall not prejudice the power of the Court to decide a case ex aequo et bono, if the parties agree thereto.

Early developments in international environmental law

In one of the earliest international environmental laws, the 1900 London Convention for the Protection of Wild Animals, Birds, and Fish in Africa was aimed at curbing potential ecological degradation contributed by unabated commercial exploitation largely dominated by features of colonial rule. Environmental interdependencies and externalities were perhaps first recognized in the bilateral context of a US–UK boundary dispute leading in 1909 to the Treaty Relating to Boundary Waters Between the United States and Canada. Article III of the Treaty stated that water "shall not be polluted on either side to the injury of health or property of the other." These two countries were again involved in the management of another environmental externality, this time air-pollution emissions. The Trail Smelter case arbitration awards were handed down in two stages, the first in 1938 and the next in 1941. In this case a Canadian company operating large smelting plants in British Columbia emitted sulfur dioxide into the atmosphere and thus caused damage to crops and led to pollution in the adjacent US state of Washington. In the decision of the arbitration panel it was declared (*US v. Canada*, 3 R Intl. Arb. Awards, 1941):

> Under the principles of international law, as well as of law of the United States, no state has the right to use or permit the use of its territory in such a manner as to cause injury by fumes in or to the territory of another or the properties or persons therein, when the case is of serious consequence and the injury is established by clear and convincing evidence.

Environmental values and environmental law

A society's perception of the role of the environment, its current status, and expectations for the future are among the major determinants of the evolution of norms, standards, and principles governing the environment. Furthermore, these "feelings and sentiments" of a society are usually weighed, by the governing local and domestic institutions, against potential tradeoffs with other competing values (or pressing problems) in according priority of attention (and resource allocation). Translation of these values occurs through the domestic polity and its interactions with international institutions. The role of economic factors then arises in more specific arrangements and policy choices. Box 4.1 summarizes the roles of environmental values, human rights, and environmental law.

The Universal Declaration of Human Rights under the UN system emerged from being a nonbinding "soft law" into a binding obligation of states 18 years after the adoption of the Declaration in 1948. Although the Declaration contains elements regarding the right to life and health, there was no mention of the environment or environmental quality. It is reasonable to believe that the state of understanding and imperatives of concern toward the environment have undergone major changes during the interim period. This is only an illustration of the state of international consensus building and decision-making and state practice. As long as the state responsibility factor is not sufficiently sensitive or in harmony with the pace of emerging problems, there are avoidable costs and adverse consequences to some or all sections of society, broadly termed (negative) externalities.

BOX 4.1

Environmental values, laws, and human rights

IEL pervades the arena of the international law of human rights, although mainly from the perspective of private international law (Degagne, 1995). The Stockholm Declaration of 1972 detailed the relationship between the enjoyment of human rights and the quality of the environment, but did not declare a "right to the environment." The condition of the environment is inextricably linked to our social and economic well-being. A human rights perspective remains an important aspect of environmental management (see Boyle and Anderson, 1996, for a collection of essays in this direction).

The following have played a significant role in the evolution of soft law norms.

1 The 1982 UN World Charter for Nature proposed that "all persons, in accordance with their national legislation, shall have the opportunity to participate, individually or with others, in the formulation of decisions of direct concern to their environment, and shall have access to means of redress when their environment has suffered damage or degradation."

2 The 1989 UN Convention on the Rights of the Child declares that states must take proper measures "to combat disease and malnutrition . . . taking into consideration the dangers and risks of environmental pollution" (see, for details, UN Doc. A/44/49, 1989, reprinted in 28 ILM 1448, 1989).

3 The 1992 Rio Declaration (Principle 1) states that human beings are "entitled to a healthy and productive life in harmony with nature." Thus, an argument to protect the environment may be asserted as a corollary to the specifications of human rights.

4 As an example of case precedence (in private international law), in 1993 the European Commission on Human Rights found that the installation and operation of a waste treatment station near the domicile of the applicant was a "nuisance" and amounted to a violation of her right to a private life (*Lopez Ostra v. Spain*, App. No. 16798/90; Report of August 31, 1993).

5 As an illustration of case law with implications for IEL, the Philippines Constitution, Section 16 of Article II of 1987 states that "[t]he State shall protect and advance the right of the people to a balanced ecology in accord with the rhythm and harmony of nature."

Legal foundations to control externalities

The following is a brief summary of the legal developments that sought to recognize the role of negative environmental externalities and provide for remedies.

The *Trail Smelter Arbitration* of 1941 (*US v. Canada*, 3 R. Intl. Arb. Awards 1905; 1941) was perhaps among the first adjudications to recognize the role of precautionary behavior even within the arena of a state exercising its sovereign rights. Air pollution from a smelter in the town of Trail in Canada resulted in damage to apple crops, among other adverse effects, on US territory. The international arbitration panel in this case observed that "under the principles of international law ... no State has the right to use or permit the use of its territory in such a manner as to cause injury by fumes in or to the territory of another or the properties or persons therein" (Id. at 1965).

The arbitration panel's position to dispense with traditional tort notions seeking causation for damage award is significant. The general principle that a state may not indulge in activities harmful to the natural environment of another state was later recognized as a non-binding (soft-law) principle of international environmental law under Principle 21 of the 1972 Stockholm Declaration:

> States have, in accordance with the Charter of the United Nations and principles of international law, the sovereign right to exploit their own resources pursuant to their own environmental policies, and the responsibility to ensure that activities within their jurisdiction or control do not cause damage to the environment of other States or of areas beyond the limits of national jurisdiction.

The Stockholm Declaration was accepted by the UN General Assembly toward formulating rules governing the international environment and the roles of states (UN GA Res. 2996, UN 27th Session, UN Doc. A/9730/1972). One of the earliest explicit statements incorporating the precautionary principle (PP) was advanced in the legislation of the Federal Republic of Germany in the 1970s.

The 1982 UN General Assembly Resolution on the World Charter for Nature advocates some of the key ingredients for the control and mitigation of negative externalities. Principle 11 of the Charter states:

> Activities which might have an impact on nature shall be controlled, and the best available technologies that minimize significant risks to nature or other adverse effects shall be used; in particular:

a) Activities which are likely to cause irreversible damage to nature shall be avoided;

b) Activities which are likely to pose a significant risk to nature shall be preceded by an exhaustive examination; their proponents shall demonstrate that expected benefits outweigh potential damage to nature, and where potential adverse effects are not fully understood, the activities should not proceed;

c) Activities which may disturb nature shall be preceded by assessment of their consequences . . . and if they are to be undertaken, such activities shall be planned and carried out so as to minimize potential adverse effects.

The evolution of modern environmental law

Modern international environmental law is largely responsive to emerging global environmental problems. However, the pace of progress in the formulation of relevant laws cannot simply be such as to respond to problems after they surface. A great deal of articulation is required at an international level to balance current and future needs in the environmental sustainability of the planet and the human environment. Unlike common law, which tends to remain "reactive, backward-looking, compensatory" in its aims, IEL is expected to be progressive and forward-looking (see Heinzerling, 1999). This primary role of IEL suggests that some of the norms of conventional international public law such as "customary law" (explained later in this section) need to be adapted for their application to the environmental arena. The role of the precautionary principle in IEL is an illustrative example of this process.

Much of IEL owes its foundations to the 1972 UN Conference on the Human Environment, held at Stockholm. Several agreements and treaties followed in subsequent years. Principle 21 of the Stockholm Declaration maintained that "[s]tates have, in accordance with the Charter of the United Nations and the principles of international law . . . the responsibility to ensure that activities within their jurisdiction or control do not cause damage to the environment of other States or of areas beyond the limits of national jurisdiction" (UN Doc. A/Conf. 48/14/Rev. 1, 1973).

In 1973, the Council of the European Communities issued a statement of principles and objectives of the Community's environmental policy, declaring that "[i]n accordance with the Declaration of the United Nations Conference on the Human Environment adopted in Stockholm, care should be taken to ensure that activities carried out in one state do not cause any degradation of the environment in another state."

The Rio Declaration

Several important principles, which started as parts of soft law and which are now evolving into international norms, were laid down in the Declaration of the 1992 Rio Conference. Box 4.2 sets out the Principles contained in the 1992 Rio Declaration concerning international legal actions to protect the global environment. Agenda 21, Background Chapter 39 of the Rio Conference suggested a few guidelines for an international legal framework toward the formulation and implementation of international environmental laws and integration with the imperatives of sustainable development, with a recognition of the features that obtain in developing countries.

Most international environmental regulatory measures rely on the provision of rules and standards; some are nonbinding soft law instruments, while others are binding target-bound activities. In the latter category, the main examples include (1) the Montreal Protocol for phasing out ozone-depleting substances by the year 2000, and (2) the 1985 Helsinki Protocol on Sulfur Dioxide to the 1979 UN Economic Commission for Europe Convention on Long-range Transboundary Air Pollution (LRTAP), which called for a 30 percent reduction in national annual sulfur emissions or their transboundary fluxes by 1993. The Montreal Protocol was the first international agreement that also provided incentives for the less developed countries to adopt technologies conducive to phasing out ozone-depleting substances.

Soft law and hard law

Hard law in international public affairs arises primarily from customs and treaties. Customs require the time-tested adoption of practices (though not in every case; see chapter 6 regarding an international water dispute resolution by the ICJ). Thus they generally require a time element for their recognition in law. On the other hand, treaties generally require about two to 12 years for their formation and adoption by various states to enter into force. An expedient recourse, sometimes more pragmatic than the above two options, is to formulate soft law. This is largely in the form of a nonbinding agreement between various countries and lays a broad framework (if any) on

The 1992 Rio Principles, with international legal implications

2 States have, in accordance with the Charter of the United Nations and the principles of international law, the sovereign right to exploit their own resources pursuant to their own environmental and developmental policies, and the responsibility to ensure that the activities within their jurisdiction or control do not cause damage to the environment of other States or of areas beyond the limits of national jurisdiction.

7 States shall cooperate in a spirit of global partnership to conserve, protect, and restore the health and integrity of the earth's ecosystem. In view of the different contributions to global environmental degradation, States have common but differentiated responsibilities. The developed countries acknowledge the responsibility that they bear in the international pursuit of sustainable development in view of the pressures their societies place on the global environment and of the technologies and financial resources they command.

15 In order to protect the environment, the precautionary approach shall be widely applied by States according to their capabilities. Where there are threats of serious or irreversible damage, lack of full scientific certainty shall not be used as a reason for postponing cost-effective measures to prevent environmental degradation.

16 National authorities should endeavor to promote internationalization of environmental costs and the use of economic instruments, taking into account the approach that the polluter should, in principle, bear the cost of pollution, with due regard to the public interest and without distorting international trade and investment.

19 States shall provide prior and timely notification and relevant information to potentially affected States on activities that may have a significant adverse transboundary environmental effect and shall consult with those States at an early stage and in good faith.

24 Warfare is inherently destructive of sustainable development. States shall . . . respect international law providing protection for the environment in times of armed conflict and cooperate in its further development, as necessary.

Source: UN Doc. A/Conf. 151/5/Rev. 1, 1992

specific subjects and general principles. Soft law generates endo-genous changes in state behavior over time. According to Carter and Trimble (1995, p. 1241), "[s]oft law is where international law and international politics combine to build new norms." In general, it is negotiated between state representatives at international institutions and does not warrant further approval by parliaments or legislative bodies for ratification. Usually, soft law forms the first step toward evolution of the corresponding hard law. Some resolutions of the 1972 Stockholm Declaration constituted only components of soft law at that time, but many of those principles have now been translated into law, as, for example, in the cases of some of the provisions of the 1982 Law of the Sea, or the 1987 Montreal Protocol on ozone depletion.

The mandatory provisions of so-called hard law can lead to "soft responsibility" (see also Craik, 1998) when there are no credible com-pliance and enforcement mechanisms. Ingredients of hard law can make it less useful than soft law if the mechanisms for verification of compliance and remedial actions for noncompliance are weak. The boundary line between soft law and hard law may not be as certain as a law classification suggests. States tend to prefer nontreaty obliga-tions as a simpler and more flexible foundation for their future rela-tions. Hillgenberg (1999) argued that international agreements not concluded as treaties (and therefore not covered by the Vienna Con-vention on the Law of Treaties; see p. 144) also play an important role in international relations. The difference lies mainly in the parties' intention to specify their relationship in a way that excludes the application of treaty or customary law on the consequences of a breach of obligations. It is a useful exercise to examine the extent to which the parties choose to abide by the stated provisions, even though nontreaty agreements are not a source of law in the sense of Article 38 (1) of the Statute of the International Court of Justice (see below). The relationship may be described as a self-contained regime whose characteristics depend on the parties' intentions in the specific case and the introduction of some of the rules of treaty law into that regime may be appropriate (Hillgenberg, 1999).

International agreements not concluded as formal treaties under section 102 of the UN Charter are not covered by the 1969 Vienna Convention on the Law of Treaties, and also do not constitute a source of law in the sense of Article 38 (1) of the Statute of the ICJ. Nonetheless, they play an important role in the evolution of soft law. States tend to signal their intentions in specific cases and go further with a "learning by doing" approach. The introduction of some of the rules of treaty law may still be appropriate in such a self-contained regime (Hillgenberg, 1999).

Customary international law (CIL)

CIL is one of the two fundamental sources of international law, the other being treaty law. *Opinio juris sive necessitatis* refers to the obligation felt by a state when a certain practice is required by international law (sometimes seen as a behavioral element in the formation of customary law). Custom is traditionally defined to comprise: (1) state practice and (2) *opinio juris*, or the belief that a specific state practice is a matter of obligatory requirement of international law. Article 38 of the Statute of the ICJ refers to "international custom" as "evidence of a general practice accepted as law." Treaty provisions can form a basis for the creation of customary law, but this is not an automatic phenomenon. In the North Sea Continental Shelf cases (*FRG v. Denmark, FRG v. Netherlands*, ICJ 3, 42–44, February 20, 1969) it was clarified that the conditions leading to the creation of the customary law based on a treaty provision include the following: (1) the provision must be of a norm-creating nature; (2) there must be widespread participation in the treaty regime, including those states that are especially affected; and (3) state practice must be consistent with the existence of the obligation.

Customary norms of international law and treaty/convention law constitute the two main elements of international law. According to the American Law Institute (ALI, 1987), Restatement of the Law (Third), Foreign Relations Law of the United States Section 102 (Restatement (Third) Article 102 (2) (US)) maintains that "customary international law results from a general and consistent practice of states followed by them from a sense of legal obligation." This varies slightly from the ICJ Statute provisions. It is useful to recall that comment (b) of the above Article 102 reads: "The practice necessary to create customary law may be of comparatively short duration, but it must be general and consistent. . . . A principle of customary law is not binding on a state that declares its dissent from the principle during its development" (ALI, 1987).

The duration, frequency, uniformity, and generality of a practice provide evidence of consistency in state practice, and thus constitute CIL (Brownlie, 1990; Aceves, 1996). The collection of international behavioral regularities (in specific areas of operation) that states practice (in more than one form, legislative, administrative, and judicial formulations and decision-making) over time constitutes CIL. At times it is easier to interpret CIL when it is expressed in negative terms, such as prohibitions of human rights violations. The role of common-alities of interests (both goals and means of achieving them), the dynamics of domestic and international political and economic fac-tors, the evolution of institutions at international and other levels, changes in development priorities among different states, and percep-tions of gains and losses of alternative courses of action (including the support of relevant populations or the influence of lobby groups) are some of the determinants of the formation of CIL, in addition to the role of international law. The application of economic analyses in each of these ingredients has yet to be fully explored in the literature on the law and economics of CIL.

Article 38 (1) of the ICJ Statute points out that the Court relies on subsidiary means that include judicial decisions and the teachings of publicists. The Court "cannot 'create' law: only States can do that, through the formation of treaty and customary rules and general principles of law. They serve merely to aid the identification of rules created by States" (Churchill and Lowe, 1988, p. 10).

In modern IEL, a few norms have risen from their earlier status as being CIL into binding mandatory legal requirements. Some of the gaps in CIL have been addressed in the form of treaty laws in appro-priate areas and state duties specified in a mandatory sense. Principle 21 of the Stockholm Declaration is now a binding obligation based on treaty laws. The 1982 UN Convention on the Law of the Sea (Articles 193 and 194) declares that states "have the sovereign right to exploit their natural resources pursuant to their environmental policies and in accordance with their duty to protect and preserve the marine environment" and "shall take measures necessary to ensure that activities under their jurisdiction or control are so conducted as not to cause damage by pollution to other States and their environment, and that pollution arising from incidents or activities under their jurisdiction or control does not spread beyond the areas where they exercise sovereign rights in accordance with (the) Convention."

As argued by Buergenthal and Maier (1990), the role of *opinio juris* is to be viewed carefully. Even when the requirement may be met from observance of a rule generally and consistently over a long period of time, it is difficult to know how widely accepted a practice must be to meet the test; "in general, the practice must be one that is accepted by the world's major powers and by states directly affected by it. There must also not be a significant number of states that have consistently rejected it" (Buergenthal and Maier, 1990, p. 23).

As an illustration of the graduation of soft law into customary law (and hence into "hard" law), let us note that the precautionary principle (PP) was considered a soft law but has now graduated to become a CIL. Specific to some environmental issues where there are binding treaties among nation-states, it clearly emerged from being a soft law into the law. The PP was elucidated in a number of international agreements (see chapter 3) and thus merits as a custom, and leading to CIL. The state practices and the rulings of the ICJ (as in the nuclear test case, *New Zealand v. France*, Order 22 IX, 95 ICJ Rep., 1995) and in the Gabcikovo-Nagymaros project case (ICJ, September 25, 1997; see also box 6.2) tend to conclusively endorse the PP as a norm of CIL (see also McIntyre and Mosedale, 1997).

Some more observations and comments may also be summarized in the interpretation of CIL. According to Schlicht (1993, p. 178), custom is "a set of behavioral dispositions inherited from the past"; "it creates entitlements and preferences which shape economic transactions" (ibid., p. 180). In their theory of CIL, Goldsmith and Posner (1998, p. 53) assumed that states act "rationally and strategically in pursuit of their perceived self-interest," largely in relation to similar kinds of behavior in other states. The absence of *stare decisis* (role of precedence) in some aspects of international law is also noteworthy (see, for example, Bhala, 1999). To the extent this feature holds, it sets its own behavioral implications. However, an indirect precedence setting is also not uncommon. For example, in international trade disputes, some of the GATT dispute panels do make reference to previous rulings and examine similarities or lack thereof between different cases.

The role of custom or consistent state practices was emphasized by Aceves (1996, p. 1062): "Custom establishes expectations regarding certain behavior. In turn, these expectations can guide economic transactions without the need for costly safeguards. Through this process, custom may contribute to economic efficiency." Further, "[t]he importance of custom . . . resides in its ability to shape the expectations of actors and constrain behavior in the absence of explicit rules" (ibid., p. 1064).

Based on an empirical study involving several countries, Knack and Keefer (1997) concluded that shared standards and norms tend to (1) reduce uncertainty in the effectiveness of transactions or their specific performance expectations, hence (2) and/or otherwise reduce transaction costs. These discussions lead to the role of trust as an efficiency-enhancing factor. However, in the international context, the societal parallel hardly lends itself to an extension. The credibility factor is more likely to be relevant; this is comprised only partly of trust and is based on considerations of established patterns of behavior.

CIL and treaties

Area- or theme-specific treaties serve to jump-start measures envisaged under agreements that would not otherwise emanate from existing CIL. In other words, treaty provisions can eventually lead to CIL and can form the precursors of ever-expanding provisions of CIL. Goldsmith and Posner (1999) suggested that customs among states appear to be less common and more fragile than customs among individuals because of vastly different sets of dynamic determinants of customs in the two configurations. They argued that:

> CIL is the label attached to behavioral regularities that emerge in various strategic settings; treaties may be labels attached to certain pronouncements that emerge in various strategic settings. . . . The main difference between the two forms of law is that CIL evolves in the absence of clear and authoritative communication between interested states, which makes it difficult to achieve cooperation or coordination, whereas treaties are a product of authoritative communication and thus are more likely than CIL to produce cooperation or coordination. (Goldsmith and Posner, 1999, p. 1172)

The role of state practice

The norm of state practice over time has severe limitations if it is sought in every environmental management issue. The reason for this is that some problems are only now being discovered and thus attempts to mitigate them have not received attention purely because of the relatively short time since they were diagnosed. This is the essence of the "fast-breaking science" argument of Hohmann (1994). States are principal actors in international policy design and implementation. The lack of a unified administrative command (luckily, perhaps, for humanity) governing world affairs necessitates an active role for methods of cooperation and coordination. Some studies (see, for example, Stein, 1982; Milner, 1991) in the theory and practice of international relations examine the issue from a rather extreme form of governance (or lack of it): anarchy. This enables some inferences about the role of governmental and intergovernmental interventions.

The economists' favorite "invisible hand" of market solutions to everything can only solve some problems (economic, environmental, or other) for some time, but not necessarily all problems at all times. The role of international institutions, assuming they are not devised or conducted as a drag on supporting systems, can be to enhance cooperation among states.

It has been argued that state practice minimizes the problems of transaction costs at the international level and is an important element in the two principal sources of international law: treaty law and customary international law. Aceves (1996, p. 1005) argued that:

> Customary international law allows states to promote cooperation in the absence of formal agreements. It minimizes transaction costs by allowing states to forgo explicit negotiations and to function even in the absence of a formal structure . . . state practice facilitates the development of governance structures that address the problems raised by transaction costs.

This assertion needs to be examined in regard to the relative effectiveness (in terms of cost, time, and meeting the specified objectives/targets) of exogenous and endogenous structures of institutional governance. If the role of international agreements and the law in various forms – all constituting exogenous institutional factors – is such that their transaction costs are very high, the efficacy of endogenous institutional governance (domestic level) remains a major normative determinant of the choice of norms for legal specifications.

The design of international environmental agreements (IEAs)

Several authors have sought to present formal models for IEAs in accordance with varying sets of stylized assumptions (unfortunately not always spelled out, since most of these assumptions are implicit rather than explicit). Using a game-theoretic approach has been the standard methodology of these modeling exercises. It is useful to design treaties which sustain a level of implementation based on self-interest where this is not a net addition to recommendations on the treaty design; this conclusion has also emerged from some of the game-theoretic models. In an interlinked approach to the provision of global environmental public goods, the models in Barrett (1997) suggest the use of disincentives such as trade sanctions for noncooperating countries in the formation and implementation of an IEA. Alternatively,

Petrakis and Xepapadeas (1996) showed that a relatively viable group of environmentally conscious countries may arrange to pay for other countries, thus forming a larger and relatively stable coalition to effect environmental improvement. However, in a multiperiod setting, the use of such incentives (if these are properly selected) could reduce the innovation initiatives of aid-receiving countries. Batabyal (2000) analyzed the role of alternative forms of international contracting in the presence of asymmetric information. He concluded that there is a crucial role for incentives administered by a supranational entity. In general, the heterogeneous nature of countries' resource endowments suggests a role for an apex coordinating mechanism (not necessarily a bureaucratic organization) at the international level which can devise proper incentives for relevant groups of countries to enable their participation and effective implementation of a desirable environmental standard or norm.

4.3 CONCEPTS AND PRINCIPLES OF INTERNATIONAL ENVIRONMENTAL LAWS

Historically, both contracts and treaties have been treated alike; they were considered consensual agreements. "A treaty is primarily a contract between two or more independent nations" (*Whitney v. Robertson*, 124 US 190, 194, 1888). However, a modern interpretation finds several important differences (see Dunoff and Trachtman, 1999). Box 4.3 provides a glossary of terms, mainly in relation to traditional expressions of legal notions and the modern use of treaty laws.

The Vienna Convention on the Law of Treaties was initiated in 1949; it took shape 20 years later, in 1969, and entered into force in 1980. If this timeframe seems a bit strange, one need only think of its companion treaty, the proposed treaty on the Law of State Responsibility, which also started its draft formation in 1949 but is still in its "draft" stages and is yet to be agreed upon for possible adoption.

The Vienna Convention on the Law of Treaties, held in two sessions in 1968 and 1969, entered into force on January 27, 1980 with 90 states having become parties to the Convention by the twenty-first century (with 47 original signatories). The full text is contained in the UN document UN Doc. A/Conf. 39/11/Add. 2. This Convention, largely a codification of prevailing customary international law, remains the primary source of law governing multilateral environmental

BOX 4.3

Legal glossary

amicus curiae: "Friend of the court"; a person or entity allowed to present arguments of relevance on an issue or issues before a competent legal authority.

inter se: Between the parties to a specific agreement or other transaction.

jus cogens: Preemptory norms of international law.

locus standi: The entitlement to represent legal interest on an issue before a legal entity.

rationale materiae: By reason of the subject matter.

res communis: An asset of global common interest but not amenable to state sovereign control.

res nullius: An asset amenable to control/acquisition/ownership or use but not yet in the possession of any entity of legal existence.

stare decisis: The principle that a judicial body should follow its own previous decisions and those of similar or greater authority.

Adoption: The formal act by which the form and content of a proposed treaty text are established. As a general rule, the adoption of the text of a treaty takes place through the expression of the consent of the states participating in the treaty-making process. The instruments of "acceptance" or "approval" of a treaty have the same legal effect as ratification and consequently express the consent of a state to be bound by a treaty.

Accession: The act whereby a state accepts the offer or the opportunity to become a party to a treaty already negotiated and signed by other states. It has the same legal effect as ratification.

Declarations: States tend to make "declarations" as to their understanding of some matter or as to the interpretation of a particular provision. Unlike "reservations," declarations merely clarify the state's position and do not purport to exclude or modify the legal effect of a treaty.

Entry into force: Typically, the provisions of a treaty determine the date of ratification by a fixed number of states (and possibly category, if any) on which it enters into force.

Ratification: Defines the international act whereby a state indicates its consent to be bound to a treaty if the parties intended to show their consent by such an act.

Treaty: Used either as a common generic term or as a particular term to indicate an instrument with certain characteristics. It has regularly been used as a generic term embracing all instruments binding in international law that have been concluded between international entities, regardless of their formal designation. Both the 1969 Vienna Convention and the 1986 Vienna Convention confirm this generic use of the term. The 1969 Vienna Convention (Article 2 (1) (a)) defines a treaty as "an international agreement concluded between States in written form and governed by international law, whether embodied in a single instrument or in two or more related instruments and whatever its particular designation." The 1986 Vienna Convention extends the definition of treaties to include international agreements involving international organizations as parties. In order to speak of a "treaty" in the generic sense, an instrument has to meet various criteria: (1) it has to be a binding instrument, which means that the contracting parties intended to create legal rights and duties; (2) the instrument must be concluded by states or international organizations with treaty-making power; and (3) it has to be governed by international law.

Agreement: The 1969 Vienna Convention on the Law of Treaties employs the term "international agreement" in its broadest sense to refer to legal instruments which do not meet its definition of "treaty."

Convention: The term can have both a generic and a specific meaning. Article 38 (1) (a) of the Statute of the ICJ refers to "international conventions, whether general or particular" as a source of law, apart from international customary rules and general principles of international law, and, as a secondary source, judicial decisions and the teachings of the most highly qualified publicists. This generic use of the term embraces all international agreements and is synonymous with the generic term "treaty."

Protocol: The term is used for agreements that are less formal than those entitled "treaty" or "convention" and could be used to cover the following kinds of instruments: (1) a protocol of signature, an instrument subsidiary to a treaty which is drawn up by the same parties and which deals with ancillary matters such as the interpretation of particular clauses of the treaty; (2) an optional protocol to a treaty, an instrument that establishes additional rights and obligations to a treaty; and (3) a protocol based on a framework treaty, an instrument with specific substantive obligations that implements the general objectives of a previous framework or umbrella convention. Such protocols ensure a more simplified and accelerated treaty-making process and have been used particularly in the field of international environmental law. An example is the 1987 Montreal Protocol on Substances that Deplete the Ozone Layer, adopted on the basis of Articles 2 and 8 of the 1985 Vienna Convention for the Protection of the Ozone Layer.

Sources: **Brownlie (1990); www.un.org/Depts/Treaty/glossary.htm (March 1, 2000)**

agreements. Box 4.4 lists important articles of the Convention that set out the rules for applying international law when multiple treaties involving different combinations of parties are to be interpreted. Article 103 of the Charter of the United Nations is mentioned in the stated article. According to this reference to Article 103, the UN Charter takes priority over any other treaty (earlier or later) to which member states are a party. Article 34 of the Convention states that "[a] treaty does not create either obligations or rights for third States without its consent." When a treaty specifies that it assumes priority over another treaty, this provision is inapplicable to states which are not a party to the treaty that contains the conflicting clause (Mus, 1998). The *lex posterior* rule of Article 30 (3) of the Vienna Convention yields priority to the UN Charter. Articles 31 and 32 of the Vienna Convention offer guidance to resolve conflicts among treaties.

Mus (1998) suggested that when a treaty interpretation appears to remain inconclusive, the *lex posterior* rule should be applied as the last resort, after exhausting the usage of Articles 31 and 32. This rule will apply only when all the contracting parties to the earlier treaty have also become a party to the later treaty. Article 30 (3) leaves open for interpretation the possibility that states have become a party to the later treaty but not to the earlier one. Article 30 remains silent on the interpretation of treaties that are adopted simultaneously. Article 41 of the Vienna Convention is entitled "Agreements to modify multilateral treaties between certain of the parties only," and lays down conditions under which some parties to a multilateral treaty are allowed to form a new treaty between them, without being internationally responsible to the other parties for the existing multilateral treaty. In general, it is useful that when formulating treaties, states should specify their acceptance or otherwise of clauses that are in conflict with other treaties to which they are parties.

BOX 4.4

Vienna Convention on the Law of Treaties, 1969

ARTICLE 30: APPLICATION OF SUCCESSIVE TREATIES RELATING TO THE SAME SUBJECT MATTER

1   Subject to Article 103 of the Charter of the United Nations, the rights and obligations of States Parties to successive treaties relating to the same subject matter shall be determined in accordance with the following paragraphs.

2   When a treaty specifies that it is subject to, or that it is not to be considered as incomplete with, an earlier or later treaty, the provisions of that other treaty prevail.

3   When all the parties to the earlier treaty are parties also to the later treaty but the earlier treaty is not terminated or suspended in operation under Article 59, the earlier treaty applies only to the extent that its provisions are compatible with those of the later treaty.

4   When the parties to the later treaty do not include all the parties to the earlier one: (a) as between State Parties to both treaties the same rule applies as in paragraph 3; (b) as between a State Party to both treaties and a State Party to only one of the treaties, the treaty to which both States are parties governs their mutual rights and obligations.

5   Paragraph 4 is without prejudice to Article 41, or to any question of the termination or suspension of the operation of a treaty under Article 60 or to any question of responsibility which may arise for a State from the conclusion or application of a treaty, the provisions of which are incompatible with its obligations towards another State under another treaty.

Sources: Vienna Convention on the Law of Treaties, UN Doc. A/Conf. 39/127, 1969; 8 ILM 679; www.untreaty.un.org. Reproduced with the permission of the UN Publications Board

Article 60 of the 1969 Vienna Treaty describes the "rules of release" of a state from legal duties, including responses to a breach of treaty. The currently uncodified "law of state responsibility" remains the source of the rules of remediation in treaty breaches. The rules of release evolve around the concept of "material breach" (MB), defined in Article 60 (3) as follows:

> A material breach of a treaty, for the purpose of this Article, consists in a) A repudiation of the treaty not sanctioned by the present Convention; or b) The violation of a provision essential to the accomplishment of the object or purpose of the treaty.

A relatively minor breach of an important provision can give rise to the right of termination, whereas a serious breach of provision not "essential" to the attainment of the objectives of the treaty does not do so (Greig, 1994).

In so far as bilateral treaties are concerned, MB is both necessary and sufficient to give the victim of that breach the option to release itself from all of its obligations under the breached treaty. However, in multilateral treaties, under Article 60 (2) of the Vienna Convention, an MB is a necessary but not sufficient condition to legitimize the release option; the MB must also either lead all nonbreaching parties to agree that their simultaneous release is appropriate, or specifically affect a party seeking release only from its obligations to the breaching party, or radically affect the future performance obligations of all parties (see Setear, 1997).

Setear (1997, p. 50) argued that "Article 60's focus upon the importance of the breached provision to the treaty's object or purpose, rather than upon the impact of the breach on the benefits and costs accruing to the parties as a result, is a rule that economizes on the need to make costly factual determinations." Setear suggested that the Article 60 rule is consistent with the recognition of the role of transaction costs that accrue in administering a treaty over time.

Efficient breach of contracts and treaties?

Is "efficient breach theory" efficient in the transaction costs (TC) sense? The "efficient" breach in contracts is treated as if the detection is a certainty, and the transaction costs are not significant; hence its provision for compensatory damages equaling the harm inflicted. This remains a suboptimal solution and there is little guarantee that an efficiency improvement (in the sense of economic surplus maximization) would indeed occur.

In the management of global commons as international collective goods, including compliance with international treaties, the role of the victim and multilateralism is sometimes hard to define. The victim may or may not be a party to a treaty, but the planet becomes the victim. An *amicus curiae* petition method must be devised in such

BOX 4.5

Conventions and their status

The status of a selection of Conventions at the beginning of the twenty-first century is summarized below.

1 Convention on Long-range Transboundary Air Pollution, adopted within the framework of the UN Economic Commission for Europe on the Protection of the Environment, concluded at Geneva November 13, 1979; entered into force March 13, 1983. Signatories 33, Parties 45.

2 Vienna Convention for the Protection of the Ozone Layer, concluded at Vienna March 22, 1985; entered into force September 22, 1988. Signatories 28, Parties 173.

3 Basel Convention on the Control of Transboundary Movements of Hazardous Wastes and their Disposal, concluded at Basel March 22, 1989; entered into force May 5, 1992. Signatories 53, Parties 133.

4 Convention on Environmental Impact Assessment in a Transboundary Context, adopted under the auspices of the UN Economic Commission for Europe, concluded at Espoo (Finland) February 25, 1991; entered into force September 10, 1997. Signatories 30, Parties 29.

5 Convention on the Protection and Use of Transboundary Watercourses and International Lakes, adopted under the auspices of the UN Economic Commission for Europe, concluded at Helsinki March 17, 1992; entered into force October 6, 1996. Signatories 26, Parties 26.

6 UN Framework Convention on Climate Change, concluded at New York May 9, 1992; entered into force March 21, 1994. Signatories 166, Parties 180.

7 UN Convention to Combat Desertification in those Countries Experiencing Serious Drought and/or Desertification, Particularly in Africa, concluded at Paris October 14, 1994; entered into force December 26, 1996. Signatories 115, Parties 159.

8 Agreement on Cooperative Enforcement Operations Directed at Illegal Trade in Wild Fauna and Flora, open to all African countries, concluded at Lusaka September 8, 1994; entered into force December 10, 1996. Signatories 7, Parties 6.

Others: The 1998 Convention on Access to Information, Public Participation in Decision-making, and Access to Justice in Environmental Matters was adopted at Aarhus (Denmark) on June 25, 1998 with 40 signatories, but by the beginning of 2000 only four had become parties (not yet in force). Another 1998 Convention, the Rotterdam Convention on the Prior Informed Consent Procedure for Certain Hazardous Chemicals and Pesticides in International Trade, was adopted at Rotterdam on September 10, 1998 with 73 signatories, but the parties were only two by the end of the twentieth century (not yet in force).

Source: Summarized from information obtained from www.un.org/Depts/Treaty/ final/ts2/newfiles/part_boo/xxvii_1.html (December 30, 1999)

scenarios to protect global environmental features. New rules may be required to this effect. One of these could involve levying "restoration fees" from offending parties. A global trust fund for this purpose may be created and administered under the UN system.

Box 4.5 summarizes the chronology of some of the major international environmental agreements, the size of participation indicated by the number of states who were original signatories, and the number that signed the ratification, in each case. This is provided to indicate the broad magnitude of gaps in the coverage of issues in the global commons, and the limited participation by states (even assuming the constraints of effective participation imposed by entries of "reservation" by some states; see the next section for details) in many of the agreements. Although a precise estimate may not be feasible at this stage, it is reasonable to conclude that the coverage of environmental features and the participation of states even under these themes is hardly a fourth of the magnitude of international participation required to wisely manage the global environmental resources and this allows environmental free-rider phenomena.

4.4 TREATY RESERVATIONS

The "reservations" clause of treaties remains one of the weakest points of international treaty law. Even when parties join protocol agreements, any state can "enter a reservation" to a future change and thereby exempt itself from the overall policy framework or Convention with respect to that specific provision.

Article 2 (1) (d) of the 1969 Vienna Convention on the Law of Treaties defines a reservation as meaning

> a unilateral statement, however phrased or named, made by a State, when signing, ratifying, approving or acceding to a treaty, whereby it purports to exclude or modify the legal effect of certain provisions of the treaty in their application to that State. (UN Doc. A/CN.4/491/Add. 1, paragraph 82, 1998)

A reservation is a declaration made by a state by which it purports to exclude or alter the legal effect of certain provisions of the treaty in their application to that state. A reservation enables a state to accept a multilateral treaty as a whole by giving it the possibility of not applying certain provisions with which it does not want to comply. Reservations can be made when the treaty is signed, ratified, accepted, approved, or acceded to. Reservations must not be incompatible with the object and the purpose of the treaty. Furthermore, a treaty might prohibit reservations or only allow for certain reservations to be made (Articles 2 (1) (d) and 19–23, Vienna Convention on the Law of Treaties, 1969, and summary from the UN website: www.un.org/Depts/Treaty.htm).

The 1969 Vienna Convention on the Law of Treaties ("1969 Vienna Convention") contains rules for treaties concluded between states. In addition, the 1986 Vienna Convention on the Law of Treaties between States and International Organizations or between International Organizations ("1986 Vienna Convention"), which has still not entered into force, added rules for treaties with international organizations as parties. Neither the 1969 Vienna Convention nor the 1986 Vienna Convention distinguishes between the different designations of these instruments. Instead, their rules apply to all of those instruments as long as they meet certain common requirements.

Article 102 of the Charter of the United Nations provides that "every treaty and every international agreement entered into by any Member State of the United Nations after the present Charter comes into force shall as soon as possible be registered with the Secretariat and published by it." All treaties and international agreements registered or filed and recorded with the Secretariat since 1946 are published in the UN Treaty Series (UNTS). By the terms "treaty" and "international agreement," referred to in Article 102 of the Charter, the broadest range of instruments is covered.

The 1999 Report of the International Law Commission (ILC) included in its chapter VI a detailed examination of "the law and practice relating to reservations to treaties," in response to the 1993 UN General Assembly resolution which sought the inclusion of this item on the agenda of the ILC. Several examples of varying situations that led to the inclusion of reservations or interpretative declarations were examined. The good-faith intentions and practices following the stipulations are considered important in the assessment of the significance of these provisions.

An empirical analysis of the treaties and invoking of the reservations clauses in the context of the Council of Europe was provided by Akermark (1999). It was observed that: (1) from 1962 to 1998, the total number of treaties was 133, of which 57 (constituting 43 percent) did not have any reservation clause; (2) of these, 45 treaties permitted specific forms of reservations, and 19 prohibited all reservations. It was found that in most cases the reservations were permitted only when a contracting party could "claim that its legislation in force presents an obstacle to the full realization of the treaty." The tendency for this feature to constitute regional customary rule was also noted.

As the Harvard Law Review Association (HLRA, 1991, p. 1544) pointed out, "although the convention-protocol approach may reduce free rider problems, it does not reduce the threat of hold-outs in the regulation of global commons." The hold-outs take different forms at different times for a state in its practice. An *ex ante* provision for this is usually made in the "reservations" process of treaty formation. The effectiveness of CITES diminished as a result of such practices: Japan exempted four species of whales and five African states exempted African elephants. The CITES equivalent of protocols was the lists of endangered or protected species. The existence of reservations tends to dilute treaty law significantly. "Treaty integrity" can hardly be preserved unless the entire treaty (with the exception of obvious impossibilities specific to some states, which may thereby seek exceptions or make use of a reservations clause) is adhered to by the contracting parties. The 1982 UN Convention on the Law of the Sea (see chapter 5) was the first document to seek a "package deal": states could neither enter reservations nor use only some of the provisions selectively. One of the "costs" of such tighter laws is that some states are unwilling to join or ratify such treaties, and others need considerable time to decide in favor of joining. It is relevant to note that it took 12 years for the Law of the Sea to enter into force.

BOX 4.6

Reservation case study: Canadian national laws

Canadian reservation: Convention on Environmental Impact Assessment in a Transboundary Context (adopted 1991, entered into force 1997).

Canada entered the following reservation in its ratification of the Convention on May 12, 1998:

> In as much as under the Canadian constitutional system legislative jurisdiction in respect of environmental assessment is divided between the provinces and the federal government, the Government of Canada in ratifying this Convention, makes a reservation in respect of proposed activities (as defined in this Convention) that fall outside of federal legislative jurisdiction exercised in respect of environmental assessment.

Several objections were lodged by different countries to the principle and practice of this reservation. Among these were Spain, Sweden, Finland, Italy, France, Norway, and Luxembourg. Among other reasons, it was pointed out that the Vienna Convention on the Law of Treaties, 1969, a type of international public law, provides in Article 19 (c) that reservations that are incompatible with the object and purpose of a treaty are not authorized. The customary principles do not allow subordination of international public law to some of the provisions of domestic law.

There are other variants of reservations allowed in international public law, as long as the party expressing "objections" to an international law is not a signatory to the contrary provisions. States which persistently object to new (noncustomary) principles of law would not be bound by such specifications of the principles or standards (see Stein, 1985 regarding the principle of the persistent objector).

4.5 INTERNATIONAL RELATIONS THEORY AND IEL

The scope for an integration of international relations (IR) theory and international law (IL) arises from the analytical content and analytical approaches of modern theories of IR, as suggested by Abbott (1989).

The interface of IL and IR attracted several authors in the 1990s (see, for example, Burley, 1993; Setear, 1996; Slaughter et al., 1998; Abbott, 1999). Modern IR (referred to as IR hereafter) focuses on the inter-actions of specific issues in a static and dynamic context, unlike the substantial traditional literature of international politics that deliber-ates systems as a whole, with "political power" as the most influenc-ing factor. Among the important ingredients of IR theory are "state rationality" and "strategic rationality." States are perceived to explore their interests both in a rational (albeit bounded rational) decision-making context as well as in a strategic context. The role of cost–benefit calculus (and hence the tradeoff of future values with current interests, and discount factors) and transaction cost analysis also comes into play in these approaches. These aspects of IR theory facilitate a meaningful description and prediction of state parties' behavior to a large extent. Analysis of "strategic rationality" (see Snidal, 1985) enables understanding of states' interdependence in a positive-sum game description of state interactions and evolution of state practices (under soft law, hard law, or neither). IR theory seeks to maintain clarity on the ingredients that constitute international state practices: international law, rules, standards, regimes of governance, and institutions.

Much the same can be stated about the commonality of IR and IL theories with modern law and economics (referred to hereafter as L&E). Among the methods common to the analysis of IL, IR, and L&E are: contract theory, game theory, public choice theory, transaction cost economics, and decision-making under uncertainty with incom-plete information (including the economics of information). It is useful to note that these methods lend themselves to a wide variety of applications in most disciplines, ranging from industrial management to psychology. The details are what makes the difference, being par-ticularly useful for a specific area or otherwise. A meaningful analysis of IEL requires deployment of the knowledge base of IL, IR, L&E, in addition to environmental economics (EE) and new institutional eco-nomics (NIE). An approximate assessment of international environ-mental law and economics (IELE) may be to express it in terms of the following equality (where the plus sign denotes the set-unionization rather than an arithmetical addition):

IELE = IL + IR + L&E + EE + NIE

One of the key formulations in IR is that of international regimes. In early descriptions, the regimes were defined by Krasner (1982, p. 186) as "sets of implicit or explicit principles, norms, rules, and decision-making procedures around which actors' expectations converge in a given area of international relations." The role of IL in this account is rather obvious, and so is that of various contracts and treaties. It is possible to subdivide regimes into relevant fields of application or other functional uses. The interactions of legal regimes and illegal regimes, or those of soft-law-based regimes and hard-law-based regimes, which involve governmental and nongovernmental entities and constitute an amalgam of regimes would be a realistic description of many issues. This definition could be improved with a more precise specification of each of its ingredients, and then analytical formulations can be formalized. The broader question is to devise and examine exogenous regimes, endogenous regimes, and the interplay of the two. In IR, regime formation needs to take into account these features. If regimes in IR are not analyzed in terms of a systems approach describing cause-and-effect factors and their relationships, the term could remain a mere tautology.

International legal disputes admit analysis under IR, just as they admit the use of the analytics of cooperative game theory and other decision-making techniques. However, a judicious mix of political institutional analysis and a narrower in-depth analysis of specific problems is what gives IR theory its strengths (see, for example, Schmidt, 1996 for an application in the US–Canada fisheries problem; and Colburn, 1997 for an explanation of several provisions of the 1995 UN Agreement on Straddling Fish Stocks, using regime theory; see chapter 5 for the Fish Stocks Agreement).

This is not to suggest that applying IR theory is a panacea or a substitute for sound judgment. If the role of institutions is subsumed to too many technicalities, there is a risk of providing simplistic and naive solutions. It is important to note, as Slaughter et al. (1998, p. 375) observed, that "[i]nstitutions that provide collective goods may be collective goods themselves, subject to the same difficulties of supply and maintenance as the underlying substantive benefits they are designed to provide." The conditions under which international regimes emerge as endogenous institutions, and the role of exogenous factors in this evolution, are issues of constant interest. The function of regimes in IR helps explain the role of incentives and constraints in state rationality, and also the roles of principals and agents and their motives in arriving at decisions under various regimes. Formal analytical models tend to assume state behavior as one of utility maximization, on the lines of standard individual-level utility maximization or a normative prescription of social welfare maximization at the aggregate level for a society. Neither are likely to hold good as real world depictions of decision-making behavior, since the normative assumptions of rationality may not hold for states in their interactions for IEAs (Dunoff and Trachtman, 1999). A number of motivations of representatives of state contributing to treaties and other agreements also are important (see some variations suggested by Stephan, 1997).

Parties in international relations tend to possess incentives for a fuzzy decision-making apparatus, and sometimes by design, in order to appropriate gains of flexibility in interpretation and implementation (or lack of it) of multilateral agreements. Parties may resort to opportunistic behavior, as long as there are incentives to do so, and there are no legal or other hindrances to control such behavior. In a value-free decision-making context, such opportunistic behavior tends to enhance the surplus for the individual decision-making entity, possibly (but not necessarily) at the expense of the rest of the agents in the international arena. The negative effects of such behavior are determinable by the existence of a "joint production function" and the relative interdependencies of actions in the static and dynamic timeframes. Kostritsky (1993) argued that opportunism tends to explain why contracting parties (potential or *de jure*) dispense with "formal, bargained-for contracts."

The negotiations for the 1982 Convention on the Law of the Sea lasted eight years, and the Convention entered into force in 1994, a total span of 20 years for the agreement/treaty to be operational. The 1994 GATT Uruguay Round Trade Negotiations took seven years. Based on similar international practices, Aceves (1996, pp. 1016 and 1065) concluded that

> States cannot make exhaustive agreements that address every contingency that may arise in the course of their relationship(s). These negotiations may take many years and the cost of such negotiations would be prohibitive. States also lack the information necessary to consider adequately all potential risk factors and developments . . . transaction costs will have a significant impact on whether states choose treaty law or customary international law in the development of international institutions.

The economic considerations enabling a state to decide in favor of joining an agreement are substantially different than those that tend to determine a breach of a treaty (Ress, 1994). There are situations, however, where a state uses as "private information" its decision to join an agreement with the motive or expectation of *de facto* breaching that agreement. The risk of loss of credibility and the corresponding long-term costs are relevant in the latter case, as long as there is a possibility of detection by other parties of such behavior. Lack of a uniformly "competent authority" in the international judicial system is one of the many factors that can undermine the application of many economic principles in international legal decisions, and applies even more so in the international environmental arena. The principle of reciprocity (*do ut des*) (see Ress, 1994, p. 290) states that the "parties to an international treaty comply with treaty obligations as long as the expected long-term benefits are greater than the costs of non-performance." It was also suggested that the costs or benefits may not be entirely monetary.

Self-implementing treaties

A treaty is self-implementing if it enables parties to continue to comply in an intertemporal sense with negligible *ex post* transaction costs for monitoring and enforcement of the treaty obligations, even when political or other institutional factors among the parties change over time. Ress (1994, p. 293) argued that this may be feasible if "the difference between the advantages reaped from the treaty and the costs of further compliance with the terms of the treaty is negative so that the advantages prevail." By the nature of the features incorporated and unspecified in a given treaty, these are usually incomplete treaties, especially in the long-term sense. Often some, though not all, gaps in treaties tend to be filled by dispute settlement panels or arbitration panels (Bos, 1980).

Treaty breaches

Treaty breaches in most cases are usually founded on *ex post* opportunistic behavior. An obvious scenario that minimizes treaty breaches is to devise treaties that are nonbinding to begin with. A nonbinding international agreement is a treaty which does not have the nature of an international law treaty (Bilder, 1981; Ress, 1994). Such treaties are not recognized under Article 102 of the UN Charter but seem to satisfy some political and moral considerations, thus forming a part of soft law. A breach of such agreements does not attract sanctions or reprisals, but gets noted among other parties, with a possible effect on some other related or apparently unrelated multilateral relations. This could elicit lack of cooperation from other parties, including nonparties to a specific agreement, and thus prove "expensive" for the breaching party in the long run (Bilder, 1981). Ress (1994, p. 286) suggested that (1) nonbinding agreements generally minimize transaction costs and (2) "the replacement of international treaties by so-called non-binding agreements is opportune when all parties have a strong interest in the fulfillment of the respective commitments." The role of *ex ante* safeguards against *ex post* opportunism in the context of formulation and implementation of treaties was examined by Ress (1994). An illustrative case is that of European Community (EC) law which, under the auspices of the European Court of Justice (ECJ), allows any member of the EC the possibility of bringing a damage or liability claim against a breaching member country and has a "preventive effect" against potential breaches. This is expected to be a cost-effective method of enforcement.

A comparison of contract law and economics with the law and economics of treaties in the international context admits certain similarities as well as dissimilarities. The treaty doctrine regarding "reservations" has no parallel in contract law. As pointed out by Dunoff and Trachtman (1999), the analogy with contracts is closer in some treaties than in others. Similarly, the theory of "efficient breach" in domestic contract law admits some merits of contract violations when the surplus created by such actions can be efficiency-improving. There is hardly a parallel for this in the treaty law so far. This situation could arise for a number of reasons, including the lack of a proper compensating mechanism to cover breaches and their restitution, and the existence of *ex post* costs (or other externalities) of precedence or of validating violations (see Ress, 1994). In behavioral terms, a few of the treaties (for example, the Montreal Protocol; see chapter 6) contain mechanisms that could enhance incentives to cooperative behavior in the sense of a repeat prisoner's dilemma (Setear, 1996; see also chapter 2).

There are several theories to explain the prevalence and extent of state compliance with international laws (see, for example, Koh, 1997). None offers a unified framework. Most explanations rely on the role of the specifications of various provisions in international treaties, both binding and nonbinding (see Chayes and Chayes, 1995). These issues are discussed in detail in chapter 9. State sovereignty is an important factor that affects the evolution and practice of state behavior; some of the major features of this topic are explored next.

■ 4.6 VOLUNTARY PARTICIPATION AND SOVEREIGNTY

It is useful to recall that the global commons comprise both *res nullius* and *res communis*. The latter consists of entities that are legally susceptible to acquisition by states but not yet under the control of territorial sovereignty. *Res nullius* consists of the high seas and other regions outside any property ownership regimes. The role of the state and its sovereign rights remains an important factor in the governance of the global commons.

Sovereignty of states is a fundamental principle of international public law. Even though the HLRA (1991) review seems to suggest it is yet another "competing value," it is doubtful whether a state would easily bargain away its sovereign rights under most pretexts of international law or its compliance. "A rule of international law generally becomes binding upon a state only if the state freely accepts that rule and submits its sovereignty under the rule" (Perrez, 1996, p. 1188). The principle of permanent sovereignty over natural resources is the fundamental principle of contemporary international public law. The writings and litigations on this issue have depicted over the years competing interests between capital-rich (or capital-exporting) countries and natural resource-rich (or mineral and other raw material-exporting) countries; there was little evidence that international concerns about sovereignty and natural resources related to the depletion of nonrenewable resources or fair "rental values" for resources extracted as a result of decolonization and sovereignty.

The UN Resolution on Permanent Sovereignty over Natural Resources remains the most important statement on states and their natural resources (and also on the legality of nationalizing foreign companies hosted in the sovereign states). This resolution of the UN General Assembly (Resolution No. 1803) was adopted on December 14, 1962 (UN Doc. A/5217, 1963; reprinted in 2 ILM 223, 1963). It declared:

> The right of the peoples and nations to permanent sovereignty over their natural wealth and resources must be exercised in the interest of their national development and of the well-being of the people of the State concerned. . . . The free and beneficial exercise of the sovereignty of peoples and nations over their natural resources must be furthered by the mutual respect of States based on their sovereign equality.

Later, in 1974, UN Resolution No. 3281 (XXIX) recognized that "each State enjoys a sovereign right," but omitted any reference to international law. As a result of this omission, contemporary international

BOX 4.7

UN Charter of Economic Rights and Duties of States

UN General Assembly Resolution 3281 (XXIX) declared in its pre-amble that it was desirous of contributing to the creation of conditions for, among other things, "the protection, preservation and enhancement of the environment." Some selected Articles of this Charter appear below.

- *Article 2 (1)*. Every State has and shall freely exercise full permanent sovereignty, including possession, use and disposal, over all its wealth, natural resources and economic activities.
- *Article 3*. In the exploitation of natural resources shared by two or more countries, each State must cooperate on the basis of a system of information and prior consultations in order to achieve optimum use of such resources without causing damage to the legitimate interests of others.
- *Article 29*. The sea-bed and ocean floor and the subsoil thereof, beyond the limits of national jurisdiction, as well as the resources of the area, are the common heritage of mankind.
- *Article 30*. The protection, preservation and enhancement of the environment for the present and future generations is the responsibility of all States. All States shall endeavor to establish their own environmental and developmental policies in conformity with such responsibility. The environmental policies of all States should enhance and not adversely affect the present and future development potential of developing countries. All States have the responsibility to ensure that activities within their jurisdiction or control do not cause damage to the environment of other States or of areas beyond the limits of national jurisdiction. All States should cooperate in evolving international norms and regulations in the field of the environment.

law recognizes only Resolution 1803 (XVII) of 1962 as a restatement of CIL. The 1974 resolution is seen as a political statement supported mainly by the nonindustrial countries.

Interpretation of permanent sovereignty as an economic concept was underlined by the UN Study of 1962 (UN, 1962), which dealt only with issues of economic rights, concessions, and nationalization of foreign companies. Perrez (1996) concluded that the principle of permanent sovereignty over natural resources did not interfere with duties and obligations under international law, and that there is no conflict with the state obligation not to cause transboundary environmental damage. Principle 2 of the 1992 Rio Declaration declares that states have "the sovereign right to exploit their own resources pursuant to their own environmental and developmental policies."

The principle of avoidance of externalities can possibly be traced back to the Roman law maxim *sic utere tuo ut alienum non laedas* (use own property so as not to injure that of another). The ICJ in the Corfu Channel case (*UK v. Alb.* 1949, ICJ 4, 22) stated the same in its assertion that the sovereignty principle implies "the obligation of every state not to allow its territory to be used for acts contrary to the rights of other states."

In developments under modern IEL, the prevalence of global accountability, in addition to the exercise of the sovereign rights of states, is a discernible feature in many international treaties/agreements. For example, Article 59 of the 1982 UNCLOS provides the basis for the resolution of conflicts regarding the attribution of rights and jurisdiction in the exclusive economic zone: "the conflict should be resolved on the basis of equity and in the light of all the relevant circumstances, taking into account the respective importance of the interests involved to the parties as well as to the international community as a whole." Furthermore, UNCLOS Article 193 on the sovereign right of states to exploit their natural resources provides that states have the sovereign right to exploit their natural resources pursuant to their environmental policies and in accordance with their duty to protect and preserve the marine environment.

As Perrez (1996, p. 1212) observed, "[t]he principle of permanent sovereignty over natural resources requires each state to respect all other states in the use of their natural resources, which inherently includes the obligation not to cause transboundary pollution." However, one limitation that remains fairly common in state practice is to exercise sovereign rights and ignore externalities if there are no obligatory requirements in accordance with international treaties or other agreements. Wolf (1997, p. 14) observed that because of the "uncertainty, complexity, and incompatibility of what is right and what is desirable," international environmental negotiations focus on "mechanisms by which one or another state of the world will result, not the magnitude or distribution of values in that state."

4.7 INTERFACE OF DOMESTIC AND INTERNATIONAL LAWS

Domestic and international laws are expected to function in their own spheres of competence. Each system of law is "supreme in its own field, and neither has a hegemony over the other" (Brownlie, 1990, p. 57). Subject appropriateness, state responsibility (and commitment) on the specific issue, and the clarity of rules of international law regarding their applicability are among the determinants of any conflicts of interpretation in the two systems on a given issue. The relation between domestic laws and international public law is clarified by the 1969 Vienna Convention on the Law of Treaties, especially in its Article 27: "A party may not invoke the provisions of its internal law as justification for its failure to perform a treaty. This rule is without prejudice to article 46." The latter states that

> 1. A State may not invoke the fact that its consent to be bound by a treaty has been expressed in violation of provision of its internal law regarding competence to conclude treaties as invalidating its consent unless that violation was manifest and concerned a rule of its internal law of fundamental importance. 2. A violation is manifest if it would be objectively evident to any State conducting itself in the matter in accordance with normal practice and good faith.

In the context of regional and domestic laws, EC Treaty Article 177 (ex. 130u) binds the EC member countries as a whole to the obligation that "[t]he Community and the Member States shall comply with the commitments and take account of the objectives they have approved in the context of the United Nations and other competent international organizations."

Some international treaties specify signatory states' obligations and the law-making roles of their respective national legislatures in the implementation of the particular treaty. For example, the UN Convention on the Law of the Sea specifies such a role in its Article 207 (1). A number of other treaties prescribe specific performance standards and/or norms of conduct for each of the participating states. Each stipulation (and a vector of such stipulations for each treaty or convention)

BOX 4.8

International treaties and US law

The definition of treaty for international law purposes is broader than that found in the US Constitution. In the US, treaties are defined in domestic law as international agreements entered into with the advice and consent of two-thirds of the Senate. The United States could enter into some international agreements that are treaties in the international sense but not necessarily in the US constitutional sense. Some of those agreements are entered into by the Executive Branch on its own authority and some by the Executive with the concurrence of both Houses of Congress.

The Vienna Convention is in force for about 90 states, not including the United States. A stalemate exists between Congress and the Executive Branch over the allocation of authority between the two branches to enter into and terminate international agreements (treaties in the international sense) on behalf of the United States. Often, the Executive Branch negotiates agreements that are intended to be binding, without the consent of two-thirds of the Senate. These agreements are entered into with the concurrence of a simple majority of both Houses of Congress ("Congressional–Executive agreements") in cases where concurrence may be given either before or after the Executive Branch negotiates the agreement. The extent of the President's authority to enter into Sole Executive agreements is controversial (see also Congressional Research Service Study of Treaties and Other International Agreements: The Role of the United States Senate (Senate Foreign Relations Committee Print No. 103–53, 1993)).

Provisions in treaties and other international agreements are given effect as law in domestic courts of the United States only if they are "self-executing" or if they have been implemented by an act of Congress having the effect of federal law. Some of the provisions in an international agreement could be self-executing while others in the same agreement are not. Even if a treaty or other international agreement is nonself-executing, it may have an indirect effect in US courts. International treaties and Congressional–Executive agreements are somewhat interchangeable.

Kontou (1996) examined the problem in the US situation created by the coming into effect of a rule of customary law that runs contrary to an existing treaty provision: the Law of the Sea Treaty signed in 1982, together with its failure to achieve enough ratifications to cause it to come into effect before 1994. A treaty under the US Constitution requires the agreement of two-thirds of the Senate, and even a presidential/executive agreement needs a vote of both Houses of Congress. Yet a President can determine that a new customary rule has formed and that the United States should adhere to it. An example of this occurred in 1993 when President Reagan proclaimed a 200-mile exclusive economic zone. The judiciary also has some power to declare customary law as part of the law.

at the international level needs to be juxtaposed with the related (if not entirely parallel or isomorphic mapping) of domestic laws. It is often the case that several international treaties do not automatically translate themselves into national laws, and this is largely because many gaps are deliberately (and sometimes inadvertently) left out in treaties, leaving a "menu" of options at the national level. A useful classification of international treaty obligations is provided by Ebbesson (1996). The distinguishing features of these obligations are: (1) balancing norms (for example, the choice of so-called best available technology, BAT); (2) prohibitions on certain pollutant emissions or on the consumption of banned/restricted items; (3) target-based environmental management, as in the case of reductions of greenhouse gases under the Kyoto Protocol; (4) standards seeking national regulation of hazardous wastes or other pollutants; and (5) maintaining a level playing field without discrimination, as stipulated for the trade–environment measures under the World Trade Organization. The milieu of state-specific features of political economy, economic, and environmental factors determines the resultant implications of IEL on domestic environmental law and enforcement.

In the US, the domestic implications of international treaty laws are rather complex in their constitutional and legal provisions. Box 4.8 highlights some of the issues in this regard.

■ 4.8 SUMMARY

IEL has made extensive use of soft law, and it is a matter of pragmatism whether soft law gradually evolves into hard law. Besides, the most important role of soft law is to affect state parties' behavioral expectations and to induce behavioral conformity over time. The risk of having no law at all or of undertaking protracted negotiations entailing long time intervals and high transaction costs is greater if comprehensive hard laws were insisted on all the time, or in the early stages of international environmental regulation. Although treaty development based on consensus among parties remains a useful method of devising international environmental legislation, more innovative methods of IEL may be required to move toward "stream-lined international rule-making" rather than traditional principles of unanimity (Dunoff, 1995). The risk of a small number of powerful nations steering the global agenda should, however, be minimized in order to ensure a wider acceptance and compliance of environmental norms. The Montreal Protocol (see chapter 6) provides an innovation of an expeditious decision-making feature. The Protocol provides for periodic review of and changes to any provisions, and also for the following decision-making mechanism (Article 2 (9) (c)):

> In taking such decisions, the Parties shall make every effort to reach agreement by consensus. If all efforts at consensus have been exhausted, and no agreement reached, such decisions shall, as a last resort, be adopted by a two-thirds majority vote of the Parties present and voting representing at least fifty percent of the total consumption of the con-trolled substances of the Parties.

It remains crucial for treaty implementation that proper informa-tion regarding compliance with the treaty obligations is available from participating states in a time-bound manner. Most treaties, however, meet with the opposite: reporting requirements are weak and where they do exist, compliance with these requirements is even weaker. The design of treaties needs to consider, in an integrated framework, information-reporting systems as well. This could form part of an *ex post* cost-minimizing approach. The application of transaction cost economics would suggest this provision.

Review Exercises

1 The US Restatement of Foreign Relations Section 102 (1) states: "A rule of international law is one that has been accepted as such by the international community of states: a) in the form of customary law; b) by international agreement; or c) by derivation from general principles common to the major legal systems of the world." Discuss the following aspects of this definition:

(i) in the evolution of the rule of international law. Is there a potential tradeoff between the number of states practicing a law or agreement or legal norm, and the time period of state practices?

(ii) in the example of the precautionary principle. Is this definition sufficient in its scope and intent to qualify the PP as a rule of international law?

2 Discuss the validity or the limitations of the assertion that CIL, by definition, "arises from decentralized and noninstitutionalized state acts."

3 What role do transaction costs play in the formation and implementation of international treaties?

4 How is the international treaty dealt with in the US government in so far as the domestic laws are concerned, and in the international legal standing of government activities? Explain the relative roles of the Executive Branch of the US government and the US Congress in the ratification of different categories of international treaties.

5 Discuss the role and limitations of "reservations" in their contributions to (a) formation of legal instruments; (b) effectiveness of international laws; and (c) *ex ante* revelation of *ex post* intentions of treaty compliance.

6 Explain the role of international relations theory in the development of IEL, with special reference to the features of sovereignty and strategic behavior.

7 Elucidate the role of economic analysis in Principle 15 of the Rio Declaration: "In order to protect the environment, the precautionary approach shall be widely applied by States according to their capabilities. Where there are threats of serious or irreversible damage, lack of full scientific certainty shall not be used as a reason for postponing cost-effective measures to prevent environmental degradation."

8 Discuss the common and distinguishing features of soft law and hard law in international public law systems. Explain the role of transaction cost economics in the formation of the two components of the law.

REFERENCES

Abbott, K. W., 1989, Modern international relations theory: A prospectus for international lawyers, *Yale Journal of International Law*, 14, 335–411.

Abbott, K. W., 1993, "Trust but verify": The production of information in arms control treaties and other international agreements, *Cornell International Law Journal*, 26, 1–35.

Abbott, K. W., 1999, International relations theory, international law, and the regime governing atrocities in international conflicts, *American Journal of International Law*, 93, 361–78.

Aceves, W. J., 1996, An economic analysis of international law: Transaction cost economics and the concept of state practice, *University of Pennsylvania Journal of International Economic Law*, 17, 995–1068.

Akermark, S. S., 1999, Reservation clauses in treaties concluded within the Council of Europe, *International and Comparative Law Quarterly*, 48, 479–514.

Barrett, S., 1997, The strategy of trade sanctions in international environmental agreements, *Resource and Energy Economics*, 19, 345–61.

Batabyal, A. A., 2000, On the design of international environmental agreements for identical and heterogeneous developing countries, *Oxford Economic Papers*, 52, 560–83.

Bhala, R., 1999, The myth about *stare decisis* and international trade law, *American University International Law Review*, 14, 845–956.

Bilder, R. B., 1981, *Managing the Risks of International Agreements*, Wisconsin: University of Wisconsin Press.

Bos, M., 1980, Theory and practice of treaty interpretation, *Netherlands International Law Review*, 27, 135–70.

Boyle, A. and Anderson, M. (eds.), 1996, *Human Rights Approaches to Environmental Protection*, Oxford: Clarendon Press.

Brownlie, I., 1990, *Principles of Public International Law*, Oxford: Clarendon Press.

Buergenthal, T. and Maier, H. G., 1990, *Public International Law*, St. Paul: West Publishing.

Burley, A., 1993, International law and international relations theory: A dual agenda, *American Journal of International Law*, 87, 205–32.

Carter, B. E. and Trimble, P. R., 1995, *International Law*, Boston: Little, Brown.

Chayes, A. and Chayes, A. H., 1995, *The New Sovereignty: Compliance with International Regulatory Agreements*, Cambridge, MA: Harvard University Press.

Churchill, R. R. and Lowe, A. V., 1988, *The Law of the Sea*, Manchester: Manchester University Press.

Colburn, J. E., 1997, Turbot wars: Straddling stocks, regime theory, and new UN agreement, *Florida State University Journal of Transnational Law and Policy*, 6, 323.

Craik, A. N., 1998, Recalcitrant reality and chosen ideals: The public function of dispute settlement in international environmental law, *Georgetown International Environmental Law Review*, 10, 551–80.

Degagne, R., 1995, Integrating environmental values into the European Convention on Human Rights, *American Journal of International Law*, 89, 263–94.

Dunoff, J. L., 1995, From green to global: Toward the transformation of international environmental law, *Harvard Environmental Law Review*, 19, 241–301.

Dunoff, J. L. and Trachtman, J. P., 1999, Economic analysis of international law, *Yale Journal of International Law*, 24, 1–59.

Ebbesson, J., 1996, *Compatibility of International and National Environmental Law*, The Hague: Kluwer Law International.

Goldsmith, J. L. and Posner, E. A., 1998, Notes toward a theory of customary international law, *Proceedings of the 92nd Annual Meeting of the American Society of International Law*, Washington, DC: American Society of International Law.

Goldsmith, J. L. and Posner, E. A., 1999, A theory of customary international law, *University of Chicago Law Review*, 66, 1113–77.

Greig, D. W., 1994, Reciprocity, proportionality, and the Law of Treaties, *Virginia Journal of International Law*, 34, 295–344.

Harvard Law Review Association (HLRA), 1991, Developments in the law: International environmental law, *Harvard Law Review*, 104, 1484–1639.

Heinzerling, L., 1999, Environmental law and the present future, *Georgetown Law Journal*, 87, 2025–78.

Hillgenberg, H., 1999, A fresh look at soft law, *European Journal of International Law*, 10, 499–516.

Hohmann, H., 1994, *Precautionary Legal Duties and Principles of Modern International Environmental Law*, London: Graham and Trotman.

Keohane, R. O., 1988, International institutions: Two approaches, *International Studies Quarterly*, 32, 379–98.

Knack, S. and Keefer, P., 1997, Does social capital have an economic payoff? A cross country investigation, *Quarterly Journal of Economics*, 112, 1251–88.

Koh, H. H., 1997, Why do nations obey international law?, *Yale Law Journal*, 106, 2599–2659.

Kontou, N., 1996, *The Termination and Revision of Treaties in the Light of New Customary International Law*, New York: Oxford University Press.

Kostritsky, J. P., 1993, Bargaining with uncertainty, moral hazard, and sunk costs: A default rule for precontractual negotiations, *Hastings Law Review*, 44, 621–45.

Krasner, D., 1982, Structural causes and regime consequences: Regimes as intervening variables, *International Organization*, 36, 185–206.

McIntyre, O. and Mosedale, T., 1997, The precautionary principle as a norm of customary international law, *Journal of Environmental Law*, 9, 221–41.

McNair, Lord A., 1961, *The Law of Treaties*, Oxford: Clarendon Press.

Milner, H., 1991, The assumption of anarchy in international relations theory: A critique, *Review of International Studies*, 17, 67–89.

Mus, J. B., 1998, Conflicts between treaties in international law, *Netherlands International Law Review*, 45, 208–32.

Perrez, F. X., 1996, The relationship between "permanent sovereignty" and the obligation not to cause transboundary environmental damage, *Environmental Law*, 26, 1187–1212.

Petrakis, E. and Xepapadeas, A., 1996, Environmental consciousness and moral hazard in international agreements to protect the environment, *Journal of Public Economics*, 60, 95–110.

Ress, G., 1994, *Ex ante* safeguards against *ex post* opportunism in international treaties: Theory and practice of international public law, *Journal of Institutional and Theoretical Economics*, 150, 279–303.

Schlicht, E., 1993, On custom, *Journal of Institutional and Theoretical Economics*, 149, 178–97.

Schmidt, R. J., 1996, International negotiations paralyzed by domestic politics: Two-level game theory and the problem of the Pacific Salmon Commission, *Northwestern Environmental Law Review*, 26, 95–123.

Setear, J. K., 1996, An iterative perspective on treaties: A synthesis of international relations theory and international law, *Harvard International Law Journal*, 37, 139.

Setear, J. K., 1997, Responses to breach of a treaty and rationalist international relations theory: The rules of release and remediation in the Law of Treaties and the Law of State Responsibility, *Virginia Law Review*, 83, 1–126.

Slaughter, A.-M., Tulumello, A. S., and Wood, S., 1998, International law and international relations theory: A new generation of interdisciplinary scholarship, *American Journal of International Law*, 92, 367–97.

Snidal, D., 1985, The game theory of international politics, *World Politics*, 38, 25–42.

Snidal, D., 1996, Political economy and international institutions, *International Review of Law and Economics*, 16, 121–38.

Stein, A. A., 1982, Coordination and collaboration: Regimes in an anarchic world, *International Organization*, 36, 279–99.

Stein, T. L., 1985, The approach of the different drummer: The principle of the persistent objector in international law, *Harvard International Law Journal*, 26, 457–80.

Stephan, P. B., 1997, Accountability and international lawmaking: Rules, rents and legitimacy, *Northwestern Journal of International Law and Business*, 17, 681–705.

United Nations (UN), 1962, *The Status of Permanent Sovereignty over Natural Wealth and Resources*, New York: UN Secretariat (UN Doc. A/AC.97/5/Rev. 2, 1962).

Weiss, E. B., 1993, International environmental law: Contemporary issues and the emergence of a new world order, *Georgetown Law Journal*, 81, 675–710.

Williamson, O. E., 1985, *The Economic Institutions of Capitalism*, New York: Free Press.

Wolf, A., 1997, *Quotas in International Environmental Agreements*, London: Earthscan Publications.

chapter five

Biological Resources and Environmental Laws

■ 5.1 INTRODUCTION

The danger of irreversibility and/or biological species extinction affects biological resources. It can never be known which of the species that have been lost might have contributed to one or more beneficial uses via ecological services, including biomedical applications for human health. When a specific biospecies becomes extinct, it is not just that species that the planet loses; the impact is felt on the ecological equilibrium, given the existence of strong ecological interdependencies. Many of the concepts and principles of ecology and ecological economics presented in chapters 1 and 3 are relevant in this context. Biophilia (see chapter 1) is a relevant background norm for the management of biotic resources. This chapter rejects the staunchly anthropocentric proposal that "animals count, but only insofar as they enhance wealth" (Posner, 1981, p. 76), unless the concept of wealth explicitly includes environmental assets (not necessarily subject to evaluation using market factors). In the absence of a comprehensive measure of wealth and in due recognition of the role of interrelationships among genetic resources (and hence the role of genetic diversity), such proposals lack merit.

Several international environmental agreements and corresponding laws in the area of biological species have been devised for about a century with the objective of biological conservation and preservation of biological diversity. Their effectiveness has been somewhat limited, but the efforts have not been of marginal significance. Trade-restrictive measures to regulate the international transfer and commercialization of biological species were among the first to be used in a range of environmental trade measures seeking to protect the ecology and the environment on a global scale. There continue to be several impediments in the specifications and implementation of rules in respect of many of the related laws. Enhanced global cooperation, in addition to the provision of stringent legal measures, is seen as a prerequisite for effective biological conservation and sustenance of biodiversity.

This chapter provides significant features of the relevant agreements and other global accords. Biological resources of land and sea are considered almost equally important. Preventive and mitigating aspects of various international actions are also examined. Some international agreements (for example, the 1982 UN Convention on the Law of the Sea) sought to include ecological integrity concepts in some of their provisions. As the theory of contracts in chapter 2 suggests, even the most "comprehensive" treaty remains "inevitably incomplete" and requires "gaps" to be filled as they are observed with state practice. The practice aspects of some international treaties are also summarized in this chapter. Further details on compliance and effectiveness are presented in chapter 9.

■ 5.2 BIOLOGICAL CONSERVATION AND CITES

The UN Educational, Social, and Cultural Organization (UNESCO) was one of the earliest initiators of global attention to biospheric aspects of the environment. In 1968, UNESCO convened the first Biosphere Conference, the Intergovernmental Conference of Experts on the Scientific Basis for Rational Use and Conservation of the Resources of the Biosphere, held at Paris (UNESCO Doc. SC/MD/9, 1969). The Stockholm Conference in 1972 emphasized, among other things, in its Principle 3, the need for international cooperation in maintaining the "capacity of the earth to produce vital renewable resources."

Wildlife and nature conservation are among the oldest subjects of bilateral and multilateral agreements between states. Some of the early regional agreements (before 1990) on bioconservation and biodiversity include the following:

- 1911 Convention for the Preservation and Protection of Fur Seals
- 1940 Washington Convention on Nature Protection and Wildlife Preservation in the Western Hemisphere
- 1951 Convention for the Establishment of a European and Mediterranean Plant Protection Organization

- 1966 Rio International Convention for the Conservation of Atlantic Tunas (ICCAT)
- 1971 Ramsar Convention on Wetlands of International Importance Especially as Waterfowl Habitat
- 1972 Bonn Convention on the Conservation of Migratory Species
- 1976 Washington Convention on the Conservation of North Pacific Fur Seals
- 1979 Berne Convention on the Conservation of European Wildlife and Natural Habitat
- 1980 Convention on the Conservation of Antarctic Marine Living Resources (CCAMLR), formed as a part of the 1959 Antarctic Treaty System
- 1985 ASEAN Agreement on the Conservation of Nature and Natural Resources

The 1971 Ramsar Convention was the first global attempt to seek agreements on habitat-based biological conservation. Under this treaty, parties agreed to promote "wise use" of all wetlands. The draft for the agreement was prepared by the International Waterfowl Research Bureau (IWRB) and the International Union for the Conservation of Nature and Natural Resources (IUCN). The parties included very few non-European countries. Financial resource limitations are among the weaknesses of the provisions' implementation, and also the agreement's expansion or integration of more parties.

The 1972 Bonn Convention was promoted by the Federal Republic of Germany on the basis of a draft report prepared by the IUCN. It came into force in 1983. The Convention seeks to protect endangered migratory species by imposing obligations on states where the species normally live. For species in Appendix I of the Convention, states must "endeavor" to take a set of measures to protect the habitats of these species. This has been considered the weakest provision of a soft law, where the aim is simply to "endeavor," with no specific targets and goals or means of achievement or monitoring implementation being set out.

Convention on International Trade in Endangered Species (CITES)

The 1973 Washington Convention on International Trade in Endangered Species of Wild Fauna and Flora (CITES) emphasizes environmental trade measures. CITES entered into force on July 1, 1975. Its preamble recognizes, *inter alia*, that wild fauna and flora in their many beautiful and varied forms are an irreplaceable part of the natural systems of the earth which must be protected for this and the generations to come; the ever-growing value of wild fauna and flora from aesthetic, scientific, cultural, recreational and economic points of view; that international co-operation is essential for the protection of certain species of wild fauna and flora against over-exploitation through international trade.

Article X allows trade (but does not obligate it) with nonparties on the basis of "comparable documentation . . . substantially conforming" with the permits of the Convention. The Convention prohibits international trade in species that are faced with the threat of extinction; these are listed in Appendix I of the Convention as "all species threatened with extinction which are or may be affected by trade." The Convention restricts trade for species listed in its Appendix II, as it was deemed that unrestricted trade could critically diminish their survival potential: "although not necessarily now threatened with extinction, [they] may become so unless trade in specimens of such species is subject to strict regulation in order to avoid utilization incompatible with their survival."

Appendix III contains a list of species that a party identifies as subject to regulation within its jurisdiction and in need of cooperative measures for protection, in accordance with Article II of the Convention. Imports from states that are not parties to the Convention are allowed only if the importers produce the documentation required under CITES. The CITES Secretariat is among the largest of the international Convention Secretariats (relative to others, some of which have a couple of employees as their full-time staff), and this factor contributes to its effectiveness. As Lang (1993) noted, its effectiveness is also due to the obligation to trade with nonparties on the same basis as parties, which provides incentives for nonparties to accede to the Convention. Sand (1997, p. 57) noted that precautionary trade measures were "feasible and necessary . . . to prevent a 'free-rider' dilemma lest unilateral bans penalize individual importing or exporting countries *vis-à-vis* their less scrupulous competitors."

The First Conference of Parties to CITES held in Berne in 1976 led to what are called the Berne Criteria. These included two resolutions, Conf. 1.1 and Conf, 1.2, which detailed criteria for adding species to and removing them from Appendices I and II. Conf. 1.2 required that listing and delisting be treated asymmetrically. It stated:

Criteria for deletion or transfer should require positive scientific evidence that the plant or animal can withstand the exploitation resulting from the removal of protection. This evidence must transcend informal or lay evidence of changing biological status and any evidence of commercial trade which may have been sufficient to require the animal or plant to be placed on an appendix initially.

At the Ninth Conference of Parties of CITES in 1994, the precautionary principle (PP) (see chapter 3) was endorsed for the first time, in a rather restricted way. This resolution, known as Conf. 9.24, proposed additional guidelines for any amendments to Appendices I and II of the Convention. Conf. 9.24 adopted the PP in the following clauses:

> Recognizing that by virtue of the precautionary principle, in cases of uncertainty, the Parties shall act in the best interest of the conservation of the species when considering proposals for amendment of Appendices I and II; Resolves that when considering any proposal to amend Appendix I or II the Parties shall apply the precautionary principle so that scientific uncertainty should not be used as a reason for failing to act in the best interest of the conservation of the species.

CITES is a nonself-executing treaty and cannot be implemented until specific legislation has been adopted by each member. This basic obligation of the enactment of appropriate national legislation, set forth in Article VIII of the Convention, has not been fulfilled by a majority of parties. According to a 1993 report by IUCN–World Conservation Union (see OECD, 1997), around 85 percent of CITES parties have incomplete or otherwise inadequate legislation for implementing the Convention. Common deficiencies observed in national legislation include, *inter alia*, the absence of appropriate penalties to deter infractions and the limited coverage of species listed in the Appendices. The failure to adopt domestic legislative and regulatory measures prevents parties from adopting the required trade measures envisaged under CITES. This inaction resulted in a number of instances of noncompliance in some of the member states, regarding the issue of export permits for Appendix I species before an import permit was obtained, and related aspects. The absence of a legal framework for implementing CITES also constrains the parties' ability to monitor trade in species. According to Article VIII.7, parties are required to provide the Convention Secretariat with an annual report containing a summary of all records of trade in specimens included in the Appendices. But widespread noncompliance has been identified as a major problem of implementing the Convention. Between 1986 and 1991, for instance, no more than 40 percent of parties submitted their reports on time

(OECD, 1997). The dispute resolution mechanisms under CITES are very weak and largely ineffective. The nonbinding nature of obligations tends to enfeeble the spirit of the Convention (see also Bacon, 1999).

An issue of importance is the state's obligations in biological species trade in relation to the provisions of the World Trade Organization (WTO), which came into existence based on an agreement of 1994, and in conjunction with those of CITES. Some WTO members are also parties to CITES, and there are a few WTO members that are not parties to CITES. For WTO members that are also parties to CITES, CITES provisions could prevail according to the principles of customary international law, with the application of the Vienna Law of Treaties (see chapter 4). According to this view, when two agreements signed by the same parties relating to the same subject matter are in conflict, the agreement later in time (*lex posterior*) is presumed to prevail.

Thus, CITES provisions could have been held to have prevailed over any conflicting GATT provisions for as long as CITES postdated the original 1947 GATT Agreement (OECD, 1997). However, Article II.4 of the WTO Agreement clarifies that it is a legally distinct agreement: "The General Agreement on Tariffs and Trade 1994 is legally distinct from the General Agreement on Tariffs and Trade dated 30 October 1947." It appears that GATT 1994 now postdates CITES, with the interpretation that a *lex posterior* approach is no longer possible. It may be argued that *lex specialis* would be applicable (despite CITES preceding GATT 1994) because specific environmental agreements are not broad-based as in the GATT. Under the principle of *lex specialis*, the more specific of two agreements tends to control, overriding an application of the *lex posterior* feature. These issues remain relevant for more years to come and are subject to interpretation in specific combinations of agreements and their provisions. (For more on the interface between trade and the environment, and on dispute resolution, see chapters 8 and 9, respectively.)

In the US, separate legislation was enacted which essentially embraces the CITES provisions. Highlights of this Endangered Species Act are provided in box 5.1.

Under Article 189 of the 1992 Treaty of the European Union (EU), a regulation of the European Community (EC) is "binding in its entirety and directly applicable in all Member States." In addition, the EU sought to ensure harmonization of the implementation of CITES by requiring its members to withdraw reservations for listed species that they held under Articles XV (3) and XVI (2) of the Convention; all EU members that are already parties to CITES complied.

BOX 5.1

Endangered Species Act, USA

The US Endangered Species Act (ESA) of 1973 is considered very comprehensive among environmental laws. CITES is implemented in the US through the ESA. In section 2 of the ESA, it was recognized that species have "ecological, educational, historical, recreational and scientific value" and that these aspects are not properly reflected in accounting for economic growth and development. The ESA and its amendments did recognize the role of integrated approaches to species conservation by adopting the notions of ecosystems and ecological interdependencies. In enacting this law, the US Congress opined that it was not a matter of economics to list endangered species and their habitats for protection. The US Supreme Court expressed a similar opinion, after examining the legislative intent: "the value of endangered species is incalculable" and "it is clear from the Act's legislative history that Congress intended to halt and reverse the trend toward species extinction – whatever the cost" (437 US 187, 184, 1978).

Despite the legislative rhetoric, there remain operational constraints in the effective implementation of the provisions of the ESA, primarily due to (1) suboptimal budgetary resource allocations at the government level; and (2) lack of further amendments to the ESA that allow some calculation of benefits and costs in order to decide on further action or inaction. Under 1978 amendments (Section 4) to the ESA, the Secretary of the Interior may "take into consideration the economic impact, and any other relevant impact, of specifying any particular area as critical habitat," and could exclude such a specification "unless failure to designate leads to extinction."

Under the ESA, private parties cannot "take" a listed species; the definition of "take" includes "to harass, harm, . . . wound." Habitat modification is considered a form of "harm." Brown and Shogren (1998) observed that government funding for the endangered species program of the Fish and Wildlife Service (the nodal agency for implementing the ESA) failed to keep pace with the number of listed species, leading to the result that after a quarter century of operation, the real budget per species dropped to 60 percent of its 1976 level. The roles of cost-effectiveness of alternate choices and decision-making under uncertainty with incomplete information have yet to be fully utilized in the governance of the activities contemplated under the ESA.

Regarding the role of economic analyses relevant for the implementation of various provisions of the Act, Brown and Shogren (1998) suggested that (1) in accordance with the Act's emphasis on an ecosystems approach rather than a species approach, economic incentives may be designed to protect or preserve ecosystems that cut across public and private lands; this approach itself may be based on identifying critical habitats for listed and unlisted species (given their ecological interdependencies); (2) economic factors (including land-use changes and spatial development) which affect potential species extinction could be identified. At the international level, the corresponding imperatives clearly suggest the need for international cooperation (and the provision of incentives for the conservation of habitats), public and private sector cooperation in each country, and a recognition of the principles of sustainable development.

However, the regulation under EU applies only to the European territory of member states, except for France, where it applies also to France's overseas departments. The overseas possessions of Denmark, the Netherlands, and the UK do not form part of the territory of those states or of the Community, and thus form separate customs regions for the inapplicability of CITES (see, for details, Burns and Mosedale, 1997). The Secretariat Report of CITES (Doc. 9.23 of November 1994) on the implementation in the EU observed rather widespread irregularities in compliance measures relating to reexport permits.

International trade policies have a major impact on the earth's biodiversity, potentially interfering with and undermining national and international conservation laws and policies. Trade liberalization can also increase exploitation of natural resources and exacerbate the associated negative impacts on biodiversity. Trade in rare wildlife species is thought to be the second or third most lucrative illegal trade in the world. Since 1992, the Center for International Environmental Law (CIEL) has advocated strong and realistic implementation of the Biodiversity Action Network (BIONET), a network of nongovernmental organizations (NGOs) that CIEL launched in 1993 in cooperation with the Sierra Club and other US environmental groups.

The conservation of biological species, focusing on endangered and potentially endangered species (with an emphasis on environmental trade measures, as in the case of CITES), addresses some of the issues involved in the sustainable management of biological resources. A broader aspect relates to the management of biological diversity, where the concept of "optimal biodiversity" is deemed to coincide with that of maximal biodiversity. The imperative of genetic diversity in the preservation of species is the key factor supporting such a concept, combined with the unknown risks and irreversibility involved in the loss of biodiversity. The next section deals with international agreements in relation to these areas of concern.

5.3 BIOLOGICAL DIVERSITY AND THE CONVENTION ON BIOLOGICAL DIVERSITY (CBD)

The potential value of future uses of biotic species (in medicine, agriculture, or other) is an anthropocentric consideration which extends to support the preservation of biodiversity. Even when there are some priority species in terms of their importance in uses for humans, their interdependencies often suggest the need to maintain all species. The economic question of "optimal biodiversity" and prioritization of species for preservation cannot be addressed without sufficient clarity about the relative future roles of different ecological and economic factors in welfare maximization forever in a sustainable sense. What can, however, be attempted is to devise cost-effective methods of broad-based conservation strategies. These include finding an optimal mix of policy instruments and information catering to these objectives, attainable at least total cost. Technical models of "optimal biotic resource exploitation" are often advocated in the context of neoclassical economic models (see, for example, van Kooten and Bulte, 2000).

Formal models also extend to the evaluation of welfare implications with and without an ivory trade ban to the states/societies affected by these alternatives. These formulations (optimization models) lead to so-called "optimal elephant stocks." However, most conclusions are based on a series of explicit and implicit assumptions; the latter simply shift the original problem to another arena and fall short of solutions that lead to robust policy prescriptions. It has already been noted in chapter 3 that the specification of time preferences and discount rates in the evaluation of future resources is a critical issue in most policy prescriptions. After considerable analytical and empirical investigations, van Kooten and Bulte (2000) observed that "[w]hether a trade ban is effective in achieving its goal of species preservation or enhancement depends crucially on the discount rate, which is an object of a country's macro-economic policies, as much as it is on the intervention by the international community to protect wildlife species" (p. 335). In addition, several unknowns and uncertainties obscure specific answers to the issue of "optimal stocks." A number of qualitative prescriptions can be made, however. These include alternative measures of species protection and their relative cost-effectiveness, provided there is a policy precommitment to preserve species and apply sound principles such as the precautionary principle (see chapter 3).

The public trust doctrine provides a rationale and legal precedent for placing ecological protection above private property rights, as argued by Hurlbut (1994, p. 398). This doctrine has been advocated in some court opinions, for example: "the duty of the state [is] to protect the people's common heritage of streams, lakes, marshlands and tidelands, surrendering that right of protection only in rare cases when the abandonment of that right is consistent with the purposes of the trust" (*National Audubon Society v. Superior Court of Alpine County*, 658 P.2d 709 (Cal. 1983)). Ecological interdependence and the requirements of ecological sustainability are fundamental features that necessitate policy action to safeguard biological resources rather than leaving them to the tyranny of market forces.

Edward Wilson (1992) rightly argued that "biodiversity is the key to the maintenance of the world as we know it." It takes several hundred thousand years to build rich ecosystems and their biodiversity. The term biodiversity seemed not to formally exist until the 1986 National Forum on Biodiversity under the auspices of the US National Academy of Sciences and the Smithsonian Institution. Biodiversity is defined by the UN Environment Program (UNEP, 1992) as "the genetic, taxonomic, and ecological variability among living organisms; this includes the variety and variability within species, between species, and of biotic components of ecosystems." It is the high diversity that ensures continuity and functioning of the ecosystem, food web, and human survival (Patrick, 1997).

Biodiversity is but one major segment of ecosystem services. These services include the conditions and processes through which natural ecosystems, and the species that make them up, sustain and fulfill human life (see Daily, 1997). New discoveries in medicine and life sciences are amongst the most important factors relevant in an appreciation of biodiversity's contribution to human society. A number of studies have tried to estimate the monetary values of medicinal plants and biodiversity for pharmaceutical and medical use (see, for example, Balick et al., 1996). These estimates vary, but the order of magnitude is several billion dollars, with or without accounting for other uses or values of biodiversity. In general, the net commercial value of plant genetic-based or other biotic resources remains very high both in the short run and in the long run. At a general level, the economic principle of conservation would require that the optimal level of biotic conservation would seek to equate marginal social cost of conservation with marginal social benefit (see, for example, Batabyal, 2000). However, this principle (akin to a canonical norm of much economic reasoning) is easier to proclaim than to undertake. The reason, aside from institutional lacunae, is the lack of estimates of the relevant costs and benefits in an ecosystem (and interlinked ecosystems), with several unknowns and uncertainties about current and future states of parameters and valuation. In order to reduce the complexity of information requirements, a pragmatic measure should seek to use cost-effective methods of biological conservation. This method requires a separate assessment of the level of conservation, based largely on ecological principles. The two exercises can be made in an iterative manner by examining the cost implications of desirable alternative measures of species conservation and selecting a pragmatic combination package consisting of cost/budget and the corresponding conservation level. Activities such as bioprospecting, undertaken by different entities, should then form part of an overall package and resources should be utilized from a mix of sharable rents and public fiscal financial resources. Several unknowns and uncertainties continue to affect the "optimal resource management" of bioresources even with these approaches, but the information requirements are considerably reduced when compared with those required to invoke equalization of marginal cost and marginal benefit, the typical rule of industrial economic activity. Let us note that such a rule generally ignores the long-term noncommercial values of resources, and tends to be misguided by the undue influence of incomplete markets and the lesser influence of missing markets.

Biodiversity is perhaps the most important segment of what is generally referred to as the ecosystem and its management, which integrates ecological, economic, and social factors of human and other life forms on the planet; it is a strongly interconnected system of earthdwellers, including humans. A general goal of ecosystem management is defined in the US Government Interagency Ecosystem Management Task Force (1995): "to restore and sustain the health, productivity, and biological diversity of ecosystems and overall quality of life through a natural resource management approach that is fully integrated with social and economic goals."

At the global level, the most significant modern environmental law in biological resources arises from the 1992 Convention on Biological Diversity (CBD). This Convention was adopted at Nairobi on May 22, 1992 and signed at Rio de Janeiro on June 5, 1992. More than 165 countries (including the EC) are parties to the Convention (excluding, among others, the USA). The Convention entered into force on December 29, 1993. The CBD defined "biodiversity" as "[t]he variability among living organisms from all sources including, inter alia, terrestrial, marine and other aquatic ecosystems and the ecological complexes of which they are part." These "ecological complexes" include diversity within species, between species, and of ecosystems, and correlate to genetic diversity, species diversity, and ecosystem diversity. UNEP (1995) summarized the definition as the variety of the world's organisms, including their genetic makeup and the communities they form.

The Convention deploys methods of action, including rules for the international transfer of genetic material defined as "material of plant, animal, microbial or other origin containing functional units of heredity – of actual or potential value." The Convention includes provisions for both *ex situ* and *in situ* conservation. The former refers to the conservation of biological materials outside their natural habitats (such as gene preservation), and the latter describes the conservation of ecosystems and their natural habitats for the maintenance of species in their natural settings. Among the important provisions of the Convention is its imposition of legal responsibility on states for the environmental impact of their activities (including those of private entities in their jurisdiction) in other states.

The Convention is viewed as an important landmark for the following reasons: (1) the genetic level of biodiversity was considered for the first time at a global level; (2) it recognized the existence of an unequal burden among countries, and that countries with the greatest biotic resources do not necessarily have the greatest available resources for protecting them; and (3) it explicitly advocated the need for global coordination, with financial and technological resources from the industrial countries. Some of the major highlights of the Convention's provisions are set out below.

Article 1 of the CBD (see www.untreaty.un.org; 31 ILM 23, 1992) states:

> The objectives of this Convention, to be pursued in accordance with its relevant provisions, are the conservation of biological diversity, the sustainable use of its components and the fair and equitable sharing of

the benefits arising out of the utilization of genetic resources, including by appropriate access to genetic resources and by appropriate transfer of relevant technologies, taking into account all rights over those resources and to technologies, and by appropriating funds.

Short of any details, the principle of "fair and equitable sharing of benefits" remains a largely nonactionable specification thus far. As discussed later, the bioprospecting and rent-seeking aspects of genetic resource exploitation, combined with misappropriations of indigenous knowledge in the use of biological products, stand out as areas of global discontent (especially between developing and developed countries). The UN (1997) paper outlined a number of unresolved and somewhat contentious issues arising out of the CBD, including the lack of clarity on so-called benefit-sharing among parties in respect of any biological exploration of a commercial nature and the use of indigenous knowledge (usually not patented), and iniquitous intellectual property regimes (IPR) possibly unsuitable for the potential process and product markets of biological products.

Article 3 of the CBD declares that:

> States have, in accordance with the Charter of the United Nations and the principles of international law, the sovereign right to exploit their own resources pursuant to their own environmental policies, and the responsibility to ensure that activities within their jurisdiction or control do not cause damage to the environment of other States or of areas beyond the limits of their national jurisdiction.

This is merely a reassertion of Principle 21 of the Stockholm Declaration and may be interpreted as a movement of the previous soft law into hard law.

Article 5 relates to cooperation on matters of transboundary externalities: "Parties shall cooperate in respect of areas beyond national jurisdiction and on other matters of mutual interest, for conservation and sustainable utilization of biodiversity." The economics of unequal mutual interest remains the key issue here. When parties do not have an equal interest in a specific species the role of cooperation is to be devised in a strategic interactive sense, with cross-linkages to other species and factors of cooperation.

Article 8 (c) sets out a provision regarding the management of biological resources for conservation and sustainable use. It states that parties should "[r]egulate or manage biological resources important for the conservation of biological diversity whether within or outside protected areas with a view to ensuring their consumption and sustainable use." Similarly, Article 10 (b) seeks to minimize impacts on biodiversity of using biological resources where it stipulates that parties should "[a]dopt measures relating to the use of biological resources to avoid or minimize adverse impacts on biological diversity."

Regarding international cooperation and the role of patents, Article 16 of the CBD reads:

> The Contracting Parties, recognizing that patents and other intellectual property rights may have an influence on the implementation of this Convention, shall cooperate in this regard subject to national legislation and international law in order to ensure that such rights are supportive of and do not run counter to its objectives.

Article 22.2 provides that it shall be implemented consistent with rights and obligations under "the law of the sea." This provision does not directly refer to the 1982 Convention on the Law of the Sea but has implications for this as well as other laws of the sea (see section 5.4).

Partly due to the influence of the CBD, the 1972 World Heritage Convention revised in 1994 its criteria for selecting sites that are significant natural habitats for *in situ* conservation of biodiversity. A number of synergies between the CBD and several international agreements are noteworthy, especially in the areas of marine and coastal biodiversity and bioconservation (see de Fontaubert et al., 1998). Some of these are:

- Ramsar Convention, 1971
- CITES, 1972
- World Heritage Convention, 1972
- MARPOL, 1973/1978
- UNCLOS, 1982
- Rio Declaration, Agenda 21, 1992
- UN General Assembly Resolution on Driftnets, 1991
- UNFCCC, 1992
- Fish Stocks Agreement, 1995
- FAO Code of Conduct for Responsible Fisheries, 1995

Bioprospecting and indigenous knowledge

One of the critical issues in the context of the CBD (as well as a few other treaties) is that of appropriate sharing of gains arising out of bioprospecting: the commercial exploitation of biotic species and their pharmaceutical use based on (often uncoded) traditional knowledge. Bioprospecting "rents" in some cases are very significant and possess the potential to finance relevant bioconservation. Owing to methodological flaws, primarily based on the assumption of uninformed or no *a priori* information regarding the potential likelihood of a plant or biotic product being employed in medicinal or related uses, Simpson et al. (1996) suggested that returns to genetic assets of bioprospecting may not be sufficient to create significant self-supporting conservation incentives. However, the fact that bioprospecting is usually based on prior knowledge (even if fuzzy) substantially enhances the value of new "discoveries" and related bioprospecting. This is illustrated by Rausser and Small (2000, p. 196), who argued that bioprospecting rents based on indigenous knowledge or other sources of information could potentially lead to sharable surplus and lead to conservation of resources as well. They also stated that "the institutions regulating bioprospecting, including systems of intellectual property rights, should reward the provision of helpful prior information, as well as the conservation of the base biological material" (ibid.). In this context it is useful to note, as Posey (1996) did, that traditional resource rights (usually in relation to indigenous peoples in different regions of the world) should protect knowledge relating to biological resources. The CBD does include the principle of prior informed consent (PIC) in resource use, but its operational use is far from being satisfactory or equitable.

Modern international public law should also seek more use of the 1989 ILO Convention 169 Concerning Indigenous and Tribal Peoples in Independent Countries; this Convention is still to be ratified by most countries, however. Its Article 4 states: "Special measures shall be adopted as appropriate for safeguarding the persons, institutions, property, labor, cultures and environment of the peoples concerned."

The market value of the agricultural seed germ plasm utilizing traditional knowledge is estimated at about $50 billion per year in the US alone (RAFI, 1994). Similarly, the pharmaceutical industry has been taking advantage of the knowledge of plant medicines on a grand scale, and estimates of commercial benefits approximate to similar magnitudes. Thus, traditional indigenous communities have been providing subsidies to a modern agricultural system that barely recognizes their contributions. The CBD in its Articles 8 (j) and 18 (4) refers to some of the indigenous peoples' requirements. Article 8 (j) requires "equitable sharing of the benefits arising from the utilization of such knowledge, innovations and practices." The operational principles for implementation of this norm are far from perfect, and a new Convention or Protocol may be called for.

The CBD provides a legal framework for a comprehensive ecosystem-based approach to conservation and addresses a myriad of complex issues related to biodiversity protection. The Convention confirms that countries have both legal control over their biodiversity and a right to share in the benefits of its use. Developing countries are some of the most biodiversity-rich, yet often lack the resources and the incentives needed for conservation. The Convention calls on governments to help indigenous and local communities protect their traditional knowledge and practices relating to biodiversity, and to establish incentives to encourage fair sharing of the benefits from those traditions.

Integrating economic and environmental policy is essential to an effective strategy for biodiversity conservation. In recognition of this need, Article 11 of the Biodiversity Convention requires parties to examine the impact of economic incentives on the conservation and sustainable use of biodiversity.

On a related issue in the special region of Antarctica, the 1980 Convention on the Conservation of Antarctic Marine Living Resources (CCAMLR) requires consensus for decision-making and does not employ the precautionary principle explicitly (unlike in the later 1992 CBD) or in its implication of reversing the burden of proof in favor of conservation. However, its Article II sets out three principles of conservation for harvesting fisheries in the region. These are: (1) prevention of population decline to critical levels that adversely affect stability of stocks of tampered populations; (2) maintenance of ecological relationships between the harvested, dependent, and neighboring species; and (3) minimization of the risks of ecosystem changes that are irreversible within two or three decades (for a detailed application of the principles, see Parkes, 2000; Bacon, 1999). CCAMLR adopts an ecosystem approach, with the implication that the Convention's governing entity must consider both the impact of biotic resource exploitation on the specific species as well as the corresponding impact on other biotic populations. However, the dispute resolution mechanisms under this regime are rather weak (somewhat similar to CITES) and the effectiveness of this regime is generally deemed rather limited (see also Bacon, 1999).

Much of the debate and policy action on biological resources conservation and preservation concerns land-based resources. However, it is well known that more species belong in the arena of marine resources. The following section deals with the international legal arrangements in the protection of these resources.

▉ 5.4 FISHERIES, MARINE LIFE, AND THE LAWS OF THE SEA

Many marine resources continue to decline at rates that are clearly unsustainable. Coral reefs are under constant threat of destruction in most locations of the world. It has been estimated that about 58 percent of reefs are at risk due to human interference. This problem is especially acute in the species-diverse ecosystems of the Southeast Asia region. In addition there is a serious loss of fisheries resources in most oceanic regions, despite the fact that overfishing was recognized as a problem of fisheries resource management at the beginning of the twentieth century. The problems identified were originally confined to the North Atlantic and North Pacific regions. Overfishing has progressed since the 1950s and the harvest has already peaked in most areas, especially in the Northwest and Southeast Atlantic. Based on information since the 1970s, the Food and Agriculture Organization (FAO, 1997) found that the annual growth rate in the harvest was about 7 percent, which is no longer sustainable.

Marine fisheries constitute an important segment of the economy in several countries, including Canada, Norway, and Iceland. Estimates of world marine production, based on total harvest, were about 82 million tons in the mid-1990s. It is important to note that another 27 million tons are discarded every year (see Rao, 2000). The benefits from a reduction of these losses would, first, enhance the survival volume of juvenile fish, and second, contribute toward sustainable harvesting of some of the species. The rising demand for fish due to the expanding human population and the increasing shortfall in supply demonstrate expected market features: rising fish prices, and thus restricting fish consumption among the poorer sections of society. This is far from conducive to equity in food consumption, considering that fish is amongst the most desirable food item for its nutritional and health value, and any effective denial of the poor can aggravate malnutrition problems and the attendant consequences (Rao, 2000).

The FAO (1997) study suggested that three factors would uphold sustainable harvesting: (1) rehabilitating the overharvested and degraded regions; (2) further exploiting underdeveloped fishing areas at an increased but sustainable rate; and (3) significantly reducing wastage. Some of these actions cannot be brought about simply by market factors themselves and require interventions such as improved technology for fish collection and storage. Fishing cooperatives or similar associations might require external assistance to upgrade their technologies.

The International Conference on the Sustainable Contribution of Fisheries to Food Security was held in 1995 at Kyoto and was represented by 95 countries. Some of the decisions included (1) the Implementation of the Provisions of the UN Convention on the Law of the Sea of 1982 relating to the Conservation and Management of Straddling Fish Stocks and Highly Migratory Fish Stocks; (2) the development and use of selective, environmentally safe, and cost-effective fishing apparatus and techniques; and (3) the allocation of resources for ensuring effective multispecies management of the commercial fisheries sector.

Oceans and marine resources

In early international actions, the US President Truman Proclamations of 1945 were the "first positive law" on the subject of an exclusive economic zone and the Continental Shelf, according to the ICJ in the North Sea Continental Shelf cases (ICJ 3, 1969). The unilateral Truman Proclamations (13 Dept. of State Bull. 485–486, 1945) stated, among other items, a concern for oil exploration and resources "conservation and prudent utilization when and as development is undertaken."

A few treaties have dealt with various aspects of the law of the sea. The 1958 Convention on the Territorial Sea, High Seas, and Continental Shelf and the 1973 Convention on the Prevention of Pollution from Ships were among the notable early treaties on a wide scale. Articles 1–3 of the 1958 Convention were regarded by the ICJ as "reflecting, or crystallizing, received or at least emergent rules of customary international law." The first Law of the Sea Conference was held in 1973, but a draft treaty was formulated nine years later in 1982 as the Law of the Sea (LOS). The 1973 International Convention for the Prevention of Pollution from Ships placed rather modest limits on ocean dumping, but the US ratification of this came after 14 years. Box 5.2 provides a list of some of the major international agreements that emerged after World War II.

International fisheries

Harvesting and conservation of international fisheries is influenced by a number of market and institutional factors. The latter include the role of international agreements and provisions of the law governing territorial waters and rights of resource exploitation. The First UN

BOX 5.2

Ocean resources and governance laws, 1946-99

- 1946 International Convention for the Regulation of Whaling, held at Washington, December 2, 1946; in force November 10, 1948; 42 ratifications.
- 1952 International Convention for the High Seas of the North Pacific Ocean, held at Tokyo, May 9, 1952; in force June 12, 1953; 3 ratifications; Protocol to the Convention, Tokyo, April 25, 1978; in force February 20, 1979; 3 ratifications.
- 1954 International Convention for the Prevention of Pollution of the Sea by Oil, held at London, May 12, 1954; in force July 26, 1958; 72 ratifications. This first international agreement dealing with marine pollution led to the establishment of the Intergovernmental Maritime Consultative Organization (IMCO) as a specialized UN agency; it was renamed the International Maritime Organization (IMO) in 1982.
- 1958 Convention on the Territorial Sea and the Contiguous Zone, held at Geneva, April 29, 1958; in force September 10, 1964; 46 ratifications.
- 1958 Convention on the High Seas, held at Geneva, April 29, 1958; in force September 30, 1962; 57 ratifications.
- 1958 Convention on Fishing and Conservation of the Living Resources of the High Seas, held at Geneva, April 29, 1958; in force March 20, 1966; 36 ratifications.
- 1958 Convention on the Continental Shelf, held at Geneva, April 29, 1958; in force June 10, 1964; 54 ratifications.
- 1958 Optional Protocol of Signature concerning the Compulsory Settlement of Disputes arising from the Law of the Sea Conventions, held at Geneva, April 29, 1958; in force September 30, 1962; 38 ratifications.
- 1972 Convention for the Prevention of Marine Pollution by Dumping from Ships and Aircraft, held at Oslo, February 15, 1972; in force April 7, 1974.
- 1973/78 International Convention for the Prevention of Pollution from Ships (MARPOL) was held in London and later modified in 1978; collectively called MARPOL 73/78; in force October 2, 1983; various equipment and discharge standards emerged from this, requiring restructuring of tanker fleet.

- 1982 UN Convention on the Law of the Sea (UNCLOS), held at Montego Bay, Jamaica, December 10, 1982; in force November 16, 1994.
- 1994 Agreement relating to the Implementation of Part XI of the LOS Convention, adopted by the UN General Assembly on July 28, 1994; in force July 28, 1996.
- 1995 Agreement for the Implementation of the Provisions of the LOS Convention relating to the Conservation and Management of Straddling Fish Stocks and Highly Migratory Fish Stocks (sometimes simply called the Fish Stocks Agreement), adopted August 4, 1995 at New York by the UN Conference on Straddling Fish Stocks and Highly Migratory Fish Stocks; not yet in force.

Sources: Compiled from Churchill and Lowe (1988); www.un.org/Depts/Treaty/ final/ts2/newfiles/frontboo/toc21.htm (February 18, 2000)

Conference on the Law of the Sea in 1958 failed to arrive at an agreement on both the concept of exclusive fishery zones, and on the extent of territorial fishing rights. This vagueness left some coastal states to try new methods and this led to international disputes. Box 5.3 provides a historical summary of the Iceland fisheries dispute with West Germany in the 1970s. Later developments are noteworthy. The UN Convention on the Law of the Sea was drafted in 1982 and entered into force in 1994. It establishes fishing and water rights within the exclusive zone of 12 miles from the coast for the adjacent sovereign states, and binding procedures for the settlement of disputes over sea resources outside the 12-mile zone. This agreement provides property rights with little obligation for the conservation of the corresponding resources. The UN Conference on Straddling Fish Stocks and Highly Migratory Fish Stocks Agreement was formally adopted on August 4, 1995. It seeks an application of the precautionary principle to monitor stocks and conserve fishery resources in sovereign and international waters.

Convention on the Law of the Sea

By the 1980s, the environmental and ecological externalities of either excessive interventions or *sui generis* consumptive resource use in the oceans was well recognized by several authors (see, for example, Underdal, 1980). The need for internationally coordinated actions

BOX 5.3

International fisheries disputes

In the late 1950s, Iceland unilaterally issued a regulation establishing an exclusive fisheries zone extending up to 12 miles around its
coasts. After diplomatic initiatives, England and West Germany concluded provisional agreements with Iceland; in these agreements
the preferential rights of Iceland were recognized in the exclusive
zone. Later, Iceland took another unilateral action in 1971 to extend its exclusive fishery zone to 50 miles, declaring bilateral agreements with England and West Germany null and void. The affected
two countries took up the issue with the International Court of
Justice (ICJ). The Court delivered its verdict (*United Kingdom v.
Iceland*) on July 25, 1974: Iceland had no right to unilaterally
exclude the affected countries in the 12-mile to 50-mile zone. The
Court observed (ICJ, 1974): "It is one of the advances in maritime
international law, resulting from the intensification of fishing, that
the former *laissez-faire* treatment of the living resources of the sea
in the high seas had been replaced by a recognition of a duty to
have due regard to the rights of other States and the needs of
conservation for the benefit of all." The ICJ determined that the
law pertaining to fisheries must accept the primacy of the requirement of conservation based on scientific data, interpreted a former
Chief Justice of the ICJ (Singh, 1988). A property rights-based
approach to the resolution of the dispute was adopted in this case,
and the Court acted as a steward for the environment in its inclusion of conservation as a requirement for fisheries management in
international waters (Konisky, 1998). Some of these guidelines
were found useful in the international agreements of the 1980s
and 1990s.

became increasingly evident. Even when the international community
waited for the development of customary international law (as it
inadvertently did when it took a quarter-century for a comprehensive
law of the sea to enter into force), this did not provide a regime for
the management of sea resources with any reasonable restraints or the
rule of law. Even when CIL evolves, it cannot usually furnish important technical details (Oxman, 1996); from the perspective of strengthening the rule of law, the customary law position is no substitute for

the goal of global ratification. The United Nations Convention on the Law of the Sea (UNCLOS) marked the beginning of modern international environmental law governing sea resources. It was opened for signature on December 10, 1982 in Montego Bay, Jamaica, after more than 14 years of preparatory work involving participation by over 150 countries. The Convention entered into force about 12 years later on November 16, 1994. Thus the UNCLOS is the result of about a quarter-century of effort. In retrospect, an application of transaction costs economics in the treaty formulation alone leads to a search for more cost-effective alternatives. The story of legal development (or lack of it) did not end there. To address some of the concerns with the Convention's seabed-mining provisions that had been raised, primarily by the industrialized countries, the UN Secretary-General convened a series of consultations which culminated in the adoption, on July 28, 1994, of the Agreement relating to the Implementation of Part XI of the United Nations Convention on the Law of the Sea of December 10, 1982. The agreement entered into force on July 28, 1996. In addition, an Agreement for the Implementation of the Provisions of the Convention relating to the Conservation and Management of Straddling Fish Stocks and Highly Migratory Fish Stocks was arrived at in 1995 (though it is not yet in force).

The provisions under the UNCLOS seek to advance the rule of law in some basic ways (Oxman, 1996). Global ratification of the Convention of the treaty can lead to a common interpretation of the rules of international law governing two-thirds of the planet, including rules of state practice; such a ratification leads parties to accept submission to international arbitration or adjudication of most disputes arising under the Law of the Sea Convention that are not settled by other means (see chapter 9 for more details).

The 1982 UNCLOS deals with marine pollution and depletion of fish stocks. Article 3 of the UNCLOS provides that "every State has the right to establish the breadth of its territorial sea up to a limit not exceeding 12 nautical miles, measured from baselines determined in accordance with this Convention." The question of residual rights is left open in accordance with Article 59.

The exclusive economic zone (EEZ) regime remains a main approach for the conservation of living marine resources. These relate to living and nonliving resources, other economic resources, marine scientific research, and pollution control. The emergence of the EEZ as a norm of zoning in ocean law is the result of state practice and the provisions of Part V of the 1982 UNCLOS. It is provided under Article 55 (the specific legal regime of the exclusive economic zone):

The exclusive economic zone is an area beyond and adjacent to the territorial sea, subject to the specific legal regime established in this Part, under which the rights and jurisdiction of the coastal State and the rights and freedoms of other States are governed by the relevant provisions of this Convention.

Article 57 defines the breadth of the exclusive economic zone: "The exclusive economic zone shall not extend beyond 200 nautical miles from the baselines from which the breadth of the territorial sea is measured." Article 119 (1) offers guidelines for fishing in the high seas outside the 200-mile zones, forming part of *res communis*.

The Convention does not directly deal with issues of marine biodiversity, with some exceptions covering living resources in part of Article 56. This Article sets duties and rights of coastal states under the EEZ regime, an important development in the international law of the seas. As observed by Juda (1996), this Article provides the coastal states "sovereign rights" for defined purposes, rather than "sovereignty" in its entirety. Juda (1996) argued that the EEZs may be politically desirable but they "are not congruent with the natural and ecological divisions of ocean space." Besides, it has been argued elsewhere that the transboundary movement of fish stocks along and across the EEZs tends to limit the usefulness of the EEZ regimes. Regarding living resources, the coastal states have a duty to ensure that EEZ resources promote "optimum utilization," based on "total allowable catch" (TAC) and renewal capacity of the sources of supply of these resources.

Article 1 (4) of the UNCLOS defines "pollution of the marine environment." In a very brief Article 192 of the Convention, unlike most other Articles, it was declared as a specification of "general obligation" that "[s]tates have the obligation to protect and preserve the marine environment."

Articles 193, 194, and 195 elaborate the principles of marine environmental protection. In particular, Article 194 recognizes the need to control environmental externalities when it includes "measures to prevent, reduce and control pollution of the marine environment" and declares, *inter alia*, that:

> States shall take all measures necessary to ensure that activities under their jurisdiction or control are so conducted as not to cause damage by pollution to other States and their environment, and that pollution arising from incidents or activities under their jurisdiction or control does not spread beyond the areas where they exercise sovereign rights in accordance with this Convention.

Other important provisions of the UNCLOS are in the following specific areas: international cooperation regarding conservation and sustainable utilization of sea resources are given, in particular, in Article 63.1 and Articles 117 to 119; conservation and sustainable utilization within national jurisdiction are specified in particular, in Articles 61.2, 62.4, and 65.

The regime of deep-seabed-mining, the theme in Part XI of the 1982 UNCLOS, has been a bone of contention among developed and developing countries. It was also declared that the mineral resources found beyond the EEZs are the "common heritage of mankind." The International Seabed Authority (ISBA) is the governing body for all such resources. Resource exploitation under the ISBA must (1) "ensure effective protection for the marine environment from harmful effects which may arise from such activities" (Article 145); and (2) be conducted "with reasonable regard to other activities in the marine environment" (Article 147 (1)). The entire Part XII, in addition to several other provisions, of the 1982 UNCLOS deals with various aspects of the marine environment and its protection.

The UNCLOS tends to give the impression that most fish stocks are confined to the EEZ of coastal states as stationary habitats (for detailed interpretations, see Churchill and Lowe, 1988). Since fish stocks migrate, greater attention is required. A brief requirement of agreed measures among coastal states for the conservation of these resources is made in Article 63. These issues came to be addressed later in the 1995 Fish Stocks Agreement. Besides, the UNCLOS could not provide sufficient specific measures to conserve global fishery resources, hence the need for the 1995 Fish Stocks Agreement.

Various new norms governing the international fisheries beyond the UNCLOS Convention include the following: the 1994 Convention on Conservation and Management of Pollock Resources in the Central Bering Sea (also called the "Donut Hole" Agreement; see 34 ILM 67, 1995); the 1995 Fish Stocks Agreement; the 1993 FAO Agreement to Promote Compliance with International Conservation and Management Measures by Fishing Vessels on the High Seas (hereafter called the 1993 FAO Agreement); and the 1995 FAO Code of Conduct for Responsible Fishing. The FAO Code, now part of soft law, consists of guidelines dealing with fisheries management, fishing operations, aquaculture development, integration of fisheries into coastal area management, postharvest practices and trade, and fisheries research. The December 1995 Kyoto International Conference on the Sustainable Contribution of Fisheries to Food Security was represented by 95 state parties and declared its intention to "apply the precautionary approach" as referred to in the FAO Code and in the Fish Stocks Agreement. The potential for the FAO Code thus appears to gain momentum to form into hard law. A few regional agreements also supplement some of the above measures. These include the 1989 Convention for the Prohibition of Fishing with Long Driftnets in the South Pacific, and the 1992 Inter-American Tropical Tuna Convention Agreement for the Reduction of Dolphin Mortality in the Eastern Tropical Pacific Ocean (also called the La Jolla Agreement).

The 1995 Fish Stocks Agreement forms an important basis for international fisheries law. It pertains to three major treaties (see Vigneron, 1998): the UNCLOS, for which this constitutes a special agreement, the 1993 FAO Agreement, and the 1994 "Donut Hole" Agreement. The preamble of the agreement states that the parties are "conscious of the need to avoid adverse impacts on the marine environment, preserve biodiversity, maintain the integrity of marine ecosystems and minimize the risk of long-term or irreversible effects of fishing operations." It requires an application of the PP, protection of marine biodiversity, and minimization of the ecological impact of fishing. Article 3 requires states to exercise their sovereign rights within the context of Article 6. More specifically, Article 6 (2) requires the parties to be "more cautious when information is uncertain, unreliable or inadequate. The absence of adequate scientific information shall not be used as a reason for postponing or failure to take conservation and management measures" (see UN Doc. A/Conf.164/37, 1995; 34 ILM 1542).

The need to manage the oceans as common property resources with global cooperation was emphasized in the Report of the Independent World Commission on the Oceans (1998), entitled *The Ocean Our Future*. The threats to oceans and marine life were reassessed. These included a set of major sources of pollution. It was estimated that, in addition to other pollutants such as discarded nuclear submarines, the quantity of petroleum hydrocarbons released into the oceans each year amounts to about 2.5 million tons. There is no indication of any let-up in the continuous increases in additions to these wastes, and as a result the sink's assimilative capacity is adversely affected. Concerted global action is thus a prerequisite for environmental sustainability of the oceans.

The World Commission on the Oceans (1998) in its report seeks attention to the "unfinished agenda of ocean law." Aspects of this include, *inter alia*, the need to elaborate international rules regarding (1) "responsibility and liability for harm to the marine environment, especially for acts not prohibited by international law"; and (2) application of the PP within the scope of existing agreements. Among the main recommendations in the Report are (p. 20): (1) that the users of ocean resources and polluters of marine ecosystems should bear the "true costs of their actions"; and (2) that management regimes incorporating the PP need to be established at the appropriate regional levels, incorporating intersectoral and interdisciplinary approaches. Recent developments in the case law affecting international laws of the sea are given in box 5.4. The first invokes the application of the Vienna Law of Treaties and the role of reservations, in addition to other legal facts.

■ 5.5 FOREST RESOURCES

Forests have the characteristics of both common property resources as well as appropriable private or national resources. The wide variety of environmental and ecological functions served and services provided by forests suggest the need for a comprehensive assessment (not necessarily monetary valuation itself) of the role of forests in affecting the environmental quality of the planet.

Two sets of competing norms affect the policies and laws governing "common property resources" (see also Hooker, 1994, for other interpretations): state sovereignty versus state responsibility, and allocative efficiency versus global equity in resource use.

The Rio Declaration of 1992 (especially its Chapter 11) and the Forest Principles negotiated at the 1992 Earth Summit in Rio (Nonlegally binding Authoritative Statement of Principles for a Global Consensus on the Management, Conservation, and Sustainable Development of All Types of Forests, UN Report A/CONF.151/26/Rev. 1, Vol. 1, 1992), both forming part of soft law, enunciated the following guiding principles for international forest policy (UN, 2000):

- the states have the sovereign right to utilize their resources, to meet their national policy objectives;
- the states have the right to economic development in accordance with their social, economic, environmental, and political conditions;
- the States have common but differentiated responsibilities regarding collective global interest and concerns related to forests;
- the States have the responsibilities to ensure that activities within their jurisdiction do not cause damage to the environment of other states or of areas beyond the limits of national jurisdiction;

BOX 5.4

Cases in international law of the sea

1. THE LEGALITY OF THE CANADIAN SEIZURE OF THE SPANISH TRAWLER *ESTAI*

Canada's marine policy is partly governed by the 1995 Coastal Fisheries Protection Act. It recognizes that the freedom of the high seas by distant-water fishing nations is subject to regulation since the living resources of the sea are not inexhaustible. Canada could take unilateral action to protect its depleting stocks of fish, as a matter of "necessity," and in its application of precautionary measures (Akiba, 1997). The state of "necessity" in international law is defined and provided by the International Law Commission (ILC): "The situation of a State whose sole means of safeguarding an essential interest threatened by a grave and imminent peril is to adopt conduct not in conformity with what is required of it by an international obligation to another state." Furthermore, "a state claiming the benefit of the existence of a state of necessity must not itself have provoked, either deliberately or by negligence, the occurrence of the state of necessity" (Report of the International Law Commission on the work of its 32nd Session, 2 Year Book of International Law Commission 34; UN Doc. A/CN.4/SER.A/1980/Add. 1, pt. 2).

Spain's application of March 28, 1995 requested the International Court of Justice (ICJ) to declare certain legislation of Canada (in particular the Coastal Fisheries Protection Act, as amended in 1994, and implementing regulations) invalid under international law. The application also asked the Court to hold that the arrest by the Canadian navy on the high seas, on March 9, 1995, of a Spanish-flag fishing vessel involving the use of force constituted a violation of international law for which Canada must make reparation. On December 4, 1998, the ICJ ruled (12–5) that it lacked jurisdiction to adjudicate the dispute. Spain relied on the declarations made by the two parties accepting the Court's compulsory jurisdiction under Article 36 (2) of the ICJ Statute.

Canada challenged the Court's jurisdiction, invoking a reservation contained in its 1994 declaration excluding from jurisdiction "disputes arising out of or concerning conservation and management measures taken by Canada with respect to vessels fishing in the NAFO Regulatory Area, as defined in the Convention on Future Multilateral Cooperation in the Northwest Atlantic Fisheries, 1978, and the enforcement of such measures."

The Court agreed with Canada that the words of an optional clause declaration, including a reservation contained therein, must be interpreted in a natural and reasonable way, having due regard to the intention of the state making the reservation at the time when it accepted the Court's compulsory jurisdiction. The Court stressed that a reservation to a declaration should be interpreted in a manner compatible with the effect sought by the reserving state. The Court found that the words "disputes arising out of or concerning" contained in Canada's reservation exclude not only disputes whose immediate "subject matter" is the measures in question and their enforcement, but also those "concerning" such measures and those having their "origin" in those matters. The Court noted that it had to determine whether the dispute had as its subject matter the measures mentioned in the reservation or their enforcement, or both, or concerned those measures or arose out of them. The Court pointed out that "measure" covered any act, step, or proceeding (including a law and its implementing regulations) and imposed no limit on the material content or on the aim pursued thereby (in this case, the conservation and management of fish). The Court was satisfied that the measures taken by Canada constituted "conservation and management measures."

On this basis, the ICJ concluded that the dispute submitted to it by Spain constituted a dispute "arising out of" and "concerning" "conservation and management measures taken by Canada with respect to vessels fishing in the NAFO Regulatory Area" and "the enforcement of such measures."

The Court gave primary importance to the effect sought by the reserving state Canada when it accepted in 1994 the ICJ's jurisdiction with its amendment of May 10, 1994. On that date, Canada filed an amended declaration accepting the jurisdiction of the ICJ. On March 9, 1995, the Canadian coastguard arrested *Estai* on the high seas outside Canada's 200-mile EEZ and declared this action (quoted in the Spanish application to the ICJ) "was necessary in order to put a stop to the overfishing of Greenland halibut (turbot) by Spanish fishermen." On April 20, 1995, Canada and the EC signed an Agreed Minute on the Conservation and Management of Fish Stocks, and later Canada repealed the application of its regulations toward proceedings against the *Estai*. In the amendment of

May 10, 1994, paragraph 2 (d) excluded "disputes arising out of or concerning conservation and management measures taken by Canada with respect to vessels fishing in the NAFO Regulatory Area, as defined in the Convention on Future Multilateral Cooperation in the Northwest Atlantic Fisheries, 1978, and the enforcement of such measures."

The ICJ opined that all elements of its Article 36 (2) must be interpreted in unity: "the principle of interpretation whereby a reservation to a declaration of acceptance of the compulsory jurisdiction of the Court is to be interpreted in a natural and reasonable way, with appropriate regard for the intentions of the reserving State and the purpose of the reservation" (ICJ Docs. CR/98, at paragraphs 43, 51–52). As Kwiatkowska (1999) observed, the ICJ's broad interpretation of the generic term "conservation and management measures" and its conclusion that the term "enforcement of such measures" entails minimal use of force may be potent to influence further development of the international law of the sea. The full text of the decision may be found on the Internet at the ICJ website: http://www.icj-cij.org.

Sources: Akiba (1997); www.icj-cij.org (December 12, 1999); Peter H. F. Bekker's brief (ASIL Insight): "International Court of Justice Rejects Jurisdiction in Fisheries Jurisdiction Case brought by Spain against Canada," obtained from the American Society of International Law's website, www.asil.org/insigh28.htm (December 12, 1999)

2. INTERNATIONAL TRIBUNAL FOR THE LAW OF THE SEA: SOUTHERN BLUEFIN TUNA CASES (*NEW ZEALAND V. JAPAN*; *AUSTRALIA V. JAPAN*), REQUEST FOR PROVISIONAL MEASURES (AUGUST 27, 1999)

New Zealand and Australia alleged that Japan had failed to cooperate in the conservation of the southern bluefin tuna (SBT) stock by undertaking unilateral experimental fishing in violation of its obligations under Articles 64 and 116 of the UNCLOS. The Tribunal was requested to prescribe provisional measures ordering Japan to immediately cease unilateral experimental fishing for SBT and to restrict its catch to its national allocation. In addition, New Zealand and Australia requested the Tribunal to declare that, pending a final settlement, the parties should act consistently with the precautionary principle in fishing for SBT, and to ensure that no action be taken that might aggravate or prejudice any decision on the merits.

In response, Japan argued that the Tribunal lacked *prima facie* jurisdiction and therefore could not prescribe any provisional measures. Alternatively, should the Tribunal find jurisdiction, Japan submitted a counter-request for provisional measures calling on New Zealand and Australia to "urgently and in good faith" recommence negotiations with Japan in order to reach a consensus on outstanding issues, including determination of a total allowable catch and national allocations of SBT stock for the year 2000. If the parties did not reach consensus within six months, Japan argued that any remaining disagreements should be referred to a panel of independent scientists.

The Tribunal held that it had jurisdiction, and also that under Article 290 (5) of the UNCLOS it has the right to prescribe provisional measures if required by the urgency of the situation. In this respect, the Tribunal noted that the conservation of the living resources of the sea is "an element of the protection and preservation of the marine environment" (paragraph 70). Therefore, the Tribunal held that, regardless of the fact that it could not conclusively assess the scientific evidence presented by the parties, provisional measures were warranted as a matter of urgency to preserve the rights of the parties and to avert further deterioration of the SBT stock (paragraph 80). The Tribunal prescribed provisional measures and ordered that all parties should refrain from conducting an experimental fishing program for the SBT stock (paragraph 90 (1)).

Judge Laing contended that in this case the Tribunal had made decisions of fundamental importance for the institution of provisional measures and "potentially of critical relevance to an aspect of international environmental law." The judge noted that "scientific uncertainty or the absence of complete proof should not stand in the way of positive action to minimize risks or take actions of a conservatory, preventative or curative nature." Judge Laing also held that by adopting a precautionary approach rather than the precautionary principle, the Tribunal had kept a certain degree of flexibility, "underscor[ing its] reticence about making premature pronouncements about desirable normative structures."

Sources: Section on international decisions edited by B. H. Oxman, *American Journal of International Law,* 93 (April 1999), 502–7; www.asil.org (international law in brief section)

- international cooperation should focus on building human and institutional capacity in developing countries to manage their forests sustainably.

The issue of international arrangements and mechanisms (IAM) to promote sustainable forest policy has been one of the themes of deliberations in the Intergovernmental Panel on Forests (IPF) and the Intergovernmental Forum on Forests (IFF). UN (2000) suggested the following sixteen elements for an IAM:

- formulation and implementation of national forest programs
- promoting public participation
- combating deforestation and forest degradation
- traditional forest-related knowledge (TFRK)
- forest-related scientific knowledge
- forest health and productivity
- criteria and indicators of sustainable forest management (SFM)
- economic, social, and cultural aspects of forests
- forest conservation and protection of unique types of forests and fragile ecosystems
- monitoring, assessment, and reporting
- rehabilitation and conservation strategies for countries with low forest cover
- rehabilitation and restoration of degraded lands, and the promotion of natural and planted forests
- maintaining forest cover to meet present and future needs
- financial resources
- international trade and SFM
- international cooperation in capacity building and transfer of environmentally sound technologies to support SFM.

Recent attempts at policy formulation

At its fourth session, the Intergovernmental Forum on Forests (IFF, 2000) suggested the following among other measures (including the adoption of economic principles, with significant implications). At a general level, they merit further development and potential operationalization in specific contexts.

1 Forest products and services (and their substitutes) should be valued through full-cost internalization; countries should

undertake analyses of the implications of such valuation on forest management and economic development, taking into consideration the potential costs and benefits of improved efficiency and sustainability of the forest sector.

2   The Forum urged countries to promote fair and equitable sharing of the benefits arising from the utilization of forest genetic resources, as defined by the Convention on Biological Diversity.

3   The Forum stressed that deficiencies in valuation in economic terms of, for example, social and ecological values, do not imply that these values are less relevant.

4   The scope of valuation of forest goods and services needs to extend beyond the limits of the forest sector and include, for example, consideration of alternative land-use options of significant social or economic value, forest products pricing, and ecological impact of substitute materials. There is a need to develop an approach to identify both costs and benefits of sustainable forest management, as well as ways to encourage countries to internalize externalities.

5   The nature and extent of illegal trade in wood and nonwood forest products, including forest-related biological resources, is a serious concern due to consequential damage to ecosystems and loss of biodiversity, among others.

Clearly, a multipronged approach is needed for a meaningful and comprehensive management of forest resources. There are hardly any hard laws to govern forests directly. The existing forest-related legally binding agreements are those of the UNFCCC and its Protocols, and those of the UN Convention to Combat Desertification. International provision of a Forest Protocol to the UNFCCC, and another in relation to the Convention on Biological Diversity, may be a useful approach to enhanced governance of forest resources, moderating climatic variations, and preserving biodiversity. Given the nature and degree of interdependencies among these features, such supplementary measures could afford enhanced environmental protection measures and also minimize transaction costs when some of the existing treaties are used for further development. Forest-rich countries tend to subsidize the provision of several benefits of forest resources (including forest-based bioresources). This implies that other countries (constituting "free-riders" specific to these environmental goods and services) are enjoying the positive environmental externalities in this case. Such phenomena do not constitute incentives to the preservation of forest resources in forest-intensive countries in the absence of a fair compensation mechanism. Thus, the development of a fair and equitable international environmental regime to ensure sustainable forest management is called for.

■ 5.6 SUMMARY

This chapter's focus has been more specifically on ecological resources, although their interaction with other components of the environment remains inextricably interlinked. Most of the international environmental agreements dealing with biological resources have evolved over about a century, yet their relative effectiveness has been relatively meager. The degree of effectiveness of international laws seems to be proportionate to the size of the "coalition" constituted by the parties to each of the agreements. Soft laws, as in the case of forest resources, have been too soft and devoid of incentives for resource preservation. Hard laws, as in the case of some of the provisions under CITES, are not hard enough when the parties to the Convention do not comply with necessary enactment of domestic laws or with supplying of relevant information to other parties.

The role of the PP should remain a critical part of biological preservation, but the application of the PP is not uniform among the different environmental laws affecting (not necessarily governing) global biotic resources (for a comparative summary of the application of the PP in international and regional contexts, see Backes and Verschuuren, 1998). An ecosystems approach generally becomes an approximation of the PP in a few cases, and it has become more acceptable in different agreements and treaties. This is an encouraging indication of future uses of the approach and biotic resource conservation.

Environmental trade measures are yet another complex issue; they are further considered in chapter 8. Lang (1993, p. 174) pointed precisely to one area of difficulty: "the problem of nations that are reluctant to join a treaty is not as easy to solve in conservation treaties not concerned with trade." Even in those treaties that use environmental trade measures, their relative effectiveness depends upon the role of private trade and governmental enforcement in the domestic context. In other words, no international law may be more binding than the strength or weakness of the domestic legal and judicial framework itself.

Review Exercises

1 Explain the roles of the following in the protection of endangered species: reciprocal state practice cooperation, free marketization of species trade, and externalities of trade practices violating CITES.

2 Justify the existence and merits of an explicit and/or implicit concept that "optimal biodiversity" equals maximal biodiversity. Explain the "costs" of achieving less than maximal biodiversity.

3 Explain the role of transaction costs in the formation and implementation of the UNCLOS. What alternatives, if any, exist to mitigate such costs?

4 Discuss the role of full-cost pricing, generalized allocative efficiency, and generalized productive efficiency in the management of forest resources.

5 Explain the role of the precautionary principle in (a) CITES, (b) the CBD, and (c) the UNCLOS.

6 Explain the limitations in the CBD in regard to the provisions of fair and equitable sharing of bioprospecting. What alternatives exist in improving such provisions?

REFERENCES

Akiba, O., 1997, International law of the sea: The legality of Canadian seizure of the Spanish trawler (*Estai*), *Natural Resources Journal*, 37, 809–28.

Backes, C. W. and Verschuuren, J. M., 1998, The precautionary principle in international, European, and Dutch Wildlife Law, *Colorado Journal of International Environmental Law and Policy*, 9, 43–86.

Bacon, B. L., 1999, Enforcement mechanisms in international wildlife agreements and the United States: Wading through the murk, *Georgetown International Environmental Law Review*, 12, 331–61.

Balick, M. J., Elisabetsky, E., and Laird, S. A. (eds.), 1996, *Medicinal Resources of the Tropical Forest: Biodiversity and its Importance to Human Health*, New York: Columbia University Press.

Batabyal, A. A., 2000, Aspects of ecosystem persistence and the optimal conservation of species, *International Review of Economics and Finance*, 9, 69–77.

Brown, Jr., G. M. and Shogren, J. F., 1998, Economics of the Endangered Species Act, *Journal of Economic Perspectives*, 12, 3–20.

Burns, W. C. and Mosedale, C. T., 1997, European implementation of CITES and the proposal for a Council regulation (EC) on the protection of species of wild fauna and flora, *Georgetown International Environmental Law Review*, 9, 389–433.

Churchill, R. R. and Lowe, A. V., 1988, *Law of the Sea*, Manchester: Manchester University Press.

Daily, G. (ed.), 1997, *Nature's Services*, Washington, DC: Island Press.

de Fontaubert, A. C., Downes, D. R., and Agardy, T. S., 1998, Biodiversity in the seas: Implementing the Convention on Biological Diversity in marine and coastal habitats, *Georgetown International Environmental Law Review*, 10 (3), 753–854.

Dickson, B., 1999, The precautionary principle in CITES: A critical assessment, *Natural Resources Journal*, 39, 211–28.

Food and Agriculture Organization (FAO), 1997, *Review of the State of World Fisheries Resources: Marine Fisheries*, Fisheries Circular No. 920FIRM/C920, Rome: FAO Fisheries Department.

Hooker, A., 1994, The international law of forests, *Natural Resources Journal*, 34, 821–77.

Hunter, C. J., 1997, Sustainable bioprospecting: Using private contracts and international legal principles and policies to conserve raw medicinal materials, *Boston College Environmental Affairs Law Review*, 25, 129–74.

Hurlbut, D., 1994, Fixing the Biodiversity Convention: Toward a special protocol for related intellectual property, *Natural Resources Journal*, 34, 379–410.

Intergovernmental Forum on Forests (IFF), 2000, *Substantive Parts of the Report of the Intergovernmental Forum on Forests (Advance Unedited Text of the IFF At its Fourth Session)*, New York: United Nations (UN Doc. E/CN.17/IFF/2000/).

Juda, L., 1996, *International Law and Ocean Use Management*, New York: Routledge.

Konisky, D. M., 1998, The UN dispute settlement system and international environmental disputes, *Journal of Public and International Affairs*, 9, 1–24.

Kwiatkowska, B., 1999, Fisheries jurisdiction (Spain v. Canada), *American Journal of International Law*, 93 (April), 502–7.

Lang, J. T., 1993, Biological conservation and biological diversity, in G. Sjostedt (ed.), *International Environmental Negotiation*, London: Sage Publications, pp. 171–83.

Noyes, J. E., 1998, The International Tribunal for the Law of the Sea, *Cornell International Law Journal*, 32, 109–82.

Organization for Economic Cooperation and Development (OECD), 1997, *Experience with the Use of Trade Measures in the Convention on International Trade in Endangered Species of Wild Fauna and Flora (CITES)*, OECD Document OECD/GD(97)106, Paris: OECD Secretariat.

Oxman, B. H., 1996, The rule of law and the United Nations Convention on the Law of the Sea, *European Journal of International Law*, 7 (3), 353–71.

Parkes, G., 2000, Precautionary fisheries management: The CCAMLR approach, *Marine Policy*, 24, 83–91.

Patrick, R., 1997, Biodiversity: Why is it important?, in M. L. Reaka-Kudla, D. E. Wilson, and E. O. Wilson (eds.), *Biodiversity II*, Washington, DC: Joseph Henry Press, pp. 15–24.

Posey, D., 1996, Protecting indigenous peoples' rights to biodiversity, *Environment*, 38, 7–9 and 37–45.

Posner, R. A., 1981, *The Economics of Justice*, Cambridge, MA: Harvard University Press.

Rao, P. K., 2000, *Sustainable Development: Economics and Policy*, Oxford: Blackwell.

Rausser, G. C. and Small, A. A., 2000, Valuing research leads: Bioprospecting and the conservation of genetic resources, *Journal of Political Economy*, 108, 173–206.

Rieser, A., 1997, International fisheries law, overfishing and marine biodiversity, *Georgetown International Environmental Law Review*, 9, 251–80.

Rural Advancement Foundation International (RAFI), 1994, *Conserving Indigenous Knowledge: Integrating Two Systems of Innovation*, Study for the United Nations Development Program, New York.

Sand, P., 1997, Whither CITES? The evolution of a treaty regime in the borderland of trade and environment, *European Journal of International Law*, 8, 29–58.

Simpson, R., Sedjo, A., and Reid, J. W., 1996, Valuing biodiversity for use in pharmaceutical research, *Journal of Political Economy*, 104, 163–85.

Singh, N., 1988, The UN and the development of international law, in A. Roberts and B. Kingsbury (eds.), *UN: Divided World*, Oxford: Clarendon Press, p. 183.

United Nations (UN), 1997, *The United Nations Convention on Biological Diversity: A Constructive Response to a Global Problem*, Background Paper of the UN prepared for the Special Session of the General Assembly to Review and Appraise the Implementation of Agenda 21, June 1997; obtained from www.un.org/ecosocdev/geninfo/sustdev/es&5bio.htm, February 15, 1997.

UN, 2000, *International Arrangements and Mechanisms to Promote the Management, Conservation and Sustainable Development of All Types of Forests*, Report of the Secretary General, UN Document E/CN.17/IFF/2000/4, New York: UN Secretariat; also at www.un.org/esa/sustdev/docsiff4.htm.

UN Environment Program (UNEP), 1992, *Report of the Intergovernmental Negotiating Committee for a Convention on Biological Diversity*, Nairobi: UNEP Secretariat.

Underdal, A., 1980, Integrated marine policy: What? Why? How?, *Marine Policy*, 4, 159–69.

van Kooten, G. C. and Bulte, E. H., 2000, *The Economics of Nature: Managing Biological Assets*, Oxford: Blackwell.

Vigneron, G., 1998, Compliance and international environmental agreements: A case study of the 1995 United Nations Straddling Fish Stocks Agreement, *Georgetown International Environmental Law Review*, 10, 581–623.

Wilson, E. O., 1992, *The Diversity of Life*, Cambridge, MA: Belknap/Harvard University Press.

World Commission on the Oceans, 1998, *The Report of the Independent World Commission on the Oceans*, Cambridge: Cambridge University Press.

chapter six

Laws Based on Environmental Phenomena

▌ 6.1 INTRODUCTION

A number of international laws emerged after some of the significant global environmental problems were identified scientifically, and in some cases after damage had already been incurred by a few sections of society. Preventive aspects of environmental management should, ideally, remain the key to efficient environmental governance. However, some problems require perceptible diagnosis in order to engage attention at the international level. This might imply the infliction of some damage by the decision time point, but it may be hard to initiate policy actions in the absence of a minimal recognition of cause-and-effect relationships (preferably with some degree of scientific certainty). The continued accumulation of greenhouse gases (leading to, among other phenomena, global warming and its adverse consequences), the depletion of the ozone layer (leading to environmental public health and other problems), the continued expansion of deserts and the role of anthropogenic factors in desertification in some regions of the world, the environmental impacts of hazardous materials (including production, consumption, and movements), and the transboundary effects of air and water pollution are some of the major themes for consideration in this chapter. A few highlights of the relevant international laws are presented below.

Many of the global environmental problems under these themes require attention in the sense of management of the global commons. Most of the concepts of economic analysis set forth in the first three chapters of the book are pertinent for each of the themes deliberated here. Among important economic principles of relevance are the precautionary principle (PP) (or, in diluted versions, precautionary measures), the polluter pays principle (PPP) (or its variants, including internalization of environmental costs or externalities), the common but differentiated responsibilities principle (environmental equity aspect), the role of transaction costs in various international treaty formulations and in their implementation, and the economics of sustainable development. Most of these concepts and principles apply in the global governance of each of the environmental phenomena, although some more vigorously than others, depending on the specific focus. Considering how little, if any, economic analysis accompanies international treaty formulation, there is a significant gap between what can be done and what is being done in this regard.

■ 6.2 GREENHOUSE GASES AND THE UN FRAMEWORK CONVENTION ON CLIMATE CHANGE (UNFCCC)

The main greenhouse gases (GHG) are carbon dioxide, methane, nitrous oxide, hydrofluorocarbons, perfluorocarbons, and sulfur hexafluoride. These have been found to cause global warming, independently and jointly. The concept of global warming potential applies to each of these GHGs (see Rao, 2000). Much of the global climatic change is attributed to the accumulation of GHGs.

Several institutions came into existence during the 1990s in response to increasing concerns about global climatic change. The UN Framework Convention on Climate Change (UNFCCC) was signed in 1992 and entered into force to become operative since 1994. Its coordinative role remains significant. A number of multilateral development finance institutions and organizations such as the World Bank and the Organization for Economic Cooperation and Development (OECD) also play important roles in this context. International agreements are also supported by the political economy aspect of potential gaps in the provision of optimal emissions consistent with global environmental sustainability. The 1999 Economic Report of the US President (1999, p. 212) stated: "Because greenhouse gas emissions contribute to changes in the global atmosphere but do not have visible local effects, national governments, even in the richer countries, come under less pressure from their citizens to regulate their national emissions alone. Without international agreements to limit greenhouse gas emissions, achieving a more prosperous world may entail ever-increasing emissions." It must also be noted that a more prosperous world may be achievable, but such a phenomenon may not be sustainable with ever-increasing emissions.

BOX 6.1

UNFCCC Article 3 Principles

In their actions to achieve the objective of the Convention and to implement its provisions, the Parties shall be guided, *inter alia*, by the following:

1 The Parties should protect the climate system for the benefit of present and future generations of humankind, on the basis of equity and in accordance with their common but differentiated responsibilities and respective capabilities. Accordingly, the developed country Parties should take the lead in combating climate change and the adverse effects thereof.

2 The specific needs and special circumstances of developing country Parties, especially those that are particularly vulnerable to the adverse effects of climate change, and of those Parties, especially developing country Parties, that would have to bear a disproportionate or abnormal burden under the Convention, should be given full consideration.

3 The Parties should take precautionary measures to anticipate, prevent or minimize the causes of climate change and mitigate its adverse effects. Where there are threats of serious or irreversible damage, lack of full scientific certainty should not be used as a reason for postponing such measures, taking into account that policies and measures to deal with climate change should be cost-effective so as to ensure global benefits at the lowest possible cost. To achieve this, such policies and measures should take into account different socioeconomic contexts, be comprehensive, cover all relevant sources, sinks and reservoirs of greenhouse gases and adaptation, and comprise all economic sectors. Efforts to address climate change may be carried out cooperatively by interested Parties.

Source: www.unfccc.int. Reproduced with the permission of the United Nations Framework Convention for Climate Change, New York, 1992

The UNFCCC specifies three categories of commitments: (1) those general commitments that apply to all parties of the Convention; (2) those specifically applicable commitments for parties listed in Annex I (39 industrial countries and economies in transition); and (3) commitments that apply to parties listed in Annex II. Box 6.1 highlights some of the UNFCCC principles and policies. The Conference of Parties (COP) under the UNFCCC became an institutional arrangement for continued multilateral negotiations and policies governing global climatic issues. The first Conference of Parties (COP-1) was held in Berlin in 1995. It was agreed that the commitments for GHG reductions were inadequate to address the problem of climatic stabilization. This Berlin Mandate was carried through subsequent COPs and the third one (COP-3), held at Kyoto in 1997, proposed a series of fairly significant (if not optimal, for some) specific targets for GHG reduction, leading to the Kyoto Protocol. In a report to the Fifth Conference of the Parties (COP-5) to the UNFCCC in November 1999, the Chairman of the Intergovernmental Panel on Climate Change (IPCC) summarized the potential adverse impacts of climate change, with some indication of differential impacts across different regions (obtained from www.ipcc.ch/press/speech11–99.htm, November 18, 1999):

1 Arid and semi-arid land areas in Africa, the Middle East, and Southern Europe become even more water-stressed than at present.
2 Agricultural production in Africa and Latin America decreases.
3 The incidence of vector-borne diseases such as malaria increases in tropical countries.
4 Critical ecological systems, particularly forests and coral reefs, undergo changes in "structure and functioning."

In addition to the broad principles under UNFCCC Article 3, its Article 4 provides a framework for "commitments" with a focus on the relatively significant role sought from the developed countries. These "commitments" include, *inter alia*, the following:

All Parties, taking into account their common but differentiated responsibilities and their specific national and regional development priorities, objectives and circumstances, shall take climate change considerations into account, to the extent feasible, in their relevant social, economic and environmental policies and actions, and employ appropriate methods, for example impact assessments, formulated and determined nationally, with a view to minimizing adverse effects on the economy, on public health and on the quality of the environment, of projects or measures undertaken by them to mitigate or adapt to climate change. (Article 4.1 (f))

Regarding financial contribution by the developed countries, part of Article 4 states:

> The developed country Parties and other developed Parties included in Annex II shall provide new and additional financial resources to meet the agreed full costs incurred by developing country Parties in complying with their obligations under Article 12, paragraph 1. They shall also provide such financial resources, including for the transfer of technology, needed by the developing country Parties to meet the agreed full incremental costs of implementing measures that are covered by paragraph 1 of this Article and that are agreed between a developing country Party and the international entity or entities referred to in Article 11, in accordance with that Article." (Article 4.3)

A provision for Joint Implementation (JI) was made in Article 4.2 (a). This provides that Annex I countries may implement measures jointly with other parties to meet the GHG stabilization objectives. The parties at COP-1 decided to establish a pilot phase of "Activities Implemented Jointly" (AIJ) in order to gain experience and possibly calibrate the scheme using a "learning by doing" approach. The scheme is based on the fact that the capital costs of reducing concentrations of GHGs vary by the method of affecting the sources and sinks in different countries. The prevention of these emissions remains a priority as long as the cost-effectiveness criteria are met. JI allows one country to reduce the emissions or enhance the sinks for the GHGs of another country party, for example forest development, and obtain accountable credits for the activity. Different forms of JI activities were envisaged and have partly been implemented during the past few years under other international agreements as well. These JIs related to the UN Convention on Desertification, the Montreal Protocol, and the 1994 Sulfur Protocol to the Transboundary Air Pollution Convention. The Kyoto Protocol of COP-3 in its Article 6 allows the transfer and acquisition of emission-reduction credits accruing as a result of GHG emission-reduction projects among Annex B parties (as per the list under the Kyoto Protocol). Many JI projects seek to create investment schemes in host countries where the investor finds a cost-effective alternative to emission reduction with higher incremental costs in the originating country or at the source of emissions.

Projects under AIJ are mainly in two groups: (1) those reducing GHG emissions through enhanced energy-use efficiency, and (2) those expanding sinks for GHG absorption such as forestry projects. The forestry schemes tend to be among the least-cost measures and are rather popular in the current scenario. However, some critics argue that the schemes are not necessarily durable or replicable beyond a small limit. Cullet and Kameri-Mbote (1998) argued that JI does not take fully into account development impacts or local needs, and that it may discourage technological innovation in environmentally sound technologies in developed countries.

The need for reducing various transaction costs remains a high priority in the design and implementation of JI mechanisms. The role of the successive COPs is critical in this phase. Dudek and Wiener (1996) recommended that the COP and national governments act to foster "multiple, non-exclusive, visible clearinghouses for JI information," and for "entrepreneurial investment management vehicles." It was also suggested that competition mechanisms should be promoted for participants with the creation of contestable market institutions via the participation of public and private institutions in the host countries. The efficacy of JI schemes can be enhanced partly with the verifiable achievement of net carbon offsets at the project level. This requires a well-defined baseline in each specific project setting. For a few plausible alternatives in defining baselines for different categories of projects, see Michaelowa (1998). Besides, much uncertainty confounds the JI schemes and their net effects.

The Economic Report of the US President (1999, p. 194) declares that "under incentive-based regulation, sources of emissions may be more inclined to develop new technology that reduces pollution at lower cost than under alternative forms of regulation." Some examples of incentive-based approaches given in the Report were tradable emission permit systems, emissions taxes, subsidies to reduce pollution, and liability rules. One would, however, consider pollution liability rules as an element of disincentives rather than incentives.

The significant development after the formulation of the UNFCCC is the Kyoto Protocol. The Protocol needs ratification from the US and a few other countries.

 ## 6.3 THE KYOTO PROTOCOL AND LATER DEVELOPMENTS

The UNFCCC constitutes a trendsetter with few binding commitments of a verifiable or specific nature. The Kyoto Protocol proceeds further to specify the nature and extent of obligations; the binding obligations are, however, specified for a horizon of five years, with some flexibility in each commitment year for the parties. It is useful to note that the Protocol does not allow any reservations to be made by the parties

(Article 26). The Protocol was adopted in pursuance of Articles 2 and 3 of the UNFCCC. Article 2.1 of the Protocol states that each party included in Annex I, in achieving its quantified emission limitation and reduction commitments under Article 3, "shall implement and/or further elaborate policies and measures in accordance with its national circumstances." This assertion tends to limit the scope of any international policies designed at the global level without due consideration of national and local features.

Under Article 4, all parties are to prepare national inventories of emissions of GHGs by source and removals by sink, stock, and flow terms. This Article also requires parties to cooperate in controlling and reducing GHGs that remain outside the purview of the Montreal Protocol. More obligations are listed for Annex I countries to limit anthropogenic emissions of GHGs. The multiyear commitment period 2008–12 allows a great degree of flexibility over time in meeting the target reductions. Cost-effective methods of meeting the obligations of individual countries can be explored at the country level. Further devolution of such methods to decentralized regional or institutional settings and the use of a multilevel and multiperiod optimization approach are meaningful in this context.

Market mechanisms are accorded recognition in the provision of emissions trading or related mechanisms, under Article 4 (2) of the Protocol. Project-based trading credits is provided under Articles 6 and 3 (10), 3 (11), and 17. Article 6 provides, *inter alia*, that any party included in Annex I may

> transfer to, or acquire from, any other such Party emission reduction units resulting from projects aimed at reducing anthropogenic emissions by sources or enhancing anthropogenic removals by sinks of greenhouse gases in any sector of the economy, provided that:
> (a) Any such project has the approval of the Parties involved;
> (b) Any such project provides a reduction in emissions by sources, or an enhancement of removals by sinks, that is additional to any that would otherwise occur; . . .
> (d) The acquisition of emission reduction units shall be supplemental to domestic actions for the purposes of meeting commitments under Article 3.

Article 10 states:

> All Parties, taking into account their common but differentiated responsibilities and their specific national and regional development priorities, objectives and circumstances, without introducing any new

commitments for Parties not included in Annex I, but reaffirming existing commitments under Article 4, paragraph 1, of the Convention, and continuing to advance the implementation of these commitments in order to achieve sustainable development, taking into account Article 4, paragraphs 3, 5 and 7, of the Convention . . .

Articles 18 and 19 are some of the provisions for dealing with noncompliance by parties, and these articles simply allow the Conference of Parties to establish any future procedures to govern noncompliance. The UNFCCC dispute resolution process is nonbinding and can be initiated by one party to the Convention. The absence of implications for noncompliance remains an important gap in the Kyoto Protocol (see also Breidenich et al., 1998).

Among the market-based instruments for GHG reduction is emissions trading. This involves, after an initial allocation of pollution entitlements, states trading their quotas with each other so as to achieve their cost-minimizing choice of target fulfillment. In an UNCTAD (1994) study that followed the 1992 UNFCCC guidelines, the key ingredients for success of the emissions-trading program were suggested as the positive role of principal GHG-emitting countries, substantial monitoring and evaluation, and the active roles of national governments. In other words, the so-called market-based approach relies very heavily on state policies and entails substantial transaction costs.

The clean development mechanism (CDM)

Article 12 of the Kyoto Protocol established the clean development mechanism (CDM) to help developing countries achieve reduction of GHGs, stating that the mechanism's purpose shall be "to assist Parties not included in Annex I in achieving sustainable development and in contributing to the ultimate objective of the Convention, and to assist Parties included in Annex I in achieving compliance with their quantified emission limitation and reduction commitments under Article 3." The CDM seeks to assist developing countries in meeting the objectives of sustainable development and simultaneously allows the Annex B parties to obtain credit for "certified emission reductions." The details are being deliberated at the national and international levels, including the COP. In principle, the CDM encourages partnerships between the North and South, and also between private and public sectors via technology and resource transfer. If appropriate measures of activity transparency and efficiency are devised to govern the CDM, the mechanism could provide benefits to all participants.

▌ 6.4 OZONE DEPLETION, THE VIENNA CONVENTION, AND THE MONTREAL PROTOCOL

The ozone factor

A World Meteorological Organization report (WMO, 1986) observed that accumulations of specific chlorofluorocarbons (CFCs) – CFC-11 and CFC-12 – in the atmosphere had nearly doubled during 1975–85. The WMO assessment predicted that continued emissions of CFCs at the 1980 rate could reduce the ozone layer by about 9 percent on a global average by 2050. The possibility that higher levels of harmful ultraviolet (UV-B) radiation could reach heavily populated regions of the northern hemisphere was also indicated. It was also assessed that high atmospheric concentrations of chlorine could result in a potentially significant redistribution of ozone, with depletion in the upper stratosphere partially offset by increases in ozone at lower altitudes.

Various CFCs are generally used as refrigerants (propane and butane), foam insulation, aerosol propellants (in air-powered spray devices), electronic goods, and degreasing solvents for cleaning. A number of major initiatives, especially the Montreal Protocol and its follow-up actions, are expected to ameliorate the crisis but the possible continuity of damage to human and biotic health is not expected to disappear for another five or more decades. Various CFCs are being replaced by the substitutes hydrochlorofluorocarbons (HCFCs), hydrofluorocarbons (HFCs), and perfluorocarbons (PFCs). The phase-out of CFCs also applies to HCFCs, but these are allowed as interim substitutes as agreed in the 1990 London meeting of the parties of the Montreal Protocol. Just like CFCs themselves, HCFCs and HFCs are both potent gases; during a span of one hundred years after they are injected into the atmosphere, a ton of CFC-11 has about 4,000 times the global warming potential relative to one ton of CO_2, and a ton of HCFC-22 will have about 1,700 times the global warming potential of a ton of CO_2.

The Montreal Protocol on Substances that Deplete the Ozone Layer (September 16, 1987) entered into force on January 1, 1989 (26 ILM 1550, 1987). Bohm (1997) observed that (1) the Montreal Protocol seeks to control CFC use and not CFC emissions, and the difference has implications for the time-lag structure of accumulations of emissions; (2) the Montreal Protocol allows trade of CFC-based products among its signatories, thus dampening the potential for greater efficiency in reducing emissions; (3) the existence of nonsignatories can propagate enhanced emissions in those countries as long as some trade in CFC-based products from those countries is allowed into the countries that are parties to the Montreal Protocol. Bohm argued that despite its popularity as a well-conceived treaty and protocol, the Montreal Protocol is suboptimal or inefficient in that it discourages signatories from effecting reductions in CFC use below the allowed maxima, and also from reducing their "net CFC-use by bringing about efficient methods for destruction of CFCs in scrapped products" (1997, p. 330). Bohm suggested that, in general, the efficiency properties of alternative "initial treaty designs" be carefully examined before one design is embarked on. This is not to underestimate the role of political factors. However, an emphasis on articulating alternatives *ex ante* tends to broaden the comprehension of issues and provides a potential optimal solution based on a larger set of options. The role of transaction costs remains an influencing factor, but it would be futile to invoke that argument for lack of analytical soundness in any setting.

In terms of major international policy initiatives launched during recent decades, it is relevant to note the Convention for the Protection of the Ozone Layer in Vienna, held in March 1985, which mandated the ratifiers of the Convention to study the harmful effects of CFC emissions on the ozone layer and to conduct scientific research to find substitutes. The Montreal Protocol extended the Vienna Convention provisions by setting targets and limits on the emissions of CFC-11 and CFC-12, with the provision that the other villains of the ozone-depletion process such as methyl chloroform and carbon tetrachloride could be included for similar regulations later. The Montreal Protocol came into force on January 1, 1989 with the following features:

- the ratifiers must reduce their annual consumption and production of CFCs to their 1986 levels by July 1993;
- from July 1993 to June 1994 and during each year until July 1998, ratifiers' annual production and consumption of CFCs should stay below the limit of 80 percent of their 1986 levels;
- from July 1998 and after, the corresponding production should be limited to 50 percent of the 1986 levels.

By the end of 1995, 149 countries had ratified the Protocol.

The Protocol was strengthened with the 1990 London Amendments, which also expanded the list of ozone-depleting chemicals. For 1997 and the following years the levels could not exceed 15 percent of the base levels of 1986, and a complete phase-out by the year 2000 was mandated. Further enhancement of actions in this direction was sought at the Copenhagen Amendments in November 1992; the initial provision of interim substitutes for CFCs, namely, HCFCs, were also sought to be eliminated, along with carbon tetrachloride and methyl chloroform, by 1996. The most significant background for effective international collective action came from the scientific evidence in 1985 for the existence of a significant ozone hole and the analysis of factors behind it. The existence of illicit trade as a result of secondary markets for some CFCs in a few countries is an area of continued concern.

Murdoch and Sandler (1997) argued that since states were already under a CFC-reduction regime prior to the Montreal Protocol of 1987 and since there were substitutes for CFCs, it was not too hard for the developed countries to comply with obligations under the Montreal Protocol, and since there were financial resources tied to compliance for the developing countries, the latter also sought to fulfill the obligations under the Protocol. The degree of scientific certainty associated with the ozone phenomenon as well as the damage arising from ozone depletion were more influential in this case (unlike the phenomenon of global climate change, where establishing evidence with the same level of certainty still seems to be awaited).

6.5 DESERTIFICATION AND THE UN CONVENTION

Land degradation and desertification

Civilizations have drawn great strength from productive land resources. Loss of productivity through mismanagement ushered once flourishing societies to their ruin. Soil-quality deterioration and consequential loss in productivity are still very important, especially for poorer countries in their prospects for development. One of the most pressing environmental issues in the world is desertification, given the irreversibility of the damage to significant geographic areas. Yet it appears to have received much less attention than the gravity of the problem deserves. According to UN data, desertification affects about one-third of the world's land area and seems to obey the phenomenon of loss of ecological resilience. There appear to be serious links between climate change and desertification. The international community seems to have paid very little heed to the causes, effects, and adverse roles of international credit-lending institutions in this colossal phenomenon.

Land degradation may be viewed as the process by which land loses some of its natural productivity as a result of excessive grazing, crop-production activities, deforestation, and waterlogging, which is usually the result of faulty irrigation practices, the lack of conjunctive use of ground- and surface waters, and inadequate drainage of irrigation water. Soil loss and land-quality degradation are attributable to many factors, but amongst the most important are water management, water-logging, and salination of soils caused by poor irrigation practices.

Definitions

UNEP (1990) defined "desertification/land degradation" as land degradation in arid, semi-arid, and dry subhumid areas resulting mainly from adverse human impact. But that is not enough. The following definitions were given for the purposes of implementing the 1994 UN Convention on Desertification held at Paris: (1) "desertification" means land degradation in arid, semi-arid, and subhumid areas resulting from various factors, including climatic variations and human activities; (2) "land degradation" means reduction or loss, in arid, semi-arid, and dry subhumid areas, of the biological or economic productivity and complexity of rainfed crop land, irrigated crop land, or range, pasture, forest, and woodlands resulting from land uses or from a process or combination of processes, including processes arising from human activities and habitation patterns such as soil erosion caused by wind and/or water, deterioration of the physical, chemical, and biological or economic properties of soil, and long-term loss of natural vegetation.

The definitions of desertification adopted by the UNEP and the Earth Summit 1992 both imply linkage between climate change and the extent of desertification. Although finding a strong relationship between climate change and desertification is a complex task, there are a few detailed studies that suggest a valid relationship between the two. Hulme and Kelly (1993) examined data provided by Tucker et al. (1991), who used a satellite index of active vegetative cover to determine the extent of the Sahara desert. It was observed that there was an increasing trend in the area of the desert that could not be explained by rainfall variations alone; deterioration of vegetative cover caused by human activity was offered as a possible influencing factor.

Worldwide estimates indicated (*World Resources, 1996–97* and *1992–93*) that faulty agricultural practices account for 28 percent of the degraded soils; causes include shortening of the fallow period during shift cultivation, cultivating sloped topographic territories with inadequate soil-quality control measures, overgrazing, and insufficient drainage of irrigation water.

The causes of desertification include overgrazing, overcultivation, misuse of irrigation water, deforestation, and the impact of urban and industrial activities. More than 100 countries (mostly in the developing world) suffer the consequences of desertification or some form of severe land degradation. The Earth Summit 1992 agreed (Chapter 12 of Agenda 21) that projects to mitigate the phenomenon will qualify for allocation from the Global Environmental Facility (GEF), but only to the extent that the projects fulfill the goals of GEF by reducing greenhouse gas emissions, preserving biodiversity, and protecting transnational waters.

Surface air temperature has increased significantly in desertified regions owing to changes in land cover and this effect has substantially affected global mean temperature. The cyclical and cumulative effects of desertification/climate change phenomena tend to alternate when we consider the decreasing sink capacity for carbon sequestration. Balling (1991) argued that, during the twentieth century, desertified areas have warmed more than other areas; these regional segments of variations in mean surface temperature significantly "contaminate" the global mean temperature record and complicate the search for the villains behind global warming.

Anthropogenic influences and direct effects of land-use changes are the most consequential components of global change. Change in land use alters local ecosystems substantially enough to contribute directly to increased concentrations of greenhouse gases. These, in turn, affect local/regional climate and atmospheric chemistry. Desertification/land degradation seem to affect the most those areas that can afford the least – mostly the poorer regions – and marginalize many societies (where the average daily per capita income is around one dollar or less).

Land degradation and desertification should be of grave concern to the national and international communities for a number of important reasons (Daily, 1995): (1) increasing crop yields and production is crucial to meeting the needs of a growing population for food, fiber, and biomass energy; (2) anthropogenic changes in land use affect biogeochemical cycles that regulate greenhouse fluxes; (3) the preservation of biodiversity and the ecosystem depends on an appropriate combination of land quality and use patterns; and (4) land is a limiting factor of economic output, and its degradation threatens to undermine economic development in less developed nations as well as global social stability.

The UN Convention to Combat Desertification in those Countries Experiencing Serious Drought and/or Desertification, particularly in Africa (simply referred to as the UN Convention on Desertification) was held in 1994 and entered into force in 1997. This Convention defined desertification as land degradation resulting from factors including climatic variations and human activities. It also defined land degradation as meaning the loss or reduction of "biological or economic productivity and complexity . . . resulting from land uses or from . . . processes . . . arising from human activities and habitation patterns." The operative agreement of the Convention includes a number of general and specific provisions applicable to most of the member countries. The general obligations of the countries include adoption of integrated approaches to affect the processes of desertification and drought, and integration of strategies for poverty reduction with these efforts, and promotion of sustainable development.

The Convention lists a number of measures to be implemented, but there are hardly any tangible obligations or means of achievement in these desired objectives. An important feature should have been a mechanism of resource mobilization for achieving the desired goals, rather than a simple appeal to the developed countries to provide financial and technical assistance. It might be interpreted that the developed countries have a moral obligation for the colonial past when monopolistic rents were extracted and repatriated from most African countries during colonial rule, and also for the current trends in exacerbating global climate changes due to unsustainable consumption and production patterns. A separate fund and technical institutional base to combat desertification need to be created if any of the objectives of the Convention are to be met.

▨ 6.6 HAZARDOUS MATERIALS, THE BASEL CONVENTION, AND THE ROTTERDAM CONVENTION

The spatial and temporal externality-inflicting and persistent pollutant features of hazardous wastes, their production, trade, consumption, and indiscriminate disposal led to the negotiations and formation of the Basel Convention in 1989. It was signed by 35 states, including the EC. The US, producer of the largest quantities of these wastes, signed but has not yet ratified the Convention. The Convention prohibits exports to nonparties unless they are subject to an agreement at least as stringent as the Basel Convention, permits transfers of wastes only with the prior notification and consent of a "competent authority" in the receiving state, and seeks to promote environmentally sound management of these wastes.

The Basel Convention concerns the management of hazardous wastes from their generation to their final disposal and, in particular, the problem of transfrontier movements of such wastes. By the nature of the problem, international cooperation between exporting and importing countries for the protection of the global environment is called for. In the Convention, the environmentally sound management of hazardous wastes is defined as taking all practicable steps to ensure that hazardous wastes are managed in a manner that will protect human health and the environment against the adverse effects which may result from such wastes. The Convention establishes a prior information and consent regime for transboundary movement of hazardous wastes, but it does not establish a ban on such trade.

The liability rules or protocol have been attempted for about seven years so far, but the precise nature of liability and compensation for offenders transporting/dumping hazardous waste is as yet unresolved. As Krueger (1999) observed, a lesson from the Montreal Protocol for the Basel Convention and any of its follow-up protocols is to impose trade restrictions as an ingredient of the "overall package of regulations designed to restrict and eventually eliminate an environmental hazard."

As Murphy (1994, p. 60) argued, the "liability regime should complement the newly created international regulatory regime governing the hazardous wastes trade to help avoid mismanagement *ab initio*; the liability regime should be grounded on a sound data base that identifies weaknesses in the international regulatory regime."

The hazardous wastes trade cannot be left to market forces; in the long run, hazardous wastes trade is inefficient both for importing and exporting states (Hilz, 1992). To establish the point that there is a cyclical damage pattern here, it was suggested that some of the so-called domestically banned pesticides that are exported to other countries revert back in the foods imported by the chemical-exporting countries.

For a wide variety of reasons, including the role of the industry, more vigorous restrictions on the trade and consumption of hazardous chemicals have not been forthcoming. Even a relatively modern agreement such as the 1994 North American Agreement on Environmental Cooperation (NAAEC) stated simply on this subject: "Each party shall consider prohibiting the export to the territories of the other parties of a pesticide or toxic substance whose use is prohibited within the Party's territory" (Article 2 (3)).

A Note by the Secretariat of the Basel Convention (World Trade Organization Document WT/CTE/W/90 July 20, 1998 (98–2863)) stated that the main determinant for classifying a waste as hazardous is its intrinsic property (i.e., it exhibits or possesses one or more hazardous characteristics of Annex III). Annex I to the Convention is presumed to be the categories of wastes that are characterized as hazardous under the Convention. Wastes that belong to any of the two categories contained in Annex II that are subject to transboundary movements and classified as "other wastes" will be controlled under the Convention. Wastes that are not characterized as hazardous using Annexes I and III for this purpose, but are defined as, or are considered to be, hazardous wastes by the domestic legislation of the party of export, import, or transit, shall be "hazardous wastes."

At its fourth meeting in February 1998, the Conference of the Parties of the Basel Convention decided to add the two lists of wastes as two new annexes to the Convention, namely Annex VIII (list A) and Annex IX (list B).

1 List A. Wastes contained in this list are characterized as hazardous under Article 1, paragraph 1 (a) of the Convention, and their designation on this list does not preclude the use of Annex III to demonstrate that a waste is not hazardous.
2 List B. Wastes contained in this list will not be wastes covered by Article 1, paragraph 1 (a) of the Convention unless they contain Annex I material to an extent causing them to exhibit an Annex III characteristic.

Annex III of the Basel Convention contains a list of 14 hazardous characteristics. The Technical Working Group noted that uncertainties linked to the interpretation of the text of some of the hazard classes of Annex III, and in the absence of internationally accepted criteria for the classes H10 to H13, may present a problem for the implementation of the Convention.

Amendment of the Basel Convention

Recognizing the increased desire and demand of the international community for a ban on the export of hazardous wastes, especially to developing countries, the second meeting of the Conference of the Parties (1994) decided to immediately prohibit all transboundary movements of hazardous wastes which are destined for final disposal from OECD to non-OECD countries, and to phase out such movements for recycling or recovery operations by December 31, 1997 and prohibit them as of that date. At its third meeting, the Conference of the Parties agreed to adopt an amendment to the Convention incorporating this export ban into the Convention itself. The parties decided to amend the Convention by inserting a new Article 4 A, which stipulates that each party listed in a new Annex VII shall prohibit all transboundary movements of hazardous wastes that are destined for operations according to Annex IV-A to states not listed on Annex VII immediately. States listed on Annex VII are the members of the OECD and the EC, and Liechtenstein.

The Fifth Session of the Intergovernmental Negotiating Committee for an International Legally Binding Instrument for Implementing International Action on Certain Persistent Organic Pollutants (POPs) was held at Johannesburg during December 4–9, 2000. Representatives from 122 countries finalized the text of a legally binding treaty that requires governments to eliminate the use of 12 harmful POP chemicals. Financial and technical assistance to developing countries is also to be provided under this agreement to enable these countries to implement the provisions. More details are available from www.chem.unep.ch/pops/.

Use of the harmonized system of the World Customs Organization (WCO)

The Conference of the Parties of the Basel Convention has given the mandate to the Secretariat of the Basel Convention to cooperate with the World Customs Organization (WCO), in collaboration with the European Commission and OECD, on matters concerning the separate identification of wastes in the harmonized system. As of today, significant progress has been made to include entries for wastes covered by the Basel Convention in the harmonized system. As a general principle, separated harmonized system subheadings should be created for hazardous wastes which are environmentally sensitive and whose transboundary movements have to be controlled or which are important in international trade.

Reasons for the occurrence of illegal traffic in wastes, including hazardous wastes, are manifold and have their roots in the following: the increasing cost of disposal and differences in disposal costs;

differences in national/domestic law and regulations; high profit margin; difficulties in proving acts as criminal; liberalization of trade; the lack of a uniform definition of what a waste or hazardous waste is; the plurality of international/regional legal instruments concerning hazardous waste and the difficulties in following their provisions; and the lack of harmonization on the enforcement side.

The absence of a fund similar to the Montreal Protocol Fund severely constrains the financial and technical capabilities of several developing countries in their strict adherence to the specifications under the Basel Convention.

The Rotterdam Convention

The 1998 Rotterdam Convention on Harmful Chemicals and Pesticides (adopted and signed September 11, 1998) constitutes a major step in moderating the trade and its effects in cases of some of the listed hazardous chemicals. Article 1 of the Convention states its objective:

> to promote shared responsibility and cooperative efforts among Parties in the international trade of certain hazardous chemicals in order to protect human health and the environment from potential harm and to contribute to their environmentally sound use, by facilitating information exchange about their characteristics, by providing for a national decision-making process on their import and export and by disseminating these decisions to Parties.

Some of these measures are proposed to be implemented using the process of prior informed consent (PIC), originally devised about a decade ago by the Food and Agriculture Organization (FAO), UNEP, and other international organizations. The PIC procedure is a means for formally obtaining and disseminating the decisions of importing countries as to whether they wish to receive future shipments of a certain chemical and to ensure compliance to these decisions by exporting countries. The aim is to promote a shared responsibility between exporting and importing countries in protecting human health and the environment from the harmful effects of such chemicals.

A voluntary PIC procedure has been operated by UNEP and FAO since 1989, based on the amended London Guidelines for the Exchange of Information on Chemicals in International Trade and the International Code of Conduct on the Distribution and Use of Pesticides.

The new PIC procedure contained in the Rotterdam Convention is an improvement of the original procedure and is based largely on the experience gained during the implementation of the original. The Convention will enter into force once 50 countries have ratified it. As a first among the multilateral environmental agreements (MEAs), governments have agreed to continue to implement the voluntary PIC procedure using the new procedures of the Convention until the Convention formally enters into force. UNEP and FAO have been assigned the responsibility for acting as Secretariat of the Convention.

The Convention requires that hazardous chemicals and pesticides that have been banned or severely restricted in at least two countries shall not be exported unless explicitly agreed by the importing country. It also includes pesticide formulations that are too dangerous to be used by farmers in developing countries. The legally binding treaty, when it enters into force, will reduce the environmental and health risks posed by hazardous chemicals and pesticides. It will protect millions of farmers, workers, and consumers in developing countries and reduce threats to the environment, according to FAO and UNEP. This will be achieved by helping governments to prevent chemicals that they cannot safely manage from being imported into their country. If a government does choose to accept an import of a hazardous chemical or pesticide, the exporter will be obliged to provide extensive information on the chemical's potential health and environmental dangers. In this way, the treaty will promote the safe use of chemicals at the national level, particularly in developing countries, and limit the trade in hazardous chemicals and pesticides.

The Rotterdam Convention on the PIC procedure for certain hazardous chemicals and pesticides in international trade was signed by ministers and representatives from 57 countries and the EC, but the Convention has not yet entered into force. No reservations may be made to this Convention, in accordance with the stipulation of Article 27. The Convention covers 22 hazardous pesticides. Article 2 defines three categories of chemicals for regulatory purposes. A "banned chemical" means a chemical all uses of which within one or more categories have been prohibited by final regulatory action, in order to protect human health or the environment; a "severely restricted chemical" means a chemical virtually all use of which within one or more categories has been prohibited by final regulatory action in order to protect human health or the environment, but for which certain specific uses remain allowed; and a "severely hazardous pesticide formulation" means a chemical formulated for pesticidal use that produces severe health or environmental effects observable within a short period of time after single or multiple exposure, under conditions of use.

The scope of the Convention, as stated in its Article 3, is to cover (1) banned or severely restricted chemicals, and (2) severely hazardous pesticide formulations. Article 13 specifies information to accompany exported chemicals and the role of customs harmonization, to be implemented in cooperation with the WCO. Article 14 states that exchange of scientific, technical, economic, and legal information concerning the chemicals within the scope of this Convention, including toxicological, ecotoxicological, and safety information, shall be facilitated; and also that information on precautionary measures, including hazard classification, the nature of the risk, and the relevant safety advice, will be exchanged among parties to the Convention.

In addition to PIC for select chemicals and their byproducts, a set of related chemicals, persistent organic pollutants (POPs), deserves attention in MEAs. POPs are chemical substances that persist, bioaccumulate, and pose the risk of causing adverse effects to human health and the environment. The use of such persistent, bioaccumulating, and toxic substances cannot constitute a sustainable development practice. POPs are chemicals or byproducts that resist degradation in the environment. They accumulate in the body fat of animals. Concentrations increase for each upward step in the food chain. The effects of consuming POPs can be serious, including harmful effects on fertility and embryo development, damage to the nervous system, and cancer.

The international coordination and regulation of specific chemicals and their products at the consumption level is a complex management problem, considering that it is difficult even in the domestic scenario of a developed economy. Dernbach (1997) analyzed the diversity of elements and lack of focus in regulating hazardous chemicals in the domestic context in the US. The number of pollutants on each legislative Act was observed to vary considerably, as seen from the list below. Some inconsistencies are perhaps inevitable and may be attributable to differences in the effects of specific pollutants in different media (indoor air, land, water, outdoor air, etc.). It was suggested that a facility-wide or cross-media approach based on pollution prevention provides a useful foundation for regulatory regimes. The regulated pollutants common to all five Acts below numbered only 49, despite the fact that their individual coverage of pollutants is substantially higher, with the total number of different regulated pollutants being 1,134. The five US Acts and their regulated pollutants are (Dernbach, 1997):

- Clean Water Act, 148
- Resource Conservation and Recovery Act, 502
- Clean Air Act, 189
- Occupational Safety and Health Act, 450
- Emergency Planning and Community Right-to-Know Act, 599

6.7 TRANSBOUNDARY WATER AND AIR POLLUTION AGREEMENTS AND CONVENTIONS

Environmental externality problems have been of special concern for states if they are in the nature of physically neighboring externalities. Many agreements and regional conventions that have evolved over the past century relate to this category. The 1979 Convention on Long-range Transboundary Air Pollution (LRTAP) held at Geneva (entered into force in 1983) sought to address some of the problems of "transboundary air pollution," which it defined as "air pollution whose physical origin is situated wholly or in part within the area under the national jurisdiction of the State and which has adverse effects in the area under the jurisdiction of another State at such distance that it is not generally possible to distinguish the contribution of individual emission sources or groups of sources" (see 18 ILM 1442, 1979).

LRTAP was the first international agreement dealing with the problem of acid rain, caused mainly by emissions of sulfur dioxide. It was also considered the first international agreement involving atmospheric environmental policy and engaging both East and West. There were no mandatory restrictions on pollutant emissions when the Convention was first formed, but its subsequent Protocols led the parties into that direction. Among the key factors in the implementation of the Convention are the exchange of information and an undertaking among parties to engage in research initiatives in order to "gradually reduce and prevent air pollution including long-range air pollution."

It is interesting to note the attempts to integrate economic and other factors with the environmental objectives under the Convention. For example, Article 7 seeks contracting parties to initiate/cooperate in research, including "the economic, social, and environmental assessment of alternative measures for attaining environmental objectives including the reduction of long-range transboundary air pollution."

All 34 states that are either members of the European Commission for Europe (ECE) or the EC have become parties to the LRTAP Convention.

All of the countries that ratified the 1985 Helsinki Sulfur Protocol to the Convention achieved the required 30 percent reduction (from their 1980 levels) in sulfur dioxide emissions by the target date of 1993 (Soroos, 1997). Reduction of nitrous oxide (in accordance with the 1988 Sofia Declaration) by a similar percentage has become a more formidable task, however. As Soroos (1997, p. 143) noted, "[t]he impact of the LRTAP regime may be less in the protocols that limit and reduce the release of acid-forming air pollutants than in the institutional processes it has set in motion."

The LRTAP Convention parties reached a new sulfur protocol in 1994. This agreement focused on the "critical loads" aspect, based on the amount of sulfur deposition that constitutes tolerance thresholds at the level of individual ecosystems and organisms, thus incorporating the important concepts of resilience and ecosystem stability. A critical load was defined (based on the UNECE Working Group on Nitrogen Oxides, February 1988; quoted in Munton et al., 1999, p. 169) as "a quantitative estimate of an exposure to one or more pollutants below which significant harmful effects on specified sensitive elements of the environment do not occur according to present knowledge."

International water resources

Unlike most other natural resources, water resources exhibit strong physical externalities due to groundwater seepage and other ecosystem links, especially within the river-basin area. A basin is usually defined as the hydrogeological system including and surrounding a river or water-resource system. Accordingly, any principle of water management needs to recognize this important feature. Similarly, the roles of riparian and downstream water users in riverwater are also tied inextricably both to limiting water supplies or flood catastrophes.

An ecosystem approach was perhaps first initiated at the international level during the 1972 Stockholm Conference. Canada and the US employed this integrated approach six years later in the Great Lakes Water Quality Agreement, and further agreements subsequently sought to do the same. In its 1993 guidelines on the ecosystem approach to water management, the UN Economic Commission for Europe (UNECE, 1993) recommended that the entire catchment area be treated as an integrated ecosystem, and the river-basin system be treated as an ecosystems continuum. The International Law Commission (ILC, 1994), in its 1994 draft Article 20, proposed that riparian states "protect and preserve the ecosystems of international watercourses." Ideally, the river-basin system is most suitable for planning an optimization of system resources for environmental sustainability and sustainable development. However, most river-basin systems tend to cut across more than two countries and involve considerable information-sharing and credible cooperative behavior among states with hydrological interdependencies, and thus they are harder to define as a single physical entity. Interpreted differently, the river-basin concept itself can be seen as an application of the precautionary principle (Teclaff, 1996), provided the integrated systems approach recognizes the role of uncertainty and irreversibility in the complete sense.

Some of the old agreements in international water allocation and management did not take into account several types of externalities. Those agreements represented "static attempts to 'regulate' without necessarily seeking to foster further cooperation" (Brunne and Toope, 1997, pp. 40–1). It was suggested that an ecosystem-oriented regime-building tends to be more useful for international water laws: "in view of states' reluctance to subject sovereignty over resources to international interests, regimes should not aim at the 'internationalization' of the resource itself."

Chapter 18 of Agenda 21 of the 1992 Rio Declaration stresses the importance of "holistic management of freshwater as a finite and vulnerable resource" and states that "in developing and using water resources, priority has to be given to the satisfaction of basic needs and the safeguarding of ecosystems" (paragraph 18.8). The principle of equitable utilization of water resources is contained in the 1997 UN General Assembly Convention on the Law of the Non-navigational Uses of International Watercourses, adopted on May 21, 1997 (UN Doc. A/51/L72, 1997). Its Article 6 contains an illustrative list of factors for the attainment of "optimal and sustainable utilization" of international watercourses:

> Geographic, hydrogeographic, hydrological, climatic, ecological and other factors of a natural character;
>   The effects of the use or uses of the watercourses in one watercourse State on other watercourse States; and
>   Conservation, protection, development and economy of use of the water resources of the watercourse . . .

The interaction of international public laws and international environmental laws in the water sector is illustrated in a landmark judgment of the ICJ, summarized in box 6.2. The Court's decision is likely to contribute toward CIL in the water-resources sector.

BOX 6.2

The Gabcikovo-Nagymaros project and the ICJ decision

This is recognized globally as the first international environmental case adjudicated by the ICJ and as the first to set a trend in international water law. The Gabcikovo-Nagymaros project originated in a 1977 treaty between the Hungarian People's Republic and the Czechoslovak Socialist Republic for the construction of a system of water dams/locks in the Danube River, the second largest river in Europe. The treaty entered into force on June 30, 1978. An important provision of the treaty was its Article 15.1, which stated: "the Contracting Parties shall ensure, by the means specified in the joint contractual plan, that the quality of the water in the Danube is not impaired as a result of the construction and operation of the System of Locks."

Alleging risks to its environment and Budapest's water supply, and claiming "ecological necessity," Hungary suspended and later abandoned the project in 1989. The Slovak Republic ("Slovakia") succeeded Czechoslovakia as a party to the agreement and denied the Hungarian claims. Slovakia initiated its own projects, and these were alleged to adversely affect the Hungarian environment and access to water. The two countries failed to resolve their differences via a mediation forum, and the matter was submitted to the ICJ for adjudication. The Court's decision was awarded on September 25, 1995 at the Hague.

Hungary advocated five arguments in support of its claim of lawful termination of the 1977 treaty via its notification of May 19, 1992. These five aspects were: the existence of a state of necessity; the impossibility of performance of the treaty; the occurrence of a fundamental change of circumstances; the material breach of the treaty by Czechoslovakia/Slovakia; and, the development of new norms of international environmental law. Hungary stated in its arguments to the ICJ that "the previously existing obligation not to cause substantive damage to the territory of another state had . . . evolved into an *erga omnes* obligation of prevention of damage pursuant to the 'precautionary principle.'" The ICJ rejected the first four arguments by applying general customary rules of the 1969 Vienna Convention on the Law of Treaties. Since the treaty itself did not contain provisions regarding its termination, this issue had to be determined on the basis of the 1969 Law of Treaties, principles of CIL, and the Statute of the ICJ.

The magnitude of environmental harm likely to be inflicted by a series of construction works was not known since Hungary never completed the works at Dunakiliti and Nagymaros. The ICJ was to weigh the merits and risks, being "mindful that, in the field of environmental protection, vigilance and prevention are required on account of the often irreversible character of damage to the environment" (*The Gabcikovo-Nagymaros Project*, ICJ, September 25, 1997; paragraph 140). The judges panel comprised 15 members. The ICJ found it difficult to support Hungary, as Hungary failed to prove threat of "grave and imminent peril" to invoke the "state of necessity" exception (defined by the ILC Draft Articles on State Responsibility, UN Doc. A/35/10, 1980) for the unilateral termination of its 1977 treaty. According to Articles 60–62 of the 1969 Vienna Law of Treaties, the treaty can be terminated only by the mutual agreement of the parties, or by the fulfillment of all conditions of abrogation specified in the treaty itself (see also chapter 2).

The ICJ did not offer any absolute priority among any of multiple objectives of the project, nor to the protection of the environment over the other objectives, because of the legal context that "neither of the Parties contended that new preemptory norms of environmental law had emerged since the conclusion of the 1977 Treaty" (paragraph 112). Some of the ICJ references to the protection of the environment include the following:

> the environment is not an abstraction but represents the living space, the quality of life and the very health of human beings, including generations unborn. . . . The existence of the general obligation of States to ensure that activities within their jurisdiction and control respect the environment of other States or areas beyond national control is now part of the corpus of international law relating to the environment. (paragraph 53)

> the Treaty is not static, and is open to adapt to emerging norms of international law. . . . The awareness of the vulnerability of the environment and the recognition that environmental risks have to be assessed on a continuous basis have become much stronger in the years since the Treaty's conclusion. (paragraph 112)

> The Project's impact upon, and its implications for, the environment are of necessity a key issue . . . new norms have to be taken into

consideration . . . not only when States contemplate new activities but also when continuing with activities begun in the past. This need to reconcile economic development with protection of the environment is aptly expressed in the concept of sustainable development. (paragraph 140)

Some authors expressed their opinion that the ICJ missed an important opportunity to interpret and express a full ruling on the stance of Hungary that invoked an application of the precautionary principle (see, for example, McIntyre, 1998; de Castro, 1998).

Sources: Bourne (1997); McIntyre (1998); Nakamichi (1998); www.icj-cij.org/ idocket/ihs/ihsjudgement/ihsjudframe1.htm (January 2, 2000). Quotations reproduced with the permission of the International Court of Justice

◼ **6.8** SUMMARY

International policies, especially environmental laws governing identified global environmental problems, tend to include both types of global commons: *res communis* and *res nullius*. However, lack of clear provisions concerning the exercise of property rights in the former, and of liability rules in the latter, are structural impediments. This is not to state that there are well-defined liability regimes in *res communis*, nor that they are less important. Clarity on the two characteristics of the global commons enables relative priority of attention to the governance aspects.

In addition, there are problems of cross-media environmental damage due to the interdependencies of biogeochemical and other systems and their components. Cross-media pollution includes (see Hohmann, 1994) the transfer, directly or indirectly, of environmental damage or hazards from one area to another or from one environmental medium (the atmosphere, the land, water resources, and the marine environment) to another, or the transformation of one type of pollution into another. A comprehensive Protocol to the UNFCCC might be useful to cover cross-media environmental damage, liability, and the provision of precautionary measures in this regard. Such a comprehensive legal regime could possibly lead to undesirable applications of the *non liquet* norm to escape state responsibilities.

The Kyoto Protocol has a prominent role through its provision of legally binding reductions in emissions of GHGs. However, the prerequisites for the Protocol's effectiveness would include greater provision of incentives for the developing countries to voluntarily accept more obligations, and more transparent specifications of verifying fulfillment of commitments by various countries. The model of the Montreal Protocol Multilateral Fund may be relevant, as long as it does not create disincentives for active innovations in a dynamic framework.

Review Exercises

1 Identify the incentives and disincentives under the UNFCCC and the Kyoto Protocol for developed country parties to fulfill their GHG reduction commitments.

2 Examine the role and applicability of the precautionary principle in the provisions under the Basel Convention on prior informed consent.

3 What constraints, legal or other, operate in the application of the integrated river-basin concept in a transboundary watercourse? Is there any role for an arbitration panel or bargaining mechanism that could enable gains to the competing or contesting parties in the allocation and usage of riverwaters?

4 Examine the existing scope for liability rules under the Basel Convention. Also, examine the application of the polluter pays principle in its different forms of potential application to hazardous waste disposal.

5 If cross-media pollution contributes to multiple environmental problems, what guidelines are relevant in the apportioning of costs for the purpose of application of the polluter pays principle?

REFERENCES

Balling, Jr., R. C., 1991, Impact of desertification on regional and global warming, *Bulletin of the American Meteorological Society*, 72, 232–4.

Bekker, P. H. F., 1998, Gabcikovo-Nagymaros project, *American Journal of International Law*, 92, 273–8.

Bohm, P., 1997, Efficiency issues and the Montreal Protocol on CFCs, in P. Dasgupta and K. G. Maler (eds.), *The Environment and Emerging Development Issues*, Vol. 2, Oxford: Clarendon Press, pp. 309–35.

Bourne, C. B., 1997, The case concerning the Gabcikovo-Nagymaros project: An important milestone in international water law, in *1997 Yearbook of International Environmental Law*, Oxford: Clarendon Press, pp. 6–12.

Breidenich, C., Magraw, D., Roley, A., and Rubin, J., 1998, The Kyoto Protocol to the United Nations Framework Convention on Climate Change, *American Journal of International Law*, 92, 315–31.

Brunne, J., and Toope, S. J., 1997, Environmental security and freshwater resources: Ecosystem regime building, *American Journal of International Law*, 91, 26–59.

Cullet, P. and Kameri-Mbote, A., 1998, Joint Implementation and forestry projects: Conceptual and operational fallacies, *International Affairs*, 74 (2), 393–408.

Daily, G., 1995, Restoring value to the world's degraded lands, *Science*, 269, 350–4.

de Castro, P. C., 1998, The judgment in the case concerning the Gabcikovo-Nagymaros project: Positive signs for the evolution of international water law, in *1997 Yearbook of International Environmental Law*, Oxford: Clarendon Press, pp. 21–31.

Dernbach, J. C., 1997, The unfocused regulation of toxic and hazardous pollutants, *Harvard Environmental Law Review*, 21, 1–82.

Dudek, D. J. and Wiener, J. B., 1996, *Joint Implementation, Transaction Costs, and Climate Change*, OECD Document OECD/GD(96)173, Paris: OECD Secretariat.

Hilz, C., 1992, *The International Toxic Waste Trade*, New York: Van Nostrand Reinhold.

Hohmann, H., 1994, Cross-media pollution and international environmental law, *Natural Resources Journal*, 34, 535–61.

Hulme, M. and Kelly, M., 1993, Exploring the links between desertification and climate change, *Environment*, 35, 4–11 and 39–43.

International Law Commission (ILC), 1994, *Report of the Commission on the Work of its 46th Session, Draft Articles on the Law of the Non-navigational Uses of International Watercourses*, UN. Doc. A/49/10, 1994.

Krueger, J., 1999, What's to become of trade in hazardous wastes? The Basel Convention one decade later, *Environment*, 41, 10–21.

McIntyre, O., 1998, Case law analysis: Environmental protection of international rivers, *Journal of Environmental Law*, 10, 79–91.

Michaelowa, A., 1998, Joint Implementation: The baseline issue, *Global Environmental Change*, 8 (1), 81–92.

Munton, D., Soroos, M., Nickitina, E., and Levy, M., 1999, Acid rain in Europe and North America, in O. R. Young (ed.), *The Effectiveness of International Environmental Regimes*, Cambridge, MA: MIT Press, pp. 155–247.

Murdoch, J. C. and Sandler, T., 1997, The voluntary provision of a pure public good: The case of reduced CFC emissions and the Montreal Protocol, *Journal of Public Economics*, 63, 331–49.

Murphy, S. D., 1994, Perspective liability regimes for the transboundary movement of hazardous wastes, *American Journal of International Law*, 88, 24–75.

Nakamichi, M., 1998, The International Court of Justice decision regarding the Gabcikovo-Nagymaros project, *Fordham Environmental Law Journal*, 9, 337–72.

Rao, P. K., 2000, *Sustainable Development: Economics and Policy*, Oxford: Blackwell.

Soroos, M. S., 1997, *The Endangered Atmosphere: Preserving a Global Commons*, Columbia: University of South Carolina Press.

Teclaff, L. A., 1996, Evolution of the river basin concept in national and international water law, *Natural Resources Journal*, 36, 359–91.

Tucker, C. J., Dregne, H. E., and Newcomb, W. W., 1991, Expansion and contraction of the Sahara Desert from 1980 to 1990, *Science*, 253, 299–301.

UN Conference on Trade and Development (UNCTAD), 1984, *Combating Global Warming: Possible Rules, Regulations and Administrative Arrangements for a Global Market in CO₂ Emission Entitlement*, UNCTAD Doc. UNCTAD/GID/8, Geneva: UNCTAD Secretariat.

UNCTAD, 1994, *Combating Global Warming: Possible Rules, Regulations and Administrative Arrangements for Global Market in CO₂ Emission Entitlement*, Report UNCTAD/GID/8, Geneva: UNCTAD Secretariat.

UN Economic Commission for Europe (UNECE), 1993, *Protection of Water Resources and Aquatic Ecosystems, Part 1: Guidelines on the Ecosystem Approach in Water Management*, UN Doc. ECE/ENVWA31, 1993.

UN Environment Program (UNEP), 1990, Global assessment of land degradation/desertification, *Desertification Control Bulletin*, 18, 24–5.

US President, 1999, *Economic Report of the US President 1999*, Washington, DC: US Government Printing Office.

World Meteorological Organization (WMO), 1986, *Atmospheric Ozone 1985: Assessment of Our Understanding of the Process Controlling Its Present Distribution and Change*, Geneva: WMO Secretariat.

World Resources, 1992–93, World Resources Institute Publication, New York: Oxford University Press.

World Resources, 1996–97, World Resources Institute Publication, New York: Oxford University Press.

part III

Integration and Synthesis

Various concepts and principles of economics, in addition to traditional concepts of law and economics, need to be integrated with possible areas of application in international environmental laws. It is not proposed here that economics should be given a hierarchical edge over all other ingredients of analysis, such as political feasibility, social acceptance, or anthropological considerations. What is advocated, however, is the need for the due recognition of a role for the economics of institutions, ecological and environmental economic principles, and rational economic decision-making criteria. An ideal global economic welfare-maximization approach usually presumes the existence of a coordination mechanism equipped with full information. Since this is not feasible in reality, attempts should be made to accomplish an optimal mix of institutions and policies that seek in a sustainable manner to achieve welfare maximization in a local and global sense. Implicit in this approach is the balance of interests of different groups or entities of economic, legal, political, or other standing.

This part comprises three chapters. Chapter 7 deals with some of the common features of international economic laws in the international public law area, and of international environmental laws in several areas. A number of potential improvements in institutional arrangements, policy formulations, and law development are suggested here, including the scope for a revision of the definition of customary international law, the role of reservations in treaties, and the use of complementary positive measures for sustainable development. The roles of multilateral development finance institutions such as the World Bank and the European Bank for Reconstruction and Development are briefly discussed in relation to their environmental contributions. In addition, chapter 7 also discusses equity among states, the application of the common but differentiated responsibilities principle, and the provision of incentives for compliance with international laws, and of disincentives for noncompliance. Chapter 8 deals with the interface of environmental laws with policies and laws governing international trade, with an attempt to reconcile the two streams. International trade liberalization and its impact on environmental quality is briefly examined in this chapter. In addition, the issues of conflict and complementarity of trade laws under the world trading system (especially in relation to the trade regime under the World Trade Organization) are explored. Dispute resolution in this context is discussed in the final chapter, which focuses on the main features of compliance, dispute resolution, and the effectiveness of international environmental laws. The importance of environmental information and the role of nongovernmental organizations (NGOs) are also discussed in chapter 9. The economics of information and the economics of incentives and disincentives are critical in the design and practice of relevant international laws, and assume greater significance in international public law relative to domestic laws and their governance. Hence the need to continue the search for the "optimal provision" of these ingredients. Good governance, if not the most "efficient" governance, remains a relatively scarce international public good. Thus, we foresee constraints on the efficient design and implementation of global public goods (which seek to ensure internalization of externalities at least "cost" and equitable and efficient allocation of resources) in terms of constraints on the design of institutional configurations that are stable and "efficient." The challenge that lies ahead is to seek these, without necessarily creating additional layers of bureaucratic organizations for the "coordination" or "enforcement" of policies and legal arrangements.

chapter seven

International Economic Laws and Environmental Laws

▌ 7.1 INTRODUCTION

International economic laws affect and partly govern national and international activities in the areas of finance, trade, and economic interdependence. Most activities tend to be influenced by the specifications of bilateral or regional agreements of economic cooperation, wherever these exist. These, however, tend to be affected by international economic laws or their operative procedures, such as customs duties in international trade. It is useful to note that there are very few international economic laws that explicitly address global economic externalities. This stands in contrast with the laws that seek to contain or mitigate global environmental externalities. It is expected to be efficient and cost-effective whenever an integration of economic and environmental laws can be achieved. However, such integrated measures affect multiple existing laws and implementation procedures. This chapter seeks to examine some of the major issues in the law and economics of the international environmental regimes, in relation to international economic laws.

The role of property rights and liability laws remains a common underlying theme in both economic and environmental laws. An interface of these laws brings to light these and other factors which tend to complement each other in achieving welfare-maximizing provisions in the legal and administrative mechanisms. Some of the existing legal provisions need to be revised for this purpose. The need to consider a core set of economic criteria in conjunction with other institutional imperatives is emphasized. It is suggested that even when so-called pragmatic requirements (such as political acceptance, popular sentiments, practicability, and other factors) are to be accommodated, a normative framework remains useful in seeking solutions or policies that tend to deviate least from a somewhat ideal setting. In such an attempt, the "costs" of such deviations or the types and magnitudes of tradeoffs become more explicit to the decision-making entities. Some of these integrated exercises rely on a heavy dose of the analytical methods of optimization and other decision-making tools, which are not elaborated in this book. This is not to suggest that mathematical derivations can form a better set of prescriptions for policy or legal provisions, but they can assist in informed judgments and supplement the role of strategic decision-making, say with some use of game theory (described briefly in chapter 2). These are some of the themes briefly addressed later in this chapter.

■ 7.2 GLOBAL WELFARE AND COMPLEMENTARITY OF LEGAL PROVISIONS

Domestic laws and international laws interact in both directions. Some countries have laws that are more effective in most features than some other countries. The differences in the provision of legal measures on the statute book are usually a necessary but not a sufficient indicator of the effectiveness of legal regimes. "Soft regimes" of government tend to compromise most provisions of the statutes to suit the conveniences of the powerful (whether political, financial, or other). These domestic "governance" features can be reflected in the implementation of international laws as well. In the absence of special incentives (such as those under the Montreal Protocol and its Fund), it may not be realistic to expect that a country party to an international treaty or other agreement will ensure greater compliance with international laws than with domestic laws. Ideally, however, it is desirable that gaps in the laws are examined and appropriate complementary measures initiated using a systems approach (or comprehensive coverage of legal measures). These gaps are thus typical for a given country, and their universalization (except at very basic levels) may not be feasible.

The ingredients of economic analysis to assist in devising a comprehensive legal framework (not necessarily all-pervading legalese) are also important if economic welfare and its integration with environmental sustainability are to be achieved. Various relevant concepts (most of which are discussed in chapters 1 to 3) constitute elements of a comprehensive approach to global welfare enhancement. They include:

- Pareto welfare improvement in the short run and/or long run.
- Intragenerational and intergenerational equity.
- Spatial and intertemporal dimensions of
  (a) generalized resource use efficiency and equity;
  (b) generalized allocative efficiency and equity.
- Integration and coordination of laws for economic and environmental governance.
- Application of the relevant principles of sustainable development and adoption of broad approaches at the country level, and in relation to global governance.
- Minimization of *ex ante* and *ex post* transaction costs of alternative policy interventions, actions, or inactions.
- Issues in the specification of objective functions, constraints, time horizons, and discount factors.
- Maximization of global economic welfare with specifications in terms of the above.
- Role of uncertainty and incomplete information and their treatment in terms of perceptions and acceptance of risks, including risk-sharing (or risk diversification) and risk-pooling (or preparing for the greatest risks).

This is merely a core checklist for consideration in any global environmental management problem, from the viewpoint of economic analysis. The design of institutional configurations, including the legal provisions for recognition of these aspects, is a major exercise in the integration of law, economics, and politics. Clearly, these normative considerations do not debar inclusion of the requirements of pragmatism or practicability. The result of approaching governance issues using this core list is to enable conscious decision-making. When suboptimal choices are to be made, they are considered second-best or their approximations rather than a set of prescriptions (whose "efficiency" properties are unknown) derived out of group dynamics involved in collective decision-making.

Some of the important elements of a comprehensive framework for legal institutions for global environmental governance are briefly outlined below. Some of these features apply to both international economic laws and international environmental laws.

1. The ICJ framework and its refinements

Some of the provisions of the ICJ Statute seem to warrant updating after more than 50 years of observance. Explicit and implicit priorities at the time the ICJ was formed differ from those of the current era. While seeking to retain the robustness and predictability of legal institutions and their norms, it is also useful to address the dynamic aspects of legal provisions. The following is one such issue.

Article 34 of the ICJ Statute specifies that "only states may be parties in cases before the Court," and that the Court shall receive relevant information from "public international organizations on their own initiative." These provisions remain serious impediments to potential contributions of competent private organizations, including several nongovernmental organizations (NGOs). The issue of allowing *locus standi* for nonstate entities is also related to any possible action based on an *amicus curiae* petition to the Court. Failure to fully appreciate the problems of global environmental externalities and the imperatives of global commons management is the major factor constraining legal actions under such stipulations. Such restrictive provisions were perhaps justified in the 1940s, when there were minimal concerns about global environmental problems and attention was more focused on disputes involving state parties.

2. Reservations in treaties

The provision of "reservations" or "declarations" in various treaties remains a complex issue. In so far as these are utilized by the parties to genuinely condition their commitment with transparent and unavoidable exclusions or contingencies, rather than implicit and strategic motives to deviate from the treaty obligations, there is merit in such provisions. In general, such provisions tend to expedite a state's ratification of the treaty and enable the treaty's entry into force sooner rather than later. There have also been a number of treaties which do not allow any specification of reservations or declarations (such as the Kyoto Protocol and the UN Convention on the Law of the Sea). Perhaps such stringency resulted in a few cases in ratification by a reduced number of parties (such as the UN Convention on the Law of the Sea) and delayed their entry into force. The main issue is whether significant exclusions of parties' obligations tend to constitute a set of secondary free-riders (within the framework of a Convention or environmental phenomenon), while seeking to minimize free-riders in the global environmental public goods arena. Another related issue is whether several or significant exclusions of some parties (such as in the case of CITES) lead a hard law toward soft law, while claiming that it remains a legally binding hard law for others. The answer to both these predicaments is largely in the affirmative. Global environmental problems could perhaps do without "reservations" and "declarations" in most cases.

3. Improved definitions of customary international law

The role of *opinio juris*, legality, morality, obligatory behavior, and other related features in the evolution of customary international law (CIL) is but one aspect of the behavioral description of CIL. Other major variants include the role of strategic behavior, the features of repeated prisoner's dilemma and other strategies in intentional cooperation, and lack of a unitary explanatory factor for the evolution of international cooperation and states' pursuit of self-interest (see also Goldsmith and Posner, 1999). Determining whether a specific law forms CIL or not is a question based on a somewhat empirical practice. In other words, most laws do not become CILs by simply declaring them to be so. Nor do the practices of a few states for some time periods enable a specific law to qualify under CIL. The issue is the threshold level beyond which it is considered a CIL, based on state practice and/ or widespread acceptance. This threshold should, normatively stated, be linked to the environmental or ecological thresholds of relevance in maintaining or affecting resilience. For example, whether rotatory forest plantation and deforestation constitute a CIL should be interpreted in accordance with existing international laws and practices, and also the implications of accepting or rejecting a norm of practice (or legal provision) for environmental sustainability features.

4. Provisions for measures to address noncompliance

In most international environmental agreements, the implications of noncompliance with stated obligations are never specified. For some states compliance is an issue of reputational significance, or it may serve other interests, but it is not the deterrence of the consequences of noncompliance that brings states into line with the stated obligations. While recognizing that there are hardly any apex-level enforcement mechanisms or organizations to levy penalties or other costs from states, the provision of disincentives will be relevant for establishing a track record of compliance or otherwise, including respect for the provisions of noncompliance. This reputational mechanism can be tied to financial or technical assistance provisions under some agreements such as the Montreal Protocol. Chapter 9 addresses further issues in the context of the optimal provision of incentives and disincentives for compliance.

5. Positive measures for multilateral environmental agreements (MEAs)

The term "positive measures" does not appear in most MEAs, nor in Agenda 21 of the 1992 Rio Declaration. The UN Conference on Trade and Development (UNCTAD, 1997, paragraph 2) sought to define these mechanisms to include not only measures to "promote full participation and compliance on the part of all parties to MEAs, but also measures which could be used to encourage a dynamic process of continuously improving environmental performance that might go beyond the obligations in MEAs." Such measures include capacity building, institutional reform, technology transfer, information management, product harmonization, and dynamic economic instruments. These are proposed to invoke dimensions of equity, in addition to efficiency, and enable wider participation of all member countries. It was also noted in this context that "failure to comply with the provisions of MEAs is rarely the result of deliberate policies of parties, but rather the consequences of deficiencies in administrative, economic or technical infrastructure" (ibid., paragraph 4). Positive measures are thus considered important supplements to meet the inadequacies of compliance and effectiveness mechanisms. Some positive measures are already in place in some select MEAs: the UN Framework Convention on Climate Change (UNFCCC), the Convention on Biological Diversity (CBD), and the Montreal Protocol. The last one allows a developing country to notify the Protocol Secretariat of its inability to fulfill its obligations as a result of inadequate implementation of Articles 10 and 10A of the Protocol relating to technology transfer. Two of the major multilateral funding mechanisms for MEAs are the Multilateral Fund under the Montreal Protocol, and the Global Environmental Facility (GEF) designated to assist in the implementation of the CBD and the UNFCCC.

■ 7.3 INTERNATIONAL ECONOMIC LAW

International economic law refers to both public international law and private international law governing a set of economic activities affecting or affected by cross-country transactions. International economic law includes laws of economic activities, governmental or intergovernmental regulation of economic transactions, and stipulations of international legal or other institutions affecting economic transactions across countries and multilateral institutions.

International economic law tends to be largely in the domain of international private economic law rather than public international law. It deals with protection of foreign properties, repatriation of profits in commerce, dispute settlement in foreign investments, equity participation and rules governing these and other sets of economic and financial matters. We do not propose to examine them here. A major group of international economic laws arises from bilateral rather than multilateral treaties, largely affecting foreign direct investments. It is uncommon to find any mention of the role of the environment in these treaties (although a few environmental hazard safety standards or corresponding potential liabilities are usually outlined).

States undertake bilateral treaties to encourage foreign investment, since customary law provides a weak legal framework for foreign investment. Sornarajah (1994, p. 142) concluded that the principle of sovereignty over economic activity that takes place within the state has not been eroded. There are currently no multilateral treaties governing foreign investment. Bilateral investment treaties (BITs) exist in large numbers and are of tremendous importance. The "substantive provisions" of a BIT specify the required standard of treatment of investment, repatriation of profits, nationalization and compensation terms, clauses requiring the protection of commitments made between the multinational corporation (MNC) and the host, and dispute resolution clauses. BITs represent a framework through public international law of what is, essentially, a private international law issue. BITs are a form of contracting between foreign investors and the host state. A contractual damages clause can set the level of damages that is consistent with the efficient outcome, but the cost to the host of breaching an agreement under a regime without contracting may be lower or higher than the optimal level, depending on the host's acceptance or internalization of accruing costs.

Although any norm, convention, treaty, or practice governing international economic activities or transactions constitutes international economic law, more specific ingredients refer to relevant treaties among countries. Environmental issues tend to overlap with some of these. Traditionally, the narrow confines of international economic law addressed issues of global commerce and expropriation of property and resources under the changing control of individuals or institutions (including relief from alien rule). International customary law provides a basis for the exercise of various property rights and liability claims. Bilateral and multilateral investment treaties are some of the special laws affecting international economic relations in specific contexts. Furthermore, the existence and role of several international economic organizations is governed by various multilateral treaties. Some of these, for example the Organization for Economic Cooperation and Development (OECD) or the European Community (EC), are regional organizations applicable to a smaller number of member countries and their economic transactions. Among the major international economic institutions are the following:

- International Bank for Reconstruction and Development (IBRD, also called the World Bank), created in 1945.
- International Monetary Fund (IMF), created in 1945.
- International Finance Corporation (IFC), created in 1956 by the IBRD to make loans to private enterprises rather than to states.
- General Agreement on Tariffs and Trade (GATT), formed in 1947, and its successor the World Trade Organization (WTO), which came into existence from 1995.

The "Bretton Woods System" of institutions comprising the IBRD, IMF, and the GATT 1947 (to distinguish it from its revised version called GATT 1994, now a part of the WTO) was launched soon after World War II to revitalize the global economy and development. US laws under the Bretton Woods Agreements Act seek to maintain substantial control over the IBRD and the IMF where the voting powers of the decision-making forum are weighted by the capital contributions from its financial resources. Accordingly, the terms of financial resource flows or eligibility for these among the developing countries are regulated by the Boards of these institutions in tune with political and economic developments from time to time. Environmental considerations are not yet fully integrated into the activities of these institutions, which do not even mention "the environment" in their articles of organizational formation (with the exception of the European Bank for Reconstruction and Development, EBRD). Chapter 8 deals with more specific issues of international development finance and environmental aspects.

International finance is closely related to international trade phenomena, and multilateral financial mechanisms affect the global environment directly and through trade regimes. The next section provides a summary of some of the implications of global financial institutional alignments.

■ 7.4 MULTILATERAL DEVELOPMENT FINANCE AND ENVIRONMENTAL LAWS

Among the most important multilateral financial institutions are the World Bank and the International Monetary Fund. Neither institution in its articles of agreement refers to the terms "environment" or "sustainable development." However, several measures have been initiated by the Bank in this direction in recent years. It can be argued that the scope for enhanced provision remains significant. As an important and largest shareholder of the Bank's capital resources, the US government tends to play a major role in effecting changes in policies at the Bank. This became more prominent in the mid-1990s (see Bowles and Kormus, 1996).

The Bank's Operational Policies Directive 4.04 of September 1995 declares: "The Bank does not support projects that, in the Bank's opinion, involve the significant conversion or degradation of critical natural habitats." The interpretation of "significant" remains rather arbitrary, and the Bank retains its own interpretation in judging itself. The inapplicability of some of the lender liability laws in environmental damage seems to be an aspect of the lack of disincentives for suboptimal environmental performance (see Rao, 2000).

The Bank's *1998 Pollution Prevention and Abatement Handbook* sets out a few guidelines and a more comprehensive framework. In addition, the Bank issued new guidelines for environmental assessment beginning in 1999. The involvement of select NGOs in sectors such as forestry was also initiated. A few new schemes, such as the Carbon Fund to reduce emissions of greenhouse gases via shifts to renewable sources of energy, are also under active formulation for implementation.

The GEF coordinated within the World Bank network was launched to address the resource needs of developing countries in their attempts to fulfill the obligations under the UNFCCC, the Montreal Protocol, and the Convention on Biological Diversity. Article 1 (6) and (9) of the GEF state the criteria for providing assistance to developing countries in their fulfillment of obligations under the UNFCCC and the CBD. These include, in addition to the criteria set by the Conference of Parties of the two Conventions, that countries must be eligible to borrow from the World Bank or an eligible recipient of UN Development Program (UNDP) technical assistance (see also Di Leva, 1998).

The general reach of customary international law and various MEAs extends to multilateral development banks (MDBs), as pointed out by Handl (1998). MDBs have an obligation to obey the provisions of international law rather than condescendingly assert at times that they, too, care for the environment. This requirement holds whether or not their respective articles of association or incorporation explicitly recognize the role of environmental sustainability of economic activities influenced by their financial or other resources. It is sometimes suggested that the MDBs cannot overstep the sovereignty of the borrowing countries in order to impose environmental conditionalities. This argument is incoherent when we recognize that the MDBs impose various forms of conditionalities (only a few of which are substantially rational or fully informed decisions) and interfere with the economic and fiscal policies of the borrower countries. The MDBs are obligated, as instruments of the international community, to avoid causing environmental harm and also to contribute toward affirmatively protecting the environment. The international legal obligations of the MDBs extend to their specific lending activities in both the state and private sectors. Thus, the IFC's role in promoting private enterprises is not without obligations to enhance the quality of the environment or to contribute to the processes of sustainable development.

International debt contracts

International debts have a number of significant environmental implications. Here we turn our attention to two potentially innovative features: (1) the design of sovereign debt contracts and incentives in coordination with environmental performance features; and (2) the provision of new articles of agreement to allow more flexible debt restructuring.

An internationalized version of the US Insolvency Chapter 9 (usually applied in relevant municipal institutions in the US) could potentially be useful to address international debt contract enforcement issues (see Raffer, 1990 for a detailed proposal). This provision could enable a public hearing of the parties involved and lead to environmentally benign policies in the borrower countries as it diminishes pressures of constrained and ecologically destructive exports for meeting debt obligations. In short, another form of debt restructuring with soft landing and transparency can be effected by this legal provision. More alternative mechanisms of debt management can also be considered, possibly provided in the *ab initio* loan contract. These alternatives in the menu are expected to enhance the borrowers' compliance to the terms of the debt contracts, minimize the disequilibrating effects of the entire loan processes, and enhance environmental sustainability and sustainable development. A useful analysis of the "menu approach" to debt relief and rescheduling can be seen in Franke (1991); this can be extended to include explicit provisions of environmental dimensions, environmental markets, and global emissions trading and their financial integration with debt instruments (Rao, 2000).

Indigenous people, knowledge, and globalization

Granting intellectual property rights to innovations and knowledge products is a conventional method of converting public goods into private goods in the industrial countries. However, patenting and commercializing is not a standard practice in many societies, especially in respect of indigenous knowledge such as the pharmacological prescriptions of tribal communities. The relevant information remains in the informal sector and is usually uncodified and unwritten knowledge. In the absence of external influences such as multinational pharmaceutical companies, the knowledge base is preserved and localized for the benefit of local people. Efforts to commercialize and globalize can potentially benefit vast multitudes of people all over the planet and deserve support. The path from wild or exotic biota to their medicinal or other commercial production can be significantly shortened, in some cases, by using the knowledge of the indigenous people. Of the 119 known pure chemical compounds being used in the world, 88 were discovered through leads from traditional and alternative medicinal knowledge (Wilson, 1992). However, the crucial issues of equity and justice as well as the rights of indigenous people cannot be ignored for ethical as well as efficiency reasons, if the methods are to be widely acceptable and expandable.

Principle 22 of the Rio Declaration declares that "[i]ndigenous people and their communities . . . have a vital role to play in environmental management and development. . . . States should recognize and support their . . . interests and enable their effective participation in the achievement of sustainable development." Some "development projects" tend to routinely dislocate the life and livelihood of indigenous people, without the latter's consent in the process. Multilateral lending institutions such as the World Bank play a significant role in these activities. The Bank issued its own Directives and guidelines relatively recently; however, the importance attached to the issues remains feeble. For example, the Bank's Operational Directive 4.01 on Environmental Assessment states that "[i]ssues related to indigenous peoples are commonly identified through the environmental assessment or social impact assessment, and appropriate measures should be taken under environmental mitigation actions." The problem lies in compliance to the Directive and in presuming that there are mitigation actions that can offset the irreversible problems that ensue from uprooting and exploiting indigenous peoples. The Bank maintains that its policy is based on the strategy of "informed participation of the indigenous people" and that a "full range of positive actions by the borrower must ensure that indigenous people benefit from development investments" (OD 4.20, Operational Manual of the World Bank, 1998).

The European Bank for Reconstruction and Development (EBRD)

The EBRD is the first multilateral development bank to have an explicit environmental mandate in its charter. The charter states that the Bank is to "promote in the full range of its activities environmentally sound and sustainable development." The EBRD has no overarching environmental policy or criteria to guide its project lending. As a consequence, the EBRD has financed projects that are inconsistent with its mandate to promote sustainable development, as documented in a report by the Center for International Environmental Law (CIEL). The EBRD's policy and procedures for public participation and disclosure of information are also rather weak.

The EBRD's failure to integrate long-term environmental goals into its operations policies undermines all other Bank efforts to promote sustainable development in Central and Eastern Europe, according to the CIEL study. The EBRD should also develop criteria and standards to ensure that the projects it funds are consistent with its sustainable development policy. Environmental assessments (EAs) are the Bank's principal tools for determining the environmental impacts of its actions, but it needs to utilize these assessments fully. Fewer than 5 percent of the Bank's projects have received full EAs. Unlike the World Bank, the EBRD does not require any discussion of global impacts in its EAs.

7.5 ENVIRONMENTAL RESPONSIBILITY OF INTERNATIONAL ORGANIZATIONS

It goes without clarification that no international organization is above international law. Accordingly, international organizations are

BOX 7.1

Developing countries and differentiated responsibilities

Common responsibilities do not always imply common obligations or standards of performance. The common but differentiated responsibilities principle among states was formally endorsed as Principle 7 of the 1992 Rio Declaration. It is the common concern of global environmental issues that brings together heterogeneous states to a common understanding in solving a problem at hand or foreseen to occur in the future. However, it is the sense of equity and differentiated responsibility that allows states to stay together in tackling the problems in the most "effective" manner. Due recognition of the varied accountability and capacity of individual states to mitigate adverse problems or prevent some problems remains an important aspect of the larger participation of states in global environmental governance. Such an element of reasoned differentiation can only enhance commitment and compliance, not reduce it, given the added sense of moral responsibility on each specific state. As French (2000) argued, the concept of differentiated responsibilities tends to promote the efficacy of common and cooperative actions.

Principle 7 of the Rio Declaration also includes an assertion that developed countries place greater pressures on global environmental resources and hence the differential responsibilities are in part due to this aspect of environmental responsibility to be addressed in greater proportion by the developed states relative to other states. The other reasons include the technical and financial resources the developed states command. The UNFCCC and the CBD also refer to the "common but differentiated responsibilities" principle. Article 3.1 of the UNFCCC specifies that the parties shall be guided, *inter alia*, by the following:

> The Parties should protect the climate system for the benefit of present and future generations of humankind, on the basis of equity and in accordance with their common but differentiated responsibilities and respective capabilities. Accordingly, the developed country Parties should take the lead in combating climate change and the adverse effects thereof.

The International Law Association's International Committee on Legal Aspects of Sustainable Development (ILA, 1995, p. 116) stated in its report: "The rationale for [the notion of common but differentiated responsibilities] lies in 'the different contributions to global environmental degradation' and not in different levels of development." Neumayer (2000) rightly argued, in the context of greenhouse gas emissions and differentiated responsibilities, that "[i]gnoring historical accountability would give a retrospective license to past emitters from developed countries to disadvantage the poorer countries." This could also imply ignoring Principle 21 of the Stockholm Declaration, whereby states should refrain from causing damage beyond their jurisdictional limits. This prescription is also consistent with the just role of property rights, which rests on the absence of negative externality-causing utilization of property and exercise of property rights (Nozick, 1974). In addition to these factors, the fact that the developed states can, in general, address problems with less drag on their economies is an important "capacity" feature. One of the important underlying aspects of differentiated responsibilities is to avoid the problem of seeking the "lowest common denominator" (LCD) or the least amount of common responsibility uniformly acceptable across states. The latter is evidently suboptimal and inefficient in resolving global problems attributed to heterogeneous groups of states. Optimal provision of incentives and disincentives can be viewed as an economic problem to circumvent underlying LCD problems. As Halvorssen (1999) suggested, allowing for differential norms (as a form of equity among unequal states) tends to avoid LCD phenomena. The economics of differential norms needs to be advanced in the approach of total welfare maximization and Pareto-efficiency.

mandated to respect international environmental laws and do not seek to promote an era of global environmental externalities and *res nullius*. These institutions have a responsibility to minimize any potential to invoke *non liquet* as a defense against environmental damage, especially transboundary damage affecting the global commons.

The fact that some international institutions have not included "environment" or "sustainable development" in their articles of formation or memoranda of agreement is neither an excuse nor does it constitute lawful conduct of activities if there is substantial disregard to universal laws and customary international laws. The existence of a treaty or relevant articles of agreement can constitute an improved "ground level" of environmental concerns and stipulations of policies, and not a "ceiling level" of relevant compliance or legal improvisations.

The contribution of international financial institutions to environmental preservation should also arise from appropriate "lender liability laws" somewhat analogous to those in the domestic laws of some developed countries. The absence of such laws should not be construed as freedom to exploit any free-rider features of the global commons, to the advantage of some of the financial institutions' shareholders and to the disadvantage of the stakeholders of the human community in general. Global equity aspects do not support such positions, which constitute a reversal of the soft law of "common but differentiated responsibilities" in the governance of the global environment.

7.6 INTERFACE OF INTERNATIONAL ECONOMIC AND ENVIRONMENTAL LAWS

In general, international economic laws should integrate environmental considerations in order that economic policies remain sustainable. Similarly, international environmental laws should incorporate economic aspects in order that environmental protection is maximized or afforded in a cost-effective manner. Ignoring economic considerations altogether could imply reduced availability of resources for economic development activities. This could also imply reduced resources for sustained environmental actions or preserving global resources, and could lead to relative vulnerability of economic systems to cater to environmental or other problems that are not necessarily contributed by anthropogenic influences. Economic progress with reasonable environmental constraints implies a transformation of inputs into outputs, and this can possibly continue with technical innovations contributing to enhanced efficiency of production. As long as this process is ensured to continue unimpeded, environmental and economic sustainability remains secure.

CIL and bilateral treaties are among the main instruments of both economic and environmental laws in international public law. Market institutions play important roles in the governance of economic resources. However, the same does not hold for environmental resources, in the absence of markets for several resources. Hence the continued need for greater recognition of environmental factors in economic laws, including those governing the functioning of the economic factor markets. Relative inefficiencies of markets in environmental resources obviate the role of supplementary laws and enforcement. Problems of irreversibility are more relevant in environmental phenomena. An interface of international economic laws with international environmental laws reveals the relative shortcomings of economic laws in their neglect of environmental factors, a prerequisite for ensuring the sustainability of economic laws themselves.

Markets and other institutions

Economic theory, in its elementary form, suggests the equalization of marginal costs of pollution abatement as a necessary condition (but not usually a sufficient condition) to minimize the total costs in achieving a given level of environmental protection (see, for example, Keohane et al., 1998). Transaction costs are critical in the selection of policy instruments, market-based or other.

Market failures may not exist, but relative inefficiencies of markets do. An efficient organization design is suggested as one that minimizes the aggregate of the two main elements of costs to society (Trachtman, 1996): transaction costs in effecting the final resource allocation (presumably the desired allocation), and the deadweight loss due to failure to provide the optimal mix of environmental protection and other goods and services. Let us consider the example of trade in wild species.

The market value of commercial transactions of wild animals and plants and wildlife products (fur skins, ivory, special forest wood, and others) runs into several billion dollars per annum, mainly driven by consumer demand from affluent developed countries. Although wildlife species are indeed renewable natural resources, they also have a critical threshold level below which a decrease in reproduction capacity becomes virtually irreversible (Sand, 1997). This leads to extinction, despite potential *ex situ* conservation with the latest scientific techniques of gene preservation, assuming this is done well in advance, before extinction occurs. The *Red Data Books*, compiled since 1966 by the Species' Survival Commission of the World Conservation Union (IUCN), document species' extinction potential and the Red List categorizes the status of a species as "vulnerable," "endangered," or "critically endangered." International trade rules to prevent a "free-rider" dilemma are necessary to prevent unilateral bans penalizing individual importing or exporting countries relative to their less scrupulous competitors (Sand, 1997). State responsibility in trade imports and exports is generally weakened not necessarily by conscious connivance with illegal traders, but states may not possess adequate resources to enforce relevant legislative actions. The alternative is not to leave the matter to the tyranny of market forces. A judicious approach would call for active stakeholder participation, with NGOs and other entities supplementing their efforts. Enhanced public access to information and environmental justice is critical in this regard.

The relative roles of domestic laws versus international laws, domestic economic laws versus domestic environmental laws, international economic laws versus international environmental laws, and international economic regimes versus international environmental regimes are some relevant issues for further investigation.

International environmental regimes

International regimes are "social institutions consisting of agreed upon principles, norms, rules, procedures, and programs that govern the interactions of actors in specific issue areas" (Levy et al., 1995, p. 274). Regimes are often viewed as enhancers of international cooperation, as possible mechanisms for alleviating failure of cooperative efforts to the collective outcomes that lie closer to the Pareto-efficiency frontier (Sandler, 1997). A number of studies concerning the relative effectiveness of international environmental regimes may be seen in Young (1999a). Young (1999b, p. 276) argued that "the capacity of a regime to contribute to an improved understanding of the problem to be solved and to evolve to handle new tasks is surely a significant determinant of effectiveness in many cases." As an illustration, the regime for LRTAP was considered relevant for depicting regime effectiveness.

The exogenous and endogenous evolution of regimes remains an area for further investigation. Similarly, the dynamic properties of regimes to address changing circumstances and new information is an important aspect of significance in the design and reform of regimes. The role of dynamic incentives and information in the evolution of regimes is an important topic for attention. The ingredients of information in international environmental regimes include those related to scientific features of environmental phenomena in relation to other environmental and/or economic factors, and feedback information from states that are parties to an international agreement (as well as information related to the free-riders in relation to one or more environmental phenomena). The scientific information is usually exogenous to the regime, but the remaining elements of information are largely endogenous to the regime. Efficient information systems generally evolve when the initial agreement includes clear specifications on the formats and frequency of information sought from parties, and when this information is supplemented by additional sources such as NGOs. The European Union can be considered an economic as well as an environmental regime. Some of the salient features of this international regime are examined below.

The European Union (EU)

Select provisions of the treaty establishing the EC (as amended and renumbered by the Amsterdam Treaty of 1999) (see, for example, Folsom, 1999) are given here. Article 5 of the Maastricht Treaty on European Union (TEU) limits the role of regional actions when these can be better formulated at EU level rather than at the national level. The 1999 Amsterdam Treaty added a Protocol on the application of the principles of "subsidiarity" and "proportionality," respectively stated (see Folsom, 1999). The latter refers to the requirement that EU action must not go beyond what is necessary to achieve the objectives of the Treaty of Rome. The former is enunciated in Article 3b of TEU:

> In areas which do not fall within its exclusive competence, the Community shall take action, in accordance with the principle of subsidiarity, only if and in so far as the objectives of the proposed action cannot be sufficiently achieved by the member states and therefore, by reason of scale or effects the proposed action can be better achieved by the Community.

The original 1957 Treaty of Rome establishing the European Economic Community (EEC) did not contain the term "environment." Early efforts on environmental standards relied upon Article 94 (legal harmonization) and Article 308 ("necessary and proper" powers clause). In 1987, the Title XIX Environment (Articles 174 to 176) Agreement specified the general policy and principles for adoption in the Community. The 1993 Maastricht Treaty on European Union (TEU), which changed the nomenclature from EEC to EC, included this statement: "Environmental protection requirements must be integrated into the definition and implementation of other Community policies." For a detailed account of developments in environmental legislation leading to and effective from the 1997 Amsterdam Treaty (which became operational in 1999), see Bar and Kraemer (1998). The detailed aspects of the EU's bridging role between domestic and international environmental policy-making is elucidated by Liberatore (1997).

Among other items, the role of cost–benefit analysis ("the potential benefits and costs of action or lack of action") in the formulation of environmental policy is outlined in Article 174 (3). Article 176 specifies that member countries may adopt more stringent environmental protection measures subject, however, to the treaty provisions.

Article 174 provides, *inter alia*, the following:

1. Community policy on the environment shall contribute to pursuit of the following objectives:

   preserving, protecting, and improving the quality of the environment; protecting human health; prudent and rational utilisation of natural resources; promoting measures at international level to deal with regional or worldwide environmental problems.

2. Community policy on the environment shall aim at a high level of protection taking into account the diversity of situations in various regions of the Community. It shall be based on the precautionary principle and on the principle that preventive action should be taken, that environmental damage should as a priority be rectified at source and that the polluter should pay.

Implementation of environmental law in the EC

In 1996 the Commission issued a communication on implementation and sought to publish periodic reports. Access to justice as well as nonjudicial ways of solving intracommunity problems were addressed. The importance of imposing sanctions for noncompliance was also considered. The European Union Network for the Implementation and Enforcement of Environmental Law (IMPEL) was created in 1992 to promote the exchange of information and operational issues leading to a coherent approach in environmental legislation and enforcement. IMPEL was subsequently called upon to examine the problems of noncompliance aspects and to provide further guidelines (for further updates, visit www.europa.eu.int/comm/dg11/index_en.htm).

A wide disparity between EC member states' environmental inspection activities has been observed. The EC envisaged a role for IMPEL in this context. The involvement of IMPEL emphasizes the

Commission's intention to involve those with implementation and enforcement responsibilities in the member states. In its communication of 1996 the Commission emphasized the importance of appropriately deterrent sanctions for noncompliance with the requirements of the Directive. Council Directive 90/313/EEC of June 7, 1990 is designed to ensure freedom of access to information and dissemination of information on the environment which is held by public authorities and to set out the basic terms and conditions on which such information should be available (some of the EC publications, coordinated by its Directorate XI, are described on DG XI's Internet site at the following address: http://www.europa.eu.int/comm/dg11/index_en.htm).

The EC Directives tend to constitute regional law for the member states. In cases of dispute, the European Court of Justice (ECJ) gives its verdict on issues of economic, environmental, or other significance. Box 7.2 summarizes a problem arising from the interface of economic and environmental issues. The Court in this case interpreted relevant articles to imply that environmental imperatives take an overriding role in relation to economic factors, as provided in the original EC Birds Directive governing habitats for birds.

▮ 7.7 MODERNIZING AND REFORMING THE LAWS AND THEIR IMPLEMENTATION

Laws are of little significance if their effectiveness and compliance are weak. Effective integration of environmental and economic laws is a prerequisite for enhanced effectiveness of laws with respect to their objectives. Such an integration also enables their cost-effective implementation. Although some developed countries have taken a few measures in this direction, most developing countries lag behind in this regard. The quality of legal institutions in some of these countries also requires upgrading of their infrastructure as well as technical support and law enforcement. The practice of international law in these countries tends to be constrained not necessarily by its separateness relative to domestic laws but by the general constraints of the legal systems themselves. It is thus incorrect to construe that some of the acts of noncompliance observed by these states result from calculated moves by parties to international agreements. This position does not absolve parties of their obligations, but an objective assessment would suggest that these parties might require assistance from some of the developed countries in strengthening the rule of law and

BOX 7.2

Economic factors and EC bird conservation: The ECJ decision

This summary is based on the judgment of the European Court of Justice (ECJ) of July 11, 1996 regarding EC Directive 79/409/EEC on the conservation of wild birds; Directive 92/43/EEC on the conservation of the natural habitats of wild fauna and flora; the delimitation of Special Protection Areas; the discretion enjoyed by the member states; economic and social considerations; and Lappel Bank.

In February 1995, the UK House of Lords referred to the Court for a preliminary ruling under Article 177 of the EC Treaty two questions on the interpretation of Articles 2 and 4 of Council Directive 79/409/EEC of April 2, 1979 on the conservation of wild birds (OJ 1979 L 103 p. 1, hereinafter "the Birds Directive").

These questions were raised in proceedings between an association for the protection of birds, the Royal Society for the Protection of Birds (hereinafter "the RSPB"), and the Secretary of State for the Environment (hereinafter "the Secretary of State") concerning a decision designating a special protection area for the protection of wild birds.

The Birds Directive, which covers all species of birds naturally occurring in the wild in the European territory of the member states to which the treaty applies, provides, in Article 2, that the member states are to take all necessary measures to maintain the population of all those species of birds at a level which corresponds in particular to ecological, scientific, and cultural requirements, while taking account of economic and recreational requirements. Article 3 of the Birds Directive provides that the member states, having regard to the requirements mentioned in Article 2, are to take all necessary measures to preserve, maintain, or reestablish a sufficient diversity and area of habitats for all the protected species.

Pursuant to Article 4 (1) of that Directive, the species mentioned in Annex I are to be the subject of special conservation measures concerning their habitat in order to ensure their survival and reproduction in their area of distribution. In particular, the member states are to classify the most suitable territories in terms of number and size as Special Protection Areas for the conservation of those species in the geographical sea and land area where the Directive applies.

According to Article 4 (2),

Member States shall take similar measures for regularly occurring migratory species not listed in Annex I, bearing in mind their need for protection in the geographical sea and land area where this directive applies, as regards their breeding, moulting and wintering areas and staging posts along their migration routes. To this end, Member States shall pay particular attention to the protection of wetlands and particularly to wetlands of international importance.

The first question is whether Article 4 (1) or (2) of the Birds Directive is to be interpreted as meaning that a member state is authorized to take account of the economic requirements mentioned in Article 2 thereof when designating a Special Protection Area and defining its boundaries. The Court observed that Article 4 of the Birds Directive lays down a protection regime which is specifically targeted and reinforced both for the species listed in Annex I and for migratory species, an approach justified by the fact that they are, respectively, the most endangered species and the species constituting a common heritage of the Community.

The Court ruled that Article 4 (1) or (2) of Council Directive 79/409/EEC of April 2, 1979 on the conservation of wild birds is to be interpreted as meaning that a member state:

1 "is not authorized to take account of the economic requirements mentioned in Article 2 thereof when designating a Special Protection Area and defining its boundaries";

2 "may not, when designating a Special Protection Area and defining its boundaries, take account of economic requirements as constituting a general interest superior to that represented by the ecological objective of that directive"; and

3 "may not, when designating a Special Protection Area and defining its boundaries, take account of economic requirements which may constitute imperative reasons of overriding public interest of the kind referred to in Article 6 (4) of Directive 92/43/EEC of 21 May 1992 on the conservation of the natural habitats of wild fauna and flora."

Sources: www.europa.eu.int/eur-lex/en/index.html (March 10, 2000); www.curia.eu.int/en/jurisp/index.htm (March 10, 2000). Quotations reproduced with the permission of the European Court of Justice developing appropriate laws and law-enforcement mechanisms. An international institutional arrangement to assist the needy states should constitute a part of the technical and financial help provided under such agreements as the Montreal Protocol. The issue of capacity building engages attention in some of the funding mechanisms under the GEF, but the focus is on technical issues and there is insignificant attention to institutions to ensure sustainable economic and environmental laws as well as their implementation.

The 1992 World Conference on Environment and Development (WCED), in its Agenda 21 (Chapter 39) dealing with international legal instruments and mechanisms, sought among other things:

1 "the further development of international law on sustainable development, giving special attention to the delicate balance between environmental and developmental concerns";
2 "the need to clarify and strengthen the relationship between existing international instruments or agreements in the field of environment and relevant social and economic agreements or instruments, taking into account the special needs of developing countries"; and
3 "The overall objective of the review and development of international environmental law should be to evaluate and to promote the efficacy of that law and to promote the integration of environment and development policies through effective international agreements or instruments taking into account both universal principles and the particular and differentiated needs and concerns of all countries."

The role of legal institutions in several developing countries is not invariant to the quality of political institutions and power centers that control various aspects of the life of the citizenry. International influences in the provision of legal institutions could possibly lay foundations for the sustainable development of the institutions themselves, so that various obligations under international law are fulfilled as a corollary to the functioning of the systems. The evolution of CIL and treaty compliance, among other things, are then better addressed in such a context.

The issue of equity in global resource allocation and the provision of common responsibilities translated into differentiated responsibilities, both *de facto* and *de jure*, and changes in scientific and economic information require laws to be dynamic rather than static. This imperative suggests regular updating and modernization of environmental and economic laws.

Harmonization of environmental standards

The regulatory processes imposing harmonization of standards seek to ensure the compatibility of products and thus minimize cases of non-compliance *ex post*. Harmonization is often misinterpreted in terms of only one of its particular cases, namely, uniform harmonization. There is a wide variety of alternatives in the harmonization of standards. The key elements include minimum standards, maximum standards, uniform and differential standards, time-bound variations in standards, prestandard harmonization, goal or objective harmonization, and multilateral agreements allowing variations in standards. Esty and Garadin (1997, p. 334) argued that "[w]ithout some harmonization of standards, individual countries will have an incentive to disregard both spillovers of harm caused by their policies and impacts they may have on the resources of the global commons."

Specific to a given scenario, the issue is one of determining an "optimal harmonization." To illustrate this, the series 14000 Environmental Standards proposed by the International Standards Organization (ISO) are unlikely to be optimal for every region of the world. This could imply a combination of distinguishable features applied to different countries and products. Among the benefits of the process are increased transparency and eventual goal-setting. The major costs include transaction costs of defining and implementing. These costs can be minimized with the use of a gradualist approach, whereby the direction of environmental harmonization proceeds at a meaningful pace, and an element of "learning by doing" is also incorporated. The latter presumes the existence of some feedback mechanisms and relevant information systems at the national and international levels, however.

▋ 7.8 SUMMARY

The role of property rights and liability rules in the governance of the global commons remains a common theme for international economic laws and international environmental laws. The issues of *locus standi* and *amicus curiae* are important in avoiding any possible *non liquet* scenarios in the management of global environmental (and hence economic) resources. Some of the provisions of the ICJ require updating to reflect these needs. Currently, there is no role for NGOs in the ICJ Statute.

The interface of international economic laws and international environmental laws is an important topic as long as the two streams do not attempt to seek to integrate or reconcile the issues (some of which are complementary and others conflicting). Sustainability of the environment and the economy at the global level cannot be achieved if the development of sustainable institutions in general, and of legal institutions in particular, is not addressed. These problems are more significant in some of the developing countries. The provision of technical and financial assistance under some of the agreements such as the Montreal Protocol or under some of the multilateral development finance mechanisms under the World Bank or other institutions is largely oblivious to the priority needs of development of the legal infrastructure in some of the developing countries. International laws tend to be obeyed not necessarily as a strategy of compliance in some countries but because the constellation of economic and environmental factors combined with the features of the existing institutions enable the outcome. Conversely, lack of compliance is not necessarily the outcome of strategic decision-making, either. With developing countries, in several cases it may be posited that their compliance with international environmental laws is just as good (or as bad) as their compliance with domestic laws.

International institutions could possibly take the initiative to provide assistance to the eligible and needy states to develop their infrastructure for law development and compliance with domestic and international laws. However, in this context, the democracy content of international institutions governing the global environment and the issue of legitimacy of international governance are also important.

Review Exercises

1 Comment on the efficacy of the implementation aspects of the following provisions in EU Law: Articles 174 to 176 of the 1987 Single European Act (formerly 130r, 130s, and 130t) of the Treaty of the European Union (TEU).

2 In the presence of high transaction costs, are liability laws likely to be (a) superior, (b) supplementary, or (c) substitutory to the role of property rights in the governance of environmental resources? Explain the rationale for your answer.

3 What are "positive measures" in the context of multilateral environmental agreements (MEAs)? Elucidate their role with reference to any of the following MEAs: (a) Convention on

Biological Diversity; (b) EU environmental law; (c) UN Convention on the Law of the Sea.

4 In a situation largely characterized by a lack of identifiable accountability for environmental damage, or in a scenario with random culprits and random victims of environmental damage, examine the relative merits and problems of creating a Global Trust Fund to mitigate such damage. What could be the potential alternative bases for resource mobilization for the financial and technical pool comprising the Fund, in addition to possible voluntary contributions?

5 Are issues of intergenerational justice equally significant in both environmental and economic laws? Explain the answer in the affirmative or negative.

6 What are the main ingredients of a "dynamic law"? Suggest a revised set of specifications using this approach for some of the provisions under the Convention on Biological Diversity.

7 The 1991 ILC Draft Articles on Liability for Injurious Consequences of Acts Not Prohibited by International Law include a crucial provision in Article 24 on harm to the environment and resulting harm to persons or property. However, in this provision, the draft text recognizes primarily the state of origin and the state affected. Extend the reasoning to include *res nullius* and *res communis* in lieu of the "state affected" and examine the scope for institutionalizing liability compensation as well as property rights in such a context.

8 Examine the validity or otherwise of the position that international environmental laws are critically important when most environmental assets or resources are not governed by market institutions. Also, if the latter were to exist, is there still a similar need for international environmental laws? Explain the rationale for your answer.

REFERENCES

Bar, S. and Kraemer, R. A., 1998, European environmental policy after Amsterdam, *Journal of Environmental Law*, 10, 315–30.
Bodansky, D., 1999, The legitimacy of international governance: A coming challenge for international economic law?, *American Journal of International Law*, 93, 596–624.

Bowles, I. A. and Kormus, C. F., 1996, Environmental reform at the World Bank: The role of the United States Congress, *Virginia Journal of International Law*, 35, 777–808.

Di Leva, C. E., 1998, International environmental law and development, *Georgetown International Environmental Law Review*, 10, 501–49.

Esty, D. C. and Garadin, D., 1997, Market access, competitiveness, and harmonization: Environmental protection in RTAs, *Harvard Environmental Law Review*, 21, 265–336.

Folsom, R. H., 1999, *European Union Law in a Nutshell*, 3rd edition, St. Paul, MN: West Group.

Franke, G., 1991, Avenues for the reduction of LDC debt: An institutional analysis, *Journal of Institutional and Theoretical Economics*, 147, 274–95.

French, D., 2000, Developing states and international environmental law: The importance of differentiated responsibilities, *International and Comparative Law Quarterly*, 49, 35–60.

Goldsmith, J. L. and Posner, E. A., 1999, A theory of customary international law, *University of Chicago Law Review*, 66, 1113–77.

Halvorssen, A. M., 1999, *Equality Among Unequals in International Environmental Law*, Boulder, CO: Westview Press.

Handl, G., 1998, Legal mandate of multilateral development banks as agents for change toward sustainable development, *American Journal of International Law*, 92, 642–65.

International Law Association (ILA), 1995, *Report of the Sixty-sixth Conference* (held at Buenos Aires), London: ILA.

International Law Commission (ILC), 1991, *ILC Draft Articles on Liability for Injurious Consequences of Acts Not Prohibited by International Law*, New York: UN Doc. A/CN.4/428, 1992.

Keohane, N. O., Revesz, R. L., and Stavins, R. N., 1998, The choice of regulatory instruments in environmental policy, *Harvard Environmental Law Review*, 22, 313–68.

Levy, M. A., Young, O. R., and Zurn, M., 1995, The study of international regimes, *European Journal of International Relations*, 1, 267–330.

Liberatore, A., 1997, The European Union: Bridging domestic and international environmental policy-making, in M. A. Schreurs and E. Economy (eds.), *The Internationalization of Environmental Protection*, New York: Cambridge University Press, pp. 188–212.

Neumayer, E., 2000, In defence of historical accountability for greenhouse gas emissions, *Ecological Economics*, 33, 185–92.

Nozick, R., 1974, *Anarchy, State and Utopia*, Oxford: Blackwell.

Organization for Economic Cooperation and Development (OECD), 1997, *Experience with the Use of Trade Measures in the Convention on International Trade in Endangered Species of Wild Fauna and Flora (CITES)*, OECD Study Report OECD/GD (97) 106, Paris: OECD Secretariat.

Raffer, K., 1990, Applying Chapter 9 insolvency to international debts: An economically efficient solution with a human face, *World Development*, 18, 301–11.

Rao, P. K., 2000, *Sustainable Development: Economics and Policy*, Oxford: Blackwell.

Sand, P. H., 1997, Whither CITES? The evolution of a treaty regime in the borderland of trade and environment, *European Journal of International Law*, 8 (1), 29–58.

Sandler, T., 1997, *Global Challenges: An Approach to Environmental, Political and Economic Problems*, New York: Cambridge University Press.

Sornarajah, M., 1994, *The International Law on Foreign Investment*, Cambridge: Cambridge University Press.

Trachtman, J. P., 1996, The international economic law revolution, *University of Pennsylvania Journal of International Economic Law*, 17, 33–61.

UN Conference on Trade and Development (UNCTAD), 1997, *Positive Measures to Promote Sustainable Development, Particularly in Meeting the Objectives of Multilateral Environmental Agreements*, Geneva: UNCTAD Report TD/B/Com.1/Em.3/2.

Wilson, E. O., 1992, *The Diversity of Life*, Cambridge, MA: Belknap/Harvard University Press.

Young, O. R. (ed.), 1999a, *The Effectiveness of International Environmental Regimes*, Cambridge, MA: MIT Press.

Young, O. R., 1999b, Regime effectiveness: Taking stock, in O. R. Young (ed.), *The Effectiveness of International Environmental Regimes*, Cambridge, MA: MIT Press, pp. 249–87.

chapter eight

International Trade and Environmental Laws

▌ 8.1 INTRODUCTION

International environmental laws and international economic laws tend to intersect in the international trade area more than any other international activity. Thus, it is of prime importance to explore the role of law and economics in this common arena. For this purpose, this chapter examines in some detail the operative features of global trade regimes and their interaction and compatibility with international environmental agreements and other international environmental laws.

Existing provisions to integrate environmental considerations in international trade laws are reviewed in this chapter with the objective of suggesting improved bases for further reforms. Popular approaches advocating trade liberalization also are examined for their environmental implications. Strategic environmental and trade policy issues, the theme of recent debate, are also discussed. Other issues explored in this chapter are the environmental externalities of trade, the internalization of environmental costs, institutional arrangements for trade regimes, and the reconciliation of trade and environmental objectives. The interface of regional and international environmental agreements, multilateral development finance, and the environmental implications of sovereign debt agreements are also briefly considered.

The concept of sustainable trade and the polluter pays principle (PPP) are discussed. Two streams of application of the PPP are examined, neither of which has yet been fully developed in the literature: the weak version and the strong version. Various provisions under the General Agreement on Tariffs and Trade (GATT) in the governance of trade and environment interactions and the resolution of corresponding international trade disputes are analyzed in detail. Most of the international trade and environment interfaces in trade disputes are seen to have failed to invoke the prerequisites of sustainable trade in terms of their standards specified under the preamble to the articles of agreement of the World Trade Organization (even in the WTO era starting from 1995).

We start with a brief summary of an experience with an international agreement that involved trade measures to protect endangered species. The roles of incentives and disincentives, compliance, monitoring, and effectiveness of the laws are among the relevant factors for an assessment. The trade effects of restrictions and the ecological effects of these laws, in addition to economic impacts, are also of interest.

8.2 ENVIRONMENTAL TRADE MEASURES AND EXPERIENCE WITH CITES

Some of the important features of the Convention on International Trade in Endangered Species (CITES) are presented in chapter 5. Here some of the experiences and the need for greater international legal coordination are examined. CITES provisions provide for regulation or restrictions (including prohibitions) of trade for Appendix I, II, and III species. The key Articles of CITES in this case are Articles III, IV, V, and VI, which provide for import and export permits and reexport certificates to regulate the trade in such specimens. Practical domestic application of the measures varies among individual parties. Parties are required under Article VIII.1 to take "appropriate measures to enforce the provisions of the present Convention." The terms of that requirement extend beyond measures limited to domestic implementation. These include additional measures to deal with cases where there is a violation of the obligations of the agreement. In such a case, the Article provides that parties are "to prohibit trade in specimens in violation of the Convention." Article XIV also provides that nothing in the Convention prevents parties from adopting "stricter domestic measures."

Regarding the effectiveness of CITES (not necessarily its cost-effectiveness, whether these costs are the direct costs of design and implementation of treaty provisions or inclusive of transaction costs), it is often argued that since the agreement took effect in 1975, no single species listed under CITES has become extinct as a result of trade. However, this is unlikely to be due to CITES alone. This possibility is more evident when we observe that many CITES parties made very little progress in meeting the four minimum conditions under Articles VIII and IX of the Convention, namely, (1) the designation of at least one management authority and one scientific authority; (2) the prohibition of trade in specimens in violation of the Convention; (3) the imposition of penalties on such trade activities; and/or (4) the confiscation of specimens illegally traded or possessed. The results of an analysis of the national implementing legislation of some 80 parties (plus six dependent territories) carried out by TRAFFIC and the World Conservation Union (IUCN), under contract to and funded by CITES, divided the countries studied into three groups (cited in OECD, 1997): (1) 15 (14 of which were OECD members) had legislation meeting all requirements for CITES implementation; (2) 41 (of which four were OECD members and a dependency) had legislation judged not to meet all the requirements; and (3) 28 (of which two were OECD members) had legislation believed generally not to meet the requirements for implementation of CITES. Since the choice of these countries was made generally (but not exclusively) on the basis of importance in wildlife trade, it would seem conservative to generalize that some four-fifths of CITES parties do not have legislation meeting all the requirements for CITES implementation.

Regarding dispute resolution, Article XVIII of CITES makes the following provision:

> Any dispute . . . with respect to the interpretation or application of the provisions of the present Convention, shall be subject to negotiation between the Parties involved in the dispute.

> If the dispute cannot be resolved . . . the Parties may, by mutual consent, submit the dispute to arbitration, in particular that of the Permanent Court of Arbitration at the Hague and the Parties submitting the dispute shall be bound by the arbitral decision.

In this context, it can be noted that, among its conclusions and recommendations, the WTO Committee on Trade and Environment suggested (as cited in OECD, 1997) that if a dispute arises between WTO members, parties to a multilateral environmental agreement (MEA), over the use of trade measures they are applying between themselves pursuant to the MEA, "they should consider trying to resolve it through the dispute settlement mechanisms available under the MEA."

The experience with international environmental agreements (such as CITES) invoking trade measures has been largely that they are of doubtful impact, although the impact on environmental trade is not too insignificant. The fact is that some of the soft provisions of hard laws, and some of the soft laws themselves, tend to lay foundations for more coherent and effective international environmental laws. The imperative of sustainable development was possibly not recognized as a concern at the formation of global trading arrangements in 1947, when the GATT was negotiated among some countries. Hence the conspicuous absence of the terms "environment" and "sustainable trade" in the original articles of agreement of the GATT. However, they are reflected in its revised institutional form, the WTO of 1995. Growing public awareness and concern over the environmental costs of trade are among the reasons for new provisions in international trade laws and multilateral trading arrangements. These are deliberated in the next few sections.

■ 8.3 Trade Liberalization and Environmental Costs

Often, it is argued that trade expansion exacerbates environmental damage through both production effects and enhanced consumption effects. While this argument has some validity, it is far from universal. The effects of increases in income, employment, and state tax revenues at the macroeconomic level, and competitive productive efficiency requirements, especially technical innovation and resource savings incentives at the competing firm level, tend to offset some of the potential adverse effects of trade. However, there are other motivational issues relating to trade and environmental policies at the state level. Imperfectly competitive trade can lead to environmental deterioration (local and global), especially when national governments resort to "rent-shifting" with lax environmental policies and protection of domestic industry competitiveness against foreign rivals. Rent-shifting models of trade occur when governments seek to enhance export revenues with manipulation of domestic economic and/or environmental policies. These models are formulated assuming that governments relax their environmental policies relative to the "first-best" rule of equalizing marginal costs of abatement with marginal costs of damage. When price competition is a dominant feature, governments may have an incentive to resort to such measures, as suggested in the literature on strategic international trade (see, for example, Barrett, 1994). Using a static framework and certainty-based model, and ignoring transaction costs, Ulph (1996) offered an analytical model to study strategic decision-making of states and firms; it was suggested that when both these entities act strategically, there could be welfare loss. When neither acts strategically, the usual "first-best" equilibrium is derived. Ulph (1997) suggested that under imperfect international competition and strategic environmental policy at state level, governments may have incentives to seek lax environmental measures in favor of their domestic producers. Ulph provided a preliminary multistage game model and, after claiming a few deviations relative to conventional economic results of the first-best variety (where strategic considerations are largely ignored), concluded that "there is a severe problem of non-robustness of results" (1997, p. 188). Among directions for further improvement of analytical methods are the consideration of dynamic multiperiod models with reasonable discounting over time, the role of reputation and credibility and their advantages relative to gains of strategic behavior, overall improvements in welfare due to predictable behavior with commitments, and realistic aspects of the influence of both the domestic and international political economy on formulations of environmental policies.

In the public goods literature, it is generally seen that participants tend to resort to free-riding, unless there are mechanisms (such as incentives and disincentives) to regulate otherwise. An analogy is often extended to the issue of global environmental goods and their governance. There are some differences, however, arising from one form or another of "issue linkage," in addition to endogenous costs and other effects of free-rider processes on the respective state economy and the environment. Often, issue linkages arise in relation to either international credit or international trade, or both. When, for example, an environmental public health problem surfaced in certain developing countries, their food exports dropped. The corresponding long-term effects on export demand cannot be ignored, either. This illustration is not intended to suggest that the environmental public health problem was the result of a specific free-rider process, but it approximates such a possibility even when there are no explicit rules allowing discrimination in international trade under the WTO regime. Changes in the terms of trade as a result of the state-influenced production of environmental public goods are important factors. To state a lemma from Alpay (2000, p. 280) in this regard:

> In an open economy, along with positive environmental externality, the production of the environmental good also generates negative externality on the free-riding country and a positive externality on the active country through terms of trade changes.

Thus, due to interactions in the international goods markets, free-riding is not always the best option for most states. This feature itself tends to counter the "tragedy of the commons" proposition (see chapters 1 and 2).

The environmental international trade effect is a combined result of four components (Copeland and Taylor, 1994): (1) a scale of production effect that increases pollution; (2) a composition (of resource use and output) effect that reflects global specialization in industries and their pollution contribution locally; (3) a technical effect that directs substitution (often, though not always) favoring cleaner technologies; and (4) interaction of these three influences. Trade liberalization combined with appropriate internalization of environmental costs promises the potential to augment global welfare in the short run as well as in the long run, and hence may be sustainable. Scale, technique, and composition (STC) effects of trade liberalization have been advocated in recent trade literature as the main determinants of the environmental effects of trade liberalization. The composition effect refers to the likely changes in industry composition (greater specialization or other effects of comparative advantage explorations) as a result of trade liberalization, the scale effect is simply the implications of trade expansion on the scale of production and trade, and the technique effect is due to changes in production methods arising out of the above and also because of the endogenous influence of stakeholders such as environmental nongovernmental organizations (NGOs). This influence operates on the system primarily from production perspectives. Environmental effects operating through consumption systems, and endogenous preferences in response to new goods in a given stationary market due to trade expansion activities, remain significant as well.

Does trade liberalization enhance or adversely affect environmental quality (at local, regional, and global levels)? There are a few answers in partial evaluation settings. The trade liberalization and consequential environmental effects of the policies of the Uruguay Round of trade negotiations were examined by Cole et al. (1998). They considered the implications for the five pollutants: nitrogen dioxide, sulfur dioxide, carbon dioxide, carbon monoxide, and particulate matter. In most of the developing countries a net increase in each of the pollutants is predicted. In the developed countries emissions of carbon monoxide, sulfur dioxide, and particulate matter are expected to fall, while emissions of the remaining two pollutants will continue to rise. The policy implications of this assessment are not clear, however. Trade expansion generally contributes to economic growth as well as environmental pollution. The real questions are about the relative cost-effectiveness of income gains and enhanced potential as well as the commitment to reducing environmental pollution at source regionally and globally. If importers use trade liberalization mainly to locate pollution-generating production in exporter countries, the game is not what was intended under the trade negotiations.

Trade and environment: Uruguay Round effects

Empirical estimates of the implications of the Uruguay Round of trade liberalizations have been explored by Cole et al. (1998). The STC effects for several countries and regions on five pollutants – nitrogen dioxide, sulfur dioxide, carbon monoxide, suspended particulate matter, and carbon dioxide – were estimated. For nitrogen dioxide and carbon dioxide the combined STC effects are estimated to increase emissions for all regions, except for nitrogen dioxide in the US. For the other pollutants, the STC effects are estimated to lower emissions in most of the developed countries but increase them for the developing countries. Approximations of the monetary costs of increased pollution of the specified five pollutants led to a relatively small percentage (less than 2 percent for most countries) of the estimated benefits of the Uruguay Round trade effects. Given the uncertainties associated with costs, it was suggested that the percentage could also extend to about three times the above. Since the costs were largely based on rather dated information and did not include the public health and related costs of pollution, they are substantially below realistic levels.

A country-risk assessment is more important for an industrial enterprise to base its industry-locating decision than environmental "safe havens" for dumping pollution. Also, the direct costs of environmental compliance are usually estimated as relatively low: at less than about 3 percent of the total costs of operation (Low, 1993). Total transaction cost is the real determinant affecting investment decisions and environmental costs are but a minor part of such a cost basket, as argued in Rao (2000b).

In general, restrictive trade policies depict a suboptimal approach to economic welfare of the parties involved when contrasted with liberalized trade policies. However, there are costs of trade liberalization, mainly in terms of its potential impact on the environment. Since most of these costs are transmitted to other states or regions as negative externalities, greater attention is required for the governance of international trade in relation to the provision of international environmental laws.

It is useful to distinguish three types of environmental externalities that deserve attention in the context of international trade (see

Runge, 1994; Rao, 2000b; see also chapter 2 for other classifications of externalities):

1 local externalities, which have their origin in domestic markets and local production units;
2 transboundary externalities, which have their origin in one domestic market but propagate their impacts to trading or neighboring regions because of trading mechanisms; and
3 global externalities, as in the case of environmental problems of the global commons, to the extent that these are attributable to international trade mechanisms.

Trade may be relevant in enhancing environmental quality, especially when the following features obtain (see also USOTA, 1992): global environmental externalities are attributable to some of the trade activities; markets do not incorporate environmental costs in the prices of products and services; there is evidence or a reasonable basis to expect that trade measures will bring about the environmental objectives; and the environmental benefits exceed the environmental pollution costs. The problem of missing markets for some environmental resources contributes to a wide range of environmental and economic externalities (see also chapters 1 and 2).

Trade liberalization is generally popular as it tends to expand and accelerate transactions of imports and exports of goods and services, thus contributing to expanded opportunities of employment and income. In this process, the efficiency of resource utilization can occur only when all the resources are properly accounted for and there are no "free goods." The feature of missing markets for some environmental goods and services makes trade a powerful conduit for negative environmental externalities. The failure to take the environmental costs into account in marketed commodities leads to a divergence between private costs and social costs. International trade can help correct some of the failures through the provision of incentives for environmental protection and promoting efficient use of resources, but it does the opposite in some cases (see Rao, 2000b).

The 1992 Rio Summit Declaration sought to "reflect efficient and sustainable use of factors of production in the formation of commodity prices, including the reflection of environmental, social and resources costs" (Agenda 21, paragraph 2.14 (c)). An assertion in its Principle 16 was inconsistent with itself: "national authorities should endeavor to promote the internalization of environmental costs and the use of economic instruments, taking into account the approach that the polluter should, in principle, bear the cost of pollution, with due regard to the public interest and without distorting international trade and investment." This may be a self-contradictory assertion since some element of distortion of the patterns of international trade is essential if existing distortions are to be corrected. That is the price we may have to pay in order to correct a wrong. The failure to recognize this imperative is to seek *status quo ante* and still dream about effecting relevant changes. According to Rao (2000b), "[i]neffective changes will, of course, lead to non-distortive impact on international trade. Disruption of the trading system will be harmful, but the imposition of one distortion (if at all) to correct another existing distortion need not be harmful."

It is clear from some of the statements of Agenda 21 (Chapter 39 on international legal instruments and mechanisms at Section 39.3 (d)) that the Rio Conference was concerned about any possible disruption of international trading patterns rather than seeking an effective integration of trade and environment issues to their mutual reinforcement and sustainable development. This is clear when we note the following extracts from Agenda 21:

> States recognize that environmental policies should deal with the root causes of environmental degradation, thus preventing environmental measures from resulting in unnecessary restrictions to trade. Trade policy measures for environmental purposes should not constitute a means of arbitrary or unjustifiable discrimination or a disguised restriction on international trade. Unilateral actions to deal with environmental challenges outside the jurisdiction of the importing country should be avoided. . . . Should trade policy measures be found necessary for the enforcement of environmental policies, certain principles and rules should apply. These could include, inter alia, the principle of non-discrimination; the principle that the trade measure chosen should be the least trade-restrictive necessary to achieve the objectives; an obligation to ensure transparency in the use of trade measures related to the environment and to provide adequate notification of national regulations; and the need to give consideration to the special conditions and development requirements of developing countries as they move towards internationally agreed environmental objectives.

Reflecting environmental costs in trade

Internalization of environmental costs does mean all or a few of the following (Rao, 2000b): inclusion of the true worth or shadow price of each of the inputs into the production system; post-production costs to consumption stage; and the costs of disposal at the terminal stage. These costs accrue or are applicable at different levels of the lifecycle. A multistage inclusion of environmental costs is one of the direct methods, but a variety of alternatives can also be contemplated.

In a competitive market, the production cost plus environmental cost method of pricing could exclude some of the producer markets. This has implications for the uniformity or harmonizing of environmental costs by all the players (at least with respect to specific commodities/goods and their substitutes) in the world market: those who seek to free-ride on the environment should not have an incentive to do so by their lower pricing of goods and services to clinch the export market. Hence the need for a global policy coordination. UNCTAD (1995) observed that internalization of environmental costs and benefits needs to be achieved within the country-specific domestic policies, environmental absorptive capacities, and time preferences involved. This may not be entirely valid, especially when there are unassimilated emissions of pollution, which is more of a global externality; greenhouse gases provide an example of this process. Again, this points to the need for an international coordination mechanism, a market-based (like emissions trading) or quota-based or target-based reduction of global environmental pollution. Export of goods produced under environmentally unsustainable conditions is unsustainable (Rao, 2000a).

Full cost internalization will rarely be optimal and that internalization should only be carried out up to the level where the incremental benefits of avoided environmental damage justify the incremental costs of environmental provisions, according to the UNCTAD (1997) report. This general economic argument could form a step in the right direction, especially when all the costs and benefits are properly taken into account. This approach is not significantly different from the generally accepted "polluter pays" principle. A pragmatic approach suggested by Elliot (1994) is that rather than seeking to front-load all the lifecycle environmental costs on the producer, it is desirable to unbundle part of these costs so that only environmental impacts which can be dealt with at the production stage of a product are internalized at the level of the producer; the costs of environmental impacts incurred at subsequent stages of the product lifecycle can be apportioned and internalized at the level of those who benefit directly from the consumption of the products concerned.

Cost externalization (CE) is the result of spreading negative externalities and is thus an unethical proposition, as argued in Rao (2000b). The polluter pays principle is an example of a measure to avoid or minimize CE in the specific context of environmental pollution costs. In its weaker form, it still admits some element of the CE phenomenon and could provide perverse incentives for emissions of pollution. Agenda 21 of the 1992 Rio Conference recommends a good deal of minimization of CE when it talks of "efficient and sustainable use of factors of production in the formation of commodity prices, including the reflection of environmental, social and resource costs" (paragraph 2.14 (c)).

The issue of internalization of environmental costs forms a special aspect of minimization of cost externalization. To relate it to much of neoclassical economic terminology, CE is an envelope of the set of externalities generated from a wider set of perspectives than simply market externalities or price externalities (Rao, 2000b). As the UNCTAD (1995) report observed, internalization of environmental costs and benefits occurs within different country-specific domestic economic and environmental policies, their development priorities, and the environmental absorptive capacities and time preferences involved.

It may not always be feasible to incorporate all the environmental costs without disruptions in the provision of otherwise affordable goods and services. Hence the need for a multilateral consensus on the types and magnitudes of environmental cost internalization that remain pragmatic in the existing system, without losing sight of the imperatives of sustainable development.

The polluter pays principle and extensions

The relative scarcity potential of the usually presumed abundant supply of environmental resources was recognized in the early 1970s at the global level. When the cost of environmental deterioration is not "adequately taken into account in the price system, the market fails to reflect the scarcity of such resources both at the national and international levels" (OECD, 1975).

The polluter pays principle (PPP) is an economic principle that seeks to ensure that pollution costs are not externalized but incurred by the polluter. The PPP was first institutionally formalized in the 1972 OECD Recommendation of the Council on Guiding Principles concerning International Economic Aspects of Environmental Policies (quoted in OECD, 1975):

> The principle to be used for allocating costs of pollution prevention and control measures to encourage rational use of scarce environmental

resources and to avoid distortions in international trade and investment is the so-called "Polluter Pays Principle" (PPP). This principle means that the polluter should bear the expenses of carrying out the above mentioned measures decided by public authorities to ensure that the environment is in an acceptable state. In other words, the costs of these measures should be reflected in the cost of goods and services which cause pollution in production and/or consumption. Such measures should not be accompanied by subsidies that would create significant distortions in international trade and investment.

Application of the PPP was institutionally advocated by the OECD (1975) for adoption in its member countries, which are typically industrial and advanced economies. According to the OECD document, (1) the principle for allocating costs of pollution prevention and control measures to encourage rational use of scarce environmental resources and to avoid distortions in trade and investment is the PPP, and the costs of these measures "should be reflected in the costs of goods and services which cause pollution in production and/or consumption"; (2) when the environmental costs are taken into account, the market fails to reflect these costs in the price system. Despite these broad principles, the issue of internalizing environmental costs in dealing with international trade in goods and services remains contentious.

The critical issue is, however, deciding which of the pollution contributions should be assessed against the polluters. It is yet a different issue whether or not the polluter can effectively internalize the costs of pollution or pass these on to others in the chain of economic linkages. Principle 16 of the Rio Declaration of 1992 seeks to internalize environmental costs and deploy the PPP: "National authorities should endeavor to promote the internalization of environmental costs and the use of economic instruments, taking into account the approach that the polluter should, in principle, bear the cost of pollution, with due regard to the public interest and without distorting international trade and investment." The 1992 EC Treaty also endorses the PPP.

Four versions of the PPP were identified by Bugge (1996): as an economic principle of efficiency; as a legal principle of "just" assignment of costs; as a principle of international harmonization of national environmental policy; and as a principle of interstate cost apportioning. It was also suggested that the PPP applies especially where Coasean bargaining solutions do not work (for example, when corresponding transaction costs are high or when there are numerous polluters).

The original motivation of the PPP foundation is generally seen as a principle of economic efficiency. The precise definition and operational interpretations continue to remain rather vague, however.

An important aspect of the design of economic instruments is the recognition of behavioral factors. These are particularly relevant in the international arena, where nations exercise sovereign rights and operate under substantial autonomy. The deployment of motivating factors for cooperation in effective coordination requires an examination of the relevant economic foundations of such behavioral factors.

According to the PPP, when the environmental costs of deterioration are not adequately reflected in the (market or administered) price system, the scarcity value of resources is not depicted; such costs should be incorporated in the assessment of goods and services. As stated in OECD (1995), the PPP is concerned with "who" should pay for environmental protection, and not with "how much" should be paid. The 1972 Guiding Principle PPP also considered the issue whether countries should have the right to use border adjustment, duties, or tariffs to offset international differences in environmental costs, and rejected it for fear of potential discriminatory trade practices. The GATT principles as well as OECD (1972) do not authorize enforcement of the PPP with regard to imports to offset the costs of pollution prevention/control measures affecting the global environment. The possibility that trade policies could affect the environmental objectives of sustainable development was not considered when the 1972 PPP was drawn up. It was a very good principle for that point in time, but its applicable forms now need revision. Natural resource conditions and environmental features specific to different countries also comprise a varying natural environmental assimilative or renewal capability of the corresponding sinks and sources (Rao, 2000b). There are two versions of the PPP, discussed below, based on Rao (2000b).

Weak polluter pays principle (WPPP)

This is a diluted version of the original PPP and is built on the premise that when pricing on the basis of full costs (production costs plus environmental costs) generates its own set of negative externalities, the latter effects may be used to partially offset the original cost elements. This allows for a limited degree of "subsidies" relative to the full cost and recognizes both first-order and second-order effects of price interventions to correct a market failure. An element of an economic feedback mechanism (both negative and positive) is utilized here in assessing the consequential effects as well. In the latter category one could also visualize the costs of forcing economic entities out of business as a result of some of the strict and rather narrow applications of "environmental principles." Thus, this characterization of the weak polluter pays principle is an aspect of integrated and pragmatic decision-making. It promises greater recognition of trade–environment interdependencies and complementarities.

Strong polluter pays principle (SPPP)

This is an extended version of the PPP which maintains that the costs of damage to the environment should be calculated on the basis of the lifecycle of the products and be paid up front by the producer/supplier (in the chain of provision, similar to the methods used in a few countries that operate multistage value-added tax (VAT)). The method of environmental cost internalization on the basis of SPPP may be neither feasible nor desirable in all production and trade scenarios.

The GATT rules tend to support externalization of environmental costs as a legitimate source of comparative (and possibly competitive) advantage, with an obsolete prescription that the parties cannot "discriminate between like products on the basis of the method of production." The GATT rules need to be amended to allow countries to object to the import of goods using production processes that create transnational spillovers. When multilateral trade policies are required to recognize internalization of environmental costs and multilaterally agreed principles of process and production methods (PPMs), environmental and trade objectives tend to have greater coherence. Economic principles such as the PPP are usually inadequate to govern socially and environmentally desirable and sustainable trade patterns. A set of broader foundations, including the rules governing tradable items, is necessary before economic principles can be properly utilized.

The "race to the bottom" and "pollution haven" hypotheses

The debate over the "race to the bottom" and "pollution haven" hypotheses (distinguished in terms of their relative motivations, the first to enhance export competitiveness and the latter to attract foreign capital) implies that states weaken their respective domestic environ-mental standards in order to attract a greater flow of investments (and thus generate employment and other rents to the leadership) and/or enhance "competitiveness" of exports. First, this is not a universal proposition even for the postulation of a hypothesis, because not every country is capital-constrained or employment-constrained to bother using such inducements for investments. Second, the cost dif-ferential attributable to different environmental standards is usually very low (about 3 percent of total capital costs, according to some studies) relative to the total cost of transactions and thus remains an insignificant factor in investment decisions. Third, it is also the case that in almost all democratic and/or developed countries, environ-mental nongovernmental organizations and civic reactions are strong enough to counteract deliberate attempts to let lax environmental standards hurt their societies (or willfully extend their negative extern-alities to others). In an empirical study for the period 1965–95 cov-ering 34 relatively developed economies, Xu (1999) examined whether stringent environmental standards resulted in loss of international competitiveness of environmentally sensitive goods (defined as those that have incurred high levels of pollution-abatement expenditures per unit output in the OECD economies). It was found that there was no perceptible change in their competitiveness over the years. This empirical study clearly rejects the "race to the bottom" hypothesis.

Weak environmental policy at a country level can eventually con-strain export potential itself via reduced productivity or lack of full complementarity of resources for optimum sustainable production (see also Brander and Taylor, 1997; the analytical model presented in their paper, however, ignores the explicit role of time preferences among trading states and focuses on renewable open-access resources). In the resource management regimes characterized by open-access renewable resources, an analytical study by Brander and Taylor (1998) noted that the traditional economic position of gains from free trade may be undermined. The full benefits, estimated in traditional economic models, of free trade accrue when each trading partner seeks to fully internalize the costs of environmental damage (Ferrantino, 1997; Rao, 2000b).

Trade sanctions are sometimes advocated as a potential credible threat to elicit cooperation on environmental issues. Barrett (1997) argued the pros and cons of such a possibility in an economic model. This form of formal issue linkage is unlikely to hold good under the WTO regime. Besides, as Barrett (1997, p. 359) pointed out, "virtually every punishment will harm signatories as well as non-signatories, and it is this fact which is the principal obstacle to sustaining international cooperation." However, this obstacle is only from the viewpoint of provision of sanctions and other forms of disincentives under trade regimes, possibly in conflict with existing laws. The provision of appropriate incentives still remains an effective alternative in achieving and sustaining international cooperation. The WTO framework may find some of the provisions discriminatory unless they are determined with reference to an international environmental agreement (IEA).

■ 8.4 REGIONAL TRADE AND ENVIRONMENTAL AGREEMENTS

Most regional trading arrangements (see Rao, 2000b) are generally more specific about trade transactions between member countries but hardly mention anything about the environmental aspects of trade. The major exception is the 1994 North American Free Trade Agreement (NAFTA). Besides specifying the environment's role in trade relations, the agreement clarifies its relationship with other international environmental agreements as well as the overriding nature of a few other international agreements.

If conflict emerges with other trade agreements, NAFTA prevails unless provided otherwise. Article 104 clarifies that NAFTA shall not prevail over the following MEAs:

1 Washington Convention on International Trade in Endangered Species (1973, 1979);
2 Montreal Protocol on Substances that Deplete the Ozone Layer (1987, 1990);
3 Basel Convention (1989);
4 Canada–US Agreement Concerning Transboundary Movements of Hazardous Waste (1986); and
5 Mexico–US Agreement on Cooperation for the Protection of the Environment in the Border Area (1983).

A few policies and legislative measures in Europe tend to clarify the interactions between regional trade laws and environmental laws. Box 8.1 summarizes a case involving such a dispute among EC member countries. This case, resolved by the European Court of Justice (ECJ), draws a clear distinction in trade involving items differentiable by their originating location and applicable laws.

BOX 8.1

Case study: The Dutch grouse case

The ECJ ruling in the Dutch grouse case (Case C-169/89, Criminal Proceedings against Van den Burg, 1990 ECR I-2143–65) is important in setting a trend in the protection and trade of environmental resources, with particular reference to potentially endangered birds and animals. The Court held that the Netherlands could not ban local sale of birds hunted legally in other member countries, even though Dutch law seeks to protect such species.

The defendant, Van den Burg, had been prosecuted for the sale of red grouse (hunted in the United Kingdom) at a store in The Hague; the sale was deemed contrary to the Dutch law that prohibits the sale of birds found anywhere in the wild in Europe. None of the EEC Directives contained a restriction on red grouse sale. Local measures are not prohibited for each of the member countries provided they are consistent with Article 36 of the EC Treaty and "in case stem from commercial policy considerations." Article 36 does not explicitly state that the interests which it protects must be located geographically in the legislating member state. The EEC Advocate General argued, *inter alia*, that "a measure unilaterally adopted by one Member State in connection with the hunting of animals in another Member State would seem at first sight to be difficult to reconcile with the principle of mutual confidence between Member States" (Van den Burg, 1990 ECR at I-2154–55).

The Attorney-General felt that only a minimal contribution was likely to be made by the Dutch ban to encourage conservation in the UK, and that the conservation benefits were disproportionate with the costs of trade prohibition. The ECJ emphasized the EEC Directive and stated in its judgment:

> Article 36 of the Treaty, read in conjunction with Council Directive 79/409/EEC of 2 April 1979 on the conservation of wild birds, must be interpreted as meaning that a prohibition on the importation and marketing cannot be justified in respect of a species of bird which does not occur in the territory of the legislating Member State but is found in another Member State where it may lawfully be hunted under the terms of that directive and under the legislation of that other State, and which is neither migratory nor endangered within the meaning of the directive.

Source: www.europa.eu.int/eur-lex/en/index.html (March 10, 2000).
Quotations reproduced with the permission of the European Court of Justice

▌ 8.5 INTERNATIONAL TRADE LAWS AND ENVIRONMENTAL LAWS

International trade laws include laws relating to multilateral trade activities and laws governing customs duties, dumping, and other trade transactions. Several of these, even by a long stretch of interpretation, escape the environment-enhancing or affecting routes (for a detailed description of world trade laws, see, for example, Bhala and Kennedy, 1998). However, a major segment of international trade does affect the environment, one way or another (for broad coverage of relevant issues, see Rao, 2000a, b). It is useful to invoke the definition of sustainable trade as a relevant guidepost for integrating trade and environmental policies.

Sustainable trade (Rao, 2000b) is a trade regime that not only takes short-term benefits and costs into account but also seeks to ensure that trade operations can be sustained for very long time horizons (or forever) without interruptions caused as a result of the trade activities themselves. It is accomplished by taking into account the adverse effects of trade activities on the environment and negative feedback to the economy. The existence and involvement of a responsible global governing entity are presumed here, since markets themselves do not usually contain the information and foresight needed to accomplish the integration of (1) economic and environmental considerations, and (2) factors and impacts associated with markets and missing markets associated with various resources, products, and services (including services of nature). A brief alternative definition of sustainable trade is the derived one: the trade mechanism that ensures sustainable development.

The World Trade Organization and trade regimes

Multilateral trade regimes that have evolved over the past half-century or more are generally governed under the new WTO system. The General Agreement on Tariffs and Trade (GATT), formed in 1947, is now an ingredient of the WTO. The GATT, which had its final act at the Uruguay Round of Trade Negotiations, ceased to exist at the end of 1994 and was superseded by a permanent and more comprehensive World Trade Organization. Other components of the WTO system that came into effect on January 1, 1995 (based on the 1994 Marrakesh Agreement establishing the WTO) are the General

Agreement in Trade in Services (GATS), the Agreement on Trade-related Aspects of Intellectual Property Rights (TRIPS), and the Agreement on the Application of Sanitary and Phytosanitary Measures (SPS Agreement).

The GATT remained deep-rooted in the articles of agreement rather than in customary international law. The basic obligation under the GATT remains the most-favored nation (MFN) clause, which was neither a codification of customary international law nor did it establish a custom; the MFN extended only to other contracting parties (Palmeter and Mavroidis, 1998). The WTO articles of agreement clarify that the WTO jurisprudence remains that of the GATT.

Two key WTO articles of agreement are:

1 Article XVI.1: "[T]he WTO shall be guided by the decisions, procedures and customary practices followed by the Contracting Parties to GATT 1947."
2 Article XVI.3: "In the event of a conflict between a provision of this Agreement and a provision of any of the Multilateral Trade Agreements, the provision of this Agreement shall prevail to the extent of conflict."

In the preamble to the Marrakesh Agreement establishing the World Trade Organization, reference was made to the importance of working toward sustainable development. It enjoins WTO members to recognize

> that their relations in the field of trade and economic endeavor should be conducted with a view to raising standards of living, ensuring full employment and a large and steadily growing volume of real income and effective demand, and expanding the production of and trade in goods and services, while allowing for the optimal use of the world's resources in accordance with the objective of sustainable development, seeking both to protect and preserve the environment and to enhance the means for doing so in a manner consistent with their respective needs and concerns at different levels of economic development.

The WTO framework provides a few environmental considerations, and little, if any, environmental constraints as such to the global trade regime. Box 8.2 summarizes some of the relevant environmental provisions, usually in the form of "exceptions" rather than conditions for fulfillment in trade activities.

BOX 8.2

Summary of WTO environmental provisions

Some of the main provisions in the WTO agreements dealing with environmental issues are:

- GATT Article XX: policies affecting trade in goods for protecting human, animal, or plant life or health are exempt from normal GATT disciplines under certain conditions.
- Technical Barriers to Trade (i.e., product and industrial standards), and Sanitary and Phytosanitary Measures (animal and plant health and hygiene): recognition of some environmental objectives.
- Agriculture: environmental programs exempt from cuts in subsidies.
- Subsidies and Countervail: allows one-time subsidies, up to 20 percent of firms' costs, for adapting to new environmental laws.
- Intellectual Property: governments can refuse to issue patents that threaten human, animal, or plant life or health, or risk serious damage to the environment (TRIPS Article 27).
- GATS Article 14: policies affecting trade in service for protecting human, animal, or plant life or health are exempt from normal GATS disciplines under certain conditions.

Article XX on general exceptions of the General Agreement on Tariffs and Trade (GATT) states that:

> Subject to the requirement that such measures are not applied in a manner which would constitute a means of arbitrary or unjustifiable discrimination between countries where the same conditions prevail, or a disguised restriction on international trade, nothing in this Agreement shall be construed to prevent the adoption or enforcement by any contracting party of measures:
> (b) necessary to protect human, animal or plant life or health; . . .
> (g) relating to the conservation of exhaustible natural resources if such measures are made effective in conjunction with restrictions on domestic production or consumption.

The chapeau of Article XX is designed to ensure that the GATT-inconsistent measures do not (1) result in arbitrary or unjustifiable discrimination, and/or (2) constitute disguised restriction on international trade. The provision of the Article as well as its interpretation when trade disputes have arisen has assumed importance over the years. It is regrettable that Article XX still has no provision for the term "environment" or for its protection, and it refers to "exhaustible resources" rather than nonrenewable resources, as Rao (2000b) argues. The concept of "exhaustible resources" was in common use at the time of the GATT 1947, but revision of the terminology is long overdue so that we not only concern ourselves with "exhaustible resources" but also pay adequate attention to nonrenewable resources in the interests of environmental, ecological, and ecosystem services.

The TBT Agreement under the WTO system governs the technical regulations relating to "product characteristics or their related processes and production methods." This Agreement would govern environmental labeling and related aspects but would not govern a regulation that prohibits imports of products based on unsustainable harvesting of fisheries since the characteristics of the fish traded are not affected by the methods of fishing. The word "environment" does appear in the articles of the TBT, unlike in the case of the GATT.

Article 8.2 (c) of the Agreement on Subsidies and Countervailing Measures (SCM) grants as "non-actionable" under the WTO Charter

assistance to promote the adaptation of existing facilities to new environmental requirements imposed by law and/or regulations which result in greater constraints and financial burden on firms, provided that the assistance:

i) is a one-time non-recurring measure;

ii) is limited to 20 percent of the cost of adaptation;

iii) does not cover the cost of replacing and operating the assisted investment, which must be fully borne by firms;

iv) is directly linked to and proportionate to a firm's planned reduction of nuisance and pollution, and does not cover any manufacturing cost savings which may be achieved; and

v) is available to all firms which can adopt the new equipment and/or production processes.

International trade and environmental disputes

Under the multilateral trade regimes governed by the GATT, it is important to recognize that the environmental exceptions broadly outlined in GATT Article XX have often been interpreted to be used in conjunction with the chapeau of that Article. In the same spirit and reasoning, it is important that the preamble to the WTO articles of agreement be used, including the need to fulfill the objectives of "sustainable development," in order that various trade–environment conflicts are properly handled in the arbitration/appellate bodies, as argued in Rao (2000b). Some misinterpretations of the GATT law (such as invoking the chapeau of Article XX and Article III of the GATT without proper analysis) and WTO law (such as ignoring the imperatives of its preamble) surfaced in the Shrimp–Turtle Appellate Body Report (see Ala'i, 1999; Simmons, 1999). A balancing of trade liberalization and environmental protection is already largely in place under WTO law, but proper application appears to be lacking. As Rao (2000b) argues, "[t]rade liberalization for its own sake is not entirely meaningful just as environmental protection in its extreme form may also be inefficient." Some recent trends in the WTO panels suggest an increasing awareness, however (see Ala'i, 1999; Rao, 2001). The Tuna II Panel was the first GATT panel to refer to the objective of sustainable development (see also box 8.4 later in this chapter).

The application in many of the GATT panels of the "national treatment" principle under Article III of the GATT did not allow product differentiation in environmentally distinguishable products and processes as such a distinction was feared to lead to disguised trade protectionist measures and/or discrimination (see, for example, the Reformulated Gas case: United States – Standards for Reformulated and Conventional Gasoline, WTO/DS2/R.29 January 1996 Panel Report; reprinted in 35 ILM, 1996, 274).

The scope of GATT Article XX is a singular limitation for the protection of the global commons via any trade-related measures. The legitimacy of what is produced and traded rather than how it is produced makes it impossible to take into account relevant environmental measures and to apply Article XX for that purpose (see also Esty, 1994). Three major tests are traditionally sought to be verified in the application of exceptions to Article XX, thus constituting GATT jurisprudence. These are described below.

1. Application of the "necessary" test

Measures required to be least trade-restrictive ("least GATT-inconsistent," according to some of the dispute resolution panels of the GATT) are among the reasonably available alternatives. The potential candidate for alternative measures with respect to which the least GATT-inconsistency is to be examined is still a moot issue in most scenarios. In the absence of transparent and precise guidelines on this test, any given proposal can be disqualified as not being "least GATT-inconsistent." The 1991 GATT Panel Report on the Tuna–Dolphin Dispute (Tuna I) elucidated (after 44 years of the impugned clause's operation) that "necessary" should imply the requirement that a state party "exhaust all options reasonably available . . . through measures consistent with the General Agreement." Later in 1992, the second Tuna–Dolphin Dispute Panel (Tuna II) stated that "in cases where a measure consistent with other GATT provisions is not reasonably available, a contracting party is bound to use, among the measures reasonably available to it, that which entails the least degree of inconsistency with other GATT provisions." A more positive specification of the test would seek GATT-consistency in relation to the objectives of the WTO Agreement and its imperatives on application of the principles of sustainable development.

2. GATT Article XX (b): Application of the "proportionality" test

A relationship between the generalized costs of intervention measures and their general benefits is suggested as prudent when testing the relevance of any environmental measure as an environmental exception. However, there are hardly any quantifiable criteria in the potential application (in a replicable or calibrated manner) of this qualitative prescription.

3. Application of the "balancing" test

Based on a comparison of costs and benefits, this is the "primarily aimed at" factor of GATT Article XX (g). This is also a largely subjective perception rather than an empirically testable hypothesis. It is useful to ensure that the parties invoking an environmental exception establish their case according to standards and guidelines, but these guidelines are yet to be devised and prescribed by the GATT/WTO. In addition, it is useful to stipulate requisite transparency factors of the proposed actions so as to avoid disguised trade protectionism.

A number of MEAs invoke trade measures for the protection of the environment. Box 8.3 provides a list of agreements which have direct or indirect implications for international trade. According to the GATT Working Group on Trade and the Environment (GATT, 1994), GATT

BOX 8.3

Multilateral environmental agreements (MEAs)

This list includes most of the relevant agreements with implications for international trade. Up to 1992, about 17 MEAs were identified by GATT (1992) as containing trade measures, starting from 1933. Each of these agreements have not been ratified by the same set of countries, however.

- International Convention for the Protection of Birds (1950)
- International Plant Protection Agreement (1951)
- Convention on Conservation of North Pacific Fur Seals (1957)
- Agreement Concerning Cooperation in the Quarantine of Plants and their Protection against Pests and Diseases (1959)
- Rio International Convention for the Conservation of Atlantic Tunas (ICCAT) (1966)
- Phytosanitary Convention for Africa (1967)
- African Convention on the Conservation of Nature and Natural Resources (1968)
- Benelux Convention on the Hunting and Protection of Birds (1970)
- Convention on International Trade in Endangered Species (CITES) of Wild Fauna and Flora (1973)
- Montreal Protocol on Substances that Deplete the Ozone Layer (1987)
- Basel Convention on the Control of Transboundary Movements of Hazardous Wastes and their Disposal (1989)
- Convention for the Prohibition of Fishing with Long Driftnets in the South Pacific (Wellington Convention) (1990)
- Convention on Biological Diversity (1992)
- UN Agreement on the Conservation and Management of Straddling Fish Stocks and Highly Migratory Fish Stocks (1994)

Sources: Updated and summarized from GATT (1992); Rao (2000b)

parties that are nonparties to any MEA may "wish to use their GATT rights if they believe they are suffering from unfair or unnecessary discrimination" and the provisions of the MEA "should not be allowed to override those rights."

Some authors (see, for example, Maruyama, 1998) suggested that Article XX of the GATT can be meaningfully reformulated by the WTO members to explicitly authorize trade-restrictive environmental measures in tune with the MEAs such as the Basel Convention, CITES, or others. As Wold (1996) pointed out, the indiscriminate application of the nondiscrimination principle of the GATT tends to work significantly against the provisions and objectives of some of the MEAs such as CITES. Based on regional or subregional ecological characteristics, some endangered species may have to be listed in the trade-ban category or other classifications (for example, chinchillas from the US are allowed for trade, but not those from Peru). This is obviously incompatible with the nondiscrimination clause of the GATT. "GATT-proofing" of environmental trade measures (including environmental labeling), as long as these measures are authorized by an MEA, was suggested by some authors (see, for example, Staffin, 1996). It may not be as important to GATT-proof an environmental measure as it is to invoke the relevant integrated application of the Articles of the WTO, including its preamble.

The GATT 1994 under the new WTO framework should provide pragmatic measures which recognize the complementarity of trade and environmental measures. Rather than playing the role of a reluctant partner in global integration issues, the WTO/GATT mechanisms should play a more responsible role with the adoption of new reforms and changes in some of the provisions under the respective articles of agreement. Are the environmental trade measures (ETMs) likely to be suitable for attaining international environmental objectives? Below are some of the prerequisites for utilizing ETMs in the governance of global trade and the environment. They are not sufficient to ensure the pattern of sustainable development, however (Rao, 2000b). Some of the elements parallel those suggested in the USOTA (1992) report.

ETMs are specially important instruments in the following scenarios:

1 those involving global externalities such as ozone depletion or accumulation of greenhouse gases;
2 lack of workable incentives for administrative or market-oriented interventions;
3 the transaction costs of achieving these environmental measures with the exclusion of ETMs exceed those with their inclusion (in conjunction with other relevant complementary programs).

GATT hardly gained or even claimed any effective integration of trade policies and environmental considerations. Even after the 1992

BOX 8.4

US Marine Mammal Protection Act and international trade measures

The 1972 US Marine Mammal Protection Act (MMPA) and its later modifications of 1988 led to a ban on the imports of tuna from some regions, including Mexico. In connection with the application of a domestic US law to the international trade aspects, two GATT Panels held that the US ban on imports of tuna from specified countries violated GATT Article XI, and that Article XX cannot come to provide relevant exceptions to the rest of the GATT Articles in this case. The GATT Panels used feeble arguments and dubious reasoning (see also Chang, 1995) in the interpretation of Article XX of the GATT. The 1991 Panel Report asserted that (1) "(a) country can effectively control the production or consumption of an exhaustible natural resource only to the extent that the production or consumption is under its jurisdiction"; and (2) "Article XX (g) was intended to permit contracting parties to take trade measures primarily aimed at reducing effective restrictions on production or consumption within their jurisdiction." As Chang (1995) argued, the Panel held implicitly that the natural resource itself must be within the territorial jurisdiction of the country employing trade measures, and the Panel's deployment of "effective" measures is not supported by the text of Article XX (g), which merely required the trade measure to be "primarily aimed at rendering domestic restrictions effective."

The 1994 GATT Panel on the Tuna–Dolphin Dispute held that the MMPA violated GATT Article XI. This Panel rejected the "extra jurisdictional" rationale of the 1991 Panel decision, but ruled against the US, using the following argument (GATT, 1994, paragraph 5.27): "measures taken so as to force other countries to change their policies, and that were effective only if such changes occurred, could not be primarily aimed either at the conservation of an exhaustible natural resource, or at rendering effective restrictions on domestic production or consumption, in the meaning of Article XX (g)." This Panel also argued:

> If . . . Article XX were interpreted to permit contracting parties to take trade measures so as to force other contracting parties to change

> their policies, . . . the balance of rights and obligations among con-
> tracting parties, in particular the right of access to markets, would
> be seriously impaired. Under such an interpretation the General
> Agreement could no longer serve as a multilateral framework for
> trade among contracting parties. (GATT, 1994, paragraph 5.26)
>
> **Sources: Rao (2000b, 2001); Chang (1995); GATT (1994)**

UN Conference on Environment and Development (Rio Conference),
GATT (1992) clarified that:

> the GATT's competence was limited to trade policies and those trade-
> related aspects of environmental policies which might result in significant
> trade effects for GATT contracting parties. In respect neither of its voca-
> tion nor of its competence was the GATT equipped to become involved
> in the tasks of reviewing national environmental priorities, setting envir-
> onmental standards or developing global policies on the environment.

The narrow focus of the GATT mandate effectively precluded the
incorporation of MEAs in trade policies. Under the GATT, six panel
proceedings involving an examination of environmental measures or
human health-related measures under Article XX were completed. Of
the six reports, three have not been adopted. Under the WTO Dispute
Settlement Understanding, three such proceedings have been completed. The following is almost a representative overview of a select
set of these disputes, based on the WTO (1999) document. In all these
cases, trade provisions of the GATT prevailed over environmental
exceptions, partly because of misinterpretations of GATT Article XX.
In many of the dispute panel reports, the rules of interpretation tended
to change with each case.

In the Canada: Measures Affecting Exports of Unprocessed Herring
and Salmon case, adopted on March 22, 1988, Canada maintained
that under its 1976 Canadian Fisheries Act, regulations prohibit the
exportation or sale for export of certain unprocessed herring and
salmon. The US complained that these measures were inconsistent
with GATT Article XI. Canada maintained that these export restrictions were part of a system of fisheries resource management aimed
at preserving fishery stocks, and hence justified under Article XX (g).
The GATT Panel found that the measures maintained by Canada were
contrary to GATT Article XI:1 and were justified neither by Article

XI:2 (b) nor by Article XX (g). Chapter 9 provides further details of the dispute settlement aspects of the GATT/WTO Charter.

▎ 8.6 SUMMARY

International trade and its liberalization remains an area of considerable significance, especially in relation to the management of the global commons. The most important interface of international economic laws and international environmental laws emerges in the arena of trade and the environment. However, the literature is largely inconclusive, both in theory and in empirical findings about the nature of interrelationships between theories of international trade, development processes, and environmental quality, as a survey by Jayadevappa and Chhatre (2000) indicated. According to Nordstrom and Vaughan (1999, p. 57), the globalization of the world economy may have "reduced the regulatory autonomy of countries, thereby making it more difficult [to monitor] environmental standards unless as part of a concerted effort among nations."

Various trade measures contained in some international environmental agreements are either too weak in their specifications or in their implementation, or both. Besides, measures to ensure compliance with these provisions do not normally attract any sanctions or penalties for noncomplying parties. This tends to perpetuate regimes of free-ridership rather than responsible environmental partnership. To bring about such a partnership, considerable additional clarifications are required of the existing soft laws and binding hard laws. The GATT/WTO regime remains the most important international trade regime, but its integration of environmental factors in trade activities is still very feeble. Shifting rules of interpretation are seen as common in the GATT dispute resolution mechanisms, which is far from conducive to predictable legal outcomes based on a set of rules and principles. Predictability of the law and greater deployment of economic and environmental principles in the GATT/WTO regime are expected to be more useful in global welfare enhancement.

Extended lender liability laws need to be applied in relation to the financial activities of international financial institutions. The potential application of *non liquet* as a defense mechanism against environmental damage caused directly or indirectly by the operations of some of the financial institutions is conducive neither to sustainable development nor to an application of the "common but differentiated responsibilities" principle, as envisaged under the soft laws.

Review Exercises

1 Examine the role and application of the weak polluter pays principle to the hazardous wastes trade under the Basel Convention, and in general.

2 Why is cost externalization iniquitous in its incidence and how does it contribute toward more inequitable allocation of resources in the context of international trade?

3 Examine the relationship between different Articles in the TBT and SCM Agreements that seek to provide environmental protection. What improvements can be made in these Articles to ensure greater effectiveness of these provisions?

4 "The Bank does not support projects that, in the Bank's opinion, involve the significant conversion or degradation of critical natural habitats." What are the shortcomings of this specification in its potential for providing environmental protection?

5 Does the phenomenon of global externalities justify a role for international environmental organizations with enforcement powers? Examine this issue in the context of international trade.

6 Examine the validity or limitations of the following statement: "Full cost internalization will rarely be optimal; internalization of environmental costs should only be carried out up to the level where the incremental benefits of avoided environmental damages justify the incremental costs of environmental provisions."

REFERENCES

Ala'i, P., 1999, Free trade or sustainable development? An analysis of the WTO appellate body's shift to a more balanced approach to trade liberalization, *American University International Law Review*, 14, 1129–71.

Alpay, S., 2000, Does trade always harm the global environment? A case for positive interaction, *Oxford Economic Papers*, 52, 272–88.

Barrett, S., 1994, Strategic environmental policy and international trade, *Journal of Public Economics*, 54, 325–38.

Barrett, S., 1997, The strategy of trade sanctions in international environmental agreements, *Resource and Energy Economics*, 19, 345–61.

Bhala, R. and Kennedy, K., 1998, *World Trade Law*, St. Paul, MN: Lexis Law Publications.

Bowles, I. A. and Kormus, C. F., 1996, Environmental reform at the World Bank: The role of the United States Congress, *Virginia Journal of International Law*, 35, 777–808.

Brander, J. A. and Taylor, M. S., 1997, International trade between consumer and conservationist countries, *Resource and Energy Economics*, 19, 267–97.

Brander, J. A. and Taylor, M. S., 1998, Open access renewable resources: Trade and trade policy in a two-country model, *Journal of International Economics*, 44, 181–209.

Bugge, H. C., 1996, The principles of "polluter-pays" in economics and law, in E. Eide and R. van den Bergh (eds.), *Law and Economics of the Environment*, Deidrecht: Kluwer, pp. 53–74.

Chang, H. F., 1995, An economic analysis of trade measures to protect the global environment, *Georgetown Law Journal*, 83, 213–31.

Charnovitz, S., 1993, A taxonomy of environmental trade measures, *Georgetown International Environmental Law Review*, 6 (1), 1–46.

Cole, M. A., Rayner, A. J., and Bates, J. M., 1998, Trade liberalisation and the environment: The case of the Uruguay Round, *World Economy*, 21 (3), 337–47.

Copeland, B. R. and Taylor, M. S., 1994, North–South trade and environment, *Quarterly Journal of Economics*, 109, 755–87.

Di Leva, C. E., 1998, International environmental law and development, *Georgetown International Environmental Law Review*, 10, 501–49.

Elliot, G., 1994, *Internalization of Environmental Costs and Implications for the Trading System*, GATT Symposium on Trade, Environment, and Sustainable Development, Geneva: GATT Secretariat.

Esty, D. C., 1994, *Greening the GATT*, Washington, DC: Institute for International Economics.

Ferrantino, M. J., 1997, International trade, environmental quality and public policy, *World Economy*, 20, 43–72.

General Agreement on Tariffs and Trade (GATT), 1992, *Trade and Environment*, Geneva: GATT Secretariat.

GATT, 1994, *Report by the Chairman of the Group on Environmental Measures and International Trade*, Geneva: GATT Doc. L/7402, BISD, 75.

Greenway, D., 1998, Does trade liberalisation promote economic growth?, *Scottish Journal of Political Economy*, 45 (5), 491–511.

Handl, G., 1998, Legal mandate of multilateral development banks as agents for change toward sustainable development, *American Journal of International Law*, 92, 642–65.

Jayadevappa, R. and Chhatre, S., 2000, International trade and environmental quality: A survey, *Ecological Economics*, 32, 175–94.

Low, P., 1993, *Trading Free: The GATT and US Trade Policy*, New York: Twentieth Century Fund.

Maruyama, W. H., 1998, A new pillar of the WTO: Sound science, *International Lawyer*, 32, 651–77.

Nordstrom, H. and Vaughan, S., 1999, *Trade and Environment*, WTO Special Study #4, Geneva: World Trade Organization.

Organization for Economic Cooperation and Development (OECD), 1972, *The Polluter Pays Principle*, Paris: OECD.

OECD, 1975, *The Polluter Pays Principle: Definition, Analysis, Implementation*, Paris: OECD Secretariat.

OECD, 1995, *Environmental Principles and Concepts*, OECD Document OECD/ GD(95)124, Paris: OECD Secretariat.

OECD, 1997, *Experience with the Use of Trade Measures in the Convention on International Trade in Endangered Species of Wild Fauna and Flora (CITES)*, OECD Document OECD/GD(97)106, Paris: OECD Secretariat.

Palmeter, D. and Mavroidis, P. C., 1998, The World Trade Organization legal system: Sources of law, *American Journal of International Law*, 92, 398–413.

Rao, P. K., 2000a, *Sustainable Development: Economics and Policy*, Oxford: Blackwell.

Rao, P. K., 2000b, *The World Trade Organization and the Environment*, London: Macmillan/Palgrave.

Rao, P. K., 2001, *Environmental Trade Disputes and the WTO*, Lawrenceville, NJ: Pinninti Publishers.

Runge, C. F., 1994, *Freer Trade, Protected Environment*, New York: Council on Foreign Relations.

Simmons, B., 1999, In search of balance: An analysis of the WTO shrimp–turtle appellate body report, *Columbia Journal of Environmental Law*, 24, 413–54.

Staffin, E. B., 1996, Trade barrier or trade boon? A critical evaluation of environmental labeling and its role in the "greening" of world trade, *Columbia Journal of Environmental Law*, 21, 205–86.

Ulph, A., 1996, Environmental policy and international trade when governments and producers act strategically, *Journal of Environmental Economics and Management*, 30, 265–81.

Ulph, A., 1997, Environmental policy and international trade, in C. Carraro and D. Siniscalco (eds.), *New Directions in the Economic Theory of the Environment*, Cambridge: Cambridge University Press, pp. 147–92.

UN Conference on Trade and Development (UNCTAD), 1995, *Sustainable Development and the Possibilities for the Reflection of Environmental Costs in Prices*, Geneva: UNCTAD Report # TD/B/CN.1/29.

UNCTAD, 1997, *Trade and Environment: Concrete Progress Achieved and Some Outstanding Issues*, Geneva: UNCTAD Report.

US Office of Technology Assessment (USOTA), 1992, *Trade and the Environment: Conflicts and Opportunities*, Report # OTA-BP-ITE-94, Washington, DC: US Government Printing Office.

Wold, C., 1996, Multilateral environmental agreements and the GATT: Conflict and resolution?, *Environmental Law*, 26, 841–921.

World Trade Organization (WTO), 1999, *Environment and Trade*, WTO Special Study, Geneva: WTO Secretariat.

Xu, X., 1999, Do stringent environmental regulations reduce the international competitiveness of environmentally sensitive goods? A global perspective, *World Development*, 27, 1215–26.

chapter nine

Compliance, Dispute Resolution, and Governance

■ 9.1 INTRODUCTION

The provision of international laws becomes an end in itself if there is negligible compliance among the entities that are presumed to abide by the laws. The next issue is the laws' relative effectiveness in relation to the explicitly stated or implicit objectives of various provisions. No doubt most laws can be seen as incomplete contracts, but if they are also unenforceable even to the extent of their specifications on desired performances from parties, they then serve little useful purpose for society.

International environmental laws are more complex and diffused relative to most domestic laws in many countries. The lack of apex enforcement mechanisms and the issue of state sovereignty suggest that several behavior factors play a role in compliance to the legal provisions. Economic incentives for compliance and disincentives for noncompliance must be integrated in treaties and other agreements that are devised from time to time in the process of developing international environmental laws. Popular participation remains an important factor in the effectiveness of various laws, as is the involvement of environmental nongovernmental organizations (NGOs). As Principle 23 of the 1982 World Charter for Nature maintained:

> All persons, in accordance with their national legislation, shall have the opportunity to participate, individually or with others, in the formulation of decisions of direct concern to their environment, and shall have access to means of redress when their environment has suffered damage or degradation. (UN General Assembly Resolution on a World Charter for Nature, GA Res. 37/7, UN GAOR, UN Doc. A/RES/37/7, 1983)

This chapter examines important provisions of various international laws regarding their compliance requirements and any measures indicating the implications for noncompliance. Dispute resolution mechanisms are important in governing the compliance aspects of parties to various international agreements. These are examined for some of the major international environmental laws. Institutional mechanisms for improved efficacy of implementation and effectiveness are also examined in general, and in relation to some of the environmental laws.

9.2 COMPLIANCE, MONITORING, AND EFFECTIVENESS

Implementation refers to activities and policies at the national/international levels geared toward specific actions contemplated under an agreement. "Self-executing" treaties are those that do not require additional national legislation to undertake implementation of an international agreement.

Compliance refers to specific actions and inactions envisaged under an international agreement that are to be implemented by the parties to the agreement. These actions include appropriate legal and administrative measures for implementing the agreement. Some measures of compliance refer to procedural aspects, while others refer to substantive aspects. If both sets of measures have a significant positive impact in terms of realizing the stated objectives of the agreement, and/or addressing the underlying problems that led to the formation of the treaty or agreement, then implementation is considered "effective." A set of measures initiated by a party to an agreement may be in compliance but not necessarily effective, while the converse is also valid (albeit rarely).

The economics of compliance may be categorized in terms of the following components for operational relevance, based on detailed economic analysis; these enable a possible comparison of alternative bases for decision-making for various entities. The relevant ingredients of costs and of benefits are:

- Marginal cost of compliance
- Marginal cost of noncompliance
- Marginal benefit of compliance
- Marginal benefit of noncompliance
- Role of incentives and disincentives

Cost elements: direct and indirect costs – fiscal and budgetary; transaction costs; private and social costs; credibility and reputation costs;

interlinkage costs; direct and indirect provisions of penalties and other disincentives (if stated in the international agreements); incremental and fixed costs; adjustment and reform costs; costs of internalization and costs of externalization of environmental consequences; differential discount rates (implicit) applied to various cost elements, and applicable differential time horizons in the implicit assessment of these cost elements.

Benefit elements: private and social benefits, benefits to the state representatives and other agents; political benefits to the state leadership/ principals; perceptions of short-term and long-term beneficial consequences to decision-makers and the domestic society; international image, reputation, and cooperation; incentives for compliance; differential discount rates (implicit) applied to various benefit elements, and applicable differential time horizons in evaluating these benefits.

Let us note that the factors contributing to a particular level of compliance and effectiveness vary, as discussed in chapter 2. The lack of formal penalties for noncompliance need not always be construed as an invitation for noncompliance of stated provisions of an agreement between parties/states. Reciprocity and issue linkage play significant roles. As Chayes and Chayes (1991, p. 320) argued: "States have dealings and continuing relationships with each other over a range of issues. . . . A reputation for unreliability cannot be confined to the area of activity in which it is earned." The existence of reputational externalities in a repeat interactive setting is often a disincentive for states in their attitude toward compliance with international agreements. An exception may, however, be found when the discount rate on time (time preference) is very high (as in some cases of potential political uncertainties).

The treatment of breaches and nonparties

The CITES agreement of 1973 limits trade in the species covered with nonparties, so that the latter do not form escape routes for the effective implementation of the agreement's provisions. The Montreal Protocol prohibits adjustments to stated targets of reduction in hazardous substances whenever exports of these to nonparties are considered. The Basel Convention also has similar provisions.

Rules and principles

Rules are usually applicable in an "all-or-nothing" sense, whenever they are sought to be invoked, selectively or otherwise. Legal

BOX 9.1

Self-executing treaties

One of the definitions of a self-executing treaty (Ebbesson, 1996) is a treaty which is unconditionally implemented without reference to domestic law provided the treaty itself is formulated in that style and enables domestic courts to specify obligations and rights precisely. Alternatively, and more commonly, a self-executing treaty may be defined as "a treaty that may be enforced in the courts without prior legislation" and a nonself-executing treaty as one "that may not be enforced in the courts without prior legislation 'implementation'" (Vazquez, 1995, p. 695).

The distinction between the two categories of treaties arose in the US judicial system as early as 1829 at the Supreme Court in the *Foster v. Neilson* case (27 US (2 Pet.) 253, 1829). According to the US Foreign Relations Law Restatement (Third) of 1987 (Section 111), "the intention of the United States determines whether an agreement is to be self-executing in the United States or should await implementation by legislation or appropriate executive or administrative action." It was also clarified by a US federal court that some provisions of a treaty may be self-executing whereas others may not be self-executing (*United States v. Aguilar*, 883 F. 2d 662, 680; 9th Circuit, 1989; quoted in Vazquez, 1995).

Vazquez (1995) suggested four reasons why the "self-executing" doctrine may imply that an international treaty may be judicially unenforceable in countries such as the US, which lack an automatic supremacy clause in the constitutional setup. The reasons identified were: (1) treaty parties formed the treaty in the spirit that it could well be nonself-executing; (2) the obligation that a treaty imposes is such that it cannot be directly enforced by the US courts; (3) the treaty-makers lack the legitimacy of powers to accomplish by the treaty what they proclaim to achieve; and (4) the treaty does not establish a private right of action and/or there is a situation of *non liquet*.

principles state a rationale for a particular decision, if such a rationale exists in the given framework of the judicial environment; they do not, however, seek to specify a particular action or direction to be followed unless the contradiction pointed out in the ruling obviates

BOX 9.2

Softening of international environmental law?

Some of the recent trends in the evolution of the soft law suggest that it is intentional on the part of the parties to maintain a "wait and watch" or "learning by doing" attitude in some environmental issues to facilitate quicker adoption of an agreement. However, this is not always the case when loosely stated provisions exist in some international treaties or other agreements. A few important points in this regard are highlighted by Szekely (1997) and summarized below.

The 1992 Convention on Biological Diversity (CBD), in its Articles on the conservation of biological resources, calls for actions which the parties "shall" undertake. Soon this spirit changes to the vague specification "as far as possible and as appropriate" (see Articles 5 to 11 and 14; the relevance of appropriateness is not contested in the specific contexts of Articles 15.7 and 18.1, as argued by Szekely, 1997). Article 20 (paragraph 3) states that developed country parties "may" provide developing countries with financial resources to enable their implementation of some of the provisions of the CBD. In the same Article (paragraph 4), developing countries are expected to implement "their commitments" depending on the "effective implementation by developed-country parties of their commitments under this Convention related to financial resources." However, there are hardly any commitments by virtue of the previous paragraph.

Article 3 of the UNFCCC provides further instances of vague commitments. The strongest of the obligations concern developed country parties, given in paragraph 2 (a), which states that these parties "shall adopt national policies and take corresponding measures on the mitigation of climate change, by limiting its anthropogenic emissions of greenhouse gases and protecting and enhancing its greenhouse gas sinks and reservoirs." Soon, however, the focus changes: "These policies and measures will demonstrate that developed countries are taking the lead in modifying longer-term trends in anthropogenic emissions . . ."

A rather extreme case of contradiction is illustrated by the admittedly "soft law" under the 1992 Nonlegally Binding Authoritative Statement of Principles for a Global Consensus on the Management, Conservation, and Sustainable Development of All

Kinds of Forests. The document seems to begin and end with con-
tradictions, right from its title. It is difficult to find any element of
"authoritativeness" for a nonbinding declaration. The term "should"
appears 55 times in the text. However, the only instance when a
mandatory-sounding provision is made relates to the right of the
states to do as they please with their forest resources; the term
"shall" appears in Principle/Element 8 (g). If the objective of the
document was to address an environmental problem, the most
assertive part need not relate to protection of sovereign rights.
Such a feeble "authoritative statement" merely led to another set
of direction-free generalities in the Fortieth Session of the Intergovernmental Forum on Forests held in New York, 2000. UN (2000)
proposes a set of "international arrangements and mechanisms,"
abbreviated to IAM, which supposedly provides a new element
in the clueless world of forest resources governance. Among the
proposed alternatives was enhancement of the legal provisions, no
matter what were to be formulated or when.

Sources: Szekely (1997); UN (2000)

an alternative choice as the only course of action to be adopted by
the affected party.

According to Dickson (1999, p. 223), "[i]f the standard stipulates
what is to be done in certain circumstances, and it does not admit of
exceptions, then it is a rule. If it states a reason which should be
considered in certain circumstances but which need not always prevail, then it is a principle." If this is accepted as a clarifying difference,
is the precautionary principle (PP) a "principle" or a "rule"? The PP is
what it claims, a principle.

International law can be strengthened not only by providing for
binding obligations on parties, but also by more sophisticated soft
laws which seek to direct the parties (with built-in incentives and
disincentives) in desired directions for achieving environmental objectives as well as reconciling these with other relevant constraints.
However, any deliberate or inadvertent action to dilute a meaningful
agreement and thus lose its effectiveness constitutes an inefficient
act of treaty formulation and legal provision. Box 9.2 illustrates the
problems with some of the existing environmental laws depicting these
inefficiencies.

9.3 Environmental Information

The positive value of information for environmental decision-making is fairly widely accepted. However, the costs of information are also significant in several cases. In the international context information assumes a special relevance, as state parties tend to retain segments of information for their strategic advantage in various negotiations, or withhold information in order to avoid any potential disadvantage. In many cases, parties do not even possess relevant information for some environmental issues, hence the need for concerted actions to evolve global strategies. The Rio Declaration of 1992 in its Principle 10 states:

> Environmental issues are best handled with the participation of all concerned citizens, at the relevant level. At the national level, each individual shall have appropriate access to information concerning the environment that is held by public authorities, including information on hazardous materials and activities in their communities, and the opportunity to participate in the decision-making processes. States shall facilitate and encourage public awareness and participation by making information widely available. Effective access to judicial and administrative proceedings, including redress and remedy, shall be provided.

Most international environmental agreements do provide for exchange of information. Article 18.3 of the CBD seeks to establish a clearing house mechanism (CHM) to promote technical and scientific cooperation through information-sharing. The Rotterdam Convention on Prior Informed Consent significantly emphasizes the information-sharing aspects.

The Ministerial Conference on "Environment for Europe" held at Aarhus, Denmark in 1998 adopted the Convention on Access to Information, Public Participation in Decision-making, and Access to Justice in Environmental Matters, in the region of the United Nations Economic Commission for Europe (ECE). It was signed by 35 states and the EC. Article 4 provides for access to environmental information, and Article 9 access to justice, the latter stating:

> In the circumstances where a Party provides for such a review by a court of law, it shall ensure that such a person also has access to an expeditious procedure established by law that is free of charge or

inexpensive for reconsideration by a public authority or review by an independent and impartial body other than a court of law.

Final decisions under this paragraph 1 shall be binding on the public authority holding the information. Reasons shall be stated in writing, at least where access to information is refused under this paragraph.

. . . each Party shall ensure that, where they meet the criteria, if any, laid down in its national law, members of the public have access to administrative or judicial procedures to challenge acts and omissions by private persons and public authorities which contravene provisions of its national law relating to the environment.

Public participation and environmental legislation

In the US, government entities are required to observe "notice-comment-and-petition" procedures under the US Administrative Procedure Act (APA) (5 USC Sections 551–706, 1988). In international decision-making this framework is very relevant (see also HLRA, 1991). Most international organizations have powers to set forth nonbinding standards, in accordance with Articles 10–13 of the UN Charter. This does mean certain parts of "soft law" are being developed without adequate "notice-comment-and-petition" procedures. Enhanced accountability and credibility of the organization as well as of global public welfare are feasible if appropriate information-flow and feedback systems are devised for this purpose.

Box 9.3 summarizes a case involving access to information under the EC laws and the ruling of the European Court of Justice (ECJ) on this matter. This illustrates the significance of information and its access accorded in the relevant laws, and provides a model for several other countries.

Nongovernmental organizations (NGOs)

It is not entirely meaningful to include all NGOs in one group and discuss their relative usefulness or otherwise in the context of environmental governance. It is just as meaningless to include all governmental institutions in one class to deliberate their (in)efficiency. Nonetheless, a representative unaffiliated transparent NGO could, for example, qualify as a cost-effective feedback mechanism for the formulation and implementation of environmental laws. This is particularly relevant

BOX 9.3

Environmental information: The ECJ decision

COMMISSION OF THE EUROPEAN COMMUNITIES V. FEDERAL REPUBLIC OF GERMANY

The EC made an application under Article 169 of the EC Treaty (new Article 226 EC) for a declaration that the Federal Republic of Germany had failed to fulfill its obligations under Council Directive 90/313/EEC of June 7, 1990 on the freedom of access to information on the environment (OJ 1990 L 158, p. 56, "the directive"), in particular Article 2 (b), Article 3 (2), third indent of the first subparagraph and second subparagraph, and Article 5 thereof.

Article 1 of the directive provides that:

> the object of this directive is to ensure freedom of access to, and dissemination of, information on the environment held by public authorities and to set out the basic terms and conditions on which such information should be made available.
> ... "public authorities" shall mean any public administration at national, regional or local level with responsibilities, and possessing information, relating to the environment with the exception of bodies acting in a judicial or legislative capacity.

Article 3 declares: "Member States shall ensure that public authorities are required to make available information relating to the environment to any natural or legal person at his request and without his having to prove an interest."

The directive was adopted into German law by the Umweltinformationsgesetz (UIG) (Law on information relating to the environment, BGBI. I 1994, p. 1490, "the UIG"), which was adopted on July 8, 1994 and came into force on July 16, 1994. The object of the UIG, according to paragraph 1 thereof, is to ensure freedom of access to, and dissemination of, information on the environment held by public authorities and to set out the basic terms and conditions on which such information should be made available. Paragraph 3 (1) (3) of the UIG provides that "public authorities" is not to include "courts, criminal prosecution authorities and disciplinary authorities." Paragraph 4 (1) of the UIG provides that "there shall be freedom of access for all to information on the environment available from administrative authorities or private persons. . . . The administrative authorities may supply information on request, allow consultation of the file or make the source of information available in some other fashion." Paragraph 7 (1) (2) of the UIG provides that there is no right to information "during judicial, criminal or administrative proceedings in respect of information obtained by the public authorities in the course of such proceedings."

The Commission initiated against the Federal Republic of Germany the procedure for failure to fulfill obligations provided for in Article 169 of the Treaty. In the petition to the Court, the Commission claimed that the UIG is an incorrect transposition of Article 2 (b) of the directive inasmuch as it removes, as a matter of principle, courts, criminal prosecution authorities, and disciplinary authorities, not only in the exercise of their judicial functions, but also in the exercise of their administrative activities, from the duty to provide access to information on the environment. The Commission argued that a court or criminal prosecution authority may have information on the environment, in particular in the form of statistics, not necessarily obtained in the context of judicial activities.

The ECJ declared in its verdict that:

> By failing to provide for access to be given to information during administrative proceedings where the public authorities have received information in the course of those proceedings,
> – by failing to provide in the Umweltinformationsgesetz for information to be supplied in part where it is possible to separate out information concerning the interests referred to in Article 3 (2) of Council Directive 90/313/EEC of 7 June 1990 on the freedom of access to information on the environment, and
> – by failing to provide that a charge is to be made only where information is in fact supplied,
> the Federal Republic of Germany has failed to fulfill its obligations under the third indent of the first subparagraph, and the second subparagraph, of Article 3 (2) and under Article 5 of Directive 90/313.

Source: Information obtained from www.europa.eu.int/eur-lex/en/index.html (March 10, 2000). Reproduced with the permission of the European Court of Justice

in the international context, where there are hardly any designated nodal legal enforcement agencies. There could also be a risk of excessive NGO involvement in the environmental governance process. This problem arises from the fact that some of these organizations undergo changes or lack stability or coherence in their approaches to real-world problems; some do not necessarily represent the will of the people or are not formed on the basis of democratic traditions. This simply points to the need for appropriate guidelines for the selection and involvement of NGOs in environmental processes. The role of NGOs in the WTO framework continues to be a moot point; although a limited role for NGOs is envisaged in Article V of the WTO Constitution, there is very limited formal interaction between environmental NGOs and the WTO. In a significant procedural improvement, the WTO Appellate Body in the Shrimp–Turtle Dispute held that NGOs could submit *amicus curiae* briefs even when the Panel did not seek such information (the previous Dispute Panel in this case had ruled that such briefs could be submitted only when they were sought by the Panel). NGOs can potentially play custodial or arbitral roles in the governance of global resources that are not necessarily contested among specific parties or states (see also Charnovitz, 1996). This role of umpire may also be relevant when some resource utilization or impending environmental problems do not involve directly contested environmental disputes.

The experience of the CITES in the utilization of select NGOs is a useful indicator of the directions to be adopted in other scenarios and in the implementation of different international environmental agreements. The resource limitations of most of the Secretariats of these agreements can be partially offset with the deployment of human capital and information systems developed in conjunction with some of the NGOs in cooperation with various governmental entities. Sands and Bedecarre (1990) described the role of NGOs as "guardians of the spirit and purpose of CITES by monitoring both compliance and enforcement."

The 1993 North American Agreement on Environmental Cooperation (NAAEC, entered into force January 1994; see 32 ILM 1480), devised as a supplementary side agreement to the North American Free Trade Agreement (NAFTA), provides for the submission of views and claims by NGOs and that NGO members may serve on the arbitration panels formed for some of the dispute resolution mechanisms (see also Raustiala, 1997). Box 9.4 provides an illustrative list of international agreements which recognized the positive role of NGOs for promoting environmental protection.

BOX 9.4

NGOs in international environmental treaties

The increasing involvement of NGOs in international economic and environmental governance during recent years is significant. This is not to indicate that some of the early agreements dating back to the mid-twentieth century were oblivious to these aspects. More formal roles have, however, been instituted during the past two decades or so. The following extracts are illustrative, though not exhaustive, of the formal recognition of the role of NGOs in some of the international agreements.

1. 1946 INTERNATIONAL CONVENTION FOR THE REGULATION OF WHALING (SEE 161 UNTS AT 62)

Article 4: "the Commission may either in collaboration with or through independent agencies of the contracting Governments or other public or private agencies, establishments, or organizations, or independently . . . study, appraise, and disseminate information concerning methods of maintaining . . . whale stocks."

2. 1973 CONVENTION ON INTERNATIONAL TRADE IN ENDANGERED SPECIES (CITES)

Article 11: "any body or agency technically qualified in protection, conservation, or management of wild fauna and flora, in the following categories, which has informed the Secretariat of its desire to be represented at the meetings of the Conference by observers, shall be admitted unless at least one-third of the Parties present object: a) international agencies or bodies either governmental or non-governmental . . . and b) national non-governmental agencies or bodies which have been approved for this purpose by the State in which they are located."

3. 1987 MONTREAL PROTOCOL TO THE VIENNA CONVENTION ON SUBSTANCES THAT DEPLETE THE OZONE LAYER

Article 11: "any body or agency, whether national or international, governmental or non-governmental, qualified in fields relating to the protection of the ozone layer, which has informed the Secretariat of its wish to be represented at a meeting of the Parties as an observer may be admitted unless at least one-third of the Parties present object."

4. 1992 UNFCCC

Article 7: same as in Article 11 of the Montreal Protocol, except for the change of subject from ozone layer to matters covered by the Convention.

5. 1998 AARHUS CONVENTION ON ACCESS TO INFORMATION, PUBLIC PARTICIPATION IN DECISION-MAKING, AND ACCESS TO JUSTICE IN ENVIRONMENTAL MATTERS

The preamble recognizes, *inter alia*, "the importance of the respective roles that individual citizens, non-governmental organizations and the private sector can play in environmental protection." The Convention also stated in its Article 3 (general provisions): "Each Party shall provide for appropriate recognition of and support to associations, organizations or groups promoting environmental protection and ensure that its national legal system is consistent with this obligation."

■ 9.4 DISPUTE SETTLEMENT MECHANISMS

International diplomacy, especially economic diplomacy, and international law tend to complement each other; they are not usually to be considered as substitutes (although such situations exist on a very few occasions). The mechanisms of dispute settlement play an important role in the enforcement of international law. There are several fora for dispute settlement among state parties, some more comprehensive than others. These are summarized below.

Forum choice

This arises when there is no *a priori* specification of a mechanism for dispute resolution, or the agreement allows for choice of forum on the part of the disputing parties (for example, NAFTA, CBD), or when the issues involve multiple agreements (MEAs and WTO obligations), or the roles of *lex specialis* and *lex posterior* are not clear because of the mixed nature of issues.

Under NAFTA, disputes (under section B of Chapter 7 and Chapter 9) relating to human, plant, or animal life or health or the protection of the environment must be resolved within the NAFTA among its members (for an analysis, see Gantz, 1999). In general, the dispute settlement provision under Article 2005 of NAFTA allows forum choice to each member state: to elect between NAFTA or WTO.

The CBD in its Article 27 (process for settlement of disputes) provides a good deal of "forum shopping" for dispute resolution, paving the way for the role of economics and politics of forum choice among contending state parties:

> In the event of disputes between Parties concerning this Convention, the Parties shall seek solution by negotiation. If they cannot reach agreement, they may request mediation by a third party. If a dispute is not resolved by these means, the Parties agree when ratifying or approving the Convention that their dispute shall be settled by Arbitration or by submission of the dispute to the International Court of Justice [ICJ]. If the Parties do not accept this procedure, the dispute shall be submitted to conciliation.

However, some of the parties may not have submitted themselves to the ICJ, and thus the jurisdiction may not be uniformly applicable. This is explained below.

International Court of Justice (ICJ)

Article 36 of the ICJ specifies the provisions regarding its jurisdiction and role in rendering justice or interpreting international law. Article 36 states, *inter alia*:

1 The jurisdiction of the Court comprises all cases which the parties refer to it and all matters specially provided for in the Charter of the United Nations or in treaties and conventions in force.

2 The states parties to the present Statute may at any time declare that they recognize as compulsory *ipso facto* and without special agreement, in relation to any other state accepting the same obligation, the jurisdiction of the Court in all legal disputes concerning:

(a) the interpretation of a treaty;

(b) any question of international law;

(c) the existence of any fact which, if established, would constitute a breach of an international obligation;
(d) the nature or extent of the reparation to be made for the breach of an international obligation.

The ICJ responds to eligible parties upon showing injury, and not to others concerned with the global trusteeship of environmental resources. This limits third-party interventions. Furthermore, international laws may admit *non liquet*: where operative law does not exist, the litigant could simply lose by default. There are hardly any institutional arrangements in the international law arena to enable completion of contracts or gap-filling, unlike in domestic law. The role of arbitration panels is only partially to supplement interpretations and contending parties generally ensure these panels do not exercise any further law-making power. Dispute resolution mechanisms are hardly methods for efficient completion of contracts, as argued by Trachtman (1999).

UN Convention on the Law of the Sea (UNCLOS), 1982

This Convention provides one of the most comprehensive (though not necessarily totally coherent) provisions in this regard. The dispute settlement provisions are provided in several Articles. Article 59 provides the basis for the resolution of conflicts regarding the attribution of rights and jurisdiction in the exclusive economic zone: "the conflict should be resolved on the basis of equity and in the light of all the relevant circumstances, taking into account the respective importance of the interests involved to the parties as well as to the international community as a whole." Compulsory procedures for dispute settlement are given in Article 287 (choice of procedure). The alternatives in the forum selection for dispute resolution are:

1 the International Tribunal for the Law of the Sea established in accordance with Annex VI;
2 the International Court of Justice;
3 an arbitral tribunal constituted in accordance with Annex VII;
4 a special arbitral tribunal constituted in accordance with Annex VIII for one or more of the categories of disputes specified therein.

This article also provides that if the parties to a dispute have accepted (or not accepted) the same procedure for the settlement of the dispute, the dispute may be submitted only to that procedure, unless the parties otherwise agree.

In addition to this, Article 296 on the finality and binding force of decisions makes the following provisions:

1 Any decision rendered by a court or tribunal having jurisdiction under this section shall be final and shall be complied with by all the parties to the dispute.
2 Any such decision shall have no binding force except between the parties and in respect of that particular dispute.

Regarding civil damages, Article 230 specifies that monetary penalties may be imposed only with respect to violations of national laws and regulations or applicable international rules and standards for the prevention, reduction, and control of pollution of the marine environment, committed by foreign vessels in the territorial sea or beyond the territorial sea, except in the case of a willful and serious act of pollution in the territorial sea.

Article 235 specifies, *inter alia*:

> With the objective of assuring prompt and adequate compensation in respect of all damage caused by pollution of the marine environment, States shall cooperate in the implementation of existing international law and the further development of international law relating to responsibility and liability for the assessment of and compensation for damage and the settlement of related disputes, as well as, where appropriate, development of criteria and procedures for payment of adequate compensation, such as compulsory insurance or compensation funds.

International Tribunal for the Law of the Sea (ITLOS)

The 1982 UNCLOS created the ITLOS (with its chambers in Hamburg, Germany) as part of its provision for an obligatory third-party dispute settlement system. The mechanism came into existence in November 1994 when the UNCLOS entered into force. An Agreement on Cooperation and Relationship Between the United Nations and the International Tribunal for the Law of the Sea was adopted by the UN General Assembly on September 8, 1998 (UN Doc. A/RES/52/521, 1998). A few cases have already been processed (details can be accessed via the UN website, www.un.org/Depts/los.htm, or seen in the ILM publications). Article 287 of the UNCLOS offers state parties a choice of four alternative third-party fora for dispute settlement: the ITLOS, the ICJ, arbitration, and a special arbitration panel of experts. However, the expert panel is allowed only in cases involving fisheries, marine environment protection, marine scientific research, and navigation. The flexibility in those fora was the result of states' inability to unanimously agree on a single mechanism, existing or new. For a detailed interpretation of the ITLOS and various aspects of jurisprudence, see Noyes (1998).

WTO Dispute Settlement Understanding (DSU)

The DSU is considered one of the central elements of the WTO system, relative to most other international organizations and also compared to the weak mechanism that existed in its predecessor, GATT 1947. The DSU includes binding treaty obligations for the member countries. Palmeter and Mavroidis (1999) provide a detailed account of several aspects of the WTO-DSU.

As a general rule, the WTO dispute settlement procedure outlined in Article 3.2 of the DSU stated that disputes will be resolved in accordance with "customary rules of interpretation of public international law." The GATT provisions and its environmental exceptions in Article XX remain largely intact under the new GATT 1994. Besides, the overarching WTO articles of agreement, and other important agreements such as the Agreement on the Application of Sanitary and Phytosanitary Measures (SPS), the Agreement on Subsidies and Countervailing Measures (SCM), and the Technical Barriers to Trade (TBT) Agreement and their interdependent interpretations, constitute the legal bases for the resolution of trade–environment disputes under the WTO system.

The Dispute Settlement Body (DSB) of the WTO is the apex-level group that offers a ruling on all trade disputes involving members. The DSU of the WTO, agreed by all the member countries of the world body, states in Article 21.1 that "[p]rompt compliance with recommendations or rulings of the DSB is essential in order to ensure effective resolution of disputes to the benefit of all Members." The DSU was officially declared by members as a "central element in providing security and predictability to the multilateral trading systems." Article 16 of the DSU prevents blockage by a single member of the DSB's acceptance of a panel report on any trade dispute. A panel report on a dispute will be deemed adopted unless there is a consensus against it. This is called "reverse consensus," which constitutes a major improvement over the corresponding feature under the GATT

1947 mechanisms for dispute settlement. Unless a disputant opts to appeal, the panel report is submitted to the DSB for its consideration and the report is automatically adopted unless rejected by a consensus of the DSB.

There has been a widely held view that the WTO mechanisms for dispute settlement are more legalistic than most other similar international institutions. However, the founding members, especially Canada, the EC, and the US, were in favor of such a system – with the intention of devising effective transparent methods of dispute resolution and averting any global effects of uncertainties in trading regimes. The DSU in its Article 3.7 states that a "solution mutually acceptable to the parties to a dispute and consistent with the covered agreements is clearly to be preferred (over the use of panel procedures)." However, some parties tend to ignore this principle of wisdom and seek to test the workability of legal and institutional arrangements.

The interpretations of the WTO panels, and its previous GATT panels has been such as to favor trade over the environment, almost invariably. The main provisions invoked in these conclusions were those of Article III of the GATT. For example, in the US Gasoline decision (US – Standards for Reformulated and Conventional Gasoline, WTO Panel Report of May 1996), it was declared that Article III.4 "does not allow less favorable treatment dependent on the characteristics of the producer and the nature of the data held by it." The panel described as "extraneous" the producer characteristics which have a bearing on the environmental consequences of trade and consumption. This is a serious proposition that ignores the environmental dimensions of alternate modes of production and their impact, perhaps disparate impact across member countries and the rest of the world. Devoid of an ecological perspective and expertise, some of the WTO panels can hardly furnish an integrated assessment or judgment on the increasingly complex issues of trade and the environment. As argued in Rao (2000), such a "free-trade" approach is unlikely to be sustainable, and this remains a structural impediment for global trade regimes over time. If such a stand as in the Gasoline Panel continues to be maintained in further decisions under the WTO framework, it may be that a new multilateral agreement can resolve the trade–environment conflicts with a reasonable reconciliation and provide new guidelines for the same. One of the constituents of the WTO is the TBT Agreement. This allows a limited distinction, subject to the usual principles of nondiscrimination, regarding "product characteristics or their related processes and production methods." Some of the additional limitations of the WTO Articles in protecting health and the environment are explored by Charnovitz (1998).

In the absence of relevant specifications and guidelines on how to conduct a cost–benefit analysis in the international context, the Appellate Body of the Gasoline case pointed to two failures by the US Environmental Protection Agency (USEPA): (1) the agency did not adequately explore cooperative measures with the disputing countries; (2) it did not take into account the costs of its regulation to foreign refiners. The role of economic analysis, assuming there is a consensus on the relevant framework and guidelines for assessing economic costs, is a somewhat remote prospect when the articles of agreement under the GATT/WTO are primarily found to be in violation, as assessed by the panels.

The substantive as well as procedural incompleteness of the provisions of the DSU were examined by Trachtman (1999). An incomplete contracts theory perspective was seen as an explanation for the prevalence of such features in some of these and related international agreements. New proposals for "due process" and "negotiation instruments" in trade and environment were advanced in another case.

In May 1996, the US effectively prohibited imports of shrimp and shrimp products from all countries that do not require shrimp trawlers to use turtle-excluding devices (TEDs). This was aimed at the preservation of the endangered species of sea turtles, which get drowned in the nets. The devices are relatively inexpensive (ranging from $8 to $75), but the dispute initiated by India, Malaysia, Pakistan, and Thailand went up to the Appellate Body, which found the US in violation of GATT Article XI (prohibition of quantitative restrictions), while the US sought exemption under GATT Article XX (b) and (g). The United States – Import prohibition of certain shrimp and shrimp products, Panel Report of May 15, 1998 (Report WT/DS58/R, paragraph 7.60) declared that "general international law and international environmental law clearly favor the use of negotiated instruments rather than unilateral measures when addressing transboundary or global environmental problems, particularly when developing countries are concerned. Hence, a negotiated solution is clearly to be preferred, both from a WTO and an international environmental law perspective."

This case was dealt with by WTO Appellate Body Report WT/DS58/AB/R of October 12, 1998. The report raised the following issues, among others (for an analysis of the report, see, for example, Shaffer, 1999):

1   The US ban on shrimp had a "coercive effect" on other members of the WTO, and the US failed to take into account different local conditions prevailing in other regions.

2   The US successfully negotiated an Inter-American Convention for the Protection and Conservation of Sea Turtles, indicating "multilateral procedures are available and feasible," but did not attempt seriously any similar multilateral treaty with other states (especially the plaintiff states in this case).

3   The application of the trade measure was "arbitrary" in that the certification process was neither "transparent" nor "predictable," and that it does not provide any "formal opportunity for an applicant country to be heard, or to respond to any arguments that may be made against it" (paragraph 180 of the report). Thus the foreign states were denied "due process" rights.

The US State Department, the nodal coordinating department of the US government, published a Notification of Guidelines in 1999. The government is in the process of formulating a multilateral treaty for the protection and conservation of sea turtles using TEDs and also providing finances and technology to enable effective implementation for the protection of the sea turtles. The roles of *ex ante* vs. *ex post* costs, acceptance of risk levels, decision-making under uncertainty, transaction costs, and cost–benefit analysis are all relevant here.

The UNFCCC of 1992

Article 14 provides, *inter alia*, the following:

> in respect of any dispute concerning the interpretation or application of the Convention, (a party) recognizes as compulsory *ipso facto* and without special agreement, in relation to any Party accepting the same obligation:
>   a) Submission of the dispute to the International Court of Justice and/or
>   b) Arbitration in accordance with procedures to be adopted by the Conference of Parties as soon as practicable, in an annex on arbitration.
>   A Party which is a regional economic integration organization may make a declaration with like effect in relation to arbitration in accordance with the procedures referred to in subparagraph (b) above.

The Kyoto Protocol to the UNFCCC provides for dispute settlement to be specified by parties (Article 18). Several potential problems and

318 INTEGRATION AND SYNTHESIS

solutions under the Kyoto Protocol dispute resolution regimes are discussed in Kalas and Herwig (2000), who noted that "because standing before the ICJ is dependent upon showing injury, cases of noncompliance by Parties with Protocol obligations . . . will be difficult to bring by other parties" (p. 64).

The Montreal Protocol provides in its noncompliance procedures (NCP) that a party need not show an injury in order to bring a complaint to the forum under the Protocol: any party state who has "reservations regarding another Party's implementation of its obligations under the Protocol" may initiate relevant dispute resolution action.

The democracy content of international institutions governing the global environment and the issue of legitimacy of international governance remains an issue in some international environmental disputes. A more participative and transparent system of decision-making is likely to reduce the demand for dispute settlement. Similarly, a more precise articulation of some of the provisions of international agreements are also likely to have a similar effect. In other words, the "market for dispute settlement" needs to be viewed from the perspectives of demand factors as well as supply factors in order to obtain integrated approaches to the problem.

▌ 9.5 Economic Incentives and Disincentives

In general, the main difference between the performance of command or highly regulated systems and market or privatized systems is in terms of the operative aspects of incentives for performance and disincentives for nonperformance. However, as argued by Binger and Hoffman (1989, p. 69), "the private rights system is itself a public institution and is dependent on public instrumentalities for its very existence."

The Montreal Protocol, the UNFCCC, and the Convention on Biological Diversity are among the international environmental agreements that provide incentives for existing parties as well as potential new parties. These are in the form of technical assistance, project and program funds, and other resources for capacity building as well as implementation of stated measures.

In the Montreal Protocol, noncompliance provisions were deliberated in the agreement. Although the enabling clause of compliance control was discussed in 1987, it was three years later that the second meeting of the parties (London Amendments) adopted a full-fledged though interim noncompliance procedure. A system of "legal innovation" in the Protocol implementation was instituted with the following main features (Lang, 1995): (1) the compliance investigation procedure may be triggered by parties suspicious of their fellow members' performance, by the Secretariat, and by a party that considers itself unable to comply fully with its mandated obligations; (2) the Implementation Committee may obtain and act upon information, including on-the-spot investigations if the suspected party agrees, or seek amicable solutions at the Committee level; (3) at the Meeting of the Parties, the options for "drawing consequences" are available. These include the issuance of cautions and the suspension of rights and privileges under the Protocol such as trade or financial assistance.

The relative effectiveness of mechanisms for monitoring and evaluation of the compliance regimes (and their verifiability) are important, unless the provisions can be generally characterized as self-interest-sustaining and self-enforcement-inducing. Institutionalized compliance regulation and control can be classified by a variety of criteria (Lang, 1995): composition and size of the control body, regulatory and control powers of the body, investigation-triggering origins of control activities, procedural duties of the (potentially) noncompliant state, causes of noncompliance, and consequences of noncompliance.

Three elements related to compliance, essentially the forward and backward linkages in connection with features of compliance itself, may be distinguished (see also Weiss, 1995): implementation, routine compliance, and effectiveness. The first refers to the legislation, the regulations, and other aspects required to implement the agreement. Routine compliance refers not only to whether countries adhere to the provisions of the agreement and implementing measures, but whether the setting of the goals and targets induced any undesirable changes in their behavior. Compliance may also be distinguished in terms of procedural compliance and substantive compliance, and it is the latter that could lead to effectiveness of the spirit of the agreement. An agreement may be declared as being complied with, but the objectives may not be attained – a case of ineffectiveness.

Why are some international environmental agreements more effective than others? There are several explanatory factors. Most begin with the design of the agreements themselves. The contractual nature of some of the provisions affects the behavior of the parties. In addition, the "normal" features of the enforcement of domestic contracts or other legal instruments in some states extend well to the international legal aspects. The composition of parties to an agreement, then, does influence its relative effectiveness.

Characteristics of the activity involved are also important determinants of an agreement's effectiveness (see also Jacobson and Weiss, 1998). As an illustration, the few limited producers of ozone-depleting substances (with substitution alternatives in their production) in the Montreal Protocol case differ substantially from the CITES case, which involves hundreds of thousands of individuals and groups, many of whom are engaged in the illicit trade of endangered species. Other determinants of effectiveness are specific features of the agreement, including information and reporting requirements, incentives and disincentives (incentives for countries to join the Montreal Protocol and participate in its implementation, contrasted with the perverse incentives and public penalties leading to private reward for diffused enforcement systems in the CITES case), and domestic factors in individual states that are parties to different agreements. In addition there are exogenous influences, such as slowdown of an economy resulting in less use of some substances – a case of enhanced "effectiveness" under degenerate solutions to the problem.

The 1992 Report of the US Federal Government General Accounting Office (USGAO, 1992) examined eight major international environmental agreements (including the Montreal Protocol, the 1979 Geneva Convention on Long-range Transboundary Air Pollution (LRTAP), and CITES). The report concluded that the monitoring authorities at the international level were unable to verify the veracity of compliance reports and assess the degree of compliance, if any. One of the explanations for limited compliance in some international agreements is based on the proposition that parties may have a common interest in deriving the benefit of proposed collective action, but may not have a common interest in incurring the monetary or other costs of providing that collective good (Olson, 1979).

■ 9.6 TOWARD EFFECTIVE INTERNATIONAL ENVIRONMENTAL LAW

One of the main sources of international public law, and hence of international environmental law (IEL), is that of customary international law (CIL), discussed in chapter 4. It must, however, be noted that there are serious limitations in the applications of CIL in the environmental arena. This is because, as Tarlock (1997) observed, IEL consists of affirmative aspirational principles (such as the imperatives of ecological sustainability and sustainable development) and allows for some degree of flexibility among states (even when such flexibility is not explicitly stated in each international agreement).

The Institute of International Law's report, "Preparatory works: Final report" (see also Vicuna, 1997), suggested increasing international recognition of the "irreversible nature" of environmental impacts of various activities, and the need to address preventive aspects. The report suggested using the following guidelines:

1 the precautionary principle (PP);
2 the common but differentiated responsibilities principle;
3 a broad framework for assessing damage and remedial measures;
4 increased access to information and public participation in environmental management.

Among these, the PP remains a rather disputed item for categorization as a customary international law (Berwick, 1998), although the stage is expected to be ready for it to graduate soon into CIL (see also its application in the international water dispute summarized in chapter 6).

Among the major ingredients for effective provision of international environmental laws are those that start with its demand aspects. An informed social and cultural ethos and value systems benign to harmonious, equitable, and fair living standards tend to minimize damage to the environment, both locally and globally. In other words, negative externalities play an insignificant role in such a utopian configuration. In the real world, however, several complex issues and anthropogenic influences on the global environment and its governance need to be confronted. Ideally, we need to devise self-enforcing agreements among parties to international environmental agreements. Self-enforcing agreements are those that recognize factors of self-interest, the threat of enforceable sanctions, low discount rates on time and repetitive interrelationships, and the net perceived immediate loss to the party in slack enforcement or compliance. There is still a need for global trusteeship mechanisms to act as moderators and/or protectors of global environmental resources. An *amicus curiae* role for a new Global Environmental Trust (GET) in anonymous damage cases and *non liquet* scenarios remains significant in this context. It is useful to recall that in the Barcelona Traction Co. case (*Belgium v. Spain*, 1970 ICJ, 3, 32; February 5, 1970) the ICJ recognized the existence of "obligations of a state towards the international community as a whole," and not necessarily confined to the consequences of actions and inactions applicable to the contending parties only. These obligations are *erga omnes*. However, in the absence of provisions for the legal standing of a global entity such as a GET or other third parties to seek justice under the ICJ, it may be harder for such wider ramifications to find a place in global environmental justice.

Major legal frameworks governing different categories of resources are:

1 international resources (bilateral, regional, and multilateral);
2 global environmental commons (environmental goods and "bads")
   • *res nullius*
   • *res communis*
   where the exploiters are individual states or groups of countries.

The provision of legal measures needs to address both preventive and mitigating aspects. The enactment of laws, treaty formation, the optimal use of reservations, and soft law versus hard law are some of these legal requirements. In addition, monitoring, evaluation, and feedback mechanisms play significant roles. Enforcement measures within the sovereign rights framework are always rather tricky. Efficient (or optimal) provision of incentives and penalties in relation to the economics of compliance (or otherwise) deserves close attention in respect of each environmental agreement or legal stipulation.

A claim for compensation for environmental damage affecting *res nullius* could arise from a "trust" to be created via a global agreement, leading to global trusteeship (Boyle, 1997). This is similar to the "public trust" doctrine that has evolved in the US since the 1970s. Historically, the public trust doctrine was founded on the Roman law concept of *res communis*, that is, global assets, by natural law, belong to all of society. This concept adheres to the belief that global common resources belong to humankind and deserve to be protected under the doctrine of public trust. The public trust doctrine enhances the state's role in environmental protection and use of appropriate regulatory instruments for this purpose (Nanda and Ris, 1976; Taylor, 1998). In a domestic regional context involving local commons, the US Supreme Court's judicial verdict in *Phillips Petroleum Co. v. Mississippi* (484 US 469, 1988) is one of several examples of the doctrine's application. This verdict also recognized the ecological principle that lands under navigable areas share environmental and ecological characteristics with nonnavigable tidal areas, given the existence of geophysical and biological interdependencies.

Let us recall that the US National Environmental Policy Act of 1969 clearly specifies "the responsibilities of each generation as a trustee of the environment for succeeding generations" (42 USC 432, 101 (b)). As Scott (1999) elaborated, the trust law doctrine holds that the decisions made for the presumed protection of others need to be characterized with greater risk aversion (see chapter 3 for related concepts and definitions) relative to the risk-acceptance level applicable for the decision-makers themselves.

Application of the public trust doctrine is still lacking at the international level. As a result, the risk-taking and negative externality-spreading activities of states and other entities continue, with relatively minimal legal interventions. Further, the contribution of current international environmental laws toward principles of compensation for environmental harm is extremely weak or nonexistent, thus paving the way for environmental free-riders (see a detailed analysis in Wetterstein, 1997). The ILC codification attempts in this arena of state liability for environmental harm have been singularly unsuccessful in reaching an agreement of draft principles and rules. Limited provisions of civil liability and the creation of the International Oil Pollution Fund are indicative of practical limitations so far. A disclaimer in the 1979 Geneva Convention on Long-range Transboundary Air Pollution in its Article 8 (f) states that "the present Convention does not contain a rule on State liability as to damage."

Static vs. dynamic law and lags in the evolution of legal treaties

The provisions of international law must keep pace with scientific developments regarding ecosystem interdependencies and the need to recognize such phenomena in an integrated manner whenever one or more components is addressed. This is a minimal requirement that needs to be fulfilled before additional considerations of ensuring system resilience and sustainability are incorporated in conjunction with the precautionary principle. Internationalization of resource management issues is not the first step in devising responsible policies; rather, recognition of the common concern and incorporating relevant provisions in the operating rules is more pragmatic (see also Brunne and Toope, 1997).

International environmental laws, including most of the regional multilateral agreements, tend to assume a unitary polity for the purpose of adoption and implementation of the agreements and the law. This remains counterfactual in most countries, especially the democratically governed ones; even these happen to be small in their geographic territories. Despite claims of the overriding nature of international law, it is simply unrealistic for such a feature to ensure effective adoption in a federal polity mandated by applicable constitutional specifications. Several issues were raised even in the application of regional laws such as those of the NAFTA and EC environmental laws (see, for example, Kelly, 1997; Visek, 1995). The NAFTA Implementation Act of 1993 (US) provides for the first time in connection with any US treaty that the individual states in the US must be informed and permitted to participate in trade matters affecting their interests. Section 102 (b) (1) (B) offers the states some procedural rights in their adherence to the provisions of the trade act. Countries such as Belgium, Canada, and Germany provide a prominent illustration of the problems inherent in this issue, even after the countries have agreed to become parties to some multilateral agreements and international legal norms. In Belgium, for example, each of the autonomous provinces must separately adopt environmental legislation; some lag behind the rest by about five years or more.

The dynamic aspect of IEL is perhaps best pronounced by the ICJ in the Gabcikovo-Nagymaros case (*Hungary v. Slovakia*, 1997 ICJ 3; February 5, 1997; reprinted in 37 ILM 162). The Court asserted (without seriously invoking the position, since neither of the contending parties sought to deploy such norms) that new scientific insights and growing risks to humankind must be recognized, and new norms evolved under international agreements or other international instruments must be taken into consideration.

Effectiveness of international agreements

Effectiveness goes beyond mere compliance in as much as it relates more closely with the objectives of the agreement; the compliance mechanism is only in relation to the stated stipulations of required actions from the parties. LRTAP is considered one of the agreements that has been effective in affecting even the policies of the parties that have an impact on the acid rain phenomenon in Europe (Young, 1999). The role of agreements and their corresponding regimes has been to redefine collective-action mechanisms, their interplay with other mechanisms of cooperation, providing for accountability for environmental impacts, and effecting institutional reforms or behavioral patterns with implications for environmental objectives.

It is useful to note that the general role of rule of law in any state has an impact on the effectiveness of IEL. Undue emphasis on procedure or form over substance could imply that IEL becomes ineffective. If state compliance with procedures does not have an impact on the desired environmental objectives, the rules and the laws are ineffective. "Positive environmental measures" (PEMs), discussed in chapter 8, play a significant role in exploiting the complementarities of legal and other provisions of treaty implementation. In other words, such measures tend to enable reduction of total transaction costs of effective implementation, and the problem then is one of devising cost-effective measures under the PEM category.

Compatibility of international and national environmental law

Several international environmental laws possess gaps in their specifications, interpretations, and operative procedures or legal enforcement at the courts (see Ebbesson, 1996). These can hardly be translated directly into enforceable domestic laws at the country level. International treaties generally constitute an ingredient of national laws. Some treaty specifications (for example, the UN Convention on the Law of the Sea, Article 207) define the competence of the country to legislate in some areas; some (for example, MARPOL, LRTAP) prescribe standards of environmental performance; some prescribe institutional and procedural arrangements (Rotterdam Convention on Access to Public Information) for enhancing environmental objectives or their fulfillment; and some require task fulfillment in terms of specified environmental goals (Montreal Protocol, UNFCCC/Kyoto Protocol). Accordingly, initial or transitory gaps (or their lack) with national laws vary in form and substance. It is not entirely a matter of national legislative reform or action that enables compliance with international treaties. The entire institutional mix, including popular participation, the cooperation of industrial enterprise, administrative efficiency, judicial competence and enforcement, and political will, is required for the compatibility of national environmental laws with international environmental laws.

International environmental regimes and developing countries

The special features of developing countries (although not entirely common among all developing countries) warrant particular attention. It is useful to recall some of the suggestions of Agenda 21 (Chapter 39) on the legal basis of infrastructural aspects of developing countries. It states:

At the global level, . . . the participation in and the contribution of all countries, including the developing countries, to treaty making in the field of international law on sustainable development [, is of essential importance]. Many of the existing international legal instruments and agreements in the field of environment have been developed without adequate participation and contribution of developing countries, and thus may require review in order to reflect the concerns and interests of developing countries and to ensure a balanced governance of such instruments and agreements . . .

Developing countries should also be provided with technical assistance in their attempts to enhance their national legislative capabilities in the field of environmental law . . . (http://www.un.org/esa/sustdev/agenda21chapter39.htm, January 1, 2000)

As already argued in chapter 7, there is an urgent need to integrate legal institutional requirements of some of the developing countries (including the role of rule of law) as an essential prerequisite toward sustainable development and possible compliance with international legal regimes, including environmental laws. Since the "level playing field" must be similar among countries, these aspects of institutional development continue to be important.

Endogenous institutional response (EIR)

Institutions are defined as: "persistent and connected sets of (formal and informal) rules that prescribe behavioral roles, constrain activity, and shape expectations" (Keohane, 1988). However, expectations about institutions also matter. Snidal (1996) argued that "institutions matter because they provide a stable environment for mutually beneficial decision-making as they guide and constrain behavior."

Broadly, two forms of institutional governance structures are relevant: exogenous and endogenous. These are not mutually exclusive, given the interactions between the two. Both tend to be influenced significantly by transaction costs. Exogenous structures admit a greater role for third parties or international collective bodies to address issues arising out of agreements or their absence. Endogenous structures are active internal mechanisms of state practice which form policies and respond to emerging issues of multilateral cooperation, coordination, and other forms of interrelationships. The concept of state practice facilitates the development of endogenous governance structures.

Exogenous and endogenous governance structures and the role of transaction costs in state practice are some of the issues examined by Aceves (1996). Hurwicz (1972) proved that are no informationally decentralized mechanisms to realize Pareto-optimal performance in economic systems involving externalities.

EIR refers to the phenomenon of institutional responsiveness to changing information and circumstances in the sustained pursuit of the stated or normal mission of any institution. This responsiveness need not arise merely from external influences; informational inputs from exogenous sources could constitute a source of change, however. If the EIR is positive, it implies that institutions can adapt rationally to change and thus minimize disruption costs and transaction costs of various categories. EIR is the institutional equivalent of the resilience phenomenon in ecological and environmental systems. Sustainable development and the evolution of sustainable institutions, including international environmental laws, require that international and domestic institutions possess the features of EIR. This should remain a short-term and long-term objective of policies and activities of international organizations and institutions. The effectiveness of IEL will form a byproduct of this feature.

Conflict in international environmental laws

It is desirable to specify an automatic clause resorting to the more stringent provisions as the obligatory requirements for resolving any conflicts among international environmental laws. This should hold unless there are international explicit laws to the contrary. The example of the US Clean Air Act is relevant in this context. Section 614 (b) of this Act states with regard to ozone-depleting substances that it "shall not be construed, interpreted, or applied to abrogate the responsibilities or obligations of the United States to implement fully the provisions of the Montreal Protocol. In the case of conflict between any provision of this subchapter and any provision of the Montreal Protocol, the more stringent provision shall govern."

 ## 9.7 CONCLUDING OBSERVATIONS

Ensuring the effectiveness of IEL remains an area of continued significance. In the global environmental arena, an "injured entity/party" need not be a state party, as often required in various legal institutions and international public laws. Since global environmental externalities do not necessarily distinguish national boundaries, and since there is scope for an otherwise liable party to invoke *non liquet* under existing laws to abdicate its environmental responsibilities, it is important that this free-rider exit be sealed. There are at least two routes to fill this vacuum. Both require the stipulation of provisions concerning (1) the legal standing/*locus standi* of interested parties (state or other legal entities), and (2) the provision of *amicus curiae*. It is likely that these improvisations will constitute cost-effective methods of global environmental protection and enforcement of international environmental laws.

The various specifications of compliance features and the somewhat vague and unenforceable noncompliance aspects of most environmental laws render even the hard laws of limited effectiveness. The articulation of integrated strategies to bring free-riders to comply with various laws is an important aspect of further development of the law. The role of economics is more vital than ever, given the significance of achieving more efficient global environmental governance.

Review Exercises

1 Explain the WTO Dispute Settlement Mechanism (DSM) in relation to the competing provisions in a specific multilateral environmental agreement of 1998 on an issue related to trade and the environment.

2 In resolving trade disputes, especially involving any form of discrimination, Article 3.7 of the WTO Dispute Settlement Understanding (DSU) makes the following provision: "The first objective of the dispute settlement mechanism is usually to secure the withdrawal of the measures concerned ... compensation should be resorted to only if immediate withdrawal ... is impracticable." In addition, Article XX of GATT 1994 provides a few environment-related exceptions, which are called "non-violation" cases. If these exceptions do not apply in a specific impugned trade measure initiated by a member country of the WTO, examine the relevant economic approaches and criteria for assessing the stated "compensation." Also, if the disputed environmental trade measure does in fact contribute (in the net contribution sense) to enhancing global environmental quality, provide an assessment of the net global welfare contribution of the trade measure, even when it violates Article XX of the GATT.

3 Evaluate the WTO-DSU from the perspective of incomplete contracts theory and identify potential fillable and other gaps in some of the provisions.

4 If the right to health is a universal right, examine the role and limitations of Articles III and XX of GATT 1994 in limiting the deployment of process-based environment-enhancement (especially in relation to impact on environmental public health) with reference to the 1948 UN Charter of the Universal Declaration of Human Rights.

5 Explain the concepts of compliance, noncompliance, effectiveness, and impact of an international environmental agreement. Explain the roles of principles, rules, and standards in these concepts.

6 Explain the concept of endogenous institutional response (EIR) and its significance in understanding the evolution of organizations and institutions in relation to specific international environmental regimes (IER). Examine EIR–IER in the context of the Montreal Protocol to the Vienna Convention on Substances that Deplete the Ozone Layer.

7 Comment on the validity or otherwise of the following assertion: "Each state benefits from a treaty but may be even better off if it breaches the treaty later on . . . international treaties can be self-policing because of the built-in threats of retaliation(s) against violations if time discount rates or the probability of leaving the game are not too high for the participants as compared to relative period benefits" (Bernholz, 1994, p. 305).

8 If the "soft law" aspects of international environmental governance are to be effective, what ingredients are (a) necessary and (b) sufficient to ensure (i) compliance with the legal provisions and (ii) effectiveness in relation to the objectives of specific soft law and its corresponding environmental management?

REFERENCES

Aceves, W. J., 1996, An economic analysis of international law: Transaction cost economics and the concept of state practice, *University of Pennsylvania Journal of International Economic Law*, 17, 995–1068.

Bernholz, P., 1994, *Ex ante* safeguards against *ex post* opportunism in international treaties, *Journal of Institutional and Theoretical Economics*, 150, 304–9.

Berwick, T. A., 1998, Responsibility and liability for environmental damage: A roadmap for international environmental regimes, *Georgetown International Environmental Law Review*, 10, 257–68.

Binger, B. R. and Hoffman, E., 1989, Institutional persistence and change: The question of efficiency, *Journal of Institutional and Theoretical Economics*, 145, 67–85.

Boyle, A., 1997, Remedying harm to international common spaces and resources: Compensation and other approaches, in P. Wetterstein (ed.), *Harm to the Environment: The Right to Compensation and the Assessment of Damages*, Oxford: Clarendon Press, pp. 78–89.

Brunne, J. and Toope, S. J., 1997, Environmental security and freshwater resources: Ecosystem regime building, *American Journal of International Law*, 91, 26–59.

Charnovitz, S., 1996, Participation of nongovernmental organizations in the World Trade Organization, *University of Pennsylvania Journal of International Economic Law*, 17, 331–56.

Charnovitz, S., 1998, Environment and health under WTO dispute settlement, *International Lawyer*, 32, 901–21.

Chayes, A. and Chayes, A. H., 1991, Compliance without enforcement: State regulatory behavior under regulatory treaties, *Negotiation Journal*, 7, 311–31.

Dickson, B., 1999, The precautionary principle in CITES: A critical assessment, *Natural Resources Journal*, 39, 211–28.

Ebbesson, J., 1996, *Compatibility of International and National Environmental Law*, The Hague: Kluwer Law International.

Gantz, D. A., 1999, Dispute settlement under the NAFTA and the WTO: Choice of forum opportunities and risks for the NAFTA parties, *American University International Law Review*, 14, 1025–1106.

Harvard Law Review Association (HLRA), 1991, Developments in the law: International environmental law, *Harvard Law Review*, 104, 1484–1639.

Hurwicz, L., 1972, On informationally decentralized systems, in C. McGuire and R. Radner (eds.), *Decision and Organization*, Amsterdam: North-Holland, pp. 297–336.

Jacobson, H. K. and Weiss, E. B., 1998, Assessing the record and designing strategies to engage countries, in E. B. Weiss and H. K. Jacobson (eds.), *Engaging Countries: Strengthening Compliance with International Environmental Accords*, Cambridge, MA: MIT Press, pp. 511–54.

Kalas, P. R. and Herwig, A., 2000, Dispute resolution under the Kyoto Protocol, *Ecology Law Quarterly*, 27, 53–134.

Kelly, M. J., 1997, Overcoming obstacles to the effective implementation of international environmental agreements, *Georgetown International Environmental Law Review*, 9, 447–88.

Keohane, R. O., 1988, International institutions: Two approaches, *International Studies Quarterly*, 32, 379–98.

Lang, W., 1995, Compliance: Control in respect of the Montreal Protocol, in American Society of International Law, *Proceedings of the 89th Annual Meeting, "Structures of World Order,"* New York.

Nanda, V. P. and Ris, Jr., W. K., 1976, The public trust doctrine: A viable approach to international environmental protection, *Ecological Law Quarterly*, 5, 296–410.

Noyes, J. E., 1998, The International Tribunal for the Law of the Sea, *Cornell International Law Journal*, 32, 109–82.

Olson, Jr., M., 1979, *The Logic of Collective Action*, Cambridge, MA: Harvard University Press.

Palmeter, D. and Mavroidis, P. C., 1999, *Dispute Settlement in the World Trade Organization: Practice and Procedure*, Boston: Kluwer Law.

Rao, P. K., 2000, *Sustainable Development: Economics and Policy*, Oxford: Blackwell.

Raustiala, K., 1997, The "participatory revolution" in international environmental law, *Harvard Environmental Law Review*, 21, 537–86.

Sands, P. J. and Bedecarre, A. P., 1990, Convention on International Trade in Endangered Species: The role of public interest non-governmental organizations in ensuring the effectiveness of the ivory trade ban, *Boston College Environmental Affairs Law Review*, 800–35.

Scott, A., 1999, Trust law, sustainability, and responsible action, *Ecological Economics*, 31, 139–54.

Shaffer, G., 1999, Notes on international trade: WTO, *American Journal of International Law*, 93, 507–14.

Snidal, D., 1996, Political economy and international institutions, *International Review of Law and Economics*, 16, 121–38.

Szekely, A., 1997, Compliance with environmental treaties: The empirical evidence. A commentary on the softening of international environmental law, *American Journal of International Law Proceedings of the 91st Annual Meeting at Washington, DC*, 234–40.

Tarlock, A. D., 1997, The influence of international environmental law on United States pollution control law, *Vermont Law Review*, 21, 759–92.

Taylor, P. E., 1998, From environmental to ecological human rights: A new dynamic in international law?, *Georgetown International Environmental Law Review*, 10, 309–97.

Trachtman, J. P., 1999, The domain of WTO dispute resolution, *Harvard International Law Journal*, 40, 333–77.

United Nations (UN), 2000, *International Arrangements and Mechanisms to Promote the Management, Conservation and Sustainable Development of All Types of Forests, Report of the Secretary General to the Fortieth Session of the Intergovernmental Forum on Forests*, New York: UN Doc. E/CN.17/IFF/2000/4.

US General Accounting Office (GAO), 1992, *International Environment: International Agreements are not Well Monitored*, Report No. GAO/RCED-92–43, Washington, DC: US General Accounting Office.

US President, 1999, *Economic Report of the President, 1999*, Washington, DC: US Government Printing Office.

Vazquez, C. M., 1995, The four doctrines of self-executing treaties, *American Journal of International Law*, 89, 695–723.

Vicuna, F. O., 1997, Preparatory works: Final report, in *1997 Yearbook of the Institute of International Law*, pp. 313–34.

Visek, R. C., 1995, Implementation and enforcement of EC environmental law, *Georgetown International Environmental Law Review*, 7, 377–94.

Weiss, E. B., 1995, Remarks on "Compliance: Control in respect of the Montreal Protocol," in American Society of International Law, *Proceedings of the 89th Annual Meeting, "Structures of World Order,"* New York.

Weiss, E. B. and Jacobson, H. K. (eds.), 1998, *Engaging Countries: Strengthening Compliance with International Environmental Accords*, Cambridge, MA: MIT Press.

Wetterstein, P. (ed.), 1997, *Harm to the Environment: The Right to Compensation and the Assessment of Damages*, Oxford: Clarendon Press.

Young, O. R., 1999, Hitting the mark: Why are some international environmental agreements more successful than others?, *Environment*, 41, 20–9.

Website Addresses

Nongovernmental Organizations (NGOs)

- **International Council of Environmental Law**
  http://www.law.pace.edu/env/icelsite/icelhome.html
- **World Wildlife Fund** http://www.panda.org
- **Center for International Environmental Law**
  http://www.econet.apc.org/ciel/index.html
- **Environmental Law Institute** http://www.eli.org/
- **Foundation for International Environmental Law and Development**
  http://www.ecouncil.ac.cr/rio/focus/report/english/FIELD.htm
- **Friends of the Earth** http://www.foe.co.

Biological Diversity

- **Biodiversity Conservation Information Service**
  http://biodiversity.org
- **Biodiversity Information Network**
  http://www.bdt.org.br/bin21/IUCN
- **Biodiversity Forum** http://www. worldcorp.com/biodiversity
- **UNESCO Bioethics Committee** http://www.unesco.org/ibc/
- **World Conservation Monitoring Center**
  http://www.wcmc.org
- **Working Group on Traditional Resource Rights**
  http://users.ox.ac.uk/~wgtrr
- **FAO Genetic Resources** http://www.icppgr.fao.org
- **Convention on Biodiversity Clearing House Mechanism**
  http://www.biodiv.org/chm.html

Sustainable Development

- **FAO Sustainable Development**
  http://www.fao.org/waicent/faoinfo/sustdev/welcome.html
- **International Institute of Sustainable Development**
  http://www.iisd.ca/

Climate, Trade, and Environment

- **World Trade Organization** http://www.wto.org
- **International Centre for Trade and Sustainable Development** http://www.ictsd.org
- **International Standards Organization** http://www.iso.ch

- **UN Framework Convention on Climate Change**
  http://www.unfccc.de
- **Intergovernmental Panel on Climate Change**
  http://www.unep.ch/ipcc/
- **US Global Change Research Information**
  http://www.gcrio.org

REGIONAL AND NATIONAL

- **Africa Network for Environment and Sustainable Development** http://www.rri.org/nesda/
- **Caribbean Environment Program**
  http://rolac.unep.mx/cepnews/ing/first.htm
- **Middle East Environment Project**
  http://eelink.umich.edu/greenlife/index.html
- **Regional Environmental Center: East and Central Europe**
  http://www.rec.hu
- **Australia Department of Environment**
  http://www.erin.gov.au
- **Environment Canada** http://www1.ec.ga.ca
- **German Federal Environment Agency**
  http://www.umweltbundesamt.de
- **USA** http://www.usepa.gov

International Environmental Treaties

- **Center for International Earth Science Information Network** http://www.ciesin.org/entri/
- **Greenpeace** http://www.greenpeace.org/~intlaw/
- **Treaties and International Covenants**
  http://untreaty.un.org/english/treaty.asp
  http://sedac.ciesin.org/pidb/texts-subject.html
  http://www.tufts.edu/fletcher/multilaterals.html
  http://www.asil.org/resource/treaty1.htm

International Environmental Legal Education

- **Asian-Pacific Center for Environmental Law**
  http://sunsite.nus.sg/apcel/
- **Australian Center for Environmental Law**
  http://www.law.usyd.edu.au/~acel
- **Center for International Environmental Law**
  http://www.igc.org/ciel

- **European Environmental Law**
  http://www.unimaas.nl/~egmilieu
- **PACE University** http://www.law.pace.edu/env/

Environmental Law Libraries

- **PACE Virtual Environmental Law Library**
  http://www.law.pace/edu/env/vell6.html
- **Sustainable Earth Electronic Library**
  http://www.envirolink.org/pubs/
- **University of Virginia**
  http://ecosys.drdr.virginia.edu/environment.html
- **US Library of Congress**
  http://www.lcweb2.loc.gov/glin/glinhome.html

Source: Adapted from www.iucn.ch (June 12, 2000)

Index